"A monumental and humane book that puts people, places and communities at the heart of its indictment of estate regeneration in London."
Andrew Wallace, University of Leeds

"Paul Watt is a leading analyst of housing policy and politics. He draws on this experience to make sense of a pervasive and troubling housing policy that is reshaping urban space and urban lives in London and beyond."
David Madden, London School of Economics

ESTATE REGENERATION AND ITS DISCONTENTS

Public Housing, Place and Inequality in London

Paul Watt

P

First published in Great Britain in 2021 by

Policy Press, an imprint of
Bristol University Press
University of Bristol
1-9 Old Park Hill
Bristol
BS2 8BB
UK
t: +44 (0)117 954 5940
e: bup-info@bristol.ac.uk

Details of international sales and distribution partners are available at
policy.bristoluniversitypress.co.uk

British Library Cataloguing in Publication Data
A catalogue record for this book is available from the British Library

ISBN 978-1-4473-2918-3 hardcover
ISBN 978-1-4473-2919-0 paperback
ISBN 978-1-4473-2921-3 ePDF
ISBN 978-1-4473-2922-0 ePub

Cover design: Clifford Hayes
Front cover image: Paul Watt, Woodberry Down estate, London
Borough of Hackney, 2018

This book is dedicated to the memory of my mum and dad – Miralda and Charles Watt – who were able to access public housing when they needed it

Contents

List of figures, tables and photographs

Figures

Tables

Photographs

Source and copyright: Paul Watt

List of abbreviations

ABI	Area-based initiative
ALMO	Arms-Length Management Organisation
ASB	Anti-social behaviour
ASH	Architects for Social Housing
BAME	Black, Asian and Minority Ethnic
CARP	Carpenters Against Regeneration Plans
CDSG	Carpenters Destination Steering Group
CEI	Comprehensive Estates Initiative
CHCTAG	Custom House and Canning Town Action Group
CPA	Christian Peoples Alliance
CPO	Compulsory Purchase Order
CPP	Clapham Park Project
DCH	Defend Council Housing
DCLG	Department for Communities and Local Government
DETR	Department of the Environment, Transport and the Regions
DHP	Decent Homes Programme
DHS	Decent Homes Standard
DIY	Do-it-yourself
DOE	Department of the Environment
FOI	Freedom of Information
GCNF	Greater Carpenters Neighbourhood Forum
GLA	Greater London Authority
GLC	Greater London Council
GP	General practitioner
HA	Housing association
HAT	Housing Action Trust
HCCHG	House of Commons Council Housing Group
HDV	Haringey Development Vehicle
HFH	Homes for Haringey
HMO	Houses in multiple occupation
HRA	Housing Revenue Account
ILD	Index of Local Deprivation
IMD	Index of Multiple Deprivation
IRA	Independent Residents' Advisor
JR	Judicial review
LA	Local authority
LBB	London Borough of Barnet
LBH	London Borough of Hackney

LBL	London Borough of Lambeth
LBN	London Borough of Newham
LBS	London Borough of Southwark
LBTH	London Borough of Tower Hamlets
LCC	London County Council
LHA	Local Housing Allowance
LSE	London School of Economics
LTF	London Tenants Federation
MBC	Metropolitan Borough Council
MHCLG	Ministry of Housing, Communities and Local Government
MP	Member of Parliament
NDC	New Deal for Communities
NES	Northwold Estate Survey
NHS	National Health Service
NS-SEC	National Statistics Socio-Economic Classification
NST	Non-secure (temporary) tenant
OO	Owner-occupation
PEACH	People's Empowerment Alliance for Custom House
PEP	Priority Estates Project
PFI	Private Finance Initiative
PPP	Public–private partnership
PRP	Private registered provider (of social housing) – aka housing association
PRS	Private rented sector
RCJ	Royal Courts of Justice
RSL	Registered social landlord – aka housing association
RTB	Right to Buy
SPV	Special Purpose Vehicle
SRB	Single Regeneration Budget
TMO	Tenant Management Organisation
TRA	Tenants and residents association
UCL	University College London
VSO	Voluntary sector organisation
WDCO	Woodberry Down Community Organisation

Acknowledgements

This book would not have happened had it not been for the interviewees, who treated me with the greatest courtesy and respect. I am especially grateful to the nearly 180 estate residents who allowed me the honour of hearing their stories. Various housing groups generously let me attend their meetings: Carpenters Against Regeneration Plans, Demolition Watch London, Focus E15, Haringey Defend Council Housing, Northumberland Park Decides, Save Northwold, Southwark Defend Council Housing, Southwark Group of Tenants Organisations. I gained insights and assistance from numerous housing and community campaigners including Paul Burnham, Hannah Caller, Wendy Charlton, Julian Cheyne, Alison Davy, Aysen Dennis, Pam Douglas, Alex Finnie, Jerry Flynn, Angie Forrester, Emily Jost, Glenn Mcmahon, Fred Milson, Simon Morrow, Tanya Murat, Tawanda Nyabango, Peter O'Kane, Joanne Parkes, Jasmin Parsons, Richard Rees, Glyn Robbins, Paulette Singer, Jasmin Stone, and John Xuareb (apologies to anyone I've omitted). I greatly enjoyed estate walking tours in the knowledgeable company of Leslie Barson, Farhan Samanani and Pablo Sendra (South Kilburn), Jessie Brennan (Thamesmead), Geraldine Dening and Simon Elmer (Central Hill), Alberto Duman (Canning Town/Custom House), and Michael Edwards (Limehouse Fields and Ocean).

Thanks to the following for their insightful comment on drafts of this book: Rowland Atkinson, Mike Berlin, Bob Colenutt, Stuart Hodkinson, Keith Jacobs, Tom Keene, Gareth Millington, Alan Morris, Ryan Powell, Andrew Wallace and Martin Wicks. I had enlightening conversations on housing and regeneration with John Aitken, Kate Belgrave, Alice Belotti, Penny Bernstock, Elena Besussi, Duncan Bowie, Jane Brake, Aditya Chakrabortty, Alex Colas, Piero Corcillo, Alex Frediani, Tom Gillespie, Kate Hardy, Debbie Humphry, Tony Manzi, Anna Minton, Suzy Nelson, Mark Panton, David Roberts and Chris Saunders. Thanks to Northwold estate residents and David Allen for contributing towards the Northwold Estate Survey.

The research was funded by various grants from Birkbeck, University of London. Transcription was expertly undertaken by Amanda Roulstone (Dragon) and Frances Bradley. I am grateful to Marcus Saraiva for creating Figure 4.1. The following libraries and their staff generously facilitated my research: British Library, Bancroft Road, Minet Library, Newham Library. I have presented material from this book at numerous conferences, seminars, housing and political meetings and feedback from these has been invaluable. Thanks also to the postgraduate and undergraduate students on my 'Cities and Urban Inequalities' module at Birkbeck on whom I tried out many of my ideas. Special thanks to Emily Watt and Caroline Astley at Policy Press who were patience personified.

My wife Tamsin and her daughter Eliza helped with the presentation of the photographs. Tamsin has been a tower of support throughout and is pleased that she has finally got her husband back.

1

Introduction

"I'm praying to god, 'don't regenerate my estate' because regeneration has become a nasty word" (Social housing tenant, at a meeting held to discuss regeneration in the Tottenham area of north London, 2016).

This statement, made by an anxious tenant, encapsulates the main theme of this book. Regeneration refers to an urban policy involving spatially targeted reinvestment in and revitalisation of physically deteriorating, economically under-resourced and socially deprived areas – in this case public/council/social housing estates. Even though some regeneration aims can be considered laudable, the practice of regeneration in London has meant that it has become a 'nasty word' among estate residents as they see their homes bulldozed and their communities scattered. Much has already been written about this topic by academics, journalists and housing campaigners, but this is the first book to provide an in-depth account of what it means for London social tenants and homeowners to *live through* the regeneration of their estates over years and even decades. It focuses on regeneration schemes that involve 'comprehensive redevelopment' – demolition of an existing estate and rebuilding it as a 'mixed-tenure neighbourhood' with large numbers of market properties for sale or rent. Such comprehensive redevelopment fundamentally changes estates in ways that residents don't expect, and are not properly told about by the politicians, officials and consultants who promote it as a way of solving London's housing crisis.

In theory, the Carpenters estate in Stratford, in the east London borough of Newham, has been 'regenerating' since 2004. In reality, regeneration hasn't properly started. Instead Newham Council has 'decanted' most of the tenants, leaving the estate half-empty for 15 years.[1] Mary and her husband (a retired elderly white working-class couple) had been living at the Carpenters estate for over 40 years, and had bought their house under the Right to Buy (RTB) policy, having first rented from the council. For Mary and her husband, regeneration had appeared to plague them in their twilight years. One question I asked my interviewees, was "who do you think is going to benefit from the regeneration?" This is Mary's reply: "I haven't got a clue, it certainly wasn't us, it wasn't for the likes of us." Michael was a middle-aged black Caribbean council tenant who lived at the Northumberland rk estate in Tottenham in the north London borough of Haringey. ichael was dismayed by the poor cleaning standards at his estate d had taken to picking up the litter in the public space outside his ck. Like Mary, Michael was entirely unconvinced by the promised generation makeover – "the money's coming in and the community's ing out". 'It's not for us' was a phrase that I heard time and time in from residents at London's 'regenerating' estates. This book traces y they said this, and what regeneration *really does* to their homes, ir neighbourhoods, to them and their families.

Housing in an unequal city

Al cities are unequal, but some cities are more unequal than others. London is one of the most unequal cities on the planet. Social, spatial and housing inequalities were prominent in London's 19th century imperial days but are now being reproduced in late 20th/ early 21st century Victorian redux manner following four decades of neoliberal urban and welfare restructuring including the last decade of austerity policies.

Housing is the most palpable manifestation of London's inequality. The street homeless bed down near the citadels of private wealth in the form of so-called 'luxury' apartment blocks – many of which are half-empty – that have proliferated to cater for the global 'super-rich' elite. It is this housing juxtaposition – zero domestic space for those who desperately need it, but an overabundance of such space for those who don't need it or even want it – which lies at the cruel heart of London's housing crisis (Dorling, 2014). Other dimensions of this crisis include high and rising levels of housing deprivation such as overcrowding, and dispossession including evictions. Deprivation and dispossession are disproportionately borne by London's multi-ethnic working-class population, who reside in the city's social housing estates,[2] or in the insecure private rental sector (PRS).

Most of London's social housing estates were purpose-built by local authorities (councils) and financially supported by central government through subsidies and loans. These council estates were developed as part of a political programme to provide decent quality housing at a rent that ordinary working-class Londoners could afford, a programme which is very much associated with the Labour Party. If London's estates were largely council-built, many are currently owned and managed by voluntary-sector housing associations – aka private registered providers of social housing (PRPs) or registered social landlords (RSLs) – as a result of the stock transfer policy from the 1980s to 2000s. Local authorities and housing associations share a primary duty to provide 'social housing' (with sub-market rents), although large housing associations, especially in London, increasingly operate along commercial lines (Manzi and Morrison, 2018). The various terms for public housing – local authority, council, state – are used interchangeably throughout the book, but the broader 'social housing' term is also employed where this is apposite.

The orthodox approach to London's housing crisis is that this is a supply-side problem – too few properties are being built: 'the city faces a need for some 49,000 additional homes a year' (Hanna et al, 2016: 3). This supply shortage results in unaffordable house prices and rents, so more market and 'affordable' housing (shared ownership and 'affordable rent') properties must be built. An alternative explanation lays in the four decades' long pursuance of neoliberal housing policies which resulted in the shrinkage of social renting, especially public housing (Watt and Minton, 2016). It is this which has resulted in the city's inability to meet the housing needs of its large low-income population consisting of the working poor and those struggling to get by on paltry out-of-work benefits. Despite London's record numbers in paid work, this work is often low-paid and insecure, part of the trend towards increasing labour market precarity. Those worst affected by poverty include Black, Asian and Minority Ethnic (BAME) groups, young people and female lone parents, all of whom are more likely to be either employed in a low-paid job or to be out of work.

London, especially inner London, had an extensive public housing sector up until the 1980s, but this declined due to the collapse in new building coupled with the sale of existing council homes via the flagship Thatcherite privatisation policy, the RTB introduced in the Housing Act 1980. During its 13 years in office, New Labour kept the RTB because it saw it as politically expedient to do so. Margaret Thatcher had tapped into popular aspirations around homeownership and Tony Blair was not going to prevent these aspirations from being realised. What is so shocking from the standpoint of Labour Party history is that during Blair's decade in power (1997–2007), a derisory 280 homes were built by local authorities in London. This compares to nearly 104,000 under both previous periods of Labour government – 1965–69 and 1974–78 – over 207,000 in total (GLA, 2019a). In fact, had the New Labour governments under Blair matched the nearly 52,000 council homes built in London from 1980 to 1990, when Thatcher was in power (MHCLG, 2019a), there would be around 5,000 households in temporary accommodation rather than the real 2018 figure of 56,880.[3]

Public housing estates have provided working-class Londoners with genuinely affordable and secure homes for over a century to an unusual extent by the standards of most major Western cities. At its peak during the early 1980s, nearly one in three London households – 770,000 – rented their homes from the council, whereas by 2011 this had reduced to just under 440,000 (Watt and Minton, 2016). By 2018, the local authority stock stood at 392,800 properties (MHCLG, 2019a). As the book discusses, there are numerous reasons for this decline, especially the RTB policy of which working-class Londoners (like Mary quoted earlier) were supposedly the beneficiaries. If the RTB changed tenures, from renting to owning, demolition and rebuilding result in a far more radical and disruptive set of physical and social changes. It is this comprehensive redevelopment form of regeneration which is causing council-built estates to disappear from London's skyline, and it is these which are the focus of this book.

Estate regeneration

Estate regeneration represents a type of urban policy that is spatially targeted at social housing estates which are suffering from physical deterioration alongside social and economic deprivation, for example high levels of poverty, unemployment, overcrowding, ill health, crime and anti-social behaviour (ASB). The aim is to improve both the area and residents' life chances by reinvesting in the built environment (upgrading homes and estate facilities), and enhancing employment, training and education, community development, health and welfare services, community safety, and so on. Regeneration incorporates varied combinations of physical, social and socioeconomic policy interventions which aim to tackle an estate's problems in a holistic, sustainable manner, as with New Labour's New Deal for Communities (NDC) programme. Estate regeneration has involved complex series of public–private partnerships (PPPs) since the 1970s, albeit the private sector role has dramatically increased in significance including in relation to the schemes that are analysed in this book.

Estate regeneration usually contains a physical renewal element involving reinvestment in the built environment, as seen in Sadiq Khan's (current Mayor of London) definition: 'the process of physical renewal of social housing estates through a range of interventions – from refurbishment and intensification, to demolition and rebuilding' (Mayor of London, 2018: 4). The physical renewal aspect has become increasingly prominent, and especially the notion that the best way to regenerate estates is to knock them down and start again: 'While estate regeneration does not necessarily always include demolition and rebuilding, the term is now frequently associated with such forms of comprehensive redevelopment' (Hanna et al, 2016: 12). This book examines this scorched earth, comprehensive redevelopment approach to estate regeneration with a primary focus on its housing and built environment-related aspects. The employment, training and education aspects of regeneration are not analysed, although issues related to community development, community safety, health and well-being are discussed.

Housing professionals and politicians from the main parties advocate estate comprehensive redevelopment as a crucial mechanism for expanding the city's housing supply and thereby 'solving' the city's housing crisis in its orthodox form – not enough properties being built (Adonis and Davies, 2015). To address this supply problem, more land must be made available to build on and where better to do this than on 'failed' social housing estates? Demolishing these estates will free up land for new housing development at higher densities and with modern design features. As estate regeneration has been effectively rebranded as 'estate densification' (Hanna et al, 2016), so the various social goals regarding improving existing residents' life chances have been downgraded (Chapter 3).

While estate regeneration in the form of demolition and redevelopment has increased the total number of new homes, most of these are market properties for sale or rent at prices way beyond those which ordinary working-class Londoners can afford (LAHC, 2015). The rest of the regeneration package is made up of 'affordable housing', which most Londoners consider to be an Orwellian sick joke – since most of this is *un*affordable in real terms. Demolition has reduced the amount of social rental housing being re-provided on the regenerated estates – the only part of the 'affordable housing' shibboleth which is truly affordable for low-income Londoners (LAHC, 2015). Demolition also means that existing social housing residents are dispossessed of their homes and displaced while only a fraction return to the new, rebuilt estates (Flynn, 2016). As estate regeneration 'unlocks' land values, it also increases private house prices and rents which make the surrounding area even less affordable, which drives out low-income tenants who are already struggling in London's toxic PRS. Estate regeneration-as-demolition has therefore contributed towards the 'state-led gentrification' of previously working-class areas of the city (Watt, 2013).

At a time of dire housing need, there are nearly 21,000 homes officially classified as 'long term empty' – vacant for over six

Photograph 1.1: Carpenters estate – Focus E15 occupation of empty flats, 2014

months – across the city (Transparency International UK, 2017). Estate regeneration has contributed towards the growing number of these empty homes. While Newham Council was decanting the Carpenters tenants in expectation of a regeneration that has never arrived, it was simultaneously displacing its homeless families out-of-borough and even outside London altogether (Watt, 2018a, 2018b). The Focus E15 housing campaign shone a light on this perverse regeneration result by occupying two boarded up flats at the half-empty Carpenters estate in September 2014 (Gillespie et al, 2018). Rather than solving London's housing crisis, estate regeneration has exacerbated it via the emptying out and loss of social housing, as Focus E15 captured by their banners outside the occupied flats – 'These People Need Homes' and 'These Homes Need People' (Photograph 1.1).

Two discourses of estate regeneration[4]

A discourse represents a set of interrelated concepts that allow us to understand the social world, but which also provide a framework and set of guidelines for acting in the world (Levitas, 2005). There are two broad approaches – competing discourses – to understanding estate regeneration involving demolition: the hegemonic 'official/mainstream discourse', and the 'oppositional/critical discourse' (Watt, 2017). The official discourse – promoted by politicians, regeneration professionals and the mass media – frames estates as 'failed places', consisting of 'failed housing', and subliminally that such estates are inhabited by 'failed people' (Hancock and Mooney, 2013; Adonis and Davies, 2015). Given such manifest failures, regeneration is a welcome panacea for residents who are only too glad to have their homes and estates knocked down. The official discourse simultaneously normalises and de-problematises regeneration as an axiomatically progressive urban policy. This approach has some academic support from studies which argue that demolition and rehousing is progressive because it offers residents a benign relocation away from poor, rundown housing and neighbourhoods to genuinely better places (Kleinhans and Kearns, 2013; Posthumus and Kleinhans, 2014; Egan et al, 2015; Lawson et al, 2015).

Critical urbanists, alongside anti-demolition housing campaigners, have constructed an alternative oppositional/critical regeneration discourse which acts as a counter-hegemonic challenge to the official discourse. While the official discourse pathologises these 'failed places' as 'sink estates', the oppositional discourse regards estates as functioning working-class neighbourhoods which are broken apart by demolition and rehousing. For critical urbanists, the 'sink estate' pathologisation acts as the underpinning rationale for demolition (Kallin and Slater, 2014; Lees, 2014). Rather than benign improvement, estate regeneration is state-led gentrification (Watt, 2009a, 2013; Lees, 2014) or 'social cleansing' (Elmer and Dening, 2016). Urban space is systematically rearranged for the benefit of capitalist developers and their local state accomplices, while the result is displacement and the erosion of the working-class right to the city (Harvey, 2012).

Both discourses – set out in Watt (2017) – can be regarded as Weberian ideal types: 'An ideal type is formed by the one-sided accentuation of one or more points of view. ... Historical research faces the task of determining in each individual case, the extent to which this ideal construct approximates to or diverges from reality' (Weber, 1949: 90). Are estates failed places, as the official discourse opines, or are they places where people want to live, as the oppositional discourse suggests?

I conducted research on the 2012 London Olympic Games that illustrated how the official discourse constructs hyperbolic claims regarding the positive benefits of regeneration which elide the many disbenefits that it brings in its wake, especially for low-income populations (Kennelly and Watt, 2011, 2012, 2013; Watt and Bernstock, 2017; Watt, 2018b). This book deepens that critique by demonstrating how comprehensive redevelopment produces *multiple discontents* for estate residents. Such discontents are systematically erased from the one-dimensional official/mainstream regeneration discourse where the only possible way forward is to knock down 'failed estates' and start again – policy by bulldozer.

My critical social scientific approach is clearly allied with the counter-hegemonic discourse (Watt, 2017; Appendix A). At the same time, the book offers a sympathetic critique of academic strands within this discourse, particularly the influential body of work on public housing demolition from scholars such as Loretta Lees, Tom Slater and Phil Hubbard (see inter alia, Slater, 2013a; Kallin and Slater, 2014; Lees, 2014; Lees and Ferrari, 2016; Hubbard and Lees, 2018). These three are leading urban geographers whose research background is gentrification and who are heavily influenced by the work of Neil Smith, for whom 'Regeneration was always ever a gentrification strategy' (cited in Lees, 2014: 921; see Smith, 2002). Their body of work can be labelled the 'anti-gentrification' perspective on estate regeneration. According to this perspective, estates are being destroyed by the onward predatory – indeed planetary – march of gentrification in the ideological guise of 'regeneration' (Lees et al, 2016). This anti-gentrification perspective has considerable analytical merits, as previously argued (Watt, 2009a, 2013). However, having conducted further research since publishing these two papers, I have become aware of the analytical blind spots and oversimplifications within the anti-gentrification perspective. By focusing so heavily on the *point of displacement* – forced removal due to demolition – this perspective illuminates what *leaving estates* means to residents, but it underplays the sociological, spatial and housing complexities of *living at* estates. It is these complexities that are foregrounded in the book's in-depth account of London's estates and their regeneration.

Rationale and methodology

The book provides an experiential perspective on estate regeneration from the epistemological standpoint of those it most affects – the residents who have to live with it over many years. This emphasis on residents' experiences and accounts represents a deliberate value-choice (Weberian 'value relevance'; Weber, 1949), and reflects my social scientific, political and ethical concerns that residents' voices are both under-represented and misrepresented within the official regeneration discourse. Therefore, while the views of politicians and regeneration professionals are presented (especially those who worked closely with residents), their views are subaltern to those of residents.

The research on which this book is based dates to 2007 but was mainly undertaken from 2012 to 2018 with follow-up work during

2019 (Chapter 4 and Appendices). The data comes from multiple sources including in-depth interviews, participant observation, an estate survey, documentary research, secondary analysis of statistical data and visual photographic data. The main methodological approach is ethnographic, rooted in qualitative in-depth interviews and fieldwork. This approach reflects an emphasis on what Max Weber calls 'verstehen' – understanding lay actors' social actions in their terms (Eldridge, 1971) – in this case, understanding how estate residents give meaning to regeneration as a social process that they live through. As such, it follows on from the qualitative methodological emphasis that several scholars have advocated (Matthews, 2012; Goetz, 2013; Glucksberg; 2017; Morris, 2019).

The main method is the in-depth interviews undertaken with 178 residents and ex-residents of social housing estates. Fieldwork comprised estate visits and participant observation at formal and informal meetings, and this fieldwork is referred to. Also referred to are findings from a resident survey undertaken at Northwold estate in Hackney in 2017. This survey involved 190 respondents, and the estate was at an early stage of regeneration (see Watt and Allen, 2018). Six people running local businesses at or near estates were interviewed, as were two filmmakers who had made films about the research estates. In addition, over 50 officials were interviewed, including local politicians, housing and regeneration professionals, community workers and volunteers.

Although the book is informed by both sociological and geographical perspectives, it is not a theoreticist project. Rather it follows in the tradition of Pierre Bourdieu, who 'advocated the *fusion* of theoretical construction and practical research operations' (Bourdieu and Wacquant, 1992: 34; original emphasis). What has been crucial in guiding my overarching perspective is the many hundreds of hours spent in regeneration-related meetings and listening to residents in interviews relating *their* experiences. These experiences are complex, and I have tried throughout to faithfully represent this complexity.

The research was undertaken at several London estates which were undergoing regeneration. The estates were not chosen in a predetermined manner, except in the sense of aiming to include ones at different stages of regeneration (Appendix A). Their inclusion reflects my long and idiosyncratic ethnographic journey through London's regeneration landscape from 2007 to 2019. This journey involved attending hundreds of meetings, sometimes several per week and sometimes in a scholar-activist capacity (Appendix A). At these meetings, I talked to residents about their experiences and then followed up by visiting them at their estates and interviewing them, provided we got on well enough. Hence the research reflects the amazing Londoners I met who generously let me hear their stories and to whom I am profoundly grateful.

The research estates range from the massive Aylesbury estate with over 2,700 dwellings, to Cressingham Gardens with just over 300. They were at various stages of regeneration, from the early planning stage to those where substantial demolition and rebuilding had occurred (Chapter 4). The 14 main research estates are as follows, along with the year that regeneration began:

- Aylesbury – 2000
- Canning Town/Custom House (an area comprising several estates) – 2000
- Carpenters – 2004
- Central Hill – 2014
- Clapham Park – 2000
- Cressingham Gardens – 2012
- East Dulwich – 1997
- Heygate – 1998
- Northumberland Park – 2015
- Northwold – 2016
- Ocean – 2000
- Westbury – 2014
- West Hendon – 2002
- Woodberry Down – 1999

Nine of the above began during New Labour's period in office (1997–2010). This is why considerable space is dedicated to examining New Labour's record on urban regeneration in Chapter 3. The remaining five schemes (Northumberland Park, Northwold and the three Lambeth estates – Central Hill, Cressingham Gardens and Westbury) were begun under the Coalition/Conservative governments and are congruent with austerity.

The above-mentioned regeneration schemes have been controversial, as reflected in how residents have challenged and even overtly resisted demolition. These estates therefore constitute what Mayer (2007: 92) refers to as 'spaces of contestation'. Another reason for the controversial nature of the schemes is because all of them – bar West Hendon – have been undertaken in London boroughs that are politically dominated by the Labour Party, the party that built many of the estates in the first place. At a meeting on the regeneration of Northumberland Park estate, a first-time attendee queried "why is our council allowing it, I thought the council was Labour?" – the amused general reply was, "*it's Labour* that's doing it". Estate demolition has been advocated and enacted by Labour councils in Hackney, Haringey, Lambeth, Newham and Southwark. These Labour councils have pursued demolition in the face of focused and sustained grassroots resident opposition (Watt, 2018c).

This has prompted radical housing campaigns – for example Focus E15 and Architects for Social Housing (ASH) – to vilify Labour councils and the Labour Party generally as being primarily responsible for the capital's social cleansing (Elmer and Dening, 2016; Watt, 2016). This critique is perfectly understandable. At the same time, it elides the opposition to estate demolition from *within* the Labour Party and affiliated trade unions such as the GMB and Unite (GMB, 2015; Koessl and Mayo, 2015). It must be remembered that the Labour Party is a broad church, one whose differences became even more apparent with the rise of Corbynism and Momentum from 2015 to 2019 (Chakrabortty, 2017; Seymour, 2017). It was such intra-Labour Party differences which led to the demise of the controversial Haringey Development Vehicle (which targeted Northumberland Park estate) via the removal of the Blairite/Progress-dominated Labour council and its replacement with a left-wing council in 2018 (Inside Housing, 2017, 2019). At several points in the book, the Labour Party's role is revisited. In party political terms, it's worth highlighting the principled and well-informed critique of estate demolition made by the Green Party, especially Sian Berry (2018).

Overview

The book revolves around three themes: the development of public housing in London and its transformation via estate regeneration; the role of place in relation to public/social housing estates; and the relationship between such housing and London's socio-spatial inequalities. These themes are addressed from a multi-disciplinary critical urbanist perspective encompassing urban/housing policy, urban sociology and urban geography.

The book is theoretically eclectic and draws upon concepts and frameworks derived from critical urbanism, Bourdieusian sociology, *verstehen* sociology, and the geography and sociology of place. Critical urbanism prioritises the critique of urban social and spatial injustice and inequality (Brenner, 2009). In this vein, it is argued that the social and physical construction of the city, including housing and the built environment, is shaped by deep structures of power and inequality derived from the imperatives of capital accumulation and neoliberalisation processes (Harvey, 1973, 1989; 2003; 2005; Jacobs, 2019).

Several Bourdieusian sociological concepts are deployed in understanding social space and physical space (Bourdieu, 1984; Savage et al, 2005; Allen, 2008; Savage, 2010, 2011), as follows.

- *Field* refers to the arenas of social engagement where people struggle for recognition (economic, educational, consumption, housing, and so on); each field is governed by distinct 'rules of the game'.
- '*Habitus* refers to socially acquired, embodied systems of schemes of disposition, perceptions and evaluation that orient and give meaning to practices' (Bourdieu, 1984: 17; emphasis added).
- *Capitals* refer to the differential types and amounts of resources that people draw upon within fields – economic (monetary), cultural (educational and embodied) and social (networks).
- *Symbolic violence*, whereby 'violence does not depend on physical coercion, but can take place when we accept domination tacitly' (Savage, 2015: 50).

In his review of the relevance of Bourdieu for urban sociology, Savage (2011: 515; original emphasis) notes how 'field theory' became increasingly important in Bourdieu's work in relation to understanding the interplay between social and physical (geographical) space, in order to 'demonstrate that fields matter concretely, that the relational power struggles they illuminate *cannot but be marked in the urban landscape itself*'. Geographical spaces – like council estates – are thus in a sense fields within the urban landscape which are configured and reconfigured by shifting class relations of domination and subordination. London council estates are working-class dominated urban spaces or fields; they are socio-spatial arenas in which working-class social practices and values are dominant and normalised (Chapter 6). What regeneration does is upend this working-class domination such that the field of the council estate is radically transformed through a process of state-led gentrification whereby the remaining working-class residents become subordinate within the new socio-spatial field of the post-regeneration redevelopment (Chapter 12).

While both critical urbanism and Bourdieusian urban sociology are highly relevant for the analysis, they share similar limitations which derive from their underpinning structural logics – labour–capital relations in the case of the former and habitus constraints in the latter. These logics render each approach overly deterministic and insufficiently attuned to how lay social actors make sense of their lives. Such structural approaches therefore need supplementing with a *verstehen* sociology filtered through a geographical lens. Verstehen sociology provides accounts of social action which are 'adequate at the level of meaning' (Eldridge, 1971: 28), and necessitates understanding actors' intentions and actions *in their terms* rather than as mere derivations from an a priori, all-encompassing, all-powerful structure – capital–labour relations, class position, habitus, and so on. Hence the emphasis placed upon how ordinary Londoners – estate residents – understand their life-worlds and everyday experiences. This *verstehen* approach has phenomenological undertones. However, the combination of materialism with *verstehen* hopefully avoids Bourdieusian criticisms of phenomenology (Bourdieu and Wacquant, 1992) and interpretivist approaches generally. As Wacquant (2019: 310) rightly says, 'The metropolis is not put together from the ground up every morning as its denizens wake up and go on with their lives'. Thus, to refashion Marx's famous epigram from *The Eighteenth Brumaire of Louis Bonaparte* (Marx and Engels, 1968), council estate residents make their own history, but they do not make it as they please; they do not make it under circumstances chosen by themselves, but under circumstances directly encountered, given and transmitted from the past.

This is the first book to provide a theoretically informed, empirically rich account of the development and consequences of estate regeneration in London.[5] By foregrounding estate residents' lived experiences and perspectives – mainly working class – the book provides an in-depth account of their discontents with the seemingly never-ending regeneration process. The book is critical in that it highlights these discontents, and in so doing corrects the existing imbalances and silences within the official regeneration discourse in which there are only winners while the losers are airbrushed out of history.

The book draws upon research undertaken at numerous estates, although it does not offer a systematic comparative case study approach such as Belotti (2016) or Tunstall (2020). Instead it emphasises the overlaps and commonalities in how residents experience *living in* public housing and *living through* regeneration. The analysis offers a typical account of residents' experiences, albeit one that is filtered through the main housing tenure groups at estates – social tenants, owner-occupiers and temporary tenants. There is no claim being made that *each aspect* of this account applies *equally* to each estate, and it is indicated where significant differences exist. The book revisits the concept of state-induced rent gap, which refers to how the 'contrast between the disinvested [local authority] housing stock in London and the highly valued land it sits on creates enormous capital accumulation potential – in other words what can be termed a "state-induced rent gap"' (Watt, 2009a: 235). The book draws upon this concept and illustrates various aspects of political economy throughout, even though it does not provide the detailed political economic analysis that Stuart Hodkinson's (2019) painstaking dissection of Private Finance Initiative (PFI) schemes achieves. The key conceptual frameworks that structure the book are now examined, beginning with place.

Place

Place attachment, belonging, images and myths

Place is a geographical space that people attribute meanings to (Cresswell, 2004). It has a multi-scalar nature whereby 'smaller places are incorporated within larger ones' (Lewicka, 2011: 211). A working definition of place attachment is 'the bonding of people to places' (Low and Altman, 1992, cited in Manzo and Devine-Wright, 2014: 1), a bonding which has cognitive, affective and behavioural psychological components. People feel that they have an affinity with certain places and this affinity often includes social interaction, although place attachment can also encompass the physical landscape. The concept of 'place attachment' is most associated with social geography and environmental psychology (Lewicka, 2011), whereas 'place belonging' is more associated with urban sociology (Savage et al, 2005; Blokland, 2017); these two concepts are used interchangeably throughout the book.

Rob Shields (1991: 60; emphasis added) proposes that complex social interactions, within and between locations, lead to the emergence of symbolic meanings which over time form a 'place image': 'The various discrete meanings associated with real places or regions *regardless of their character in reality.*' Place images are partial, exaggerated and even stereotypical in nature. While stereotypical place images are routinely deployed by 'outsiders' who live elsewhere, the place images of residential 'insiders' are refracted through their experiences of living in a place; the latter allow for greater depth, nuance and ambivalence (Watt, 2006). As Relph (1976) argues, insiders have a more authentic relationship to place. Place images can also coagulate and ossify into a more or less stable 'place myth', for example 'True North, Strong and Free' in relation to Canada (Shields, 1991). The ossified place myths regarding public housing estates – summarised in the pejorative 'sink estate' label (Slater, 2018) – are crucial to understanding the symbolic meaning that estates have.

As Lewicka (2011: 211) argues, 'the majority of researchers dealing with people–place bonds focus on one place scale only and avoid comparisons of attachments to different place scales'. By contrast, this book examines residents' place attachments at three different scales: the home, the estate as a neighbourhood, and the intermediate scale of blocks of flats and rows of houses which subdivide estates. It is the latter intermediate scale which Kusenbach (2008) argues is especially important for local social interaction.

Home is associated with the domestic space of the dwelling and is 'an exemplary kind of place where people feel a sense of attachment and rootedness. Home, more than anywhere else, is seen as a center of meaning and a field of care' (Cresswell, 2004: 24). Home involves notions of safety and what Giddens refers to as 'ontological security', defined as 'a sense of stability and continuity as well as the ability to make changes contributing to a sense of control and a comfortable home environment' (quoted in Morris, 2019: 69–70).

Neighbourhood, community and belonging

The neighbourhood is an identifiable residential place that has a local dimension involving social interaction and the use of amenities: 'a geographically circumscribed, built environment that people use practically and symbolically' (Blokland, 2003: 213). Neighbourhoods vary in size from 1,000 to 30,000 people (Watt and Smets, 2014), and this book treats each estate as forming a neighbourhood.

If 'neighbourhood' has an inherent spatial component, 'community' is a much broader term that can operate at multiple spatial scales (the national community or the village community), or even with no spatial reference whatsoever, as with interest communities (cycling community) or identity communities (trans community). Unlike neighbourhood, community therefore does not necessarily have to include a spatial component, although it often has done within urban studies, including community studies (Blokland, 2017). Post-war community studies identified working-class 'urban villages' in major Western cities (Young and Willmott, 1957; Gans, 1962). By comparison, the contemporary urban neighbourhood is a less important fulcrum for social identities and practices due to globalisation and heightened spatial mobilities, especially among the middle classes (Savage et al, 2005; Watt and Smets, 2014). Some have suggested that the interlinkage of community with locality is antiquated and fails to recognise the complexity of contemporary cities: 'As city dwellers we operate in many communities. Often these have a locational hook, such as where we live or where our children go to school, but we're also in lots of others' (Brearley, 2017: 90).

Such mobility and multiplicity do not, however, mean that contemporary cities are devoid of neighbourhood place attachment/ belonging or that notions of 'community' are redundant (Watt and Smets, 2014; Blokland, 2017; Morris, 2019; Watt, 2020a). Even if contemporary urban areas do not form close-knit urban villages, this does not mean that the neighbourhood is irrelevant. Residential 'locational hooks' still count, and especially for deprived and marginalised populations such as the poor, unemployed, lone parents, the elderly, sick and disabled – in other words, those groups that tend to spatially concentrate at social housing estates (Chapters 5 and 6; Forrest and Kearns, 1999; McKenzie, 2015). Long-term working-class residents also often express a 'sense of community', 'defined by strong social ties with people in the area, capacity to call on neighbours for assistance, trust of neighbours, a sense of safety and strong place attachment' (Morris, 2019: 2; see Cattell, 2001; Back, 2015; Romyn, 2016). Length of residence has been identified as 'the most consistent positive predictor of attachment to residence places (usually neighbourhoods)' (Lewicka, 2011: 216), while 'ageing in place has been found to be critical for intensifying place attachment' (Smith, 2009: 144). Given that the contemporary working classes are generally less geographically mobile and materially poorer than the middle classes, they are more likely to develop positive neighbourly social relations over time (Young Foundation, 2010).

The working-class relationship to the neighbourhood is a *traditional* form of place belonging based upon residential longevity and historical rootedness – 'I belong in this neighbourhood because I have always lived here'. Such traditional place belonging is crucial to understanding how working-class estate residents relate to their neighbourhoods in London (Chapter 6). It's also possible to have this traditional place belonging based upon knowing people locally, even while expressing nostalgic views regarding how 'community' is not as strong as it used to be in the past (Watt, 2006).

By contrast to working-class traditional belonging, Savage argues that the middle classes have an *adoptive relationship* to place belonging, predicated upon moving into a neighbourhood and opting to belong to it – hence 'elective belonging' (Savage et al, 2005; Savage, 2010). Unlike traditional belonging, elective belonging is based upon choice – 'I belong in this neighbourhood because I have chosen to come and live here'. Elective belonging means that middle-class households straddle the routes/roots antimony; by being geographically mobile and flowing along routes, but then *choosing* to put down roots in an area because of its aesthetic appeal (beauty, sense of authenticity, and so on). Elective belonging also incorporates an ethical dimension as 'middle class people claimed moral rights over place through their capacity to move to, and put down roots in, a specific place which was not just functionally important to them but which also mattered symbolically' (Savage, 2010: 116). Elective belongers are distinct from rootless, here-today-and-gone-tomorrow 'transients'. In Bourdieusian terms, the middle classes choose certain neighbourhoods because these facilitate a socio-spatial fit between their habitus and various fields (education, housing, and so on) such that they feel 'at home' and comfortable living in certain urban or suburban areas (Watt, 2009b). This fit has been identified in London neighbourhoods which express the belonging patterns of different middle-class fractions (Butler and Robson, 2003; Jackson and Benson, 2014; Jackson and Butler, 2015).

Watt (2009b) argues that elective belonging inadequately captures the hierarchical nature of class, space and place, and invokes the notion of 'selective belonging': 'a spatially selective narrative of belonging that is limited to a given space within a wider area ... That space is invested with a positive place image that the wider locality is considered not to share' (Watt, 2010: 154). Selective belonging expresses how fractions of the urban and suburban middle classes engage in 'spatial disaffiliation' (Atkinson, 2006), whereby they distance themselves from geographically proximate, 'risky' poor and BAME populations via living in exclusive and exclusionary 'oases' or 'bubbles' such as affluent streets, securitised apartment blocks and gated communities (Butler, 2003; Atkinson and Blandy, 2017; Corcillo, 2020).

Inequalities, class and values

London's social housing estates are multi-ethnic spaces and have become more so since the 1970s, and many interviewees were from BAME backgrounds. Race/ethnicity therefore features throughout the book, not least since this is such a prominent aspect of London's inequalities: 'Ethnic minorities experience employment and housing disadvantage in *every* London borough, with housing inequalities being particularly notable' (Elahi and Khan, 2016: 3; original emphasis). Compared to white British people, overcrowding is higher among all

BAME groups in London, but especially among Bangladeshi, Pakistani and black African households (GLA Intelligence, 2014). BAME groups are also more likely to be both unemployed and working in low-paid jobs in London (Chouhan et al, 2011; Quereshi et al, 2014; Tinson et al, 2017). Gender relations are also important, partly related to labour market experiences, but also in relation to social housing estates as supportive, non-judgemental spaces for working-class women (Gosling, 2008; McKenzie, 2015).

While race, gender and disability are all important for understanding inequalities at London's estates, the book's primary emphasis is class inequality, and especially working-class experiences. Council estates in Britain, including London, have deep historical and contemporary sociocultural and symbolic associations with the working class (Ravetz, 2001; Watt, 2008; McKenzie, 2015). Sociological understanding of the contemporary British working-class experience has been heavily influenced by the work of Bourdieu (Skeggs, 1997; Charlesworth, 2001; Allen, 2008). One of the most influential Bourdieusian-inspired works on housing is *Housing Market Renewal and Social Class* by Chris Allen (2008). This provides a powerful critique of the Housing Market Renewal Pathfinder regeneration programme in Liverpool. For Allen, working-class people's limited economic capital, and hence proximity to economic necessity, shapes how they relate to the social world – the 'choice of the necessary' (Bourdieu, 1984). Working-class and middle-class predispositions towards housing are therefore opposites rooted in distinct relationships to being, with the former representing a practical necessity-based adherence to *home* juxtaposed to the middle-class symbolic orientation to the *housing market*:

> middle-class people, whose class position is constituted on the success of their consumption practices, view the market for houses as a space of positions and, it follows, engage in struggles for position within that social space. ... To this end, the market for houses is constituted as a *symbolic economy*. ... On the other hand, working-class people, who are faced with an economic world that urgently demands to be dealt with on a very practical day-to-day level ('you just try to get by from day to day, I can't see beyond tomorrow'), relate to houses in a practical and matter-of-fact way and are therefore basically unable to perceive houses as anything other than dwelling space, that is, a place to live. (Allen, 2008: 6–7)

Allen's critique of the regeneration professional/politician *misrecognition* – of what problematic urban space is and whether it *needs* regenerating – is highly relevant to the findings reported in this book (Chapter 8).

In *The Weight of the World*, Bourdieu and colleagues (1999) offer a multi-layered account of poverty and exclusion, including in the French social housing 'grands ensembles' – the equivalent to British council estates. The book's subtitle is *Social Suffering in Contemporary Society*, and suffering – rather than distinction – is 'the name of the game' as far as the dominated classes are concerned: 'their value is their suffering, their habitus is produced out of necessity in cramped spaces' (Skeggs, 2011: 502). Much contemporary working-class life in the UK *is* framed by suffering, poverty and deprivation, plus widespread insecurity via employment and housing precarity (McKenzie, 2015; Skeggs, 2015; Watt, 2018a, 2020b). This suffering has been exacerbated by the last decade of austerity policy:

> much of the glue that has held British society together since the Second World War has been deliberately removed and replaced with a harsh and uncaring ethos. A booming economy, high employment and a budget surplus have not reversed austerity, a policy pursued more as an ideological than an economic agenda. (Alston, 2019: 1)

Not only are the contemporary working classes in Britain exploited and deprived, they are also *symbolically devalued* via a surfeit of class hatred stereotypes – chavs, welfare mums, scroungers, and so on (Skeggs, 2015).[6] Symbolic devaluation is promulgated by politicians, right-wing think tanks and 'poverty porn' TV programmes, and has accelerated under austerity as the 'deserving' poor were demarcated from the 'undeserving' poor by the Coalition Government's 'strivers v. scivers' binary discourse (Hancock and Mooney, 2013; Tyler, 2013, 2015; Crossley and Slater, 2014).

In her excavation of symbolic devaluation, Skeggs (2011: 503) argues that the working class are positioned as 'the abject, the use-less subject who only consists of lacks and gaps, voids and deficiencies, sentimental repositories, sources of labour, negative value that cannot be attached or accrued and may deplete the value of others through social contagion' (see Skeggs, 1997, 2014 , 2015). Skeggs is discussing personhood, but her analysis can also be applied to working-class neighbourhoods – especially council estates (McKenzie, 2015). This devaluation has a spatial component in relation to territorial stigmatisation, discussed below, whereby the eponymous council estates become the symbolic sump depository of all that is *valueless* in British society (Watt, 2006, 2008). Or rather valueless from the perspective of the mass media and outsiders generally who lack the authentic relationship to place that insiders – such as long-term estate residents – possess (Relph, 1976; McKenzie, 2015).

As Skeggs (2015) argues, class analysis is or should be centrally concerned with relations of 'exploitation, domination, dispossession, devaluation' – these relations are illustrated throughout the book. At the same time, there are considerable problems with the Bourdieusian-inspired approach to the working class (that Skeggs recognises), since the 'choice of the necessary' 'is effectively a deficit model in which the working class is treated as an absence, i.e. lacking both cultural and economic capital and therefore incapable of making distinctions, unlike the case of the dominant classes' (Watt, 2006: 778). Charlesworth's (2000: 4) bleak account of deindustrialised Rotherham exemplifies this deficit model: 'this sense of nothingness, of abuse, of fracture, of damage is at the heart of working people's sense of life, of their being-in-the world'. The Bourdieusian working class, as represented by Allen and Charlesworth, is overdetermined by economic necessity and symbolic violence, and there is no scope within this approach for any kind of independent positive evaluation of working-class lives or places.

Are there any analytical ways out of this Bourdieusian-inspired cul-de-sac of despair? Three ways are posited, each of which informs this book's theoretical architecture. The first is to develop what Flint (2011: 88) refers to as 'an approach which recognizes, and is not afraid of, nuance and contradictions in accounts of social class', as Paton (2014) and McKenzie (2015) highlight in their working-class ethnographies. The second is to focus on values and valuation more broadly, rather than to fixate on the devaluation of working-class lives and spaces by powerful others (Flint, 2011; Glucksberg, 2013, 2017; Skeggs, 2014, 2015; McKenzie, 2015). This requires academics to recognise 'values beyond value', in Bev Skeggs' (2014) memorable phrase. In other words, to acknowledge and celebrate those aspects of working-class lives which are outside economic value and the impersonal logic of capital accumulation. One key value is caring, a gendered practice: 'Caring offers us a different way of being in the world, relating to others as if they matter, with attentiveness and compassion, beyond exchange' (Skeggs, 2014: 13). The third is to acknowledge the role of *feelings* in working-class lives, positive as well as negative (Back, 2015). These three emphases regarding working-class lives – as nuanced and contradictory, being valued and valuable in their own terms, and constituted by feelings – are central to the analysis of council estates in this book. London estates are *not* 'estates from hell'. Instead they are sociologically prosaic places of working-class 'getting along' and 'getting by' (Watt, 2003, 2006; Glucksberg, 2013; McKenzie, 2015).

The book examines the mundane aspects of everyday life on estates, aspects which are written out of the official regeneration discourse where wholesale eradication and transformation is the only way forward. Thus, it's important to understand 'why everyday life matters' at estates while at the same time not losing sight of the very real injustices that the working class are subject to (Back, 2015). Indeed, it is only by better appreciating what working-class people *value* – their housing, homes and neighbourhoods – that one can fully understand why being dispossessed of these things via comprehensive redevelopment makes the difference that it does.

Urban inequalities: marginalisation

Since the 1970s, urbanists investigating a wide range of Western cities have highlighted how social housing estates are linked to marginalisation processes in relation to poverty, labour market exclusion, crime and territorial stigmatisation (Power, 1997; Lupton, 2003; Smith, 2005; Musterd et al, 2006; Watt and Smets, 2017; Hess et al, 2018). The US public housing 'projects' have been singled out as epicentres of intense urban poverty, crime and racialised disadvantage (Rainwater, 1970; Hirsch, 1983; Wilson, 1987; Urban, 2012; Vale, 2013).

One of the most influential accounts of urban marginality is *Urban Outcasts* (2008) by Loïc Wacquant (see Flint and Powell, 2019). In his book, Wacquant focuses on how 'advanced marginality' is produced and lived out in the US inner city (South Side of Chicago), and French periphery (Parisian banlieues). Such urban marginality takes an ideal-typical form encompassing six dimensions: increasing wage-labour insecurity, disconnection from macroeconomic trends, territorial stigmatisation, the dissolution of place, loss of hinterland and social fragmentation. According to Wacquant, public/social housing estates – such as Robert Taylor Homes in Chicago and La Corneuve grand ensemble in the Parisian periphery – form the locales of a nascent 'precariat' whose employment contracts are insecure and who live in anomic places characterised by limited informal social support and intense social dysfunctionality.

A key implication of Wacquant's book is that despite certain similarities (physical design and housing tenure), the black Chicago hyper-ghetto and the more ethnically heterogeneous 'anti-ghetto' of the Parisian banlieues are *not* equivalent spaces in relation to the variegated patterns and processes of marginality – social context, policy and politics matter. What the state does or does not do represents a crucial driver in generating and shaping marginalisation processes. With respect to racism, crime, poverty and welfare state withdrawal, the US hyper-ghetto has no direct European equivalent (Flint and Powell, 2019).

This book focuses on two of Wacquant's place-related concepts – 'territorial stigmatisation' and the 'dissolution of place' – although it also refers to wage-labour insecurity and the precariat (Chapter 5). On territorial stigmatisation, 'advanced marginality tends to be concentrated in isolated and bounded territories increasingly perceived by both outsiders and insiders as social purgatories, leprous badlands at the heart of postindustrial metropolis where only the refuse of society would agree to dwell' (Wacquant, 2008: 237). Wacquant's concept of territorial stigmatisation has been hugely influential (Kirkness and Tijé-Dra, 2017), including in relation to council estates in the UK (Crossley and Slater, 2014; Slater, 2018; see Watt 2020c for a critique). Such stigmatisation has also helped to drive the regeneration agenda in Britain in terms of eradicating so-called 'failed estates' (Hancock and Mooney, 2013; Kallin and Slater, 2014; Lees, 2014; Dillon and Fanning, 2015).

The 'dissolution of place' is 'the obverse side of territorial stigmatization ... the loss of a humanized, culturally familiar and socially filtered locale with which marginalized urban populations identify and in which they feel "at home" and in relative security' (Wacquant, 2008: 241). In such estates, place – in the sense of a shared, meaningful locale – retreats so that residents are left in vacant spaces dominated by 'mere survival and relentless contest' (Wacquant, 2008: 241). Thus convivial, mutual social relations have broken down under the combined weight of material deprivation and external stigmatisation, as some analyses of UK public housing estates have suggested (Coleman, 1990; Power, 1997; Power and Tunstall, 1997).

Wacquant's work has undoubted analytical and rhetorical power. It also has various problems, including that it neglects housing (Powell and Robinson, 2019), an omission this book aims to contribute towards correcting. Furthermore, although Skeggs (2011) does not refer to Wacquant in her paper on class and values, her critical commentary of Bourdieu could be applied to *Urban Outcasts*, which, like *Weight of the World*, snuffs out agency as the nascent precariat are ground down by state withdrawal and entombed within their marginal urban spaces. Along with Bourdieu, Wacquant offers a deterministic and culturally thin account of working-class life and spaces. Not only does

Wacquant downplay everyday agency (Flint and Powell, 2019), but he neglects informal and formal processes of resistance, often female-led, in the US hyper-ghetto (Feldman and Stall, 2004). Several studies of stigmatised housing estates challenge Wacquant's notion that residents internalise externally generated stigmatisation (Hastings, 2004; Garbin and Millington, 2012; Morris, 2013; Watt, 2020c).

In-depth accounts of what *appear* – from the outside – to be anomic urban spaces of advanced marginality reveal belonging, a sense of community and even pride (Watt, 2006; Morris, 2013, 2019; McKenzie, 2015; Kirkness and Tijé-Dra, 2017). From Wacquant's perspective, there is little space within the spaces of advanced marginality for any kind of positive values or agency. Wacquant (2019: 310) would undoubtedly dismiss such an emphasis as 'a romantic vision of the poor as deft, habile, and resilient when they are beaten down and their lives bent out of shape by brutal policies'. On the contrary, I suggest that it is only by taking account of values and agency that one can arrive at a deep and nuanced sociological understanding of advanced urban marginality.

Urban inequalities: gentrification and the elite city

Gentrification refers to the simultaneous reinvestment in a neighbourhood's built environment and an upwards shift in the neighbourhood's demographic from working class to middle class (Lees et al, 2008). Having been begun by 'pioneer gentrifiers' of modest economic means during the 1960s to 1970s (Glass, 1964), gentrification has since swept through many working-class London neighbourhoods, particularly in the inner east and south of the city (Hamnett, 2003; Butler and Robson, 2003; Hanna and Bosetti, 2015). These neighbourhoods have not only become more middle class, but they have also become whiter as has happened in areas with traditionally strong black identities, such as Hackney (Wessendorf, 2014), Brixton and Peckham (Jackson and Butler, 2015).

London's gentrification transformation has been caused by multiple factors. These include the massive expansion in financial services (Hamnett, 2003) which has driven gentrification upmarket in those areas where ultra-affluent finance professionals have displaced the pioneer gentrifiers, as with the 'super-gentrification' of parts of north London (Butler and Lees, 2006). New-build residential development has also played an important role in London's gentrification (Hamnett, 2003; Butler and Robson, 2003; Davidson, 2008, 2010). In addition, urban regeneration has been extremely significant and has resulted in state-led gentrification, for example in 'regenerated' areas such as Stratford in east London, which was radically transformed by the 2012 Olympic Games (Kennelly and Watt, 2012; Watt, 2013; Bernstock, 2014; Cohen and Watt, 2017). State-led gentrification means the restructuring of urban space for the benefit of property developers, elite and middle-class groups, and results in dispossession and the forced displacement of low-income groups (Hackworth and Smith, 2001; Glynn, 2009; Slater, 2013a). Estate demolition has contributed towards state-led gentrification (Watt, 2009a, 2013; Lees, 2014; Lees and Ferreri, 2016).

As gentrification has broadened and deepened in London, it has spawned a mini-academic industry dedicated to fine-tuning the spaces, places and lifestyles of London's burgeoning middle classes (see inter alia Butler and Robson, 2003; Davidson, 2008, 2010; Jackson and Benson, 2014; Wessendorf, 2014; Jackson and Butler, 2015; Corcillo, 2020). In some ways, this research reveals the difficulties in making generalisations about gentrification, gentrifiers and the urban middle classes. At one extreme are 'marginal professionals' in arts and welfare with fragmented careers and low economic capital, some of whom live in social housing estates (Watt, 2005; Chapters 5 and 6), while at the other extreme are wealthy banking and finance super-gentrifiers who live in privileged enclaves (Butler and Lees, 2006).

The increasingly dominant architecture of new-build residential developments in London and south-east England is of high-density, high-rise apartment blocks, either private or mixed tenure (Corcillo, 2020; Scanlon et al, 2018; Allen and Watt, Forthcoming). These are securitised developments where the management companies' primary goals are enhancing residents' security (concierges, gates, CCTV), and catering to their exclusive leisure desires (private gyms, pools) (Atkinson and Blandy, 2017). The dominant socio-spatial tendencies in such developments are spatial disaffiliation (Atkinson, 2006) and selective belonging (Watt, 2009b). In such new-build developments, economically affluent middle-class fractions socially distance themselves from proximate multi-ethnic working-class areas and people (Davidson, 2008, 2010; Allen and Watt, Forthcoming). Spatial disaffiliation and selective belonging feature in new-build, mixed-tenure developments as private owning/renting gentrifiers live in their cocooned oases and bubbles, separated off from their social rental neighbours. This separation is architecturally ensured by having different tenure blocks and 'poor doors' (separate entrances), while there is also evidence of class antagonism directed against social renters (Kilburn, 2013; Awofolaju, 2014; Osborne, 2014; Corcillo, 2020; Chapter 12).

London's gentrification has taken an intense corporate form – 'gentrification on steroids' (Watt and Minton, 2016: 218) – characterised by accelerating house prices, rents, capital flows and displacements which has no equivalent in the rest of the UK. Lees and colleagues (2016: 80) refer to 'hyper-gentrification' as 'an accelerated taking over of land which is bigger, faster, and much more destructive than the traditional narratives of gentrification'. As Lees and colleagues argue, London's hyper-gentrification results from transnational flows of real estate capital including the activities and presence of the super-rich rather than merely the middle classes. The super-rich are an elite class of 'high net worth individuals' – with $1 million (£660,000) in non-property wealth – who make up around 1 in 20 of London's population (Atkinson, 2020). What distinguishes the super-rich is their financial assets, including prime London real estate properties many of which stand empty – a damning testimony of the city's housing crisis (Dorling, 2014; Atkinson, 2020).

Scholars of the elite/super-rich argue that London has experienced a *qualitative change* at the top of the social hierarchy during the last 20 years: 'it now seems somewhat quaint that we should still alight on the middle classes as the primary agents of urban social change in a time in which research shows they are increasingly eclipsed by ... [a] transnational elite' (Cunningham and Savage, 2017: 25–6). London is a hot spot for overseas investment, including flows of illicit money: 'The London property market attracts billions of pounds of overseas investment each year, with much of this investment driven by corruption' (Transparency International UK, 2017: 63). Twenty-first century London is witnessing a fundamental remaking of urban space for the benefit of the super-rich elite, many of whom are overseas investors (Cunningham and Savage, 2017; Atkinson, 2020). Therefore, as well as becoming increasingly gentrified, London is becoming an 'elite city'. The elite transformation of the city is even taking place in formerly iconic working-class areas, including Elephant and Castle in south London, an area which has been heavily regenerated (Glucksberg, 2016; Transparency International UK, 2017). All of this change at the top of London's socio-spatial hierarchy results in dispossession and displacement for the dominated classes.

Dispossession: expulsions, displacement and un-homing

The dispossession – expulsion – of the working class from their homes and neighbourhoods dates to the late 19th/early 20th century whereby the urban poor were cleared from the 'rookeries' to facilitate the development of major railway stations. Slum clearance and dispossession were also prominent during the post-war period in relation to urban renewal (Chapter 3).

If dispossession is far from novel, it has taken on a new lease of life under contemporary neoliberalism via what David Harvey (2003) calls 'accumulation by dispossession'. This includes how the held-in-common goods and services which formed the mainstay of the Keynesian welfare state – public housing, land, nationalised industries, and so on – have been privatised and sold off to the highest bidder, either individually (as in the case of the RTB) or collectively (via demunicipalisation, outsourcing, state-led gentrification, and so on) (Hodkinson et al, 2013; Hodkinson, 2019). In *Expulsions*, Saskia Sassen (2014: 1) argues that 'new logics of expulsion' have arisen under neoliberalisation and globalisation, as opposed to the Keynesian welfare state era which was 'driven by a logic of inclusion' (Sassen, 2014: 212).

A key vector of expulsions – and contemporary BAME and white working-class experience – is displacement from homes and neighbourhoods. Displacement refers to involuntary or forced residential relocation: 'what happens when forces outside the household make living there impossible, hazardous or unaffordable' (Hartman, 1982, cited in Slater, 2009: 294–5). Displacement can be caused by evictions, which occur either by formal legal action or informally by landlords asking tenants to move or changing the locks (Desmond, 2016). As Marcuse (1986) notes, displacement also results from gentrification-induced economic pressures such as rent hikes and physical processes including demolition.

Using Sassen's framework, I identified 'six distinctive logics of expulsion' in relation to research on contemporary housing and homelessness in London (Watt, 2018a: 69). Several of these logics of expulsion are illustrated throughout the book:

1. Reduced capacity of low-income Londoners in housing need to enter social rental housing.
2. Lengthening stays in insecure temporary accommodation.
3. Escalating evictions in the PRS.
4. 'Recurrent displacement' – households being forced to move several times.
5. Geographical extension of displacement beyond the immediate scales of home and neighbourhood to the metropolitan and regional scales.
6. Expulsion from the homelessness support aspect of the welfare state.

One key driver of accumulation by dispossession is regeneration, which critical urbanists equate with neoliberal restructuring involving third-wave, state-led gentrification (Hackworth and Smith, 2001; Glynn, 2009; Slater, 2013a). Such state-led gentrification, including via estate demolition, has been a significant factor behind displacement in London (Flynn, 2016; Lees and Ferrari, 2016; Watt, 2018a).

By contrast, the official regeneration discourse regards demolition as offering residents a benign relocation away from 'failing places' (Adonis and Davies, 2015; McLaughlin, 2015; Watt, 2017). Several academic studies have also challenged the above-mentioned critical displacement approach for implying 'that these residents have little or no agency, and tend to be "victims" of market and/or political forces' (Kleinhans and Kearns, 2013: 168). Thus several studies have highlighted how tenants are able to exercise choice and agency within the relocation process such that it is not as coercive as the state-led gentrification approach argues (Kearns and Mason, 2013; Kleinhans and Kearns, 2013), a finding which has particular resonance in the Dutch case (Posthumus and Lelevrier, 2013; Posthumus and Kleinhans, 2014). This begs questions regarding the roles of power, agency and control within the regeneration and relocation process (Chapter 10).

Displacement has thus far been conceived in terms of spatial relocation. However, as Davidson (2009) argues, this reduces a *meaningful* socio-spatial phenomenon to a spatial event which ignores phenomenological questions regarding why and how physical relocation matters? As he advocates, 'This requires a move to reassert the place in di*splace*ment. In short, there is a need to ask why displacement matters at all: what does a loss of place constitute? How is a loss of space differentiated from a loss of place?' (Davidson, 2009: 226; original emphasis). Davidson's approach leads towards the crucial analytical insight that people can *feel displaced* prior to any physical relocation, and even if they remain in or return to the same neighbourhood (Chapters 10 and 12).

Feeling displaced prior to any physical relocation allows for a recognition of displacement as a process rather than a simple before-and-after spatial event. This emphasis is captured by the concept of 'un-homing', defined as the 'process by which material and/or imaginary components of home are unintentionally or deliberately, temporarily or permanently, divested, damaged or even destroyed' (Baxter and Brickell, 2014: 134). Un-homing refers to a process whereby homes can lose their value over time – of no longer feeling at home, a feeling which can exist prior to physical relocation (Atkinson, 2015). Un-homing can occur due to landlord disinvestment – a lack of upkeep of the dwelling's physical structure whereby homes are financially and materially neglected – which in turn prompts physical displacement as renters are pressurised out of what they feel are no longer their homes (Huq and Harwood, 2019). In other words, their homes have *become* 'non-homes'.

Un-homing focuses on the domestic scale of the home, but indirect forms of displacement can also occur at the neighbourhood scale via what Marcuse (1986) refers to as 'displacement pressure'. Low-income residents can feel that their neighbourhood has changed, notably because of gentrification, even if they are not themselves *directly* affected by evictions, rent hikes, and so on (Davidson, 2009; Kennelly and Watt, 2012). Such displacement pressure therefore captures Davidson's emphasis on feeling displaced at the neighbourhood scale, a feeling that can occur while one remains in situ (Pull and Richard, 2019).

'Displacement anxiety' is a further conceptual tool that I use to help understand the meaningful nature of displacement. I introduced this term when analysing the pre-relocation displacement experiences of people living in temporary accommodation in London, including in the city's supposedly regenerating estates. This concept:

> refers to a *prospective* ruptured sense of place – of home and/or neighbourhood – as a result of a potential, forced external real-world move. It is not equivalent to what Marcuse (1986) calls 'displacement pressure' since this is a collective sense of 'being out of place' linked to seeing how a neighbourhood's character is gentrifying. Instead displacement anxiety refers to the *subjective response to the threat of immanent direct displacement* – the feeling that potential displacees have once they have either been told their home will be demolished, or when they are given notice to quit. Such displacement anxiety generates a profound sense of ontological insecurity as people literally do not 'know their place'. (Watt, 2018a: 74; original emphases)

Displacement anxiety is a useful notion when discussing the psychosocial nature of displacement (Chapter 10).

Trying to remain in place – *immobile* – is one response that low-income groups can exercise when gentrification and displacement pressure occurs (Davidson, 2009; Slater, 2009). This raises crucial issues regarding *control* over space. Paton (2014: 193) uses 'the term elective fixity to refer to the degree of control people had over their residential location, which ensures that they continue to live in their neighbourhood'. She argues that the working-class people in her study of gentrification in Glasgow had 'poor elective fixity' in relation to their ability to remain fixed in their neighbourhoods (Paton, 2014: 2014). In later chapters, we see how displacement and elective fixity play out at London's estates.

The structure of the book

Part I presents a policy analysis of public housing and regeneration. This explores how and why estate regeneration came about and provides the political-economic context for understanding residents' experiences. Chapter 2 examines public housing in relation to *housing policy*, while Chapter 3 analyses estate regeneration with reference to *urban policy*. Policy is analysed at both national and local scales with reference to London. These chapters are theoretically located within a critical urbanist perspective that emphasises welfare state restructuring via the spatially uneven epochal transition from the post-war Keynesian welfare state to contemporary neoliberalism. As Hodkinson (2019: 6) argues, 'Nowhere has this neoliberal agenda been more fervently pursued than in the realm of housing'.

Chapter 2 presents a diachronic perspective on the expansion and contraction of London's public housing from the late 19th century until the present day and addresses the question, 'how can the rise of fall of public housing in London be understood and explained?' The key argument is that public housing – the already 'wobbly pillar' of the welfare state – has been systematically privatised, demunicipalised and now regenerated such that it is a shadow of its former self. Chapter 3 argues that estate regeneration has gone through distinct phases since the 1970s, but that contemporary 20th century schemes involving demolition (comprehensive redevelopment) – which are the focus of this book – are clearly identifiable with state-led gentrification processes and outcomes. Chapter 3 also unpacks and critiques the various rationales for comprehensive redevelopment. Chapter 4 summarises the London research boroughs and estates.

Part II analyses residents' experiences of living in London social housing estates *before regeneration*. This includes understanding what values beyond value such spaces hold in relation to housing and place (Skeggs, 2014). Chapter 5 considers various themes relevant to marginalisation and inclusion, including residualisation, socio-tenurial polarisation, social exclusion and diversity. Residents' labour and housing market experiences are foregrounded. The key argument is that working-class tenants positively value council housing because, unlike the PRS, it provides long-term security as well as genuinely affordable rents. Chapter 6 examines estates as valued places with reference to residents' place attachments and belonging. Three spatial scales are scrutinised: the domestic home scale, the scale of the estate qua neighbourhood, and the intermediate intra-neighbourhood scale. Many residents expressed traditional place belonging and even a sense of community, connected to their residential longevity. While Chapters 5 and 6 highlight residents' positive valuations of housing, homes and neighbourhoods, Chapter 7 explores how estates have also become devalued places due to overcrowding, landlord neglect, enhanced population transience, crime and disorder, and also through symbolic devaluation via territorial and tenurial stigmatisation. In summary, Part II demonstrates how most social tenants and owner-occupiers positively valued their existing homes and neighbourhoods, even if such valuation was neither unqualified nor universal.

Part III focuses on residents' experiences of *living through regeneration* and addresses the following question: 'what does regeneration *do* to residents, their homes and neighbourhoods?' Chapter 8 approaches this question with reference to the beginning phase of regeneration, which includes consultation. It argues that disillusionment often sets in among residents, not least in relation to consultation processes that are regarded as one-sided, confused and confusing. In moving beyond the early stage, Chapter 9 analyses what happens once regeneration gets underway. It demonstrates the multiple ways that regeneration is experienced as physical, social, symbolic and psychosocial *degeneration*. The physical fabric of homes and estates crumbles, familiar neighbours leave and are replaced by a shifting gallery of new faces, while estates become urban dystopian locations for film and TV productions. The result is that the features of estate life that residents previously valued disintegrate, while the devalued aspects are intensified and eventually dominate residents' sense of place. Chapter 10 examines residents' experiences of displacement from their homes and neighbourhoods, both with reference to their feelings of displacement before they move out, and their spatial relocation. Although such displacement experiences are mixed, not least along tenure lines, there is extensive and intensive pre-location displacement anxiety, stressful relocation processes, and post-relocation dissatisfaction including grieving for lost homes. Chapter 11 focuses on how and why residents resist demolition and with what effects. Such resistance contributes towards broader struggles over the right to the city.

Chapter 12 provides a coda to Part III by critically examining the aftermaths of regeneration with reference to the creation of new places and inequalities at West Hendon, Woodberry Down and Carpenters estates. West Hendon and Woodberry Down are both highly unequal and fragmented places. The Carpenters estate is an example of a long-standing regeneration scheme where remaining residents live in a degenerated space, still waiting for 'regen' to arrive. The Conclusion summarises the key findings and suggests policy recommendations.

PART I

Policy analysis and research context

2

Housing policy: the rise and fall of public housing

This chapter outlines the rise and fall of public housing in London with reference to national and local housing policy. Two historical periods are identified: an expansionary period that covers the first 80 years of the 20th century, followed by a contractionary period from the 1980s until the 2010s. This periodisation is theoretically located within the development of the Keynesian welfare state and that form of welfare state's unravelling under neoliberalisation, an unravelling that has intensified under recent austerity policies. Before outlining this periodisation, it is first contextualised with reference to housing as the 'wobbly pillar' of the welfare state.

The wobbly pillar of the welfare state

Most nation states rely upon market and informal housing provision, with the latter prominent in the Global South. It is only within the cities and towns of the Global North that public/social housing has existed to any substantial extent. Public housing was a key part of post-war welfare states in Western capitalist societies (Harloe, 1995; Balchin, 1996). Many Northern European cities – and North American and Australasian cities to a much lesser extent – are physically marked by the presence of public/social housing estates (Urban, 2012; Jacobs, 2019). During the 1950 to 1980s, these estates were often large-scale and took a modernist architectural form (Urban, 2012; Hess et al, 2018). Public housing was also prominent in the former state socialist regimes in Eastern Europe, although the collapse of these regimes has resulted in wide-scale housing privatisation (Balchin, 1996; Hess et al, 2018).

Social housing is provided at sub-market costs due to state legislation and funding (although owner-occupation has also been heavily subsidised by the state in numerous ways; Merrett, 1982). Public/social housing entails the decommodification of housing in capitalist societies in that citizens can meet their basic need for shelter without having to pay market costs (Esping-Andersen, 1990; Jacobs, 2019). Decommodified public/social housing is most prominent in the social democratic and corporatist/conservative welfare state regimes

Northern Europe, rather than in the liberal welfare state regimes of North America or the marginal welfare regimes of Southern Europe (Esping-Andersen, 1990; Balchin, 1996). This pattern is linked to how workers' political parties (social democratic, labour and communist) were able to extract key concessions from capital, especially in the post-war period. By contrast, the US Democrat Party has never seriously challenged the sanctity of private property. Public housing in the US never moved beyond explicit residual provision for low-income groups and has been largely geographically restricted to the major US cities (Harloe, 1995; Urban, 2012; Vale and Freemark, 2012; Vale, 2013; Robbins, 2017).

Even in the Northern European heartlands of welfare capitalism, public/social housing never gained the universalist status of health and education. In the words of Torgersen (1987), public housing is the 'wobbly pillar' of the welfare state. There is no National Housing Service analogous to the National Health Service (NHS) in the UK. Although there has been national housing policy, this has been filtered through local government, as discussed below. Up until the 1980s, housing in the UK went through a substantial stage of *decommodification* allied to the expansion of public rental provision in the form of local authority/council housing. Since then, public housing has *recommodified* due to neoliberalisation, as this chapter argues.

Towards housing decommodification: the expansionary period of public housing

Municipalism and labourism

Victorian London was infamous for overcrowding and insanitary conditions in its working-class areas and justly deserved Wohl's (1977) label as the 'eternal slum'. Philanthropic landlords, such as Guinness and Peabody, housed workers at 5 per cent levels of return during the Victorian era, but substantial change only came via state intervention towards the end of the 19th century (Wohl, 1977; Porter, 1994). Key legislation includes the 1890 Housing of the Working Classes Act which facilitated slum clearance and public housebuilding on the cleared sites, and the 1919 Addison Act which introduced Treasury subsidies to finance public housebuilding (Bowley, 1944). Local government reform helped to promote the cause of public housing in London, especially the creation of the London County Council (LCC) in 1889 (Porter, 1994). An early fruition of the 1890 Act was the inspiring and still-standing Boundary estate, London's first council

Photograph 2.1: Boundary estate, 2013

estate, built in Shoreditch (in present-day Tower Hamlets) by the LCC from 1890 to 1900 (Photograph 2.1).

As Bowley (1944) demonstrates in her seminal account, public housing only developed slowly, incrementally and unevenly in Britain up until the 1940s. This slowness and unevenness were linked to how state provision was driven by local authorities, which were highly politically variable and not necessarily the most effective delivery agents for public housing (Bowley, 1944). Local authority housing provision has been heavily predicated on local politics and whether the Labour or Conservative Party ruled the town hall. In addition to trade unions, the inter-war formation of Labour as the major political party of the working class in Britain was assisted by ward-based organising via local state 'welfare on the rates' provision (Savage, 1987). Public housing provision was a key part of Labour's electoral appeal in northern cities and towns such as Sheffield (Backwith, 1995) and Preston (Savage, 1987), as it also was in London: 'The Labour Party's most effective way of building support [in London] without recourse to trades unions was through municipal action, particularly housing' (Weinbren, 1998: 43). For most of the 20th century, the London Labour Party actively promoted and enacted council house provision as an integral part of the local welfare state – municipal socialism. The major expansion of public housing took place in London under the auspices of the LCC (under continuous Labour control from 1934 to 1965), plus the later efforts of the Greater London Council (GLC), again especially under Labour rule (Power, 1982). Labour-controlled local authorities – first the Metropolitan Borough Councils (MBCs) (1889–1965) and later borough councils – also played a vital part in London's public housing expansion (Young and Garside, 1982; Parker, 1999).

The social geographies of public housing and working-class formation are intertwined with party politics (Watt, 2001). The early 20th century LCC emphasised building large estates at the city's edge, such as Becontree in Dagenham and St Helier in Merton (Porter, 1994; Olechnowicz, 1997). It was only after 1934, when Labour captured the LCC, that sustained attention was given to public housebuilding in the inner core. The scale and quality of the LCC inter-war estates means that this forms 'one of the more remarkable achievements in London's government, and contributed much to the marked improvement of conditions between the wars for the capital's working classes' (Porter, 1994: 311). The LCC's efforts, plus the activities of MBCs and borough councils, has resulted in the spatial concentration of council estates in the inner eastern and southern boroughs with their large working-class populations and Labour Party political hegemony. If local welfarism helped to forge links between the Labour Party and the city's working class, the estates also contributed towards tenants developing a working-class identity, partly as a reaction to nearby middle-class snobbery (Olechnowicz, 1997). The LCC struggled to get Conservative-controlled MBCs to build estates in the suburbs, not least due to middle-class opposition, as occurred in the case of Woodberry Down (Parker, 1999). By 1939, the LCC had built nearly 100,000 homes in London, while the MBCs had provided another 35,000 and housing associations 20,000 (LCC, 1961). The early 20th century local state provided a substantial bedrock to the Keynesian welfare state *prior* to the latter's post-war fruition.

Keynesian welfare state

Hundreds of thousands of houses were either destroyed or damaged in London during the Second World War resulting in an acute housing crisis (White, 2008). If war damage was the immediate spur to the huge post-war expansion in public housebuilding, the political driver was the 1945–51 Labour governments' desire to implement a national welfare state. Council housing formed a central plank of this agenda, as implemented by local authorities. The combination of the national welfare state with the LCC's and MBC's municipal socialism resulted in a staggering wave of public housebuilding in London – 170,723 local authority homes were built from 1945 to 1961 representing nearly nine tenths of the city's 191,488 post-war increase (LCC, 1965: 98). The LCC alone built 103,852 homes, with another nearly 66,871 provided by the MBCs. Nearly three quarters of London's post-war municipal housebuilding was located within the boundaries of the LCC – 125,903 homes (LCC, 1965: 99).

Coupled with the pre-war LCC expansion under Herbert Morrison, Labour's greatest municipal welfare achievement was large-scale enhancement of public housing in the capital from 1934 to 1964. By March 1962, the LCC, MBCs and the City of London combined had provided a total of 245,444 dwellings within the LCC boundaries (LCC, 1965: 97). Using the enlarged GLC boundaries, nearly 485,000 London households rented from the council in 1961, a huge number by international standards, representing over 18 per cent of the total (Table 2.1). Nevertheless, the PRS remained the largest tenure in 1961, housing over 42 per cent of all London households (Table 2.1), and 64 per cent in inner London (Hamnett, 2003; GLA Intelligence, 2015). It was the huge but declining inner London PRS that formed the epicentre of the city's housing problems during the 1950s and 1960s – multiple occupation, overcrowding, lack of facilities (hot water and bath), plus evictions which accelerated following the partial decontrol of rents brought in by the Conservative's 1957 Rent Act that resulted in 'Rachmanism' (Jephcott, 1964; Holland, 1965; Banting, 1979). Jephcott (1964) highlights how housing stress in the PRS was disproportionately faced by immigrants from the New Commonwealth, Pakistan, and Ireland. By contrast, most council tenants were living in high-quality housing during the 1950s (Holland, 1965). Nevertheless, 165,000 families remained on the LCC's waiting list by 1956 (LCC, 1961). If London's housing problems were by no means eradicated by the 1960s, they were dented by the sheer scale of municipal housing provision: 'The LCC did not build almost a quarter of a million houses as an aspect of its planning function, but because the people of London looked to it as a provider of homes' (Nevitt and Rhodes, 1972: 238).

Under the London Government Act 1963, the LCC was wound up in 1965 and replaced by the GLC, which had responsibility for suburban outer London as well as inner London. There are many reasons for this local government reform, but the Conservative

Table 2.1: Housing tenure in London (households), 1961–2011

Tenure	1961	1971	1981	1991	2001	2011
Local authority (N)	484,992	659,020	769,996	644,510	516,242	439,727
Housing association (N)	–	–	102,430	154,657	274,129	346,266
Social rented (N)	484,992	659,020	872,426	799,167	790,371	785,993
Local authority (%)	18.2	24.9	30.7	23.3	17.1	13.5
Housing associated (%)	–	–	4.1	5.6	9.1	10.6
Social rented (%)	18.2	24.9	34.8	28.9	26.2	24.1
Private rented (%)	42.4	34.1	15.1	12.2	14.3	25.1
Owner-occupied (%)	36.3	40.4	48.6	57.2	56.5	49.5
Other (%)	3.0	0.6	1.5	1.6	2.9	1.3
Total (N)	2,658,166	2,649,825	2,505,274	2,761,129	3,015,173	3,266,173

Source: Census (GLA Intelligence, 2015)

Party's desire to end Labour's long-run dominance of the LCC played an important part (Rhodes, 1972; White, 2008). It was Labour's unbroken 30-year control of the LCC that had enabled it, alongside the Labour-controlled MBCs, to create municipal socialism in London and especially in its inner core. By comparison, the longest period of national party rule has been the 13 years of New Labour governments from 1997 to 2010. Labour's LCC's hegemonic rule contributed towards the building of nearly 250,000 council properties in the very heart of the capital – *not* in the periphery, unlike many European cities (Power, 1997; Wacquant, 2008; Urban, 2012). This is one of the main distinguishing spatial features of London, whose imprint remains today in the still dense numbers of social rental housing in the city's inner neighbourhoods.

The post-war welfare state expansion meant that the number of London households renting from the local authority increased massively from nearly 485,000 in 1961 to nearly 770,000 in 1981 such that it was the second largest tenure at 31 per cent (Table 2.1).[1] If one adds in the 102,000 households renting from housing associations, social renting accommodated over 870,000 London households in 1981 or 35 per cent of the total. Owner-occupation accounted for

49 per cent, while the PRS had shrunk back to only 15 per cent. In inner London, the council-rented sector was the largest tenure by 1981 at 42 per cent of households (Hamnett, 2003). Most of the 1961-81 metropolitan-wide increase was due to building of estates by the GLC and borough councils, again especially under the periods of Labour control. Several inner London Labour councils, such as Camden, Islington and Lambeth, were dissatisfied with the rate of new council housebuilding. They therefore engaged in 'municipalisation', whereby they bought up private houses and flats located in streets ('street properties') to convert them into council housing (Watt, 2001; Hodkinson, 2019). Not only did this expand public housing, it also helped to prevent early gentrification that was occurring in parts of Camden and Islington during the 1960s to 1970s (Glass, 1964).

Figure 2.1 provides a breakdown of local authority households by borough for 1981. Nearly 54,000 households rented from the council in Southwark, almost two thirds of the total. Southwark had 20,735 more council-renting households in 1981 compared to 1961 (GLA Intelligence, 2015), suggesting an annual provision of around 1,000 new council homes. This huge expansion included the two large-scale modernist estates south of the Elephant and Castle – Heygate and Aylesbury. Tower Hamlets added nearly 18,000 council homes from 1961 to reach 43,421 in 1981 – the largest proportion in London at 82 per cent. Four boroughs (Brent, Haringey, Islington and Newham) – each politically dominated by Labour from 1965 onwards – more than doubled their number of council-renting households from 1961 to 1981 (GLA Intelligence, 2015). It was during this period that Newham council built the Carpenters estate, Barnet built West Hendon and Haringey built Northumberland Park. This dramatic expansion meant that accessing public housing became a normal rite of passage for working-class Londoners during the post-war period (Chapter 5). Therefore, as Hodkinson (2019: 25) argues, 'public housing went beyond bricks and mortar, to embody a collective intervention against the exploitation by private slum landlords that significantly decommodified access to shelter and provided a foundation for working-class social reproduction'.

London's council estates are dissimilar to their French and US equivalents. Although social housing is extensive in Paris (roughly a fifth of the total), unlike London it is limited in the inner core and is instead predominantly located in the peripheral areas (Bourdieu et al, 1999; Wacquant, 2008; Garbin and Millington, 2012). By London standards,

Figure 2.1: Households renting from local authority by London borough, 1981 (N)

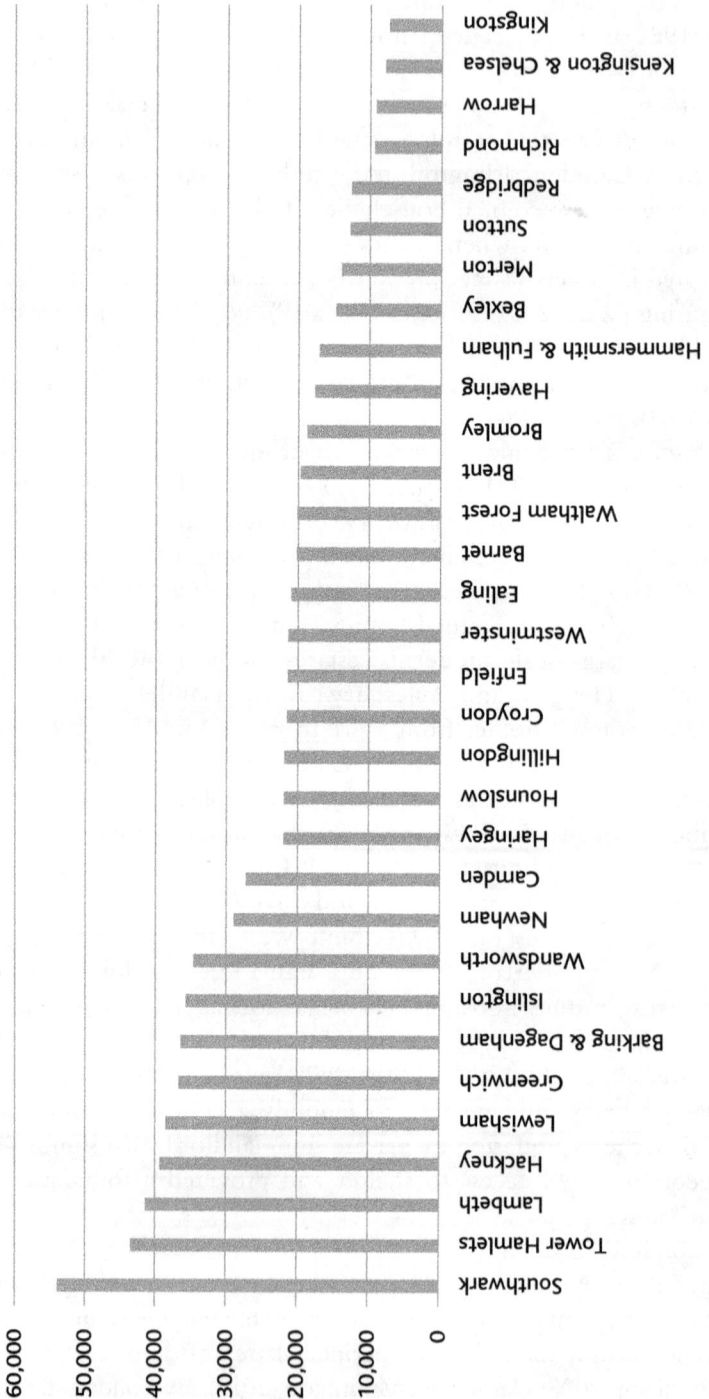

Southwark	
Tower Hamlets	
Lambeth	
Hackney	
Lewisham	
Greenwich	
Barking & Dagenham	
Islington	
Wandsworth	
Newham	
Camden	
Haringey	
Hounslow	
Hillingdon	
Croydon	
Enfield	
Westminster	
Ealing	
Barnet	
Waltham Forest	
Brent	
Bromley	
Havering	
Hammersmith & Fulham	
Bexley	
Merton	
Sutton	
Redbridge	
Richmond	
Harrow	
Kensington & Chelsea	
Kingston	

Source: 1981 Census (GLA Intelligence, 2015)

42

US cities built much smaller numbers of public units. At London's 1981 peak of nearly 770,000, local authority housing accounted for over four times the size of the New York City Housing Authority, which owned and managed 178,000 homes and is by far the largest public housing authority in the US (Robbins, 2017). In fact, London's early 1980s' peak was over half the entire US total of 1.4 million public housing units, and dwarfed that of the Chicago Housing Authority, the second largest US public housing provider with over 40,000 units (Vale and Freemark, 2012). US public housing never achieved the same broad working-class acceptance as in London (Vale, 2013). In Chicago, for example, the projects formed a distinctly racialised African-American 'second ghetto' (Hirsch, 1983). By contrast, London council housing, at least up until the 1960s, was the preserve of a 'white working class', albeit one that was ethnically differentiated, for example due to the presence of the Irish (Watt, 2001). It was only from the 1970s onwards that London council housing developed its contemporary multi-ethnic character (Chapter 5).

While the post-war period saw a massive expansion in public housing supply, there were nevertheless problems on many London estates associated with poor design, construction cost-cutting and lack of facilities (CDP, 1976; Dunleavy, 1981; Ambrose, 1996; Boughton, 2018; Tunstall, 2020). This was worsened by later funding cuts (Towers, 2000). Although municipalisation boosted the council stock, many of the acquired street properties were run down by their previous private landlords and needed extensive maintenance, as in Hackney (Harrison, 1983), Camden (Watt, 2001), and Islington (Hodkinson, 2019). The GLC, as well as inner London councils, struggled to let their rundown street properties, which resulted in around 20,000 empty council homes being squatted by the late 1970s (Kearns, 1979). These housing quality factors – plus cuts in funding, poor housing management and the impact of recession and unemployment – all contributed towards the growth of 'problem estates' in London during the 1970s (Chapter 3; Attenburrow et al, 1978; DOE, 1981).

Recommodification: the contractionary period of public housing

Local government proto-Thatcherite housing policy

The popular notion of a post-war Labour–Conservative 'Butskellite consensus' on welfare and housing is mythical, especially after 1953 when policy divergences regarding public and private renting became pronounced (Banting, 1979; Jones, 1992). These political differences were prominent in London such that Conservative-led councils pursued proto-Thatcherite recommodification housing policies – a nascent form of local state neoliberalisation. Thus, while the contractionary period of public housing is rightly associated with Thatcherism, its origins can be traced back to Conservative local government policies during the 1960s and 1970s (Passmore, 2015; Murie, 2016).

The GLC experienced alternating Labour and Conservative control from 1965 until it was abolished in 1986 under Thatcherite local government reforms. Labour controlled the GLC for just over half the period (1964–67, 1973–77 and 1981–86). Therefore, the London local government reforms meant that Labour's unassailable 30-year control of metropolitan-wide government under the LCC was halted and this enabled the Conservatives to unravel its municipal socialist achievements, none more so than in the area of public housing, the LCC's jewel in the crown. This unravelling occurred during the periods when the Conservatives controlled the GLC (1967–73 and 1977–81) and the borough councils, and it took three forms: the encouragement of homeownership; running down the existing stock in terms of size, funding and maintenance; and raising council rents to market levels (Power, 1982; Passmore, 2015).

A common misperception is that council house sales began with the Housing Act 1980 which gave sitting tenants the right to buy their council homes at substantial discounts. In fact, 'the issue of the sale of council houses is very nearly as long-lived as their construction' (Merrett, 1982: 118). In England, around 61,000 public dwellings were sold to sitting tenants on a discretionary basis between 1952 and 1970, and another 210,000 by the end of the 1970s (Jones and Murie, 2006). These discretionary sales were pushed by the Conservative Party when in government, but also by Conservative-controlled councils in London and Birmingham, including via granting mortgages (Murie, 2016). Labour had a more ambiguous position, since the Parliamentary Labour Party accepted the 'superior virtues of home ownership' (Merrett, 1982: 122) from the mid-1960s. Some commentators, such as Boughton (2018: 170), have misinterpreted the post-war legislative toing and froing by citing Labour's 1959 Manifesto as going 'further' than the Conservatives by 'offering every tenant "a chance ... to buy from the Council the house he lives in"'. This notion of post-war Labour complicity in discretionary council house sales supports the specious argument for a Butskellite consensus on housing policy. It fails to examine the historical record when Labour and the Conservatives were in power, both nationally and locally (Banting, 1979; Power, 1982; Passmore, 2015; Murie, 2016). As Merrett (1982) shows, Labour implemented many challenges to sales, at both the national and local levels, and these were especially significant in London.

Power (1982) and Passmore (2015) highlight the crucial role played by party politics in relation to London public housing during the 1960s and 1970s. As Figure 2.2 shows, discretionary sales of council properties expanded when the Conservatives controlled the GLC from 1967 to 1973, contracted rapidly when Labour was in control from 1973 to 1977, only to increase again under the Conservatives from 1977 to 1979. Power (1982) and Passmore (2015) demonstrate how sales were greater at Conservative-controlled borough councils and lower (even non-existent) at Labour boroughs.

The second aspect of proto-Thatcherite policies was shrinking the GLC stock and funding and maintenance depletion (Towers, 2000). More estates became rundown during the 1960s to 1970s, a process which was enhanced by Conservative cuts when in control of the GLC and by central government cuts imposed by Labour in the late 1970s. The London Government Act 1963 provided for the transfer of the LCC/GLC stock to whichever borough council that stock was located in. Although London Labour MPs and councils lobbied against this transfer, it was pushed through by an alliance of the GLC under Conservative control and Michael Heseltine as Secretary of State for the Environment during the early 1980s (Hansard, 1981, 1985). Southwark Council was the largest recipient of GLC dwellings from 1980 to 1983 – 23,631 were transferred which increased its stock to 62,555 (Hansard, 1983). Hackney Council had the second largest GLC transfer of 17,814 dwellings (taking its 1983 total stock to 46,350). This GLC to Hackney transfer included Woodberry Down, which at nearly 2,000 properties was one of the largest estates in Europe. Lambeth received 15,301 GLC properties (including the similarly large Clapham Park estate), which took its total stock to 48,760 (Hansard, 1983). Cash-strapped inner London councils, like Southwark, Hackney and Lambeth, were ill-prepared and under-resourced to take on board such rapid huge increases in council housing (Hansard, 1985; Towers, 2000).

Roll back to roll on and on neoliberalism

If the state housing system expanded and solidified in the post-war period up until the 1980s, it has systematically contracted and unravelled since due to 40 years of neoliberal privatisation, marketisation and demunicipalisation policies. These policies were introduced under

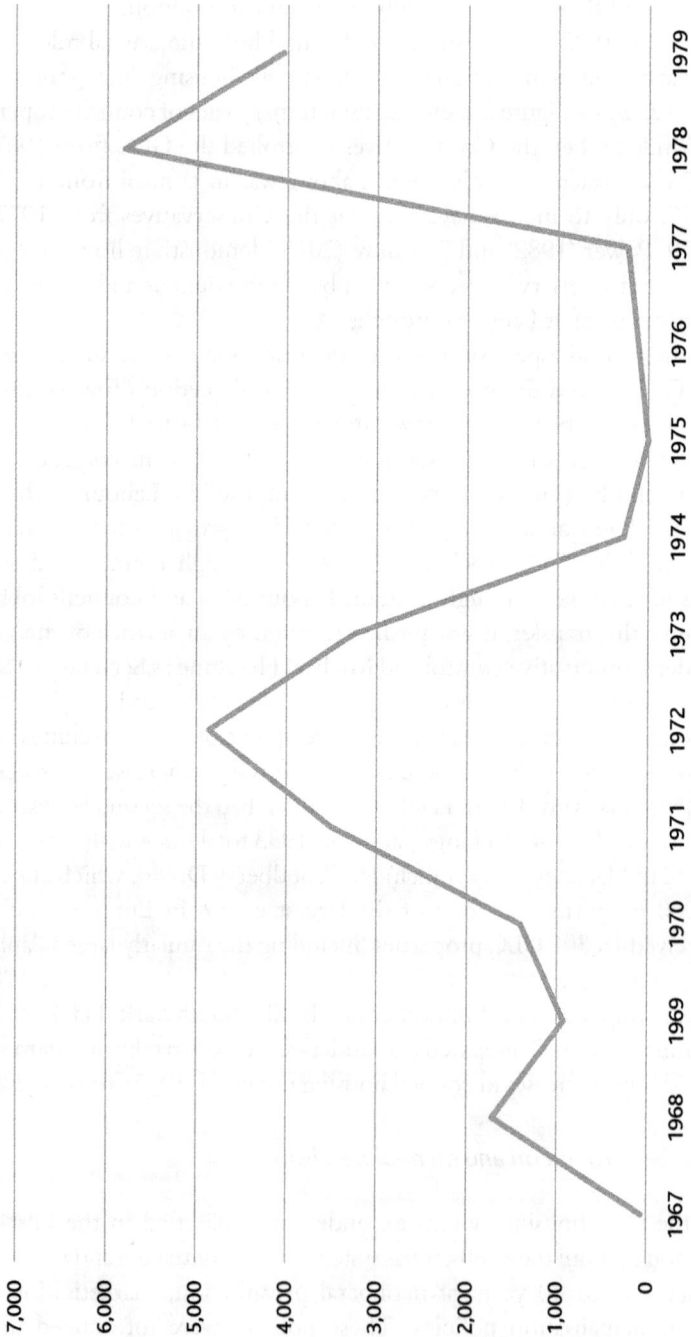

Figure 2.2: Annual sales of council properties by the Greater London Council, 1967–79 (N)

Source: Adapted from Power (1982: 256–7)

Conservative governments from 1979 to 1997. New Labour largely continued these policies, albeit in modified form, but they were then intensified under post-crash welfare austerity cuts and restructuring, The net effect has been a dramatic shrinkage of public rental households, down from 770,000 in 1981 to 440,000 in 2011 in London.

The early 'roll-back' phase of neoliberalism (Peck and Tickell, 2002) lasted from 1979 to the mid-1990s and was characterised by the rolling back of public welfare via privatisation and marketisation policies, which particularly impacted on public housing (Hodkinson, 2019). National public expenditure on housing, excluding benefits, decreased by 60 per cent in real terms from 1979–80 to 1993–94, compared with substantial real increases in expenditure on social security, health and education (Balchin, 1995: 9–10). The RTB policy formed a key plank in Thatcherism as 'popular capitalism' (Murie, 2016). Conservative governments were not content to privatise the public housing stock via the RTB – they also wanted to take the town hall out of the direct day-to-day provision and management of social housing (Hodkinson et al, 2013). Hence, the stock transfer policy of transferring council properties to housing associations was introduced via Estate Action and the 1988 Housing Act (Pawson and Mullins, 2010). Transfer meant housing associations used 'private finance to buy and renovate all or some of a local authority's homes' (National Audit Office 2003, cited in Watt, 2009a: 234). Transfer was dependent on a majority decision of tenants who voted in a ballot. Under the Conservatives, housing associations began to gain the main responsibility for owning, managing and producing social housing rather than local authorities. Stock transfer amounted to demunicipalisation and quasi-privatisation since former publicly owned council housing was transferred to increasingly commercially oriented housing associations (Ginsburg, 2005; Manzi and Morrison, 2018).

'Roll-out neoliberalism' (Peck and Tickell, 2002) began under the Conservatives during the 1990s, but was accelerated under New Labour. In order to ameliorate the negative impacts resulting from roll-back neoliberalism – increasing unemployment, homelessness and crime – the state employed governmentality techniques to re-include socially excluded populations and places, often via mobilising the 'community' through third way communitarianism (Chapter 3; Wallace, 2010a, 2010b). While New Labour encouraged 'aspirational' working-class homeownership via the RTB, it regarded council housing as irredeemably 'Old Labour' and hence unworthy of support, unlike the NHS or public education (Ginsberg, 2005). As well as maintaining the RTB, New Labour accelerated the stock transfer programme (Watt, 2009c). Thus, unlike *all* previous 20th century Labour governments, New Labour neither encouraged nor financed the expansion of local authority housing. Consequently, the public housing aspect of the Keynesian welfare state was cut adrift with disastrous consequences for working-class Londoners who could no longer access this key aspect of class reproduction (Hodkinson et al, 2013; Watt and Minton, 2016).[2]

Unsurprisingly, numbers on local authority waiting lists went up every year in London, from over 181,000 in 1997 to over 380,000 in 2012, when one in ten London households was on the list (DCLG, cited in Watt and Minton, 2016). While numbers of applicants have subsequently declined, this resulted from the Localism Act 2011, which removed nationally prescribed rules on access to social housing in favour of local authorities setting their own increasingly restrictive rules (Hodkinson and Robbins, 2013). Nearly 51,000 applicants in seven London boroughs were either struck off waiting lists or told they were ineligible (Inside Housing, 2014). This recalibration has involved prioritising the 'deserving poor' (those in paid work and ex-armed forces personnel), as opposed to the 'undeserving poor' (the unemployed, lone parents), as in Newham and Waltham Forest (Watt, 2018a, 2018b, 2020b; Humphry, 2020).

The implementation of austerity cuts and housing reforms by the Coalition Government (2010–15) in the wake of the 2008 crash ended New Labour's third-way version of neoliberalism. This was replaced by state withdrawal, localism and the Big Society (Dillon and Fanning, 2011) – or 'Do-it-yourself (DIY) communitarianism'. The result was an intensification of neoliberalisation via 'austerity urbanism' (Peck, 2012), resulting in increased poverty and deprivation (Alston, 2019). By promoting 'affordable housing' (affordable rent, shared ownership, and so on), no grant was given to social housing via the 2011–15 Affordable Homes Programme (Shelter, 2019). Consequently, the number of starts on new social rented homes in England slumped from almost 36,000 in 2010–11 to just 3,000 in the following year and a mere 950 in 2015–16 (National Housing Federation, 2017). Housing associations use cross-subsidies from private developments (including in regeneration schemes) to try and deliver social rented homes, but at a fraction of the early 1980s levels (Figure 2.3).

The 2012 introduction of 'self-financing' for local authority's Housing Revenue Account (HRA) helped to increase local authority housing investment from a low of £3.3 billion in 2012–13 to £4.6 billion in 2016–17 (in real terms), although the latter was still way below the £8 billion-plus for 1980–81 (Chaloner et al, 2019: 25–6).

The shifting funding regime is reflected in a recent uptick in public housing completions:

> During the 1970s local authorities commonly completed in excess of 100,000 new dwellings per annum and in 1980–81, ... 75,000 dwellings were completed. By 1999–00 completions had fallen to just 60. The reforms to the Housing Revenue Account in 2012 have seen completions rise to almost 2,000 per annum in recent years. (Chaloner et al, 2019: 26)

While this rise in completions is welcome, it is from an appallingly low base. Furthermore, the HRA self-financing reforms loaded billions of pounds of debt onto local authorities, which means that tenants have to repay this debt through their rents, which in turn reduces councils' fiscal capacity to maintain existing homes or build new stock (Swindon Tenants Campaign Group, 2016).

London's deepening housing crisis has prompted several councils to deploy various complex funding mechanisms to build council housing again, including Special Purpose Vehicles (SPVs) (Hackett, 2017). However, rather than providing genuinely public housing, SPVs add a novel twist to neoliberalisation via what Beswick and Penny (2018) refer to as 'financialised municipal entrepreneurialism' or 'demolishing the present to sell off the future' – as in the case of Lambeth Council's estate regeneration/demolition programme (Chapter 4).

The contraction of public housing in London[3]

Public housing peaked in 1981 when nearly 770,000 London households rented their homes from the council (Table 2.1). By 2011, this had reduced to nearly 440,000, just 14 per cent of London households, lower than in 1961. While the housing association sector expanded from 1981 to stand at 346,000 in 2011, this expansion was insufficient to counterbalance the public rental decline. Furthermore, much of the housing association expansion was not a net addition, but merely a reshuffling between landlords via stock transfers. Social housing has therefore declined in both absolute and relative terms from 1981 to 2011: down by over 86,000 to just 24 per cent. This contraction has occurred while London's population expanded from just over 6.6 million in 1981 to nearly 8.2 million in 2011 (Census; GLA Intelligence, 2015). In 2011, the PRS overtook the social rental sector, the first time this has happened since 1981.

The radical shrinkage of local authority housing (and to a lesser extent social renting generally) in London is well covered in the existing literature, so will only be discussed in broad outline (see inter alia Ginsberg, 2005; Davis, 2013; Hodkinson et al, 2013; Murie, 2016; Bowie, 2017; Boughton, 2018; Hodkinson, 2019; Shelter, 2019). This shrinkage is due to four main factors: demolitions (mainly due to regeneration), the collapse in new building, RTB sales, and stock transfers.[4]

According to Fenton et al (2012), demolitions accounted for a definite loss of 6,000 social housing properties in London from 2002 to 2010, plus a further potential loss of 20,000 giving an overall maximum of 26,000. Their analysis also suggests that 'demolition was most intense in the poorest neighbourhoods in inner London' (Fenton et al: 375). Over the same period, there were 49,000 sales to tenants (largely RTB) suggesting that the latter was the greater cause of social/ public housing reduction in London. For the later 2011–17 period, 7,350 local authority properties and another 3,846 PRP properties were demolished giving a total social housing reduction of 11,196 (MHCLG, 2019a). By comparison, RTB sales were 15,140 over the same period (MHCLG, 2019; see below). We can estimate that somewhere in the region of 17,196 to 37,000 social rental properties were lost in London due to demolition from 2002 to 2017. The LAHC (2015: 14) report shows that 30,431 social rental properties were originally located on 50 demolished London social housing estates from 2004 to 2014. It's therefore likely that the above higher estimate of 37,000 is closer to the gross social rental stock lost in London due to demolition from 2002 to 2017. Further aspects of social housing losses due to demolition and regeneration are discussed in Chapters 3 and 4. The following examines the reduction in local authority housing due to the collapse in building, RTB sales and stock transfers.

While the shrinkage of new public housebuilding began during the 1980s, there was a substantial lag as already agreed schemes went ahead. In England 74,835 local authority dwellings were built in 1980–81, as were 16,370 in London – over three and a half times the number built by private firms (Figure 2.3). Ten years later, council building in London collapsed to 1,750 and then to 20 in 1996–97, the last year of Conservative government. This already dire situation worsened from 1997 to 2010 under New Labour when a paltry 340 council homes were built in London (Figure 2.3). Instead of addressing chronic social housing shortages in London, New Labour focused on addressing social housing 'low demand', a problem that only affected certain northern cities (Watt and Jacobs, 2000). Despite housing associations' political valorisation under both Thatcher and Blair as constituting the main

Figure 2.3: Housebuilding in London, 1980–2017 (N)

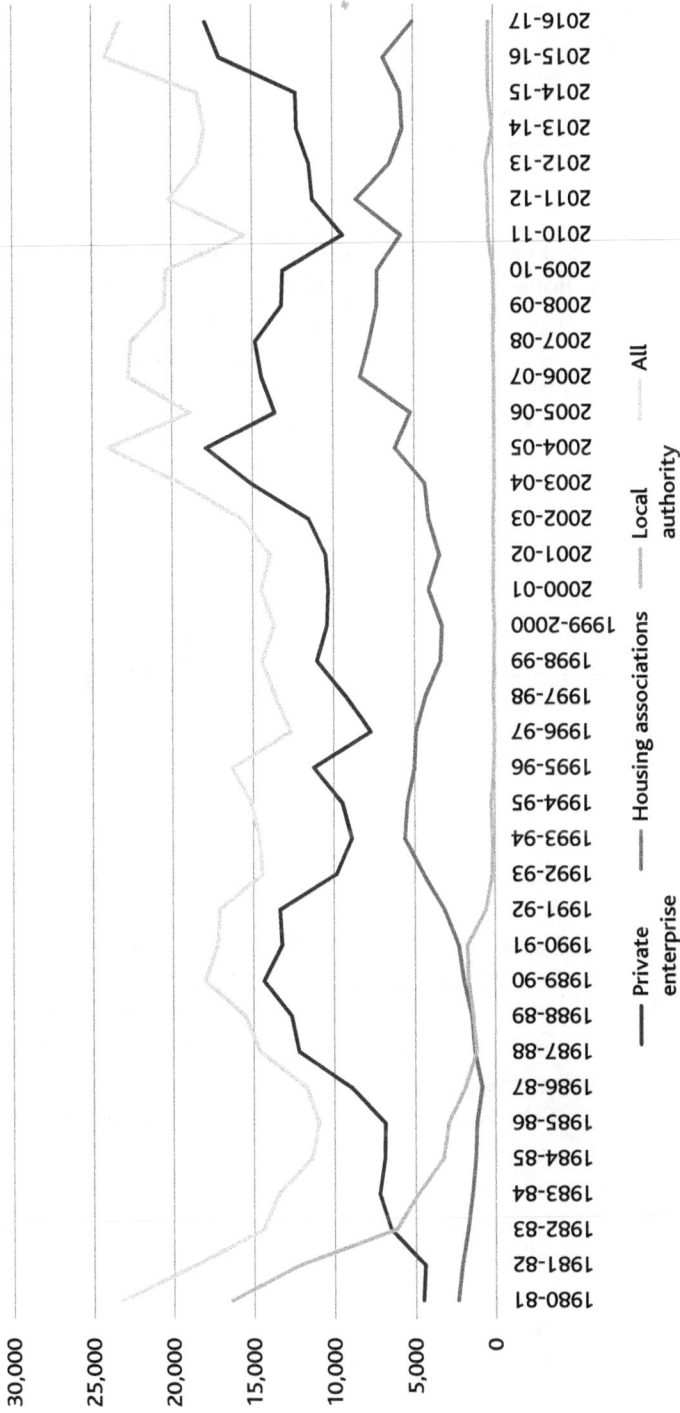

Source: MHCLG (2019a)

providers of social housing, they have never made up for the shortfall in municipal provision in London, as Figure 2.3 shows.

The RTB resulted in the sale of 285,217 council flats and houses by 2016–17, over a third of the 1980 London stock (Figure 2.4), and in aggregate terms more significant than losses due to demolition, as discussed earlier (Fenton et al, 2012). RTB sales had been slow in inner London during the early 1980s (Forrest and Murie, 1991: 118– 19), but picked up in the second half of the 1980s. Tragically for working-class Londoners, New Labour supported the RTB, but not new public housebuilding. As Copley (2014) notes, between 1998 and 2011 almost 100 council homes were sold in London for every new home built. Nevertheless, New Labour reduced the maximum discounts available; in London, these went down from £50,000 in 1997 to £38,000 in 1999 and £16,000 in 2003 (Jones and Murie, 2006). Reduced discounts and other restrictions, coupled with rapidly increasing house prices, slowed sales to a low of 397 in London in 2008–09 (Figure 2.4). The Coalition Government subsequently raised the maximum discount in London to £100,000 in 2012 (£75,000 across the country) (Murie, 2016). As a result, sales expanded although at a greater pace in London than England (Figure 2.4). Buying their home under the RTB has become much more appealing for London council tenants given the huge house price gains that can result, with ex-tenants in Hackney becoming 'property millionaires' (Mortgage Finance Gazette, 2019).

Figure 2.5 shows RTB sales for 1980–2017 by borough, indicating the large volume of sales in Barking and Dagenham, mainly accounted for by popular house sales at the giant Becontree estate. It's remarkable how many deprived London boroughs recorded massive sales whereas they had only sold less than 400 each by 1985 (Forrest and Murie, 1991), for example Southwark (17,130 sales), Tower Hamlets (14,489) and Newham (14,100). This level of sales is counterintuitive given the high poverty levels at many of these boroughs' estates. Such sales occurred due to generous discounts, but also because of the commercial exploitation of the RTB involving, 'companies offering tenants cash incentives in return for vacating the property upon completion of the right to buy purchase' (ALG, 2003: 4). Jones (2003) estimates that there were as many as 20 companies operating in London that accounted for 6 per cent of annual RTB sales in inner London. Another aspect of such RTB exploitation is 'Regeneration led right to buy – where RTB applications are put in to make a cash gain when the properties are bought back for a regeneration scheme' (ALG, 2003: 4). The ALG research indicates that RTB applications increased at many London

Figure 2.4: Annual Right to Buy sales in London and England, 1980–2017 (*N*)

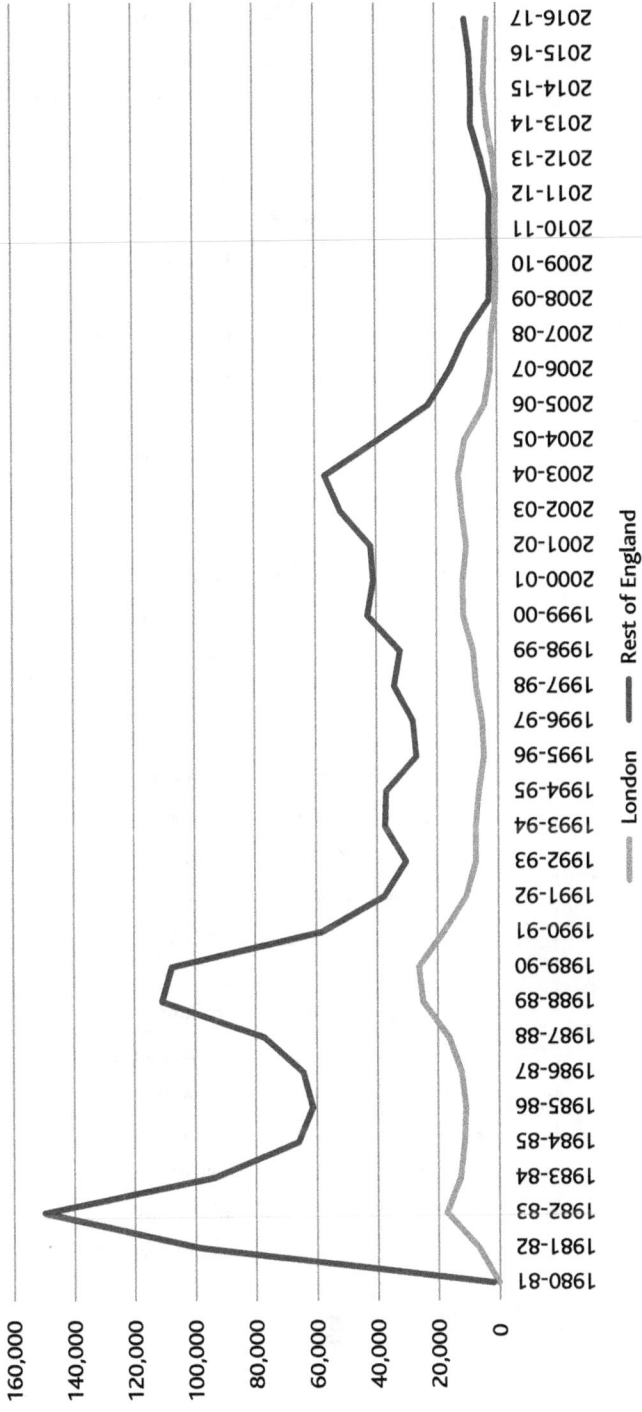

London ——— Rest of England

Source: MHCLG (2019a)

Figure 2.5: Right to Buy sales by London borough, 1980–2017 (N)

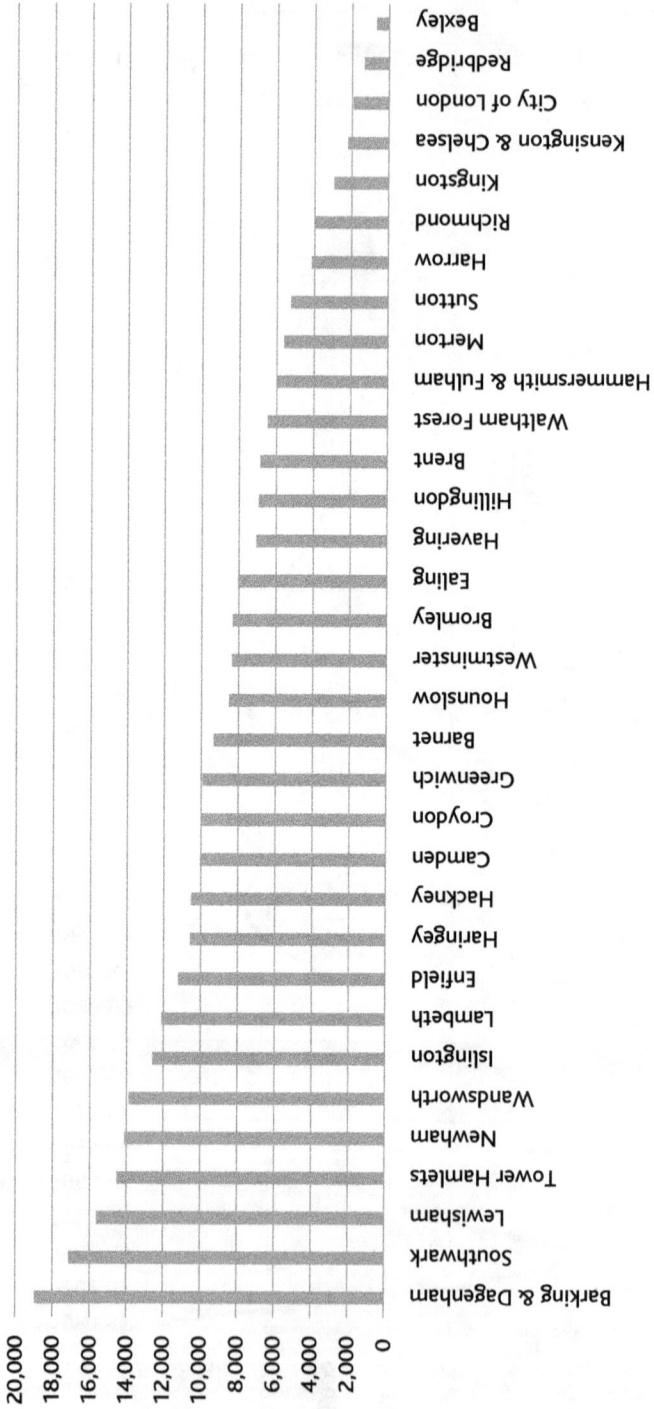

Borough	
Barking & Dagenham	
Southwark	
Lewisham	
Tower Hamlets	
Newham	
Wandsworth	
Islington	
Lambeth	
Enfield	
Haringey	
Hackney	
Camden	
Croydon	
Greenwich	
Barnet	
Hounslow	
Westminster	
Bromley	
Ealing	
Havering	
Hillingdon	
Brent	
Waltham Forest	
Hammersmith & Fulham	
Merton	
Sutton	
Harrow	
Richmond	
Kingston	
Kensington & Chelsea	
City of London	
Redbridge	
Bexley	

Source: MHCLG (2019a)

estates following the announcement of regeneration (including demolition). While this may be due to tenants wishing to make a cash gain, as the ALG report suggests, it is also highly likely to be connected to private finance companies' and estate agents' exploitation of the RTB. Several of the research estates experienced a surge in RTB applications following the regeneration/demolition announcement (Chapter 4). This aspect of the RTB has received insufficient attention from the anti-gentrification perspective (Hubbard and Lees, 2018; Elliott-Cooper et al, 2020).

Resales of RTB properties by sitting tenants have been higher in inner London than elsewhere (Jones and Murie, 2006). As the original RTB owners sell up and leave, often for suburban London and beyond, so ex-council properties have been bought by private landlords, a process that was enhanced by the expansion of buy-to-let mortgages and the commercialisation of the RTB (GMB, 2013). In addition, some RTB out-movers had sufficient capital to buy a new suburban home while also renting out their old council property, which meant they became absentee landlords. Copley (2019) estimates that more than 54,000 RTB homes (42 per cent) were privately let. Instead of the RTB creating a 'property owning democracy' in London, it has spawned a 'private landlord owning plutocracy' (Watt and Minton, 2016). The latter has contributed towards the multi-tenure nature of estates – PRS tenants living alongside RTB owners and council tenants – albeit with mixed results, as discussed in later chapters.

New Labour re-energised the previous Conservative demunicipalisation programme as part of its so-called 'modernisation' agenda (Pawson and Mullins, 2010), and in so doing pushed neoliberalisation deeper into Labour's urban heartlands including London (Hodkinson et al, 2013). Prior to 1997, only one borough had transferred its housing stock to a housing association – Conservative-controlled Bromley in 1992 (Watt, 2009c). The 2000 Housing Green paper, *Quality and Choice: A Decent Home for All*, aimed to transfer 200,000 local authority dwellings per year to housing associations (Davis, 2013). New Labour was thus determined to push forward on previous Conservative reform of local government 'aiming to privatize local services and shift delivery away from local authorities' (Wilks-Heeg, 2009: 30).

The main mechanism that New Labour used to encourage demunicipalisation was the Decent Homes Programme (DHP), discussed later. This programme compelled local authorities to reinvest in their stocks to take them up to the Decent Homes Standard (DHS), but they received no additional central government funding to assist them. Instead, each council had to pursue one of three 'stock options': large-scale voluntary transfer (stock transfer to a housing association); create an Arms-Length Management Organisation (ALMO); or devise a PFI contract (Pawson and Mullins, 2010; Hodkinson et al, 2013; Hodkinson, 2019). New Labour's underpinning rationale was shifting governance arrangements further along the direction of demunicipalisation, weakening local government and levering in private finance for social housing, all continuations of previous Conservative neoliberal policy (Wilks-Heeg, 2009; Hodkinson, 2019). These three options enhanced demunicipalisation and privatisation because they ruled out direct public investment by councils in their stock – the so-called 'fourth option'. The latter was promoted by the House of Commons Council Housing Group (HCCHG) (2005) and Defend Council Housing (DCH) and was supported by the Trades Union Congress and many Labour MPs, but to no avail with New Labour's ruling ideologues (Hodkinson, 2019).

The DHP prompted London councils to transfer slices of their housing stock as a means of accessing the funds they desperately needed to refurbish their extensive, rundown and under-invested council estates. Nearly 68,000 homes were transferred from 1998 to 2007 (Watt, 2009c). London tenant populations were more attuned to the importance of council housing, and vigorous anti-transfer campaigns took place in several inner London boroughs (Chapter 11). Stock transfer entails the sale of public land which can then be turned into prime development sites by the new housing association landlords working in partnership with private developers – a process of state-led gentrification which capitalises on the state-induced rent gap (Watt 2009a).

Public housing conditions

Thatcherite neoliberal policies had a much greater impact on housing compared to all the other areas of the welfare state (Balchin, 1995). Despite mounting evidence of backlog in repairs, real-term investment in social housing in 1997–98 was just 45 per cent of the 1980 total (Mullins and Murie, 2006: 52). Conservative government disinvestment in existing local authority housing was estimated to have resulted in a backlog of repairs of £19 billion in England by 1997 (NAO, 2010).

Since 1997, reinvestment in and maintenance of the existing public/social housing stock has occurred in a spatially uneven and less than satisfactory manner. New Labour's DHP was its main policy vehicle to reverse previous disinvestment, while its estate regeneration programme was its secondary policy (Chapter 3). When the DHP began properly in 2001, there were an estimated 1.7 million 'non-decent' homes in the social rental sector (42 per cent), made up of 1.2 million council and 500,000 housing association properties (Wilson, 2009: 4). The DHP aimed to ensure that by 2010 all social tenants in England would be living in a 'decent home' such that:

- it meets the statutory minimum standard for housing;
- is in a reasonable state of repair;
- has reasonably modern facilities and services;
- and provides a reasonable degree of thermal comfort. (Wilson, 2009: 3)

The DHP resulted in £20 billion investment in repairs and modernisation of over 2.5 million homes and was undoubtedly an improvement on the Conservatives' systemic under-funding and neglect (Hodkinson, 2019). Labour politicians have praised the DHP (Raynsford, 2016), while Boughton (2018: 244) argues that 'the Decent Homes Programme is something in which Labour can take justifiable pride – a scheme in whose modest title but practical objectives improved the lives of millions'. Despite such achievements, the DHS was not particularly high (Wilson, 2009), while the DHP only covered internal features (for example, kitchens, bathrooms, heating) rather than estates (NAO, 2010). Furthermore, DHP reinvestment was too little and too late for far too many London council tenants, as is now explained.

We saw above how New Labour's rationale in introducing Decent Homes was only partially to remedy the desperate housing needs of deprived council tenants. Had Labour wished to improve the latter's lives quickly, it could have granted the funds directly to local authorities – the fourth option (HCCHG, 2005). Instead, New Labour introduced the three stock options – transfer, ALMO and PFI – to deliberately shift housing governance further down the privatisation and demunicipalisation routes. This elaborate governance rearrangement resulted in delayed social housing improvements. The initial 2000 target for the DHP was that all homes in the social housing sector should be 'decent' by 2010. Instead, the complex governance arrangements took years to implement. Consequently, the programme missed its target dates and took far longer than originally planned.

The DHP did not actually start until 2001, four years after Labour was first elected. The 2010 target was revised in 2006 due to 'complexities' of the programme, such that 95 per cent of social homes would be decent by the end of 2010 (NAO, 2010). This 2010 revised target was also not met, 'because it has taken longer for local authorities to put in place and implement their preferred route for delivery and for some ALMOs to achieve the required inspection rating, and because of the length of the process in place to access funding' (NAO, 2010: 7). Despite Labour Housing Ministers' reassurances, DHP progress was slow in the council sector (Wilson, 2009). As Figure 2.6 shows, the national percentage of non-decent local authority homes reduced from 49 per cent in 2001–02 to 41 per cent by 2004–05, while the equivalent London figures are 55 per cent down to 46 per cent. In fact, it was only during its third term in office (2005–10) that New Labour made substantial progress in reducing both the national and London non-decent percentages (Figure 2.6). Counterfactually, had Labour lost the 2005 election, its DHP impact would have been minimal after eight years in office.

The quality of local authority stock was on average poorer in London than the rest of the country (Figure 2.6). The situation was much worse in certain inner London boroughs: 95 per cent of stock was non-decent in Hackney in 2001–02, as was 76 per cent in Tower Hamlets in 2002–03 (DCLG, 2010). Both boroughs therefore had disproportionately poor-quality housing stock, but also large numbers of estates with tenants living in deprivation due to overcrowding, unemployment and low incomes (Chapters 3 and 4).

If London had greater levels of non-decent homes at the start of the DHP, it substantially lagged behind the rest of the country in meeting the DHS, as Figure 2.6 shows. Whereas England had 16 per cent non-decent local authority dwellings by 2009–10, London had 25 per cent – the largest regional percentage. All London boroughs had reduced their Decent Homes backlog by 2009–10, but there were still 11 boroughs with more than 30 per cent non-decent homes by 2009–10 (DCLG, 2010). Even by 2016–17, 10 per cent of London's local authority homes were non-decent – including 34 per cent in Lambeth and 21 per cent in Haringey – compared to just 5 per cent in England (Local Government Association, 2020). The DHP resulted in lengthy delays, especially in London. Consequently, the pace of home improvements for many London council tenants has been glacial and for a minority virtually non-existent, rendering blanket claims of 'success' wishful thinking. Furthermore, the interaction of the DHP with regeneration schemes was to have an even worse impact on tenants at regeneration estates (Chapter 9).

Several housing and regeneration managers and professionals were interviewed. They acknowledged that the council housing stock was

Figure 2.6: Local authority non-decent dwellings in London and England, 2001/02–2009/10 (%)

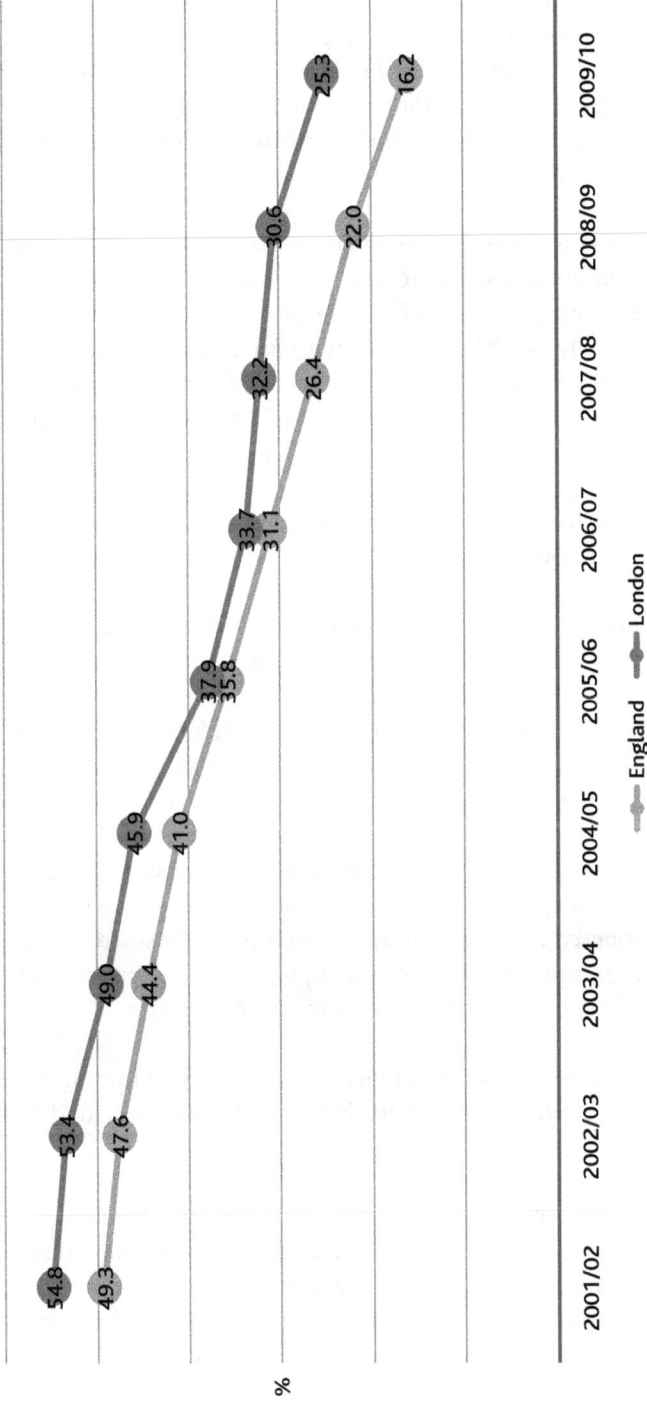

Source: DCLG (2010)

rundown due to insufficient investment over a long period of time and that major maintenance problems remained in London *despite* Decent Homes and the various regeneration programmes involving refurbishment (Davis, 2013; Hodkinson, 2019; see Luba, 2012, on Southwark). A private sector regeneration manager who had "worked on a majority of estates in London, probably most of the worst ones" felt strongly about this:

> 'There is nothing wrong with estates, they have just been abandoned and left to rot. You know doing this work [regeneration] you will be surprised what ... Well you probably won't be surprised what I have seen around many of the local authorities, working in different boroughs and the conditions people now live in. They may have a roof over their head, but Christ, you know its poverty.'

He went on to describe how council properties had received insufficient reinvestment over many years:

> 'The physical structure was pretty good, the structure of most of them are better than what I would class as the new-build – I wouldn't personally buy a new-build. But over the years, they [council properties] haven't been kept up to a decent standard. Like you go in, the rewiring in some of the cases was 30 years old, still using black and red wiring, kitchens haven't been changed to a decent standard for 10 to 15 years, old windows, bathrooms never been changed, no money put into it. There was no money put into a property, even if you were to rent it privately you'd expect to go into a decent standard of property. The councils just at the time weren't looking after their properties.'

This view was endorsed by a retired London Senior Housing Manager for Councils who explained the decline in maintenance funding from the late 1980s:

> 'There was a huge persistent sustained underfunding of the management and maintenance allowances. Now that's very nerdish, but basically it was the amount of money that was notionally available to manage and maintain the estate. I'm not talking about the big major repairs, I'm just talking about ongoing maintenance quality of the estates. And that

was hugely underfunded and increasingly so, and as the stock began to age, they became increasingly inadequate.'

As he went on to say, this lack of funding had progressively worsening consequences as the stock aged. The Housing Director of an inner London local authority confirmed the long-term lack of investment which the council was trying to rectify: "there has been, for all kinds of reasons, traditionally a lack of investment in the stock, so not only do we have a massive stock, but it's crumbling and decrepit, and thinking about how we actually manage that in the future and retain that scale has been a tricky challenge". This Director reflected on the significance of DHP vis-à-vis planned, sustained maintenance:

> 'I think it's less about Decent Homes and it's more about a proper planned approach to maintenance. If you had your own house, you recognise that it's probably wise to do the external painting before the window frames start to rot because you're going to save yourself some money in the long term. There wasn't necessarily that planned approach [in council housing] and to be frank with you, we're only just putting in place a proper planned maintenance programme now [2013]. So we're playing catch-up and thereafter we'll put in place that cyclical decoration programme, window renewal whatever it might be. So, I think there was maybe a lack of planning and a pragmatic approach to stock management. Also, I think traditionally there has been in all local authorities an under-investment.'

Conclusion

The expansionary period of public housing in London lasted throughout the first eight decades of the 20th century and reached its apogee under the post-war national Keynesian welfare state. This period saw substantial housing decommodification whereby council housing became a key feature of the metropolitan welfare state. As a result, renting from the council became a welcome and normalised part of working-class Londoners' housing experiences (Chapter 5).

Such housing decommodification started to be undermined during the 1960s to 1970s. A form of housing 'nascent neoliberalisation' was in train in London and other cities (notably Birmingham) *well before* Margaret Thatcher walked into 10 Downing Street. She was effectively nationalising the recommodification strategies – privatisation and financial cuts – of previous Conservative local governments. From 1979 onwards, central government Thatcherite neoliberalisation policies, not least the RTB, facilitated wholesale housing recommodification. New Labour largely continued such policies with the partial exception of the DHP. Despite its headline national reinvestment improvements, the DHP was also slow and partial, especially in London. These limitations became even more apparent under estate regeneration (Chapter 9); the latter is the subject of the next chapter.

3

Urban policy: estate regeneration

This chapter reviews the various urban policy programmes which have attempted to renew and regenerate London's deprived estates. The chapter begins with a brief overview of 'old' urban renewal in its post-war slum clearance form, and its 'new urban renewal' form as estate regeneration. It then traces the development of estate-based programmes from the 1980s to the 2010s, and in so doing employs a binary early-contemporary periodisation. The early period (1980s to 1990s) included relatively generous public subsidies. Contemporary regeneration dates from the late 1990s to 2010s and is the primary focus of this book. It was during this period that the private sector was expected to undertake the heavy lifting in terms of regeneration funding. The analysis concentrates on the New Labour years since this is when most of the research schemes in this book began. Following this chronological account, the next section examines the hegemonic 'official discourse' on estate regeneration and excavates the underlying rationale for such regeneration in London. Aspects of the 'entrepreneurial city' are then briefly examined in London, and the concept of the 'entrepreneurial borough' is introduced. The penultimate section compares early and contemporary estate regeneration schemes, including with reference to differential mixed-tenure outcomes, while the final section examines what regeneration-as-demolition costs residents both in financial and human terms.

From old to new urban renewal[1]

Post-war urban policy in Western capitalist societies consisted of renewal programmes which involved tearing down inner-city 'slum housing' which in many cases was replaced with public/social housing estates, typically of modernist architectural design (Hirsch, 1983; Urban, 2012). While such urban renewal often resulted in improved housing, it also erased established working-class neighbourhoods, as seen in Herbert Gans' (1962) classic study of the West End of Boston. Urban renewal and resultant displacement destroyed working-class support networks and generated grieving for lost homes and communities (Fried, 1966; Marris, 1986). Fullilove (2016) has employed the concept of 'root shock' to highlight the racialised, destructive impacts of urban renewal on black communities in US cities.

The development of large-scale post-war public/social housing estates was based on a utopian modernist vision (Campkin, 2013). However, this vision swiftly faded and from the 1970s onwards many of these estates came to be widely regarded – by politicians, the mass media and academics – as failed areas of dense poverty and crime, in both the US and Europe (Rainwater, 1970; Wacquant, 2008; Vale, 2013; Hess et al, 2018). 'Neighbourhood effects' were identified during the 1980s whereby low-income tenants were said to be doubly disadvantaged – not only by their own poverty and deprivation, but also by the *spatial* poverty and deprivation of their residential neighbourhood (Manley et al, 2013). In other words, a neighbourhood poverty effect over and above any individual poverty effects (Wilson, 1987). The suggested causal mechanisms for neighbourhood effects include lack of suitable role models, and insufficient connections to paid employment since out-of-work public tenants are spatially clustered together with other unemployed tenants like themselves. In Robert Putnam's terminology, tenants have a surfeit of 'bonding capital' to fellow poor tenants 'like them' and a deficit of 'bridging capital' to socially dissimilar others – that is, those in work and in high-paying jobs (Putnam, 2000).

Neighbourhood effects have provided the questionable intellectual rationale and justification for the eradication of spatial concentrations of public housing via 'new urban renewal' policies (Hyra, 2008). These involve demolishing public/social housing estates and redeveloping the areas into mixed-tenure neighbourhoods, for example in the US Hope VI programme during the 1990s and 2000s (Vale, 2013; Manzo, 2014a, 2014b; Robbins, 2017). New urban renewal has become the policy orthodoxy regarding social housing estates and has spread out from the US to European and Australian cities (Bridge et al, 2012; Darcy, 2013; Watt and Smets, 2017). A prominent consequence of new urban renewal programmes involving demolition is displacement whereby social tenants are spatially relocated, either nearby or further afield (Goetz, 2013; Kearns and Mason, 2013; Posthumus and Lelevrier, 2013; Morris, 2019). In some cases, social tenants have gained the 'right to remain' in or 'right to return' to the redeveloped neighbourhoods (Posthumus and Lelevrier, 2013; Glucksberg, 2017). In other cases, this right was conditional on being a 'good tenant' (paying rent, not being engaged in criminality, and so on) such that 'bad tenants' did not return (Shamsuddin and Vale, 2017).

The redeveloped areas are mixed-tenure neighbourhoods consisting of new private properties and a proportion of rebuilt social housing.

The aim of such neighbourhoods is to promote 'mixed communities' comprising the remaining/returning social tenants who live alongside incoming private homeowners. This social mixing is meant to result in 'positive gentrification' (Davidson, 2008), whereby poor/working-class tenants benefit from living in close proximity to affluent/middle-class homeowners, for example via increasing bridging capital and raising aspirations (Watt, 2017).

Despite the all-pervasive policy emphasis on creating mixed-tenure neighbourhoods, there is widespread academic scepticism as to how much positive post-regeneration social interaction across tenure/class divides occurs (Davidson, 2010; Bridge et al, 2012; Paton, 2014; Watt and Smets, 2017). In her review of the British literature, Colomb (2011: 233) concludes, 'There has been little, or no evidence, of increased social interaction between residents of social housing and the owner-occupiers of the newly built housing units'. Instead of creating mixed communities, the post-regeneration landscape generates new intra-neighbourhood inequalities and distinctions, for example inter-tenure stigmatisation and mutual suspicion (Paton, 2014; Jeffery, 2018). Several London studies have found little evidence of social mixing in new-build, mixed-tenure schemes (Kilburn, 2013; Awofolaju, 2014; Corcillo, 2020). Instead, these studies have identified prejudice and stigma directed against social tenants by high-income private owners and renters who blame the former for noise, ASB and making the neighbourhood look 'down-market'.

Early estate regeneration: 1980s to 1990s

The regeneration of council-built estates became a prominent issue in Britain as early as the 1970s. A series of official reports identified 'problem estates' characterised by high levels of poverty, crime and ASB (vandalism, graffiti, drunkenness, neighbour quarrels, and so on) (Attenburrow et al, 1978; DOE, 1981). Many of these estates needed physical upgrading. They also became a problem for housing managers because they were unpopular with tenants, and became 'difficult-to-let' (or 'hard-to-let') resulting in empty properties and above-average turnover rates.

Visiting US academics, such as Oscar Newman, drew simplistic decontextualised parallels between UK council estates, such as the Aylesbury in south London, and US public housing projects (Campkin, 2013). In *Utopia on Trial*, Alice Coleman (1990) offered a one-dimensional, albeit highly influential, environmentally determinist analysis of estates in Southwark and Tower Hamlets. She identified correlations between design features (tower blocks) and 'social malaise' (graffiti) but ignored social factors like poverty and deprivation. It's noteworthy that Coleman's supposedly benign control estate with houses – Blackbird Leys in Oxford – was subject to rioting a few years later (Power and Tunstall, 1997).

Kintrea (2007: 267) has identified 'at least a dozen significant housing related policies and programmes in operation that were relevant to the improvement of area quality' in England from 1975 to 2000. These regeneration programmes varied in aims, size, funding and geographical scope. The Priority Estates Project (PEP) began in 1979 and focused on housing management (Power and Tunstall, 1995). Estate Action was introduced in 1985 and was far more ambitious and well-funded; it included physical renewal and refurbishment as well as stock transfer (Kintrea, 2007). Another programme involving stock transfer was Housing Action Trusts (HATs), which were introduced in two waves from 1989, the first wave being far less successful than the second (Tiesdell, 2001; Hull, 2006). HATs aimed to take some of the 'worst estates' out of local authority control for 5–10 years and put them under control of a HAT, which would renovate them and then sell them back to a housing association or private landlord (Tiesdell, 2001). The original intention was that the Conservative Government would impose HATs on tenants and local authorities. This prompted a powerful grassroots tenant opposition, notably at the Ocean estate in Tower Hamlets, which resulted in a government climbdown on their forced imposition (Woodward, 1991; Tiesdell, 2001; Watt, 2018c). HATs were subsequently modified, and these second-wave HATs were introduced in six local authority areas, including three in London (Stewart and Rhoden, 2003; Hull, 2006).

The regeneration programmes that were introduced during the 1990s, such as City Challenge and the Single Regeneration Budget (SRB), were broader-based than Estate Action or HATs in that they incorporated a strong community engagement emphasis, reflecting roll-out neoliberalism (Peck and Tickell, 2002). City Challenge and SRB included area-based initiatives (ABIs) which focused on council-built estates, such as the Peckham Partnership SRB in Southwark discussed later, and the Central Stepney SRB (Chapter 4). Like Estate Action and HATs, these SRB schemes involved stock transfers to housing associations. What Estate Action, HATs and SRB also had in common was substantial levels of central government funding which, allied to local government top-up money, resulted in estate schemes being largely publicly funded (Hull, 2006). Another important feature of these early schemes was that many resulted in a net reduction in density, which facilitated the redevelopment of houses as well as flats, as discussed later.

How successful were these 1980s to 1990s regeneration programmes? Generic assessments suggest that aggregate poverty and deprivation alleviation was limited – largely a matter of preventing things getting worse (Lupton, 2003; Kintrea, 2007). Specific programme evaluations, however, indicate more positive changes, for example in relation to devolved housing management in PEP estates (Power and Tunstall, 1995), while second-wave HATs had some success in relation to housing quality improvements and community development (Stewart and Rhoden, 2003; Hull, 2006). Let us now turn to examine these early regeneration programmes in the London context.

London's estates

The problems faced by London's estates during the 1980s to 1990s were substantial. In addition to chronic underinvestment, there were numerous hard-to-let flats, empty and squatted properties, burnt-out cars and high levels of tenants applying for transfer at the 'worst estates' (Harrison, 1983; Forman, 1989; Green, 1997; Jacobs, 1999; Watt, 2001). Nationally, council estates represented areas of concentrated deprivation and many of these were in London, as a Department of the Environment (DOE) report demonstrated (Harvey et al, 1997). This report found that deprivation in England was disproportionately higher in local authority housing areas, even though half of deprived local areas comprised other tenures apart from council housing. Harvey and colleagues (1997) identified 1,370 deprived local authority estates of which nearly two thirds (879) were in London. Figure 3.1 shows the 31 local authorities with 12 or more deprived estates in 1991. Of these 31, 21 were London boroughs with Hackney (112), Southwark (101) and Tower Hamlets (100) each having 100 or over. These three London boroughs, along with Islington (75), Lambeth (75) and Camden (47), had 510 deprived council estates – 37 per cent of the England total and more than the rest of the country combined.

If the DOE report highlighted the scale of the deprivation problems facing London's council estate residents by the 1990s, it also showed the under-representation of the city's estates in targeted funding programmes, such as Estate Action, HATs, City Challenge and SRB. London had the *lowest proportion* of deprived estates in receipt of such regeneration funding from 1986 to 1994 – just 14 per cent (127 estates) compared to a national average of 25 per cent. In other words, London had 64 per cent of England's deprived estates, but only 14 per cent

Figure 3.1: Local authorities in England with 12 or more deprived estates, 1991 (N)

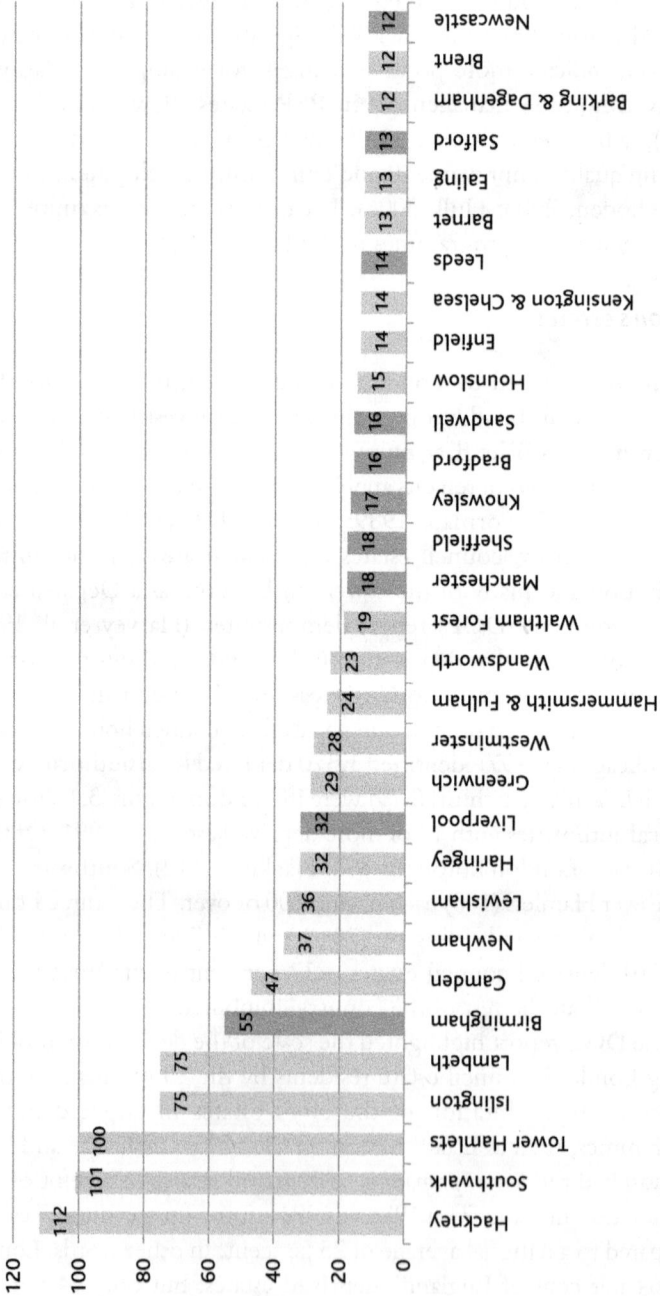

Local authority	N
Hackney	112
Southwark	101
Tower Hamlets	100
Islington	75
Lambeth	75
Birmingham	55
Camden	47
Newham	37
Lewisham	36
Haringey	32
Liverpool	32
Greenwich	29
Westminster	28
Hammersmith & Fulham	24
Wandsworth	23
Waltham Forest	19
Manchester	18
Sheffield	18
Knowsley	17
Bradford	16
Sandwell	16
Hounslow	15
Enfield	14
Kensington & Chelsea	14
Leeds	14
Barnet	13
Ealing	13
Salford	13
Barking & Dagenham	12
Brent	12
Newcastle	12

Note: London boroughs in light grey; England local authorities in dark grey.
Source: Adapted from Harvey et al (1997: 23, Table 13)

of related national funding: 'the figures suggest that there has been a more complete targeting of resources on the most deprived estates in *regions outside London*' (Harvey et al, 1997: 26; emphasis added). Therefore, despite the very significant overconcentration of deprivation at London's council estates, alongside the city's over-representation of non-decent local authority dwellings (Chapter 2), national regeneration funding tended to skirt around – rather than target – London's estates. Let's now examine two examples of early 1980s to 1990s regeneration schemes which did take place at some of London's 'worst estates'; the first is in Hackney and the second in Southwark.

Comprehensive Estates Initiative in Hackney, 1992–2003

The Comprehensive Estates Initiative (CEI) was based on five system-built large estates including Holly Street and New Kingshold. These were estates that would have appeared among Hackney's 112 deprived estates. Holly Street was built by Hackney Council in the 1970s. During the period leading up to the CEI, 80 per cent of its tenants had applied to transfer, turnover was nearly three times the borough average, and a quarter of properties were either voids or squatted (Jacobs, 1999: 112). New Kingshold was built by the GLC during the 1960s and was later transferred to Hackney Council (Chapter 2). Towers (2000: 117) notes how demolition at New Kingshold was presaged by post-transfer neglect (as discussed in relation to Woodberry Down and Clapham Park estates in Chapter 7):

> Behind a demolition decision often lies a history of neglect. Halston Point and Thornhill Point were 22-storey tower blocks, part of the New Kingshold estate in Hackney. [...] In 1982 it was transferred to the borough council. Within a short time the support system the GLC had provided disappeared – resident caretakers were removed, gardeners no longer looked after the grounds, repairs didn't get done. By the early 1990s the blocks had deteriorated appallingly – disrepair and vandalism had wrecked the blocks; the lifts broke down repeatedly; flats were infested with cockroaches; and several had been burnt out by fires deliberately started. Unsurprisingly tenant pressure was intense and the blocks were dynamited in 1995.

Niall (one of my interviewees) had lived at New Kingshold estate during the 1980s and 1990s and he described poor housing conditions and extensive squatting: "That was one of the criticisms that the tenants had of Hackney Council that they weren't preventing a high level of squatters taking over void properties on the estate."

The CEI policy process is the subject of a penetrating study by Keith Jacobs (1999), while he and Tony Manzi also published a follow-up study of Holly Street (Manzi and Jacobs, 2009). The CEI was largely publicly funded and involved a combination of demolition, rebuilding and refurbishment. It resulted in a net reduction in density alongside a shift away from council to housing association tenancies. Jacobs (1999) and Manzi and Jacobs (2009) are broadly positive about the CEI since it resulted in substantial housing improvements for tenants. Tower blocks were demolished at Holly Street and New Kingshold and replaced with houses, a popular change with tenants. Jacobs (1999) is nevertheless aware of the CEI tensions and problems, for example delays in repairs at Holly Street. He also highlights the limitations of tenant participation, including tenants expressing cynicism and distrust, as well as weariness at the number of meetings they were expected to attend.

In her evidence to the London Assembly's Housing Committee Investigation into Social Housing Estate Regeneration, Pat Turnbull (2014) provides an in-depth resident perspective of how the CEI unfolded; her account reflects several themes that are tackled in this book. She was chair of the tenants and residents association (TRA) for New Kingshold and her account gels with Jacobs' comments on the often frustrating nature of participation. Turnbull also highlights how many of the promised improvements – regarding homes and estate facilities – either never happened or only happened following tenant campaigning. She emphasises the negative psychological impacts: 'the stress of living on an estate being demolished … should never be underestimated' (Turnbull, 2014: 6). In terms of longevity, Turnbull (2014: 5) notes how the New Kingshold experience was over relatively quickly: 'compared to the typical regeneration scheme nowadays the whole thing took a much shorter space of time, a few years'. This is only one aspect of how the early schemes differ from contemporary ones, as examined later.

Peckham Partnership SRB in Southwark, 1994–2004

The Peckham Partnership SRB focused on five estates in Southwark. Arbaci and Rae (2013) use Peckham (including this scheme) as an example of a London social housing area which has been regenerated, but *not* gentrified. Housing conditions, training and employment improved due to regeneration, which meant that the area's deprivation score reduced. This benefited the local, largely BAME population who remained in situ: 'the resident population within social housing has remained largely the same throughout the process, with minimal displacement' (Arbaci and Rae, 2013: 472). Hence Peckham has not witnessed a large influx of affluent owner-occupiers, via gentrification, as occurred at Arbaci and Rae's Islington case study.

While Arbaci and Rae (2013) rely on secondary analysis of official statistics, Luna Glucksberg (2013, 2017) provides a detailed ethnographic account of the Peckham SRB regeneration process and effects.[2] Her rich, polysemic study highlights the manifold divergences and contradictions both *between and within* the various 'stakeholder' groups – politicians, professionals and tenants. Glucksberg's interviews suggest that some tenants were happy to leave the area because of crime and deprivation in Peckham, a view supported by my own interview with an ex-Regeneration Officer who worked on this scheme:

> 'There was a high level of crime and anti-social behaviour, it was a very, very, very tough environment. The flats themselves had some of the usual problems that you had at that time. There was a district heating system that was pretty inefficient. There was constantly cockroach infestation and that goes with the heating system. In Southwark, something like 80 per cent of the first lot of people said, "this is my big opportunity", and they moved off permanently.'

Nevertheless, as Glucksberg (2017) highlights, other tenants valued their existing homes and neighbourhoods and did not want to leave. Homes were of a generous size, as the ex-Regeneration Officer commented: "[they had] very big rooms, generous rooms, everybody had kitchens that you could have a table in and sit and have a family meal in the kitchen". By comparison, tenants complained that the new flats on offer were 'little more than chicken coups' (Southwark News, 1998). As the Officer notes, issues also arose because of the reduction in council homes and shift towards housing association assured tenancies, which many council tenants baulked at, an issue that has emerged in later schemes (Chapter 8).

The official view that the SRB area was '"empty" and needed "community building" 'does not tally with the ethnographic record' (Glucksberg 2017: 96). Tenants had to struggle to obtain the 'right to return' (Glucksberg, 2017), hardly indicative of a place where residents did not value their neighbourhood (Southwark *News*, 1998). Glucksberg's account, allied to my own research on local newspaper coverage, also indicates that tenants experienced the regeneration process as far more problematic and damaging – socially and psychologically – than the official account suggests, in relation to losing existing valued estate facilities, living in a deteriorating physical environment and suffering from increased crime and ASB (Southwark News, 1998, 2000a, 2000b, 2002). All these negative themes resonate with my arguments regarding 'degeneration' in Part III. Nevertheless, as Arbaci and Rae (2013) argue, the Peckham Partnership SRB did not result in the wholesale state-led gentrification that later regeneration schemes have, including those in this book. This theme will be returned to later.

Contemporary estate regeneration: 1990s to 2010s

New Labour

By the time of New Labour's arrival in government in 1997, there had been over 20 years of dedicated ABIs, many concentrated on council-built estates. Although these included several of London's 'worst estates' (as above), by and large they did not include the research estates in this book (Chapter 4). Partial exceptions were the Ocean estate, three of whose blocks fell under the Central Stepney SRB (later in this chapter, and Chapter 4), and Northumberland Park, which received some Estate Action funding. Therefore, not only did the research estates – like the Aylesbury, Carpenters, Clapham Park, West Hendon and Woodberry Down estates – suffer from the aggregate depletion of public housing investment under the Thatcher and Major governments, but they were also bypassed for central government regeneration funding. Putting it crudely, they were left to rot. New Labour changed this – at least in theory – partly by introducing the DHP, but also by initiating a complex raft of regeneration programmes, several of which targeted the research estates in this book.

New Labour launched an ambitious range of urban policy programmes to regenerate cities and tackle social exclusion in deprived neighbourhoods, especially council estates (SEU, 1998; Colomb, 2007, 2011; Kintrea, 2007; Hodkinson, 2019). These included the NDC and the National Strategy for Neighbourhood Renewal, which were targeted at areas of concentrated social exclusion (Watt and Jacobs, 2000). New Labour maintained and extended the previous 1990s' Conservative emphasis on community participation. Under New Labour, 'community' became a strategic third way concept underpinning both regeneration and welfare 'modernisation' (Imrie and Raco, 2003, Wallace, 2010a, 2010b; Dillon and Fanning, 2011). 'Strong communities' were viewed as mitigating the uncertainties of globalisation, whilst being important sites for the cultivation of 'active', responsible citizens (Fuller and Geddes, 2008). 'Community' therefore became the all-purpose social problem solution. Roll-out neoliberalism peaked under New Labour via an expectation that regeneration would reinvigorate area-based communities – as signified by the name of its flagship programme, the New Deal for Communities. However, these area-based communities could not consist of 'failed' council estates. Instead they had to comprise mixed-tenure communities of social tenants *plus* homeowners (Lupton and Fuller, 2009; Bridge et al, 2012). As discussed above, such tenure mixing would supposedly alleviate neighbourhood effects and raise social aspirations among deprived and workless social rental households.

Despite New Labour's lofty urban policy ambitions, it was unwilling to dedicate sufficient public funds to address the massive task of estate regeneration. Therefore, it increased private sector investment via stock transfers, PFI 'outsourced regeneration', and other PPPs where council land is sold (or long-leased) to a private developer (Watt, 2009a, 2013; Hodkinson, 2019). The results were the deepening and widening of the neoliberalisation and privatisation of public housing. Furthermore, previous housing supply policy failures had to be rectified, especially in London, such that regeneration began to spatially shift away from being focused on estates per se towards plugging gaps in the city's housing supply – hence the growing linkage between estate regeneration and densification (Bennington et al, 2004; Bowie, 2010, 2017; Hanna et al, 2016).

New Deal for Communities[3]

Tackling social exclusion was a main New Labour policy aim. It was famously symbolised by Tony Blair's visit to the Aylesbury estate in Southwark shortly after being elected in 1997 to begin the process of including these 'excluded' people and places (Campkin, 2013). The Aylesbury subsequently became one of the NDC areas. The NDC programme covered 39 of the most deprived neighbourhoods across England, including ten in London (Lawless et al, 2010; Lawless and Beatty, 2013). NDC populations suffered from poverty, high unemployment, poor health, high crime/ASB and fear of crime levels. The programme's overarching aim was to reduce the gaps between the 39 NDC areas and the rest of the country in relation to six themes: housing and the physical environment, crime, the community, education, health and worklessness.

The NDC was designed to address criticisms of previous regeneration programmes: that they were short-termist, lacked sufficient funding, were too geographically spread out, and were top–down. By contrast, the NDC operated over a ten-year period and each scheme had substantial funding of around £50 million. The six SRB rounds covered 1,000 areas, whereas the NDC focused on just 39 areas. The NDC also placed far more emphasis on community participation: 'by forging strong local alliances and ploughing back the knowledge and experience gained, NDC aims to enable local people to take charge of their own future' (ODPM, 2003: 2).

The national NDC evaluation suggests that it had some successes, notably in relation to place-based outcomes, but less so for people-based results (Lawless et al, 2010; Lawless and Beatty, 2013; CRESR, 2015). There is also a disjunction between the positive survey results, and more critical case study findings, including at several London NDCs (Bennington et al, 2004; Dinham, 2005, Watt, 2009a; Wallace, 2010b). These case studies highlight several criticisms of the NDC aims and results, for example tensions between top–down fiscal and governance frameworks and the needs and wishes of NDC residents (Fuller and Geddes, 2008). Such tensions were acute at the large estate-based London NDCs, three of which are research estates in this book – Aylesbury, Ocean and Clapham Park.

Housing and the physical environment was the single largest theme in financial terms, accounting for 31 per cent of all national NDC expenditure up until March 2008, although nine of the ten London NDCs spent above the average on this theme (Cole et al, 2010). The emphasis on housing and the physical environment in London reflects two factors. First that several London NDCs were located at large council estates which were extremely physically rundown due to long-term disinvestment (Ambrose, 2002; CPP, 2013; Watt, 2020c). Second, the housing emphasis 'reflects the priorities of local residents, concerned not only about the condition of the housing stock but also the consequence of poor housing for their health, well-being and safety' (Bennington et al, 2004: 1). Residents wanted their chronically poor housing conditions to be addressed, including overcrowding, as well as to see an increase in the social housing supply (Bennington et al, 2004). NDC officers thought that the programme had underestimated the extent of housing problems in some London areas and failed to predict how important housing was for residents (Bennington et al, 2004; CPP, 2013).

In addition to refurbishment, several London NDCs (including the three mentioned above) involved proposals for major physical renewal including demolition of existing council blocks and building new private flats for sale to cross-subsidise refurbishment (Watt and Wallace, 2014). The large size of the London NDC estates, coupled with their rundown condition, resulted in substantial funding gaps between redevelopment/refurbishment costs and NDC finance: 'the sums were reported to "just not add up"' (Bennington et al, 2004: 13). It superficially appeared that New Labour was pouring more public money into estate regeneration than previous Conservative governments. However, the £50 million plus NDC area budget was below the funding for the three earlier London HATs, which had equivalent-sized populations. For example, the HAT funding for 1,629 properties in Tower Hamlets was £123m (Hull, 2006: 2328), compared to £56m NDC funding for the Aylesbury estate with 2,700 properties.[4] It must also be remembered that the NDC had another five themes to address in addition to housing and in this sense was more ambitious than HATs.

Given New Labour's ideological restrictions on local authority borrowing, the NDC housing funding gap was aimed to be filled via stock transfers to housing associations which had greater capacity to borrow private finance (Ginsburg, 2005). This strategy was put forward at the three NDC research estates with numerous unsatisfactory results, at least from the residents' point of view. In line with New Labour thinking, NDC officers and council staff thought that creating mixed-tenure communities was desirable and inevitable, even though they acknowledged that there would be displacement of existing residents plus an influx of new affluent homebuyers (Bennington et al, 2004). Officers realised that tensions could emerge, which they indeed did: "I think there is a certain amount of, I suppose it's natural animosity about, it's like a social engineering thing, a sort of gentrification process and people are asking 'why are they bringing the rich in?'" (NDC resident; Bennington et al, 2004: 25). In a global city such as London, which was already suffering from an overheating property market and widespread gentrification, New Labour's NDC inevitably resulted in state-led gentrification, underpinned by the exploitation of state-induced rent gaps (Watt, 2009a).

Austerity

Under the 2010–19 austerity policies of the Coalition and Conservative governments, central government regeneration programmes largely ceased (O'Brien and Matthews, 2016). This meant that estate regeneration had to be based on levering in large-scale private funds. As local authorities and housing associations came under greater pressure to increase densities and thereby 'solve the housing crisis', they turned more and more to private developers as their regeneration partners. This includes complex funding mechanisms such as SPVs, as in the cases of Lambeth and Haringey (Chapter 4; Hackett, 2017; Beswick and Penny, 2018).

Sadiq Khan, the Labour Mayor of London since 2016, introduced a new funding and regulatory regime in *Better Homes for Local People – The Mayor's Good Practice Guide to Estate Regeneration* (Mayor of London, 2018). This guide contains an acknowledgement that things have not exactly gone smoothly: 'we know estate regeneration can result in disagreement, which can leave residents feeling they have not been properly consulted, social housing being lost, and displaced tenants and leaseholders getting a bad deal' (Mayor of London, 2018: 2). Hence the emphasis on ensuring that 'residents are at the heart of any proposals for regeneration on their estate' (Mayor of London, 2018: 2), including mandating ballots for schemes involving mayoral funding. However, the commitment to ballots was not something that the Mayor and his team had originally championed, but was instead a response to housing campaigners' grassroots pressure, for example Demolition Watch London (Watt, 2018c). Given that most research regeneration schemes in this book were introduced prior to the 2018 guide, the post-2018 phase will not be discussed in any detail.

From community new deals to estate densification projects

This section examines the hegemonic official discourse on estate regeneration as promulgated by politicians and the regeneration industry with a focus on London (see Introduction). This discourse is unremittingly positive about how 'successful' comprehensive redevelopment involving large-scale demolition is. As David Lunts, Executive Director of Housing and Land at the GLA, says:

> As we all struggle to meet the scale and complexity of London's housing challenges, it is heartening to see the huge number of successful estate regeneration projects that are underway in the capital. From Kidbrooke to Woodberry Down, Clapham Park to Grahame Park, South Acton to West Hendon, there are estates being transformed all across London. (Cited in McLaughlin, 2015: 1)

The high-profile *City Villages* report (Adonis and Davies, 2015) includes contributions from several prominent Labour Party council leaders who have pursued demolition. The authors rhapsodise about the potential housing supply benefits that London could gain, as well as the creation of new 'sustainable city villages', from knocking down *even more* London council-built estates. These estates are described throughout the report as 'notorious', 'failed', 'sink', 'mono-tenure' and 'dysfunctional', with barely a reference to any empirical evidence for such sweeping generalisations and lazy stereotypes. London's council estates have not been 'mono-tenure' since RTB in the 1980s (Chapter 2), while the research estates in this book had between 12 and 33 per cent owned properties (Table 4.1). The key underlying rationale from the *City Villages* report – and from the official regeneration discourse generally – is that estates have failed and therefore the only solution is to knock them down and start again.

Place myths and neighbourhood effects

This rationale relies upon a prominent place myth (Shields, 1991), one that constitutes the 'common sense' doxa (Allen, 2008) through which regeneration professionals, local politicians and the mass media view and interpret council/social estates – as being the spatial locus of the 'inner-city' problem (Romyn, 2019). This doxa is central to how regeneration-as-demolition becomes a metaphor for healing the socio-spatial scars that estates supposedly form in the urban fabric (Furbey, 1999). This place myth – as framed by the stigmatising 'sink estate' label (Slater, 2018) – operates along five dimensions, whereby estates are branded as the following:

1. 'excluded/poor spaces' dominated by concentrated poverty, worklessness and social exclusion where low aspirations flourish;
2. 'overcrowded spaces' dominated by insufficient domestic space;
3. 'derelict spaces' dominated by mono-tenure properties and infrastructure which are both in a state of terminal decay;
4. 'rough/problem spaces' dominated by crime and ASB;
5. 'devalued/blank spaces' dominated by a value deficit and marked by absences and gaps (resources, services, social capital, community, and so on).

Place myths, like any myths, hide far more than they illuminate. Some London social housing residents are poor, unemployed and overcrowded; estates' communal resources are too often inadequate;

crime and ASB do occur; many estate homes and public spaces are rundown (Chapters 4, 5 and 7). However, the place myth elides how none of these issues are *monopolised* by social housing and its estates in such a grossly unequal city as London. In terms of tenure, the PRS has increasing numbers in poverty, witnessed the biggest increase in overcrowding from 2001 to 2011 and has the most overcrowded households, and also the worst housing conditions (see inter alia GLA Intelligence, 2014; Hanna and Bosetti, 2015; Minton, 2017; Orr, 2018; Watt, 2020b).

The spatial emphasis on 'poor places' reproduces the exaggerated urban policy emphasis on neighbourhood effects. Academic analysis reveals that the significance of neighbourhood effects is highly questionable in the reproduction of disadvantage among social housing tenants (Bridge et al, 2012; Manley et al, 2013; Watt, 2017). One of the most rigorous UK quantitative studies concluded that anti-poverty policy should target individuals because:

> We found no evidence that the segregation of poor individuals into deprived neighbourhoods and neighbourhoods with high concentrations of social renting has negative effects on labour market outcomes, once we had control on individual characteristics. Consequently, we found no evidence that it is beneficial for individual labour market outcomes to mix homeowners and social renters within neighbourhoods. (Van Ham and Manley, 2010: 257)

Furthermore, as Slater (2013b) argues, the 'cottage industry' of neighbourhood effects research elides how the *causes* of poverty, crime and ASB, poor communal resources and maintenance lie *not* in the estates and their inhabitants, but rather in wider social, economic and political forces and structures. Many of the issues which have dogged estates – and which the place myth fuses together – are due to deep structural inequalities of class, racism and gender, inequalities which have been exacerbated by 40 years of neoliberalisation and the last decade of austerity policies (Harvey, 2005; Alston, 2019). People are not poor because they live on estates – they are poor because benefits have been cut to the bone while poverty-level wages have expanded alongside greater job insecurity (Smith, 2005; Tinson et al, 2017; Alston, 2019). People move to estates because they are homeless or living in expensive and insecure poor-quality PRS housing; social renting represents a welcome escape from such conditions (Chapter 5). The fact that many social tenants are overcrowded is not due to social housing, but because of the latter's paucity under austerity (Orr, 2018). Estates are not rundown because of some inherent process of physical decay which magically just targets social housing – they are rundown because they have received inadequate investment by their landlords over many years.

The socio-cultural nature of the regeneration logic is identified by Campkin (2013) in his analysis of regeneration in London. He draws upon Julia Kristeva's theory of abjection, in which the 'abject' is 'what disturbs identity, system, order' (cited in Campkin, 2013: 13), while 'Abjection refers to spatialised processes through which the subject, or society, attempts to impose or maintain a state of purity' (Campkin (2013: 13). Hence the socio-cultural heart of regeneration is the attempt to reimpose order on the disorderly city and in so doing make it a purer, cleaner space, more akin to the sanitised spaces of suburbia (Sibley, 1995).

If the inner city is the main socio-spatial repository of the disorderly city, the council estate is the stereotypical fulcrum of the inner-city problem (crime, disorder, poverty) in media and political narratives: 'Inner-city estates with armed gangs. For many, these are the real no-go areas of our society. These are the places where we really feel unwelcome, intimidated and unsure' (David Cameron, 2008, cited in Romyn, 2019: 143). Estates in all their urban unruliness are the opposite of suburbia; they are spaces of concentrated difference where abject bodies and practices are located – lone mothers and youths hanging around. By contrast, 'The dominant place image of suburbia, especially in Anglo-American culture, remains one of order based on social homogeneity, whiteness, heterosexual couples, political conservatism, materialism and insular self-satisfaction' (Watt, 2007: 81).

The doxic nature of the estate place myth provides a simultaneous rationale and justification for their eradication. Comprehensive redevelopment means that these 'failed places' can be made to 'succeed' via the swing of the wrecker's ball. Get rid of estates and the inner-city problem itself magically disappears (Romyn, 2019). As seen in later chapters, this pathologised approach to estates represents a fundamental *misrecognition* of how working-class people experience their homes and neighbourhoods in London.

Regeneration rationale[5]

The rationale for estate regeneration – in the form of demolition and rebuilding – in London is four-fold. First a socio-spatial rationale containing two overlapping themes: a communitarian emphasis on creating or recreating neighbourhood-based communities, and tackling disadvantage in the form of spatially concentrated poverty, deprivation, crime and ASB. Erasing estates would eradicate such spatial concentrations of disadvantage. The typical metric for identifying deprivation is an area-based measure such as the Index of Multiple Deprivation (IMD) (Smith et al, 2015). This effectively means that the IMD has become a governmental tool to help identify which estates should be knocked down on the basis that their deprivation scores are *too high* relative to average borough or city scores. Therefore the IMD operates as a WMD – a weapon of mass destruction (Chapter 4). By demolishing existing homes and building new ones for sale, regeneration will create mixed-tenure 'sustainable communities' or 'balanced communities' (G15, 2016: 29). Area-based disadvantages – including putative neighbourhood effects – are neatly eliminated.

The second rationale is architectural/design. Modernist estates are outdated and 'ugly' and comprise poor-quality homes. Their spatial configuration is deficient because estates are 'poorly integrated' into the surrounding area. Moreover, the actual buildings do not meet modern environmental standards. Therefore, existing 'eyesore' estates can be replaced with 'popular' streetscapes consisting of better-quality, energy-efficient homes.

The third regeneration-as-demolition rationale is that public funding to improve existing social homes or build new ones is unavailable. This has been a constant feature of neoliberalisation, but has worsened under austerity. Austerity has cut local authority finances to the bone, resulting in councils having limited funds to either refurbish their existing housing stock or provide new stock. The only way out of this dilemma is for councils and housing associations to lever in whatever private sector investment they can, and comprehensive redevelopment offers this opportunity. Demolition and rebuild is also preferable since in the long term it is more cost effective, while it facilitates the realisation of the other regeneration aims.

The final rationale is densification – using regeneration to provide higher housing densities on the footprint of existing estates. This aim relates to the supply-side emphasis on providing more homes for London's rising population, which will 'solve' London's city-wide housing crisis. Given the strictures on 'building out' due to the Green Belt, a potential land source is located on estates. Since many estates were built during the 1960s and 1970s, a period when London's population was declining, they were built at relatively low density with generous helpings of green space. Estates can be densified in two ways: first by infilling non-residential spaces, such as green areas or garages, and second by demolishing part or all of the estate and then rebuilding at a higher density. While infilling allows for an uplift in the number of new homes, some analysts think its potential is limited (Hanna et al, 2016). It also fails to achieve the previously mentioned social and architectural/design objectives. Therefore, comprehensive redevelopment involving large-scale demolition becomes the default preferred option.

What is the relative weight of this four-fold rationale? The densification aim was absent during the early phase of estate regeneration during the 1980s and 1990s. Schemes such as CEI and Peckham Partnership SRB resulted in a net loss of units, but also replacement houses rather than flats. Densification became more important under New Labour, as did the first socio-spatial aim, as seen in the NDC. Since New Labour, however, the socio-spatial aim has greatly diminished in significance, while the densification aim has become even more important as London's housing crisis has deepened. Therefore, rather than creating new deals for communities, à la New Labour, estate regeneration has morphed into 'estate densification projects' (Hanna et al, 2016). This has occurred under the fiscal pressures of radically scaled-back central government regeneration funds (O'Brien and Matthews, 2016), coupled with GLA pressures to increase the number of new homes (Bowie, 2010, 2017). As a result, urban policy in London has de facto become housing policy. The long-term policy failures which characterise the housing crisis – not building enough homes, especially genuinely affordable homes – are now supposed to be rectified by knocking down the homes of some of London's poorest and most vulnerable inhabitants – social tenants.

The twin emphasis on densification and 'solving' London's housing crisis has had a little-recognised geographical scale-jumping effect. Instead of estate regeneration coupling physical renewal together with tackling residents' social exclusion at the neighbourhood scale, the scale leaps upwards to the borough/city levels whereby meeting the extant housing needs/wants of borough residents for new homes ('affordable' and market) will simultaneously contribute towards solving the city-wide housing supply shortage. This scale-jumping ties in with other local state goals, as now discussed.

Urban renaissance: the entrepreneurial city and entrepreneurial boroughs

Estate regeneration is only one strand of recent urban policy, the other being 'urban renaissance' (Colomb, 2007). Urban renaissance, which reached full fruition under New Labour, involves large-scale downtown renewal strategies. The latter falls within the New Urban Politics notion that the local state promotes the 'entrepreneurial city' via enhancing private economic development (Harvey, 1989; Davidson and Martin, 2014). London has pursued entrepreneurial city strategies, for example via the 'spectacular' staging of the 2012 London Olympic Games (Kennelly and Watt, 2011; Cohen and Watt, 2017). The emphasis on the beautification and securitisation of public space in Stratford (Kennelly and Watt, 2013) amounted to the wholesale transformation of urban space – what Merrifield (2014) calls 'neo-Haussmannisation'.

One trend over the last 20 years is how individual London councils have pursued entrepreneurial city strategies but at the spatial scale of *the borough* – hence they operate as what can be termed 'entrepreneurial boroughs'. This can be seen in how councils strive for the revitalisation of their borough town centres with the intention of creating new retail and leisure destination hubs to supposedly rival the West End. Examples include the Elephant and Castle in Southwark and Stratford in Newham, both of which include upmarket private apartment blocks catering for the global super-rich and upmarket gentrifiers (Bernstock, 2014; Glucksberg, 2016).

How do entrepreneurial city/borough strategies dovetail with estate regeneration? The early regeneration schemes, such as CEI, spatially focused on the estates themselves. However, as entrepreneurial borough strategies have become more prominent, so the spatial focus has tilted away from the estates per se towards how the latter fit (or more precisely 'don't fit') into borough-scale urban renaissance aims. Estate regeneration is thus no longer primarily undertaken for residents to meet their 'collective consumption' (Lowe, 1986) needs for improved housing; but instead to renew estates as part of entrepreneurial borough aims. In fact, social housing estates literally stand in the way of the neo-Haussmannisation of urban space (Merrifield, 2014), and must be bulldozed for urban renaissance goals to be met. The next chapter discusses several examples where estate ABIs are undertaken in synergy with entrepreneurial borough strategies.

Comparing early and contemporary estate regeneration schemes involving demolition and rebuild

This penultimate section compares early and contemporary estate regeneration schemes – respectively those which were begun in the 1980s and 1990s compared to those begun during the late 1990s to 2010s. One key difference relates to the twin roles played by density and types of homes being redeveloped. The earlier schemes involved a loss of dwellings and a concomitant net reduction in density, a situation that is fundamentally different from contemporary schemes which involve a large increase in density, as per London-wide trends throughout the 2000s (Bowie, 2010). The total number of units under the Peckham Partnership SRB reduced by over 18 per cent from 4,532 to 3,694 (Glucksberg, 2017: 75). An ex-Regeneration Officer said, "it was about demolishing really substandard housing and building good-quality housing that was actually at a lower density than the density that was there". There was a near-identical percentage reduction at the Hackney CEI – down 17 per cent from the original 5,473 (Jacobs, 1999: 9–10). Such reductions are in stark contrast to the increased numbers and densities found in contemporary schemes (see later in this chapter, and Chapter 4).

Since increasing density was not a goal, the earlier schemes could build replacement *houses* instead of flats, as in the Central Stepney SRB, where the houses were extremely popular with the overcrowded Bangladeshi population (Edwards et al, 2003). An ex-Regeneration Officer who worked at the Stonebridge HAT in Brent (Stewart and Rhoden, 2003) said, "we were still going for low density, and building lots of houses – that would never happen today". The increased density in contemporary schemes is achieved by building up in the form of flats, often high-rise (Scanlon et al, 2018).

A second key difference is the restricted role of the private sector in the earlier schemes in relation to both funding and housing development. These were largely publicly funded, mainly from central government regeneration programme budgets. As an ex-Regeneration Officer says of the Peckham SRB, "it was a Tory government, and it's almost entirely publicly funded". The Hackney CEI was devised and part-funded by Hackney Council with other funding from central government programmes such as Estate Action; just 18 per cent of funding was private (Jacobs, 1999: 9). The restriction imposed by the Conservative Government was demunicipalisation – that the council stock had to transfer to a housing association, as occurred with the Central Stepney SRB (Edwards et al, 2003). Instead, contemporary regeneration schemes rely upon complex PPPs with private developers and/or housing associations (see inter alia Watt, 2009a, 2013; Adonis and Davies, 2015; McLaughlin, 2015; Derbyshire et al, 2016; Hackett, 2017; Beswick and Penny, 2018; Hodkinson, 2019; Nelson and Lewis, 2019). One PPP model involves the sale (or long lease) of council land to a private/corporate developer (often with a partner housing association) which builds market housing on the land, whose sale cross-subsidises social housebuilding and/or refurbishment. This model featured in the Heygate and Woodberry Down schemes, as well as West Hendon and Canning Town, and was the council's desired but unrealised approach at the Carpenters estate. Other approaches include creating an SPV (Lambeth, and Haringey with the Haringey Development Vehicle (HDV), stock transfer to a housing association (Clapham Park), or PFI 'outsourcing on steroids' (Hodkinson, 2019). In each PPP, although some public funding might be included (for example SRB at Woodberry Down), the contemporary schemes are financially dominated by private funding arrangements – hence these constitute either direct or indirect privatisation vehicles.

The early and contemporary schemes each produce mixed-tenure neighbourhoods, but with very different tenure mixes due to the differential funding arrangements. Figure 3.2 compares the two early outlined schemes (CEI in Hackney and Peckham SRB in Southwark), with two later schemes begun under New Labour (Woodberry Down and Heygate) in the same respective boroughs (Jacobs, 1999; Glucksberg, 2017; 35% Campaign, 2018; Nelson and Lewis, 2019). There were substantial losses in the number and percentage of council homes in both the CEI and Peckham SRB, but these were partly ameliorated by increases in housing association rental properties, resulting in a net loss of 35 per cent social renting in the CEI and 29 per cent in Peckham (Figure 3.2). However, social tenants remained in the majority in each case (75 per cent and 83 per cent respectively). Although private market homes increased, these only accounted for 21 per cent in the CEI and 17 per cent in Peckham. Therefore, the tenure mix remained heavily weighted towards social rental homes, which formed a large majority – rather than market homes for sale.

The tenure-mix pattern is fundamentally different in the two contemporary schemes where private funding was far more significant. Social tenants formed a substantial majority in each case pre-regeneration – 67 per cent at Woodberry Down and 84 per cent at Heygate. The former will shrink to 20 per cent by the end of the scheme while the latter is a paltry 3 per cent. Market homes will form the majority post-regeneration – 60 per cent at Woodberry Down and 78 per cent at the Heygate. There are significant differences between the Woodberry Down and Heygate schemes, notably the extreme 92 per cent loss of social rental units at the latter compared to just 15 per cent at Woodberry Down; hence the contemporary schemes are by no means uniform in their tenure changes. Despite such differences, the two later schemes remain fundamentally distinct from the two earlier ones in terms of the changing tenure mix. The early schemes'

Figure 3.2: Change in housing tenure at 50 demolished social housing estates in London (2004–14), and at two early (CEI and Peckham SRB) and two contemporary (Woodberry Down and Heygate) regeneration schemes in Hackney and Southwark

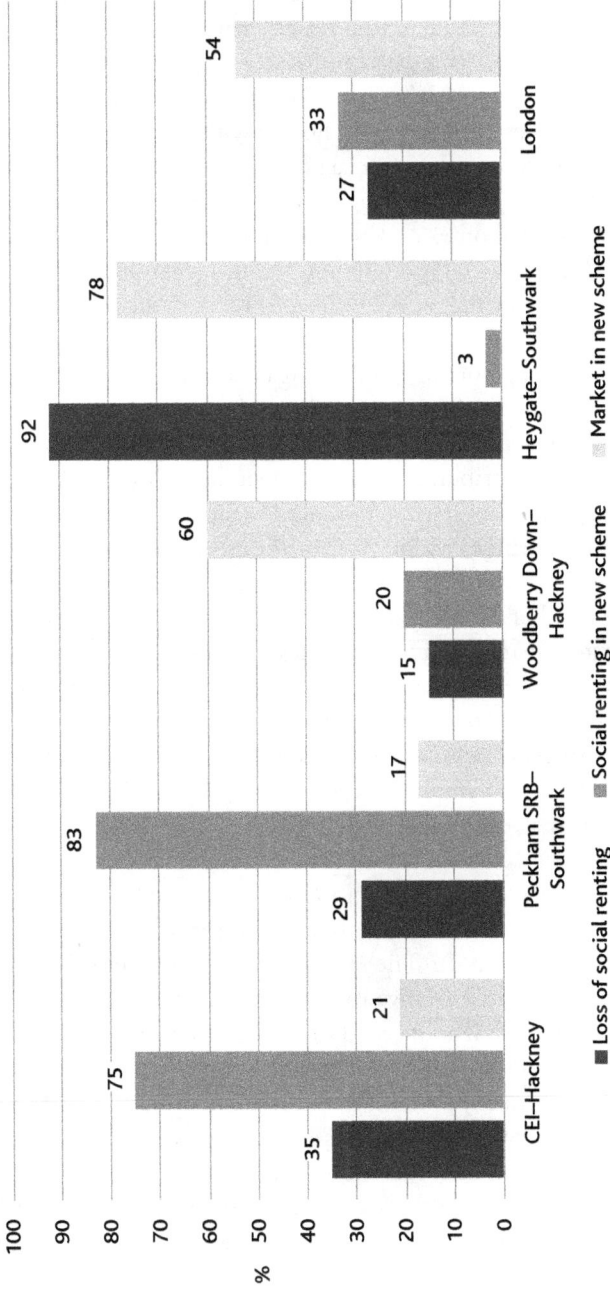

Source: CEI (Jacobs, 1999: 10); Peckham SRB (Glucksberg, 2017: 75); Woodberry Down (G15, 2016: 48; Nelson and Lewis, 2019: 14); Heygate (35% Campaign, 2018); London (LAHC, 2015: 14)

primary foci and effects were renewing estates and re-providing social renting rather than gentrification (Arbaci and Rae, 2013), whereas the later ones represent extensive state-led gentrification *masquerading* as estate regeneration.

It could be suggested that the two contemporary schemes are atypical, worst-case examples. We can gauge whether this is the case by comparing them with data from *Knock It Down or Do It Up?* (LAHC, 2015), a London-wide report.[6] This report compares the number of original homes with proposed homes with planning permission at 50 demolished council-built social housing estates for 2004–14, that is the contemporary period. It suggests that 30,431 social renting and 3,186 market (RTB) homes originally existed at the 50 demolished estates (LAHC, 2015: 14); the summary findings regarding change of tenure are presented in Figure 3.2. The LAHC data shows a near-doubling in the total number of housing units at the regenerated estates – up to 67,601 – hence 'solving the housing crisis'. It also shows an increase in 'affordable' homes (social rent, affordable rent and intermediate) up to 31,438, albeit a mere 411 units increase or just over 1 per cent – hence marginally contributing towards meeting housing need. However, this aggregate uplift in affordable housing disguises the substantial differential changes within this notoriously amorphous category (Watt and Bernstock, 2017). This uplift is accounted for by a large increase in the number of affordable rent and intermediate (including shared ownership/shared equity) properties. But social renting – the only *truly affordable* element within the fuzzy 'affordable' category – *declined* by 8,296 units or 27 per cent (Figure 3.2). By comparison, market homes for sale or rent increased over ten-fold to 36,163. Social renters will thus shift from being in a large majority (nine tenths) to a minority (one third) at each redeveloped estate, while market properties will form 54 per cent of the new homes – again indicative of London's contemporary estate regeneration as de facto state-led gentrification.

How do these London-wide figures compare to the two contemporary schemes (Figure 3.2)? The 92 per cent loss of social housing at the Heygate is extreme relative to the London 27 per cent average, while the 15 per cent Woodberry Down reduction is below the London average. The social/market weighting balance in these two examples is in both cases more pronounced than the London average. The Heygate and Woodberry Down examples are less weighted towards social homes and more to market provision than the London total. They both represent stark cases of estate regeneration as state-led gentrification, albeit that the Heygate is more extreme. What is also significant is how the one-third average for social renting at London's demolished/

re-rebuilt estates is very different from the two early schemes where, to reiterate, social tenants formed a clear majority – three quarters or more – in the redeveloped neighbourhoods (Figure 3.2).

Regeneration costs

One report policy has atypically put a monetary cost to the impacts of displacement arising from demolition and rehousing. It concluded that the:

> impact value of upheaval through rehousing from a London estate due to regeneration is in the order of £15,000 to £20,000 per average resident. Given the current statutory Home Loss Payment for tenants is £5,300, there is a case for Home Loss Payments for tenants to be increased three- or four-fold. (Hanna et al, 2016: 47)

This represents an important acknowledgement of the financial costs of demolition and displacement and how tenants are short-changed by rehousing. At the same time, Hanna et al (2016: 47) underplay the human costs: 'The impact of earlier death can be a real and unfortunate result of displacement, especially for older people, but is rare'. In fact, Appendix B of their report details the extensive and all-too-real nature of the estate regeneration discontents that I highlight in Part III – that living in a half-empty estate is anxiety-making, and that displacement is stressful, health-damaging and results in loss of local connections, and at worst premature death. According to Hanna et al (2016: 63): between 1 and 3 per cent of movers will die early; between 10 and 25 per cent will experience increased ill health; between 15 and 25 per cent will live in fear on a part-empty estate; and between 66 and 100 per cent will lose local social connections.

We can start to put some flesh on the health-damaging nature of these abstract percentages by referring to the two contemporary estate regeneration schemes above (Heygate and Woodberry Down) where a combined total of 3,174 households will eventually be displaced due to demolition. If we take the London average number of 2.5 people per dwelling (Mayor of London, 2019), this means that 7,935 people will be displaced at these two estates. Using the percentage impacts from Hanna et al (2016) above, we can estimate that somewhere between 79 and 238 people will die prematurely, and between 794 and 1,994 will suffer from ill heath due to demolition and displacement at the Heygate and Woodberry Down regeneration schemes. In terms of premature deaths, there will therefore be around one to over three times the equivalent 72 lives lost due to the 2017 Grenfell Tower fire, a devastating event that Hodkinson (2019: 1) refers to as 'social murder'. Each displacement-related early death – whether 79 or 238 lives lost – is not 'rare' but is instead a needless tragedy for those people and families so affected.

Conclusion

Urban policy has played a significant role in the redevelopment of London's public housing, and many estate regeneration research studies have been undertaken. In building upon and extending the existing research, this chapter has uniquely traced the shifting rationales, funding and governance arrangements that estate regeneration has gone through. Rather than forming a seamless whole, as has hitherto been assumed, a key shift has been identified between those early schemes from the 1990s, such as the Hackney CEI and Peckham SRB, and the contemporary schemes which are the focus of this book.

The early schemes were spatially focused on estates and their residents, had relatively generous public funding and resulted in fewer dwellings. They produced mixed-tenure neighbourhoods whereby the tenure mix was weighted towards social renting, while incoming private owners/ renters formed a minority. By contrast, the 21st century schemes have become progressively less focused on the estates themselves and more concerned with meeting London's housing supply shortfall. This process began under New Labour and has been intensified under austerity conditions. Current schemes are therefore estate densification projects reflecting how urban policy has increasingly *become* housing policy. New Labour's communitarian emphasis, which peaked with the NDC, has become much less prominent since 2010. The contemporary schemes have resulted in qualitatively different mixed-tenure neighbourhoods whereby the tenure mix is weighted towards incoming private owners/renters rather than the re-provision of homes for existing social tenants – hence the result is state-led gentrification. The early public sector-dominated regeneration/demolition schemes were also completed in a much shorter period – around ten years – as opposed to two to three decades for the private funding-reliant contemporary schemes which are dependent upon the vicissitudes of market sales (Chapters 4, 9 and 12). The final section highlighted the human costs arising from displacement related to demolition, costs that are illustrated in Part III. The next chapter provides a summary of the research estates and their boroughs.

4

The research boroughs and their estates

The research focused on seven London boroughs – referred to as the 'main research boroughs' – while less extensive research was undertaken in four 'supplementary boroughs' (Figure 4.1). Six of the main boroughs – Hackney, Haringey, Lambeth, Newham, Southwark and Tower Hamlets – have been among the most deprived local authority areas in England for decades. These six are part of the cluster of 'inner East boroughs' that Hanna and Bosetti (2015: 9) identify as having 'the highest proportions nationally of children and old people living in poverty'. These boroughs also contain large BAME populations that are disproportionately disadvantaged in terms of housing and employment (Chouhan et al, 2011; Elahi and Khan, 2016).

Despite their enduring social problems, there has also been some reduction in the extent of poverty and deprivation in the six inner East boroughs over the last 20 years which reflects how 'poverty rates have increased in outer London and decreased in inner London' (Hanna and Bosetti, 2015: 6). Table 4.1 shows the national ranking of the seven main research boroughs based on their average area-based deprivation scores in the 1998 Index of Local Deprivation (ILD) and 2015 IMD. Leaving aside Barnet as an outlier, these featured among the 20 most deprived local authority areas in England in 1998, with four appearing in the ten most deprived areas. By the 2015 IMD, the ranking of their average scores had all improved such that only Hackney and Tower Hamlets remained among the 20 most deprived areas (Smith et al, 2015: 58). As Hanna and Bosetti (2015: 11) argue, the reduction in poverty in inner London boroughs is likely to be at 'least partly explained by an influx of wealthier, more professional households. It is unlikely that such a sharp reduction in poverty could be explained solely by existing residents moving up the labour market'. In other words, the gentrification which has swept through inner London during the last 30 years is a major explanatory factor (Introduction).

The result of these changes is that the six inner East boroughs are characterised by sharp social polarisation – acute poverty and deprivation juxtaposed to wealth and affluence arising from gentrification and also the growing presence of the super-rich.

Figure 4.1: Map of London research boroughs

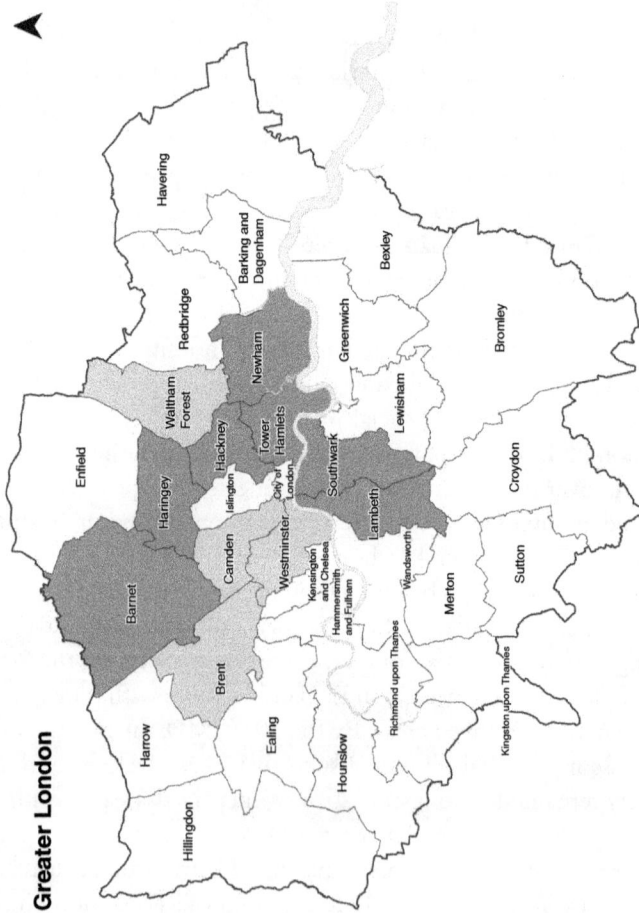

Note: Dark grey = main boroughs; light grey = supplementary boroughs
Source: © Crown Copyright/database right 2013. An Ordnance Survey/EDINA supplied service.

Table 4.1: Rank of main research boroughs in 1998 Index of Local Deprivation (ILD) and 2015 Index of Multiple Deprivation (IMD)

London borough	1998 ILD	2015 IMD
Newham	2	23
Hackney	4	11
Tower Hamlets	6	10
Southwark	8	40
Lambeth	12	44
Haringey	13	30
Barnet	130	172

Note: The 1998 ILC and 2015 IMD methodologies and rankings are not directly comparable. The 1998 ranks are based on 354 English local authorities, whereas the 2015 ranks are based on 326 English local authorities; in each case, 1 is the most deprived local authority.

Source: DETR (1998) and MHCLG (2015)

Although much of the boroughs' poverty and deprivation remains located in social housing estates, the PRS has witnessed an increasing share of poverty (Chapter 5).

Of the seven main boroughs, the outlier is Barnet, which is a classic suburban outer London borough. As Table 4.1 shows, Barnet had a nationally mid-range deprivation ranking in both 1998 and 2015. Nevertheless, Barnet's poverty/low income rate increased from 2001 to 2011, and it also experienced a reduction in managers and professionals (Hanna and Bosetti, 2015). This change reflects how the traditional inner–outer London geographical divide – with the former more deprived than the latter – has narrowed since 2001, reflective of inner London gentrification and the suburbanisation of poverty (Butler and Robson, 2003; Millington, 2011; Watt et al, 2014; Hanna and Bosetti, 2015).

Barnet is also an outlier in terms of housing. As discussed in previous chapters, the other six main boroughs had large concentrations of council housing; four were in the top five local authorities in England for having the largest percentages of deprived council estates in the 1990s (Chapter 3). Figure 4.2 shows housing tenure for the seven main research boroughs in 1981 and 2011, while Figure 4.3 shows their local authority housing stock in 2018.

This chapter summarises the boroughs and estates from which the empirical research is drawn. The main research estates are shown in Table 4.2. Nine of the regeneration schemes began during New Labour's

Figure 4.2: Housing tenure in main research boroughs, 1981 and 2011 (%)

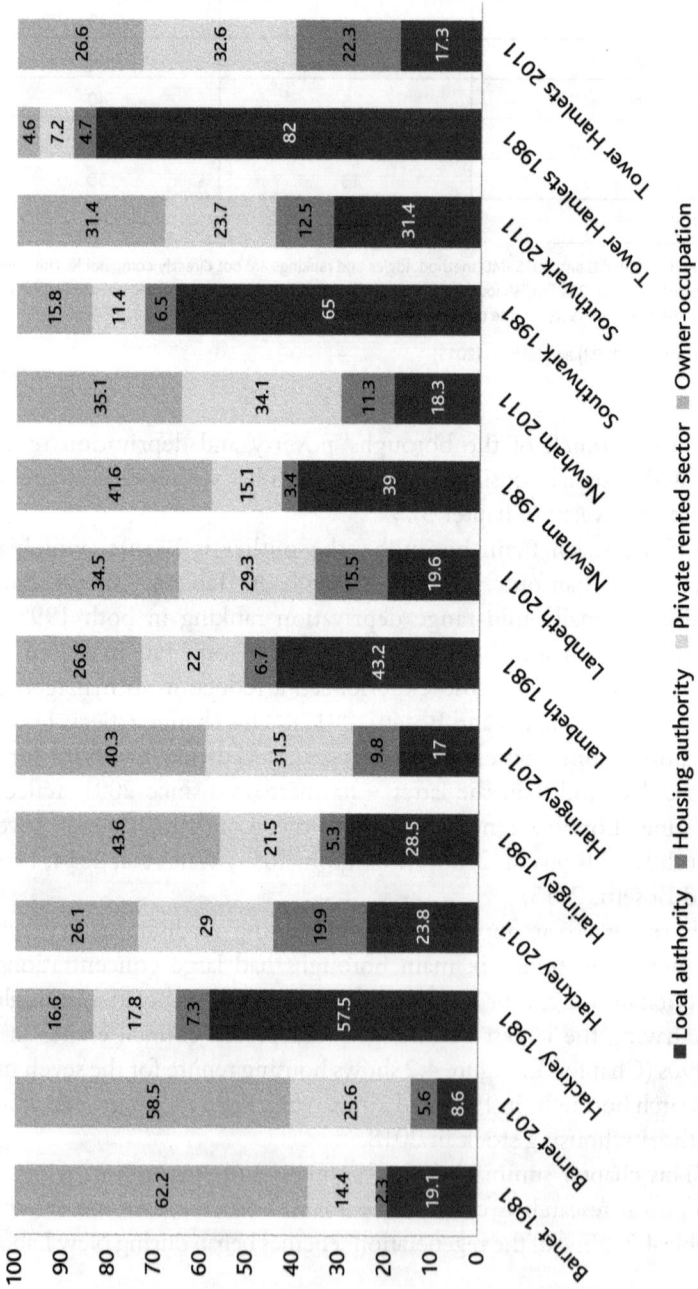

	Barnet 1981	Barnet 2011	Hackney 1981	Hackney 2011	Haringey 1981	Haringey 2011	Lambeth 1981	Lambeth 2011	Newham 1981	Newham 2011	Southwark 1981	Southwark 2011	Tower Hamlets 1981	Tower Hamlets 2011
Owner-occupation	62.2	58.5	16.6	26.1	43.6	40.3	26.6	34.5	41.6	35.1	15.8	31.4	4.6	26.6
Private rented sector	14.4	25.6	17.8	29	21.5	31.5	22	29.3	15.1	34.1	11.4	23.7	7.2	32.6
Housing authority	2.3	5.6	7.3	19.9	5.3	9.8	6.7	15.5	3.4	11.3	6.5	12.5	4.7	22.3
Local authority	19.1	8.6	57.5	23.8	28.5	17	43.2	19.6	39	18.3	65	31.4	82	17.3

■ Local authority ■ Housing authority ▨ Private rented sector ▨ Owner-occupation

Source: Census (GLA Intelligence, 2015)

Figure 4.3: Local authority housing stock in main research boroughs, 2018 (*N*)

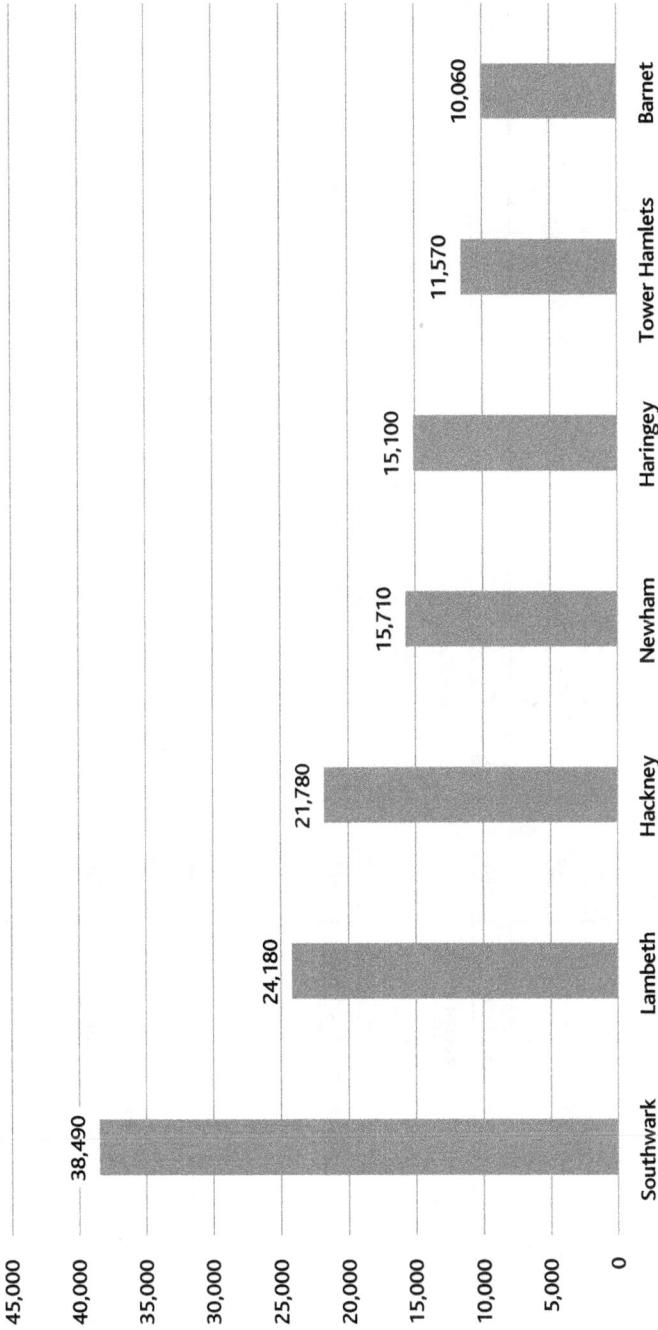

Source: MHCLG (2019a)

Table 4.2: Profile of main research estates

Borough	Estate	Period built	Local authority builder	Homes	Tenure mix before regeneration: % social rent/owner	Hectares (rounded)	Expected regeneration period at 2017–19
Barnet	West Hendon	1960s	Barnet	649	74/26	13	2002–29
Hackney	Northwold	1934–60	LCC	579	74/26	–	2016–unsure
Hackney	Woodberry Down	1946–1960s	LCC	1,980	67/33	26	1999–2035
Haringey	Northumberland Park	1960s–1970s	Haringey	1,337	78/22	23	2015–18
Lambeth	Central Hill	1967–75	Lambeth	456	71/29	7	2014–unsure
Lambeth	Clapham Park	1930s–1960s	LCC/GLC	1,997	73/27	36	2000–34
Lambeth	Cressingham Gardens	1971–78	Lambeth	306	68/32	4	2012–unsure
Lambeth	Westbury	1960s	GLC	242	74/26	–	2014–unsure
Newham	Canning Town/Custom House	1940s–1970s	West Ham MBC and Newham	1,787	82/18	–	2000–unsure
Newham	Carpenters	1960s	Newham	705	73/27	9	2004–unsure
Southwark	Aylesbury	1963–77	Southwark	2,700	88/12	24	2000–35
Southwark	East Dulwich	1930s	LCC	753	87/13	6	1997–2020
Southwark	Heygate	1970–74	Southwark	1,194	84/16	10	1998–2025
Tower Hamlets	Ocean	1949–1960s	LCC	1,565	70/30	31	2000–20

Note: Number of homes, tenure mix, hectares and end dates are best approximations; these often fluctuate between documents.

Sources: Various

period in office, and the remaining five began in 2012–16 (Introduction). It's impossible to provide anything other than a thumbnail sketch of each estate and its regeneration scheme. The latter involves a shifting gallery of partner organisations – developers, housing associations, consultants, and so on – while the masterplans often go through several iterations. Table 4.2 indicates the estimated regeneration period at 2017–19 (where available). Not only are these time periods invariably longer than the original projections, but they are not necessarily congruent with what has transpired in real terms. Both Carpenters estate and Custom House schemes in Newham have been running for many years but zero redevelopment has occurred. Chapter 12 looks at the Carpenters, West Hendon and Woodberry Down estates in detail, and this chapter begins with these three and their respective boroughs.

Newham

Newham has been described as a 'classic "inner city" authority' (Travers, 2015: 249). The closure of the Docks in the 1960s–1970s and the subsequent collapse of large-scale industry resulted in widespread poverty and deprivation (CDP, 1976). Historically, Newham represents the quintessential east London working-class area with a paternalistic local politics of 'Labourism' whereby, 'The prevailing ethos was one of "benevolent neglect"' (Marriott, 1991: 3). The local councils embarked on an extensive period of new public house building during the early post-war years. This included extensive systems-building and high-rise blocks, especially in the west of the borough in Canning Town, Custom House and Stratford (CDP, 1976; Dunleavy, 1981). By 1981, nearly two fifths of all Newham households were council tenants (Figure 4.2). While the council increased the numbers of units, design and quality were often poor, as symbolised by the partial collapse of the Ronan Point tower block in 1968, which killed four people (CDP, 1976; Dunleavy, 1981). Dunleavy (1981) details Newham Council's less than sensitive response to the housing fallout from this disaster, indicative of entrenched paternalist Labourism.

Politically, Newham is a de facto 'one-party state' (Leach, 2006: 157), with Labour ruling the council in an unbroken period since 1965, the only London council with such a record (Travers, 2015). From 1995 to 2018, it was also effectively a 'one-person state' given that it was ruled by Sir Robin Wales, first as Leader of the Council and later as Mayor (Leach, 2006). The Wales' council represented a toxic amalgamation of the worst excesses of Labourist paternalism with

New Labour neoliberalism (Research for Action, 2018a) – what can be termed 'local state authoritarian neoliberalism'.

Newham Council pursued an urban renaissance, entrepreneurial borough strategy centred upon the 'arc of opportunity' which focused on two townships – Stratford and Canning Town (LBN, 2008; Bernstock, 2014). Stratford has been the focus of several regeneration programmes dating back to the 1990s' City Challenge, but this intensified during the 2000s via the Stratford City programme and the 2012 Olympic Games. The Wales' council promoted a 'resilience' agenda involving low taxation, urban competitiveness and *reducing* social renting. The council funded its neoliberal policies by floating on a sea of debt, courtesy of LOBO (Lender Option Borrower Option) loans (Research for Action, 2018b). These policies have contributed towards increasing polarisation – heightened poverty, deprivation and homelessness for its existing multi-ethnic working-class population, combined with state-led gentrification in the Stratford and Canning Town areas (Watt, 2013, 2020b; Bernstock, 2014; Watt and Bernstock, 2017; Research for Action, 2018a).

Newham Council demonstrated an antipathy towards social housing estates, blaming them for creating 'ghettos of worklessness' and high levels of 'benefit dependency' (cited in Watt and Bernstock, 2017). This antipathy embraced a reluctance to prioritise social rental provision in new development schemes, and emptying out and knocking down existing council estates under the guise of regeneration. Of the local authorities in this book, Newham has been among the most explicit in its disdain for social housing and pursuance of a state-led gentrification agenda. By 2011, the proportion of council housing halved from 1981 to just 18 per cent, while the PRS more than doubled to 34 per cent (Figure 4.2). By 2018, Newham had 15,710 council properties (Figure 4.3). My research in Newham focused on the Carpenters estate in Stratford and the estates in Canning Town/Custom House, both of which fall within the 'arc of opportunity'.

Carpenters estate[1]

The Carpenters estate has just over 700 units and dates to the 1960s when Newham Council built three 22-storey tower blocks (Lund Point, Dennison Point and James Riley Point), low-rise blocks and terraced housing (Photograph 4.1). In 1997, Carpenters residents voted to form a Tenant Management Organisation (TMO) that took over minor management functions, such as repairs. In 2005, when the estate was last fully occupied, council tenants occupied 73 per cent of

Photograph 4.1: Carpenters estate – view from Lund Point, 2012

properties, 14 per cent were leasehold flats and 13 per cent freehold houses (Table 4.3). Rates of owner-occupation were, however, higher in the houses, two thirds of which were owned (LBN, 2012).

By the early 2000s, Carpenters residents were complaining about the poor state of the flats, especially the high-rise blocks (Chapter 8). Newham Council acknowledged the flats were in a poor state but argued that it lacked sufficient funds to refurbish them (LBN, 2012). Regeneration supposedly began in 2004 and a masterplan was developed. Demolition of the whole estate – including the houses and low-rise flats, as well as the tower blocks – was the council's preference. The council began decanting tenants from 2005, originally from James Riley Point (the tower block in the worst condition). As Table 4.3 shows, more than half of properties (55 per cent) were empty by 2012, and by 2018 only 99 council tenants remained. By contrast, the number of freeholders in houses has remained constant – as in the case of Mary (Introduction). Leaseholders reduced from 98 in 2005 to 59 in 2018. Displacement has therefore been heavily differentiated by tenure, with most council tenants decanted by 2018.

From 2011 to 2013, the council entered a partnership with University College London (UCL) which aimed to build a new campus on the Carpenters site, meaning total demolition. Apart from this short-lived

Table 4.3: Carpenters estate – housing tenure and empty properties, 2005–18

Tenure	2005 N (%)	2012 N (%)	2018 N (%)
Secure (council) tenants	514 (73)	158 (22)	99 (14)
Leaseholders	98 (14)	66 (9)	59 (8)
Freeholders	93 (13)	96 (14)	93 (13)
Non-secure tenants	0	0	55 (8)
Other tenures	0	0	5 (1)
Empty properties	0	385 (55)	399 (56)
Total	705	705	710

Source: 2005 and 2012 data adapted from LBN (2012). 2018 data supplied by LBN – FOI request by Paul Watt, reference FOI/E30871, 8 June 2018

UCL period, the Carpenters scheme has lacked a redevelopment partner. Therefore, despite the extensive decanting, there has been no demolition or redevelopment. It's little wonder that this half-empty estate has become such a potent symbol of the city's housing crisis (see Introduction).

Canning Town and Custom House

Canning Town/Custom House is in the south west of Newham and is another of the council's major regeneration areas. This riverside area suffered from the closure of the docks and deindustrialisation during the 1970s and 1980s (CDP, 1976). When regeneration began in 2000, poverty and deprivation were high, although a strong sense of community and place identity also existed within a somewhat insular working-class area (Cattell, 2001). The area included several council estates; over three quarters of the housing was social rented (LBN, 2008).

The Canning Town/Custom House regeneration programme began in 2000 and 'was in response to the areas being seriously disadvantaged, largely being in the lowest decile of the Index of Multiple Deprivation [IMD]' (LBN, 2020) – a good example of the IMD operating as a WMD (Chapter 3). The regeneration scheme is a £3.7bn project involving the demolition of up to 1,700 existing homes (mainly social rental), and the development of 10,000 new homes (mainly market properties) (LBN, 2013) – Photograph 4.2. Canning Town was part

Photograph 4.2: Canning Town and Custom House – regeneration billboard, 2013

of New Labour's 'Mixed Communities Initiative', while some homes were refurbished under a PFI scheme (LBN, 2008; Hodkinson, 2019). While there has been substantial redevelopment involving a private developer partner in Canning Town, resulting in new homes being built since 2012, there has been no development partner at Custom House (LBN, 2020).

Freedom of Information (FOI) data on the Canning Town/Custom House regeneration indicates that of the original 1,787 properties in the area, half (911) had been demolished by 2018 (767 council rented and 142 RTB properties).[2] FOI data also suggests that of the 677 new properties built by 2018, 402 were for private sale or rent, while 245 (36 per cent) were 'affordable'. Of the latter, just 89 were social rented (13 per cent), while another 115 council homes have been refurbished.[3] The loss of social rented homes has been massive – down by nearly 90 per cent. The Canning Town/Custom House regeneration scheme proved extremely controversial among council tenants and many of the things that they originally feared (break-up of existing community, displacement, no council housing reprovision) have come to pass (Chapter 8).

Barnet

Barnet is an outer London suburban borough with a strong middle-class presence and large owner-occupied housing sector (Figure 4.2). Apart from two periods, Barnet has had a Conservative council since 1965. Of the main research boroughs, Barnet had by far the smallest proportion of public housing in 1981 – just under one fifth, reflecting its long-term Conservative control. Council housing halved to 9 per cent in 2011. Even adding in housing association property, social renting accounted for only around 14 per cent of total households in 2011. The owner-occupied sector has shrunk back slightly since 1981, while the major expanding tenure is the PRS.

Barnet's council stock has been managed by Barnet Homes, an ALMO, since 2004. In the early 2000s, the council embarked upon a large-scale regeneration/demolition programme at its largest council-built estates, with the following rationale:

> Our estate regeneration schemes will see the dismantling of our largest mono tenure council estates which have proved to be unpopular and limiting in terms of opportunities for residents living on them. These *failing* post war estates, Grahame Park, West Hendon, Stonegrove/Spur Road and Dollis Valley will be replaced by mixed tenure estates with new social housing, but also opportunities for entry level and market home ownership. (LBB, 2010: 7; emphasis added)

The rationale for demolishing these so-called 'failing estates' was underpinned by the Council's 2000–2003 Housing Strategy, which provided 'unequivocal evidence of the close association between the highest deprivation levels in Barnet and our largest social housing estates' (cited in LBB, 2015: 17) – another case of the IMD operating as a WMD. Residents were said to be 'cut off' from their surrounding area, hence the 'need' to 'develop balanced communities by diversifying tenure mix' and to 'break down the barriers that currently exist between these large estates and surrounding communities' (cited in LBB, 2015: 17).

Given the relative paucity of public housing in Barnet to begin with, the council's estate regeneration programme represents the largest proportional demolition scheme in London. During the 2011–17 period, Barnet demolished 858 local authority properties, the fourth highest level of any London borough (MHCLG, 2019a). By 2018, Barnet had just over 10,000 local authority properties left (Figure 4.3).

The estate regeneration programme will lead to a net reduction of over a thousand social housing homes (from 2,671 to 1,650; LBB, 2016; my calculations). Research in Barnet focused on the West Hendon estate, although I also visited Grahame Park on several occasions.

West Hendon estate[4]

Prior to regeneration, West Hendon was the second largest estate in Barnet (after Grahame Park) with 680 properties, 649 of which were included in the final regeneration programme. The estate was built in the 1960s and sits in between a main road (West Hendon Broadway) and the Welsh Harp area of natural beauty. It consisted of low-rise blocks of flats and maisonettes, plus a tower block and terraced houses; many blocks were of concrete construction. The estate was subject to a comprehensive renewal scheme involving demolition which began in 2002. One effect of the scheme was an acceleration in RTB applications from 52 over 1995–2001 to 51 in 2002 alone following consultation (ALG, 2003: 23). Barrett London was the eventual private developer and Metropolitan Housing Trust was the housing association.[5] In 2006, these two organisations formed the Barrett Metropolitan Limited Liability Partnership for the joint venture purposes of delivering regeneration.

Regeneration took far longer than originally envisaged. Although some demolition and rebuilding had occurred by 2014 when I first went to West Hendon, most of the estate remained standing. At this point there was clear evidence that residents cared both for their homes and the estate environment (Photograph 4.3; Chapter 6). The number of Barnet Homes' secure council tenants reduced from 478 to only 212 by 2013, alongside the same number of non-secure tenants (NSTs) who had been placed on the estate on a temporary basis (Quod, 2013, cited in Watt, 2018a).

Figure 4.4 shows housing tenure before and after regeneration at West Hendon. The total number of properties is projected to increase by nearly 3.4 times from the original 649 to 2,194. Within this large expansion, the total number of 'affordable' homes will increase to 615, largely due to the upping of low-cost homeownership from zero to 353 units. In stark contrast, the number of social rental homes will decline by 45 per cent from 478 to 262, a much greater reduction than the 27 per cent London-wide average (Chapter 3). The number of market homes at West Hendon will increase by over nine times from 171 (RTB) to 1,579. The proportion of social rental homes in the new scheme will shrink to a mere 12 per cent compared to 74 per

Photograph 4.3: West Hendon estate – gardens, 2014

cent originally, while the percentage of private homes will increase from 26 to 72 per cent.

How do these changes compare to the Heygate and Woodbury Down schemes examined in Chapter 3? West Hendon's 45 per cent social rental loss is lower than the 92 per cent at Heygate, but much greater than the 15 per cent at Woodberry Down. The 12 per cent on-completion social renting at West Hendon is also in between Heygate (3 per cent) and Woodberry Down (20 per cent). Market homes will account for a massive 72 per cent – again in between Heygate (78 per cent) and Woodberry Down (61 per cent). West Hendon is a stark example of regeneration as state-led gentrification, albeit a less extreme case than the Heygate but more pronounced than Woodberry Down.

Of the original council tenanted homes at West Hendon, FOI data shows that 193 had been demolished by September 2019 (Photograph 4.4), and that all but one of the secure tenants had moved into a new-build home on the redeveloped estate.[6] If this rate of return to new homes is impressive by the Heygate's lamentable standards (Chapter 3), the overall loss of social rental homes at West Hendon means that it's de facto impossible for every council tenant to exercise the right to return in the future.

The regeneration has prompted high-profile resident opposition, including protest groups such as 'Our West Hendon', while estate

Figure 4.4: West Hendon estate – original and proposed housing tenure (before and after regeneration) (*N*)

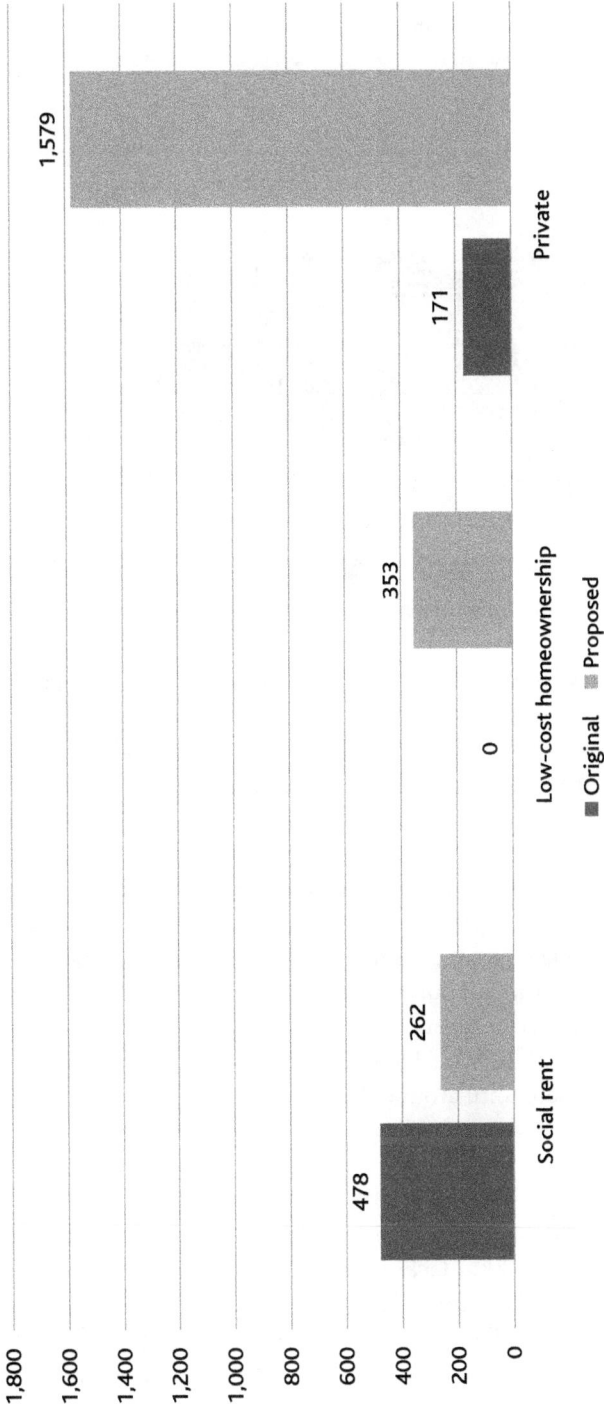

Source: LBB (2017), and email from Barnet Council (19 September 2018)

Photograph 4.4: West Hendon estate – demolition, 2019

leaseholders mounted three Compulsory Purchase Order (CPO) challenges. At the second CPO, a Labour councillor gave evidence (on the basis of FOI requests) that although the land for Phase 3 of the scheme was valued at over £12.3m, the council had sold it to Barrett Metropolitan for just £3 (Worden, 2017: 51)! West Hendon has been singled out as a particularly poor example of the capital's estate regeneration (Wainwright, 2016), and was visited by Jeremy Corbyn and Sadiq Khan on this basis: 'The Mayor of London said he was "shocked" by the controversial West Hendon estate in a visit where he and the Labour leader met residents and announced new guidelines for estate regeneration in the capital' (Hendon & Finchley Times, 2018). The West Hendon scheme began in 2002 and is not due to complete until around 2029.

Hackney

Hackney has dramatically changed over the last four decades. During the 1970s and 1980s, Hackney was a byword for inner-city poverty, deprivation and far-right racism (Harrison, 1983). Although Hackney remains deprived (Table 4.1), it's also currently identified with 'hipster gentrification' and ethnic 'commonplace diversity' (Wessendorf, 2014). Gentrification has escalated in many parts of the borough since the

1980s (Butler and Robson, 2003; Wessendorf, 2014). In fact, Hackney had the largest increase in managers and professionals of all London boroughs from 2004 to 2014 (Hanna and Bosetti, 2015).

Hackney's housing transformation has been remarkable. Whereas nearly three fifths of households rented from the council in 1981, less than a quarter did so in 2011 (Figure 4.2). Most of this reduction is accounted by RTB sales, but the remainder is due to stock transfers, and demolitions dating back to the 1990s' CEI. During the 1980s and 1990s, Hackney Council was a byword for poor management, including of its large, rundown housing stock (Jacobs, 1999; Raynsford, 2016). Like many other inner London councils during this period, Hackney found itself encumbered with large amounts of stock which had transferred from the GLC, including the two research estates: Woodberry Down located in the north east corner near Haringey, and Northwold in Clapton. Since 2011, Hackney Council has embarked on an extensive 18-site Estate Regeneration Programme involving cross-subsidy from building market homes into affordable homes provision (McLaughlin, 2015; Barke, 2017). One result has been extensive demolition; Hackney had the sixth highest demolition level of local authority housing in London at 661 units during 2011–17 (MHCLG, 2019a). Nevertheless, Hackney still had nearly 22,000 council properties by 2018 (Figure 4.3). Social renting accounted for 65 per cent of households in 1981, but this declined to 44 per cent in 2011.

Woodberry Down estate

Woodberry Down was built in stages from the 1940s to 1970s (LBH, 2014). It was begun by the LCC in the teeth of local Conservative and middle-class opposition and was a post-war model LCC estate with a range of public facilities including schools and healthcare centres (Parker, 1999). Woodberry Down was the largest estate in Hackney, with 1,980 homes spread across 57 blocks and intercut by the major Seven Sisters Road (Photograph 4.5). By the start of regeneration planning in 1999, one third of the homes had been sold under the RTB, and there was also a surge in RTB applications following the prospect of redevelopment (Jones, 2003).

The impetus for comprehensive redevelopment lay in how Woodberry Down suffered from 'a maintenance backlog costed at some £150 million' (URBED, 2007: 3), while a structural survey identified substantial physical problems at 37 of the 57 blocks (Belotti, 2014). Initially, Woodberry Down formed part of an SRB scheme, and was also one of New Labour's 'Mixed Communities Initiatives' whereby

Photograph 4.5: Woodberry Down estate – condemned local authority blocks (view from new housing association blocks across Seven Sisters Road), 2018

the emphasis was placed on private sector cross-subsidy (Woodberry Down Regeneration Team, 2009; Mixed Communities Evaluation Project Team, 2010). Hackney Council had four original regeneration aims (LBH, 2002: 2):

   i.   realising a substantial capital receipt for the Woodberry Down School site;

  ii.   achieving in due course a substantial part of its Decent Homes Target as Woodberry Down is 10% of the Council's Housing Stock;

 iii.   rehousing homeless families through the additional social housing created by the programme;

 iv.   achieving corresponding savings in temporary accommodation for the homeless.

In practice, while the council took Woodberry Down out of its DHP, this did little for residents who had to endure poor-quality homes for years (Belotti, 2014). By 2014, helping the homeless via additional social housing provision was no longer on the council's Woodberry Down regeneration agenda (LBH, 2014), and in fact there will be a net reduction in social renting (Chapter 3). The promised 'Community Based Housing Association' (Woodberry Down Regeneration Team, 2009) never materialised, while the eventual social housing partner was Genesis Housing Association, one of the increasingly commercial

G15 group of large London housing associations (Manzi and Morrison, 2018). Woodberry Down has effectively morphed from a housing needs/community development regeneration scheme into a state-led gentrification project where the private partner is Berkeley Homes, an up-market property developer (Chakrabortty and Robinson-Tillett, 2014; Nelson and Lewis, 2019). Having begun in 1999, the scheme is expected to complete in around 2035.

Several assessments of the Woodberry Down scheme are available (see inter alia Belotti 2014; Chakrabortty and Robinson-Tillett, 2014; Quod, 2014; WDCO and Eastside Community Heritage, 2015; ASH, 2017; Nelson and Lewis, 2019; Social Life, 2020). These accounts range all the way from the fulsomely positive Quod (2014) report (commissioned by the developer), to 'Class War on Woodberry Down' (ASH, 2017). To date, the most penetrating account remains that by Belotti (2014), who provides an in-depth analysis of residents' profoundly stressful regeneration and rehousing experiences.

By early 2019, 530 decanted council tenants at Woodberry Down had returned to new housing association homes, representing 29 per cent of the 1,798 new-build properties (Social Life, 2020: 25). Of the remainder, 1,052 were privately owned, and 216 were in shared ownership. At the 'old estate', 269 (21 per cent) of the 1,259 remaining properties were void (Social Life, 2020: 25). Of the 990 occupied properties at the old estate, 361 were rented by secure council tenants, 190 were in private ownership and 437 were occupied by non-secure tenants. According to Hackney Council, 'probably less' than 15 secure tenants had moved elsewhere in Hackney, and none had moved outside of Hackney.[7] FOI data shows that most of the leaseholders had moved away from the estate since only three had relocated to shared-equity properties on the redeveloped part of the estate by June 2018.[8]

Northwold estate

Northwold is an LCC-built medium-sized estate in the increasingly gentrified Clapton area. It has 579 properties (a quarter owned), divided between 20 red-brick blocks of 4–5 storeys. Northwold was one of Hackney's stock transfer estates – to Clapton Housing Association in 1998, which was subsequently absorbed into the Guinness Partnership housing association. Following transfer, the new landlord made various improvements, such as putting in lifts. In 2016, the housing association proposed a regeneration scheme; one 'option' involved extensive partial demolition. The latter was vociferously challenged by the Save Northwold campaign, a group of residents who were active from summer 2016 to late 2018. Following this concerted resistance, the housing association withdrew the demolition plans in favour of infilling plus demolition of just two homes (Hackney Citizen, 2018).

Research at Northwold involved interviews and a resident survey which was designed in liaison with the Save Northwold campaign. The Northwold Estate Survey (NES) was undertaken in summer/autumn 2017. One hundred and ninety questionnaires were completed giving a 33 per cent response rate. The results and methods are summarised in *Northwold Estate, Hackney: A Report on Residents' Attitudes to the Estate and its Potential Redevelopment* (Watt and Allen, 2018).

Haringey

Haringey is the most spatially polarised of all the research boroughs. It is fissured by a stark east–west divide between the poor Tottenham area with a large BAME population and where most of the social housing estates and temporary accommodation is located, and the wealthy western areas of Highgate, Crouch End and Muswell Hill (Dillon and Fanning, 2011; Haringey Fairness Commission, 2020).

Haringey had the second smallest local authority stock after Barnet in 1981, just 29 per cent with another 5 per cent housing association (Figure 4.2). By 2011, council housing had reduced to 17 per cent, while the housing association sector had increased to nearly 10 per cent. Nearly a third of households were in the PRS in 2011, many in poor housing conditions. In 2006, Haringey council set up an ALMO – Homes for Haringey (HFH) – to manage its stock; there were over 15,000 local authority properties in 2018 (Figure 4.3). Tottenham contains the heavily stigmatised Broadwater Farm estate – 'Britain's most notorious estate' (Hendry, 2019) – which formed the epicentre of two major riots in 1985 and 2011 (Power, 1997). The 2011 riots occurred due to the police killing of Mark Duggan, a Broadwater Farm resident. The political fallout from these riots prompted the regeneration of 'troublesome' Tottenham (Dillon and Fanning, 2015). The regeneration of Tottenham can be viewed as part of an entrepreneurial borough strategy which has included the stadium-led regeneration scheme at Tottenham Hotspurs Football Club (Panton and Walters, 2018).

Various regeneration schemes took place in Tottenham during the New Labour years, including an SRB scheme at Northumberland Park estate (Dillon and Fanning, 2011). This large estate forms the core of the Northumberland Park ward, the poorest ward in Haringey and one of the most deprived in the country. It was this estate which formed the focus of my research in Haringey and it was also the locus of the controversial HDV SPV regeneration scheme. The HDV was announced in 2013 and consisted of a 50–50 partnership between Haringey Council and Lendlease, a major international property developer (Inside Housing, 2017). The HDV included comprehensive redevelopment of Northumberland Park estate and surrounding area. This comprised the proposed demolition of 889 council, 276 leasehold and 252 private homes on (or near) the estate (Inside Housing, 2017). Northumberland Park is a somewhat disparate 1960s–1970s estate – with mainly low-rise blocks plus houses and a couple of tower blocks – located near the revamped Tottenham Hotspurs football stadium. Like many estates of this period, Northumberland Park is generously landscaped with green space in between the blocks (Photograph 4.6). As well as being poor and deprived, there are extensive resident concerns regarding community safety, cleaning, crime and ASB (PPCR Associates, 2016). Following sustained campaigning by residents and left-wing Labour Party members, the HDV was cancelled by the newly elected left-wing Labour council in 2018, and regeneration ceased at Northumberland Park (Inside Housing, 2017, 2019). In addition to Northumberland Park, I also conducted limited field and interview research at Broadwater Farm estate.[9]

Photograph 4.6: Northumberland Park estate, 2016

Lambeth

Lambeth is another inner London borough that has become increasingly gentrified (Butler and Robson, 2003; Jackson and Butler, 2015). In 1981, 43 per cent of households lived in council housing with another 7 per cent in housing association property. Lambeth has seen a large reduction in council housing, which accommodated less than a fifth of households in 2011. Nevertheless, it still had over 24,000 local authority properties by 2018, the third highest number in London (Figure 4.3). The housing association sector expanded to 16 per cent, partly due the stock transfer of several major estates during the 2000s, including Clapham Park. Research focused on Clapham Park and Cressingham Gardens estates, and to a lesser extent on Central Hill and Westbury.

Clapham Park estate[10]

Clapham Park was one of the unwanted GLC estates transferred to Lambeth Council during the 1980s. It was the largest estate in the borough with nearly 2,000 properties. The original eastern part of the estate and smaller southern section were built by the LCC during the 1930s (Gater, 1937), while the western section was mainly built during the 1950s (Photograph 4.7).

Photograph 4.7: Clapham Park estate (west), 2016

By the 1990s/early 2000s, Clapham Park had become a deprived inner-city estate with rundown, poorly maintained properties, crime (including crack houses), and a general air of abandonment and alienation (Toynbee, 2003; Beaumont, 2006; Clapham Film Unit, 2010; CPP, 2013).

Clapham Park became one of London's ten NDC neighbourhoods with a focus on community development, tackling crime and improving housing. Despite the poor housing conditions, the arrival of NDC money saw a flurry of local estate agents persuading tenants to buy under the RTB (Toynbee, 2003), indicative of the commercial exploitation of the RTB in London (ALG, 2003); over a quarter of homes were owned by 2006. The Clapham Park NDC housing rationale included demolition and development of extensive private housing for sale in Clapham Park west, coupled with refurbishment of Clapham Park east and south. Clapham Park Project (CPP, 2013) ran the social aspects of the NDC with considerable success, notably in relation to reducing crime and fear of crime. It also laid the groundwork for stock transfer from Lambeth Council to a purposely created housing association – Clapham Park Homes (part of Metropolitan Housing Partnership) – which was due to deliver housing renewal and refurbishment. The proposed transfer resulted in a bitter struggle which culminated in a majority 'yes' vote of tenants (59 per cent) in 2005.

Objections to stock transfer and to the various subsequent masterplans by residents and housing activists have focused on the planned large-scale demolition of the west, as well as defence of the estate's generous green space and numerous trees (Watt, 2009a; Clapham Film Unit, 2010). Although demolition was supposed to have been completed by 2013, there have been numerous delays such that much of the west remained standing at the time that I last visited in late 2018. By then, temporary tenants made up a significant proportion of the population in the western section.

The 2008 plan included a net uplift of just three social rental units, but the 2019 plan increased the 2008 number by 229 social rental units, in line with mayoral guidance, while the number of market homes was increased by 139 units (GLA, 2019b). The proposed final scheme will double the overall density, but will also increase the amount of social housing by 16 per cent, which is impressive by the typical net reductions outlined in this and the previous chapter. However, social rented properties will still only account for 42 per cent of the total, while market homes will be 47 per cent (GLA, 2019b). Having originally expected to be completed by 2017, it's estimated the regeneration scheme will last until 2034.

Cressingham Gardens, Central Hill and Westbury estates[11]

These three estates form part of the six small-to-medium sized estates that Lambeth Council included in its estate regeneration programme involving 1,480 homes (LBL, 2015b). The council's rationale for this programme was mainly densification and solving the borough's and city's housing crisis, while also arguing that it lacked the funds to maintain the homes up to the Decent Homes Plus standard. This is a good example of scale-jumping since the council is focusing on 'helping the homeless' elsewhere in the borough and enhancing the social housing stock, rather than estate community development as with the NDC (Chapter 3). Lambeth's regeneration programme is financially and organisationally based upon creating an SPV: 'Homes for Lambeth (HfL), a council-owned, speculative real estate company that will demolish existing public housing stock and deliver mixed-tenure developments, creating ambiguous public/private tenancies that function as both homes and the basis for liquid financial assets' (Beswick and Penny, 2018: 612–13). Existing secure council tenants will move onto Homes for Lambeth assured tenancies if they return to the redeveloped estates (Local Dialogue, 2016).

Cressingham Gardens is a low-rise estate of 306 properties in the south of the borough in Tulse Hill. It was designed in the 1970s by Ted Hollomby, the borough architect (Photograph 4.8). Nearly a third of the properties were owned, while seven properties had been left empty for over a decade (LBL, 2015b: 2). Cressingham Gardens was first identified for regeneration in October 2012 and the original rationale pointed to the poor condition of some of the properties, and also 'because the cost of delivering the Lambeth Housing Standard would be prohibitive and refurbishment works alone would be unlikely to resolve fundamental conditions and design flaws of the properties' (LBL, 2015b: 2). The rationale subsequently extended to densification via building more homes.

Lambeth Council employed Social Life (2013, 2015) as consultants and their reports identified a strong sense of community at Cressingham Gardens, and also that 81 per cent of residents wanted to stay with repairs done, while only 10 per cent wanted to leave the estate (Social Life, 2013). Residents were consulted on five options – ranging from refurbishment to total demolition – but the council subsequently removed the refurbishment options for which it lost a judicial review (JR) appeal in 2015 (Douglas and Parkes, 2016). Despite well-organised and proactive opposition to demolition via the Save Cressingham

Photograph 4.8: Cressingham Gardens estate – Brockwell Park in background, 2013

Gardens campaign, Lambeth Council is pursuing its demolition-centred approach (Sendra and Fitzpatrick, 2020).

Central Hill is situated in the south of the borough in Crystal Palace and is the largest estate in the council's estate regeneration programme, consisting of 456 homes (29 per cent owned). The reasons for including Central Hill in the programme 'include the poor state of repair of many properties on the Estate and the opportunity to build more homes, due to the relative low density of the Estate, given its location and public transport accessibility levels' (LBL, 2015a: 1). A consultation survey on behalf of the council indicated that 49 per cent supported the full rebuilding of the estate while 38 per cent were against, although this was differentiated by tenure with 55 per cent of council tenants supporting rebuilding, but only 31 per cent of owners and 35 per cent of private tenants (TCC, 2016). However, a survey by residents themselves identified only two people out of 150 who wanted demolition (Moore, 2016). Although Central Hill has been run down due to inadequate maintenance, it's also received architectural praise for being 'beautifully designed' (Moore, 2016), and is visually light years away from the 'sink estate' stereotype (Photograph 4.9), as is Cressingham Gardens. ASH (2018) produced a detailed alternative

Photograph 4.9: Central Hill estate, 2015

to demolition based upon refurbishment and infilling, which the council rejected.

Westbury is a small ex–GLC estate in the north of the borough. It has 205 homes divided between two 20-storey towers and several low-rise blocks. It is the latter with its 82 flats (50 tenanted, 32 leasehold) that is the focus of the regeneration rather than the towers. Densification was a key rationale: 'Westbury Estate was included in the Council's estate regeneration programme in December 2014 because there is considerable potential for intensification and provision of additional new homes' (LBL, 2015b: 13).

Southwark[12]

Like Hackney and Lambeth, Southwark is an inner London borough that has witnessed a dramatic social transformation during the last 40 years. The northern part of the borough was a centre of the docks and this has now been replaced by high finance, the leisure industry (including Tate Modern), the GLA and a plethora of new luxury apartment blocks including the Shard (Atkinson, 2020). The decline in local authority housing has been dramatic; down from nearly two thirds of all households in 1981 to just under one third in 2011 (Figure 4.2). Nevertheless, Southwark remains by far the largest council landlord in

London, with 38,490 properties in 2018, accounting for nearly one tenth of the city's 392,800 total (Figure 4.3).

The middle of the borough around the Elephant and Castle township area has undergone intense regeneration as part of the council's entrepreneurial borough strategy (Glucksberg, 2016). This area had two nearby 'brutalist' modernist estates – Heygate and Aylesbury. Their demolition forms part of what Merrifield (2014) calls the 'neo-Haussmannisation' of urban space in working-class south London (Campkin, 2013; Transparency International UK, 2017). Research in Southwark focused on these two estates plus East Dulwich.

In his *City Villages* report, Adonis (2015: 13) mentioned 'notorious "sink estates", where living conditions were chronically – often scandalously – bad, such as the Heygate and Aylesbury estates at Elephant and Castle'. Such 'notorious' reputations helped to justify demolition at each of these so-called 'sink estates' (Campkin, 2013). The Heygate had nearly 1,200 homes and was heavily stigmatised by the mass media and politicians – 'muggers' paradise' (BBC, 2011) – in a manner which bore scant relation to residents' lived experiences (Heygate Was Home, 2014; Romyn, 2016). It was subject to a long-running, controversial regeneration scheme from the late 1990s which involved Lendlease as the final private developer partner. Although lauded by Peter John (2015), the Leader of Southwark Council, this scheme has become the capital's poster-child for estate regeneration as state-led gentrification involving breaking up the existing community, minimal social housing and extensive displacement outside the borough and London for leaseholders (Heygate Was Home, 2014; Flynn, 2016; Lees and Ferrari, 2016; Romyn, 2016; Minton, 2017). In a crowded field, the Heygate demolition stands out for the magnitude of its social housing loss and large percentage of market homes in the new redevelopment (Chapter 3). The last leaseholder was CPOd out of his flat in 2013. Photograph 4.10 shows one of the blocks awaiting demolition in 2014. By 2019, the estate had been demolished and a new development – Elephant Park (due to complete in 2025) – stood in its place. Prices at Elephant Park start at £569,000 for a studio flat and go above £1 million, while *all* 51 units in one block were sold to overseas' investors (Transparency International UK, 2017).

The massive Aylesbury estate with 2,700 homes was the scene for Tony Blair's post-election 'challenging social exclusion' speech in 1997 (Campkin, 2013) (Photograph 4.11). It was the subject of an NDC scheme which involved a stock transfer to a housing association as well

Photograph 4.10: Heygate estate – awaiting demolition, 2014

Photograph 4.11: Aylesbury estate, 2015

as the demolition of large number of homes, plus selling off part of the land to build 1,000–1,500 private flats for sale (Watt and Wallace, 2014). Anti-transfer campaigners had concerns regarding privatisation, gentrification and 'social engineering' and, despite widespread resident recognition that the Aylesbury needed extensive refurbishment, 73 per cent of tenants voted against transfer in 2001.

While the NDC improved certain aspects of life at the Aylesbury, such as education, crime and fear of crime, it made scant progress regarding housing conditions (Social Life, 2017; Watt, 2020c). Following the 'no vote' against transfer, Southwark Council decided it lacked sufficient funding to refurbish the estate, and in 2005 it chose demolition as its preferred option. The combination of stock transfer and demolition has resulted in one of the most protracted activist campaigns in London's regeneration 'war of attrition' (Watt, 2018c). The Aylesbury has been the subject of two CPO inquiries (2015 and 2017; Hubbard and Lees, 2018), as well as the occupation of empty flats in 2015. Alongside the Heygate, the Aylesbury has become a by-word in London for estate regeneration as state-led gentrification (Lees, 2014). Regeneration will be completed around 2035.

East Dulwich (Photograph 4.12) had over 753 homes and was one of the ex-GLC estates that was reluctantly transferred to Southwark Council in the 1980s. The estate is in East Dulwich, an established middle-class neighbourhood (Jackson and Benson, 2014). Regeneration at East Dulwich began in 1997 under the government's Capital Receipts Initiative which led to the controversial Southwark Estate Initiative. Regeneration initially involved refurbishment and the demolition of just one block (LBS, 2005), but morphed into demolishing another five blocks (totalling 107 homes). Residents

Photograph 4.12: East Dulwich estate, 2014

vigorously campaigned against this with the result that four of the five blocks were saved (South London Press, 2005). Refurbishment has continued since then.

RTB percentage sales at each of the three Southwark estates was among the lowest in the estate sample: Aylesbury (12), Heygate (16) and East Dulwich (13). However, as witnessed at several London estates, one by-product of regeneration involving demolition was a dramatic increase in RTB applications at all three estates (ALG, 2003).

Tower Hamlets[13]

Like Southwark, its opposite London riverside borough, Tower Hamlets has witnessed a massive transformation such that it is now one of the epicentres of London's financial economy in Canary Wharf, as well as new-build housing development in Docklands. This economic restructuring resulted in wide-scale gentrification of the East End leading to sharp social polarisation between multi-ethnic working-class locals and affluent newcomers (Butler and Robson, 2003; Hamnett, 2003). BAME groups (including the large Bangladeshi population) in Tower Hamlets are especially disadvantaged in terms of poverty, unemployment and poor housing conditions (Chouhan et al, 2011; Elahi and Khan, 2016).

In 1981, there was an East European state socialist level of public housing since over four fifths of households rented from the council (Figure 4.2), the largest proportion in London. Tower Hamlets Council pursued a controversial stock transfer programme during the 2000s, with nearly half of transfers rejected by tenants. Nevertheless, transfers and RTB sales meant that by 2018 Tower Hamlets council stock of 11,570 properties was astonishingly only slightly larger than that of Barnet (Figure 4.3). This dramatic shrinkage, alongside extensive new private housebuilding, meant that the percentage of local authority housing plummeted to just 17 per cent in 2011, while 22 per cent were housing association rented (Figure 4.2).

Research in Tower Hamlets mainly focused on the Ocean estate, located in Stepney in the heart of the East End. The Ocean was built by the LCC during the 1950s and was one of the GLC estates transferred to the borough councils – Tower Hamlets – during the 1980s. The Ocean was the largest council estate in Tower Hamlets consisting of 1,565 flats in over 40 blocks (LBTH, 2005). Since the 1970s, the Ocean had been plagued by severe housing problems including damp, infestation and disrepair, partly stemming from being built quickly and cheaply, as well as chronic social problems including poverty, overcrowding (especially among the Bangladeshi community) and drug abuse (Ambrose, 1996, 2002). Such problems meant that the Ocean estate became a prime candidate for regeneration.

The Ocean has been the site of three major regeneration programmes. First it was included in the first wave of HATs in the late 1980s, an inclusion that Ocean tenants successfully opposed (Woodward, 1991). Following the aborted HAT, three of the large Ocean blocks in the worst condition were included in the Central Stepney SRB whose primary focus was the adjacent Limehouse Fields estate; these three blocks were demolished (Edwards et al, 2003). The Central Stepney SRB programme resulted in genuinely improved housing and health conditions, especially among the area's overcrowded Bangladeshi population who appreciated having new houses rather than flats (Ambrose, 1996, 2002; Edwards et al, 2003). The role of private finance in this programme was limited such that there was no major uplift in private homes for sale (Chapter 3).

Despite the Central Stepney SRB, Ocean residents continued to suffer from poor housing conditions, overcrowding and poverty. Consequently, the estate formed the epicentre of the Ocean Estate NDC in 2000 (LBTH, 2005). A large emphasis was placed upon redevelopment of the housing stock but, as with the Aylesbury and Clapham Park estates, the NDC funding was insufficient and hence a stock transfer to Sanctuary Housing Association was mooted. This involved a large-scale renewal scheme including extensive demolition and substantial private housing. Given these large-scale tenure changes, plus how the resultant social homes would be flats and not houses (unlike the Central Stepney SRB), tenants rejected transfer following a politically charged anti-transfer campaign in 2005. As elsewhere in London, one effect of the proposed demolition was an acceleration in RTB sales (ALG, 2003: 21; Jones, 2003). By 2005, 30 per cent of the Ocean properties had been bought under the RTB (LBTH, 2005).

Following the 'no vote', residents were effectively penalised since the housing part of the Ocean NDC programme came to an abrupt halt whilst a new 'Regeneration Trust' was set up. It took until 2010 before Tower Hamlets Council (plus residents) selected East Thames consortium (East Thames Housing Association and Bellway Homes) to put in place a £220m regeneration scheme involving redevelopment plus refurbishment of 1,200 existing council homes (East Thames, 2016). This is less a state-led gentrification vehicle than the earlier Sanctuary scheme (Watt, 2009a), but still involved demolition of 338 homes at Sites E and F, and a later demolition of three blocks with 120 homes at Site H which were originally due to be refurbished (GLA,

2010, 2014; East Thames, 2017). I estimate that the completed scheme (expected around 2020) will involve a net loss of 55 social rental homes, and net increases of 422 private, 129 shared ownership/shared equity and 92 affordable rented properties.

Supplementary boroughs

In addition to the main boroughs, limited research was undertaken in four supplementary boroughs (Figure 4.1).

- Brent – South Kilburn estate, another large London NDC estate. In the post–NDC period, South Kilburn was subject to large-scale redevelopment including demolition (Telemaque, 2015; Samanani, 2017).
- Camden – Regents Park estate in the south of the borough; part of this estate is due to be demolished to make way for the High Speed 2 railway (London Geographies, 2018).[14] In addition, one council tenant was interviewed who had been rehoused from Bacton estate in Kentish Town due to regeneration (Wainwright, 2016; Karakusevic Carson Architects, 2017). See Watt (2001, 2003, 2005, 2006) for an extensive analysis of council housing in Camden.
- Waltham Forest – two small regeneration/demolition estates: Marlowe Road (BBC, 2015), and Fred Wigg and John Walsh Towers (McKenzie and Hussain, 2018).
- Westminster – Churchill Gardens estate, which was subject to a partial demolition proposal in 2014.

Comparing the estates

The 14 main research estates are of different sizes and spatial configurations (Table 4.2). They range from the Aylesbury, one of the largest estates in the UK with 2,700 units spread across 24 hectares, to Cressingham Gardens with 306 properties on just four hectares. In the European context, large estates have been defined as 1,000 units and above (Hess et al, 2018), and this definition is used here to distinguish between large estates and small to medium–sized estates with fewer than 1,000 properties, as below.

Large estates

- Aylesbury
- Clapham Park

- Heygate
- Northumberland Park
- Ocean
- Woodberry Down

Small to medium-sized estates

- Carpenters
- Central Hill
- Cressingham Gardens
- East Dulwich
- Northwold
- Westbury
- West Hendon

This somewhat crude binary distinction highlights several physical features of the estates. First, the small to medium estates are characterised by their easy walkability; one can walk from one end of the estate to the other in around 5–7 minutes. By contrast, walking between the extreme points of the large estates can take 15 minutes or more. Second, the large estates comprise multiple blocks which are intersected by roads, in some cases major roads. This effectively fractures the supposedly singular 'estate' into several sections – as in the case of Clapham Park. Third, the small to medium estates tend to have clearer external boundaries. One result of this physical features is how residents of the large estates sometimes struggled with the notion that their estate had a *singular* place identity, whereas the latter was more apparent in the small to medium estates. As discussed in later chapters, this large/small to medium estate distinction proves useful when examining place attachment.

Resident interviewees

Socio-demographic details for the quoted interviewees are included in Appendix B. The resident interview sample is extensive but *not* statistically representative. A summary of 157 interviewees' socio-demographic characteristics is provided in Table 4.4, based on them being divided into four main tenures:[15]

- social tenants ($n = 97$) – current local authority and housing association tenants; most of the latter were previously council tenants who became housing association tenants due to stock transfers, regeneration or rehousing;

- RTB owners ($n = 28$) – ex-council tenants who bought their homes under the RTB;
- NSTs (non-secure tenants, $n = 21$) – located in social housing estates undergoing regeneration on a temporary basis; in previous decades they would have been council tenants, but are now 'would-like-to-be' social tenants;
- owner-occupiers ($n = 11$) – these are people who bought their homes on the market from RTB owners when the latter sold.

Table 4.4: Profile of estate interviewees by main housing tenures (%)

	Social tenants	Right-to-Buy owners	Non-secure tenants	Owner-occupiers (market)
Gender				
Female	57	61	81	64
Male	43	39	19	36
Age				
20–29 years	3	0	19	0
30–39 years	6	0	19	27
40–49 years	16	18	52	55
50–59 years	27	36	10	9
60–69 years	32	14	0	0
70 years and over	16	32	0	9
Ethnicity				
White British	55	36	19	36
White Other	9	11	14	18
Black/Black British	26	39	34	18
Asian/Asian British	3	11	19	9
Other	7	3	14	18
Household status				
Couple	13	48	0	20
Couple + children	7	16	38	5
Lone parent	17	0	33	0
Single person	60	36	29	30
Other	3	0	0	0

Table 4.4 Profile of estate interviewees by main housing tenures (%) (continued)

	Social tenants	Right-to-Buy owners	Non-secure tenants	Owner-occupiers (market)
Length of time at estate				
Under 1 year	0	0	9	18
1–4 years	6	0	29	9
5–9 years	4	0	48	18
10–19 years	28	7	14	45
20–29 years	23	36	0	0
30–39 years	18	14	0	9
40 years and over	21	43	0	0
Total N = 100%	97	28	21	11

Note: percentages subject to rounding errors.

The interviewees are broadly reflective of the multi-ethnic, working-class nature of London's estates, albeit that they are weighted towards elderly and long-term residents. Female interviewees dominate all tenure categories, especially among the NSTs. Nearly half of both social tenants and RTB owners were aged 60 or over, while one third of RTB owners were aged 70 or over. There were no RTB owners aged under 40 and only 9 per cent of social tenants were under 40. The older profile fits the national picture for RTB owners (Jones and Murie, 2006). By contrast, the NSTs were much younger, with 19 per cent aged under 30 and no one over 60. The owner-occupiers are a middle-aged group dominated by couples and nuclear families.

What stands out is the social renters' and RTB owners' residential longevity. Nearly two thirds of social tenants had lived at their estate for 20+ years, 39 per cent had done so for 30+ years and 21 per cent for 40+ years; only 10 per cent had lived there for less than ten years. This compares to London-wide social renters' lengths of time in current home of just 24 per cent (20+ years) and 10 per cent (30+ years) (GLA, 2019a). Residential longevity is even more pronounced among RTB owners; 93 per cent had lived on their estates for 20+ years, 57 per cent for 30+ years and 43 per cent for 40+ years! Again, this is far longer than London-wide owner-occupiers' time spent in current home – 22 per cent for 30+ years (GLA, 2019a).[16] Such residential longevity among the social renters and RTB owners is striking, especially given that nearly two fifths of all London households have lived in their current homes for less than five years (GLA, 2019a). These interviewees are therefore not statistically representative of their respective tenures in London. This longevity also suggests that the sample are likely to have an embedded traditional form of place belonging in neighbourhoods (Chapter 6). By contrast, the NSTs have much shorter residential periods. Even then, 62 per cent had been on their estate for five or more years, indicative of the increasing periods of time that London's homeless are remaining in so-called temporary accommodation which is fast becoming a tenure of destination in its own right (Watt, 2018a).

Regarding household status, 60 per cent of social tenants were single – never married, divorced, separated or widowed – compared to over a third of the RTB group. Nuclear families (couples with children) are not prominent in either tenure, although couples (many elderly) account for nearly half of RTB owners. Lone parents account for 17 per cent of social tenants, but no RTB owners. By comparison, one third of NSTs were lone parents and another 38 per cent nuclear families. This indicates how working-class families with children are increasingly excluded from accessing social housing, unlike in previous periods (Chapter 5).

Just over half of social tenants were white British, but only 36 per cent of RTB owners. Over half of the latter were from BAME backgrounds. By comparison, two thirds of NSTs were from BAME backgrounds, while only a fifth were white British. The latter is indicative of the racialised nature of housing precarity which disproportionately affects established BAME groups and recent migrants (Watt, 2018a, 2018b, 2020b). In terms of ethnicity, the sample includes very few South Asian heritage interviewees, while non-English-speaking residents are also unrepresented, a group which is prominent on certain London estates (Gidley, 2013). The next chapter moves onto the research findings.

PART II

Estates before regeneration

5

Marginalisation and inclusion

Since the 1970s, social housing estates within Western capitalist cities have been linked to marginalisation processes in relation to poverty and deprivation. This chapter examines marginalisation at London's estates with reference to three analytical frameworks: residualisation, social exclusion and socio-tenurial polarisation. While acknowledging that such approaches have considerable credibility – especially in socioeconomic terms – the chapter develops a multi-stranded critique of how they frame and analyse marginalisation. This critique embraces three main themes: employment and class; social inclusion and diversity; and tenure preferences. This critique draws upon interview data regarding tenants' labour and housing market experiences. The final section focuses on the shifting interrelationship between homelessness and social housing.

Public housing and marginalisation

The marginalisation of UK public housing has been examined through various analytical frameworks including residualisation (Forrest and Murie, 1991), social exclusion (SEU, 1998) and socio-tenurial polarisation (Hamnett, 2003). Residualisation means public renting transformed during the 1970s to 1990s from general needs housing, catering for a broad swathe of the working class, to a residual 'tenure of last resort' for a poor, largely 'non-working class' (Forrest and Murie, 1991). The latter include deprived and socially marginalised groups that were too poor to enter owner-occupation – the unemployed, sick and disabled, lone-parent families, the homeless, BAME groups, unskilled workers, and so on (Forrest and Murie, 1991; Hamnett, 2003).

If residualisation began during the 1970s, it intensified during the 1980s due to a series of policy and social developments. The Housing (Homeless Persons) Act 1977 contributed towards residualisation by allowing those with 'priority need' greater access into local authority housing thereby eroding its base in the general population (Somerville, 1994; Fitzpatrick and Pawson, 2016). The RTB was a key policy driver of residualisation because it allowed better-off tenants in more affluent rural and suburban districts to buy their houses, leaving behind a rump tenure of older, decaying council flats in inner-city areas (Forrest and

Murie, 1991; Murie, 2016). Public housing also became residualised *within the welfare state* since it suffered more from Thatcherite cuts than any other welfare area (Balchin, 1995), as discussed in previous chapters. In addition to these policy factors, deindustrialisation was a major cause of residualisation (Forrest and Murie, 1991). Council tenants became unemployed not *because* they lived in public housing, but because this tenure disproportionately housed those sections of the manual working class who lost their jobs due to deindustrialisation and the 1970s–1990s' recessions (Todd, 2014). Hence the non-working class became clustered in council estates (Forrest and Murie, 1991).

The disadvantages poor tenants faced by living in rundown estates were not merely socioeconomic, but had broader characteristics, as captured by the multivalent notion of social exclusion. Tackling social exclusion became a key aim in New Labour's urban policy (Chapter 3; SEU, 1998; Levitas, 2005). Council estates were targeted as crucibles of social exclusion where the poor, workless and those engaged in criminality and ASB were said to spatially cluster together (Watt and Jacobs, 2000). Spatial clustering supposedly reinforced social disadvantages, hence New Labour's policy emphasis on creating mixed-tenure communities via urban regeneration, as in the NDC case.

Residualisation and socio-tenurial polarisation in London

Hamnett (2003: 148) argues that inter-war and post-war council housing in London was 'a desirable and scarce commodity and families competed to gain access'. However, this desirability waned during the 1970s and 1980s. Hamnett uses census data from 1971 to 1991 to identify a process of socio-tenurial polarisation between better-off owner-occupiers and a residual, increasingly impoverished council tenant population:

> it was only in the 1970s that the social composition of council housing began to change as the skilled manual workers began to move into home ownership and council housing opened up to the less skilled, the unemployed, ethnic minorities and single parents who would hitherto have been largely excluded on various grounds. The social gap between the two tenures then began to open up in a dramatic fashion. ... Council renting has ceased to be a desirable tenure for many skilled and junior white-collar workers who have either moved into ownership or moved out of Inner London, and it has become home to many of

those who, thirty years ago, were effectively excluded from
council housing. In the process it has become increasingly
socially residualised. (Hamnett, 2003: 148)

The proportion of the economically inactive in council housing
rose from 29 per cent to 57 per cent from 1971 to 1991, thereby
confirming residualisation: the 'council sector is now dominated by
those who are not in the labour force, by virtue of either long-term
unemployment, retirement, ill health, disability or single parenthood'
(Hamnett, 2003: 149). Nearly half of housing association households
were also economically inactive by 1991. In other words, social renting
increasingly housed the non-working class of workless households
outside the labour market, as New Labour emphasised via its social
exclusion agenda (SEU, 1998; Levitas, 2005). Hamnett (2003: 190–91)
also notes how socio-tenurial polarisation in inner London had taken
a micro-spatial form via the juxtaposition between gentrified streets
and council estates: 'two-income professional or managerial owner-
occupied households can be found living only a few streets away from
deprived council estates with high levels of economic inactivity'.

Hamnett's (2003) account of council housing residualisation and
socio-tenurial polarisation is based on census data for the 1971–91
period. However, several important aspects of employment and housing
have changed since the early 1990s. First is how the 1980s/early 1990s
period represents the nadir of unemployment and worklessness for
social housing estate residents both in London and nationally (Tunstall,
2020). This period witnessed particularly high levels of unemployment
associated with deindustrialisation which hit London's working-class
council tenants hard (Watt, 2003). Since then, the city's post-industrial
service economy has dramatically expanded and this expansion has, at
least to some extent, allowed social tenants (and their adult children)
to gain paid work (Smith, 2005; Gunter and Watt, 2009; Tunstall,
2020). Second, a focus on council housing alone is less germane given
the expansion of the housing association sector, not least due to stock
transfers; this necessitates examining the broader 'social renting' tenure.
Third, council estates are no longer mono-tenurial due to RTB sales
and resales. London's estates are more mixed in terms of tenure, class
and ethnicity than they were during the early 1990s (Hamnett and
Butler, 2010; Gidley, 2013; Rosbrook-Thompson and Armstrong,
2018). Hence socio-spatial equations between council renting (as
tenure) and estates (as spaces) are no longer credible. Fourth, the PRS
has increased substantially since the 1990s; hence a bi-tenurial focus
on social renting and owner-occupation is too restrictive.

In taking the London housing tenure story forward, I refer to the 2017 NES findings (Watt and Allen, 2018), and also undertake a secondary analysis of several reports which have used 2011 Census data (GLA Intelligence, 2013a, 2013b; Travers et al, 2016). Table 5.1 uses 2011 Census data to highlight several of the demographic and socioeconomic variables that Hamnett (2003) associates with residualisation and socio-tenurial polarisation (GLA Intelligence, 2013a, 2013b). The table demonstrates how the social rental sector remains fundamentally distinct from owner–occupation, and to a lesser extent from the PRS. One quarter of all social renters were lone-parent households in 2011, compared to just 7 per cent of owner-occupiers and 10 per cent of private renters. The long-term sick and disabled comprise 12 per cent of social renters, but a mere 1 per cent of owners and 3 per cent of private renters. The retired make up over a fifth of both social renters and owner-occupiers, but only 5 per cent of private renters; this reflects how the latter has a much younger age profile than the other two tenures (GLA Intelligence, 2013a). The never worked/long-term unemployment rate is 16 per cent for social renters, much higher than both owner-occupiers (2 per cent) and private renters (6 per cent).

Table 5.1: Elderly, lone-parent households, economic activity and NS-SEC by housing tenure, London, 2011 (% of total unless otherwise indicated)

	Social rent	Owner-occupied	Private rent or rent free	Total
Age 65 years and over	21	24	5	19
Lone-parent households	26	7	10	13
Economically active	55	75	84	73
Employed	46	74	79	68
Part-time employees as % of total employees	33	12	14	16
Economically inactive	45	25	16	27
Retired	21	22	5	17
Long-term sick or disabled	12	1	3	4
NS-SEC 6 and 7 (semi-routine and routine occupations)	34	14	17	20
Never worked/ long-term unemployed	16	2	6	7

Source: Census (GLA Intelligence, 2013a, 2013b; my calculations)

In terms of employment, one third of employed social renters were working part-time in 2011 compared to only 12 per cent of owners and 14 per cent of private renters. This suggests that the expansion of non-standard 'poor work' (Shildrick et al, 2012) which has characterised London's post-industrial economy has been especially significant among social tenants, as discussed later. Finally, and as Hamnett's earlier analysis suggests, one third of social renting households were headed by those in semi-routine/routine occupations (NS-SECs 6 and 7) compared to 14 and 17 per cent respectively for owner-occupiers and private renters. In conclusion, the two polar tenures in 2011 remained social renting and owner-occupation, as the socio-tenurial polarisation thesis suggests, with private renting in between, albeit closer to owner-occupation than social renting.

Nevertheless, social renters' aggregate socioeconomic circumstances improved in certain ways from 1991 to 2011. Whereas the majority of council tenants were economically inactive (retired, looking after home or family, long-term sick and disabled, students) in 1991, this reduced to 45 per cent among social renters in 2011 (although still much greater than the 25 per cent among owner-occupiers and 16 per cent of private renters). However, nearly half of all economically inactive social renters in London in 2011 were retired (GLA Intelligence, 2013a), and most of these are likely to have been employed when they were younger. While both owners and private renters were more likely to be in employment than social renters, nearly half of the latter (46 per cent) were in paid work in 2011 (GLA Intelligence, 2013a: 4). This suggests that the notion of social renters' blanket exclusion from paid work, that Hamnett emphasises, has become less apposite.

We can examine this further with reference to the NES findings, which also include a spatial estate focus as well as tenure focus (Watt and Allen, 2018). The NES shows that 35 per cent of Northwold Household Reference Persons were economically inactive, lower than the 45 per cent London average for social renters (Table 5.1). The NES tenure breakdown demonstrates an important tenure effect since housing association tenants were far more likely to be both unemployed (8 per cent) and economically inactive (38 per cent) than leaseholders (0 per cent and 16 per cent respectively). However, *the majority* (54 per cent) of Northwold housing association tenants were in paid employment, as were 84 per cent of leaseholders. The above analysis shows that workless households are less prominent in 21st century London social housing estates than they were during the early 1990s nadir period (Tunstall, 2020).

One recent report on low-income households in London (based upon earning under 60 per cent of national median income after housing costs) indicates that poverty rates were substantially higher among social tenants compared to either owners or private renters in 2011 (Travers et al, 2016). However, the report also shows that rapidly rising market housing costs have pushed more private renters into poverty across London from 2001 to 2011, while social renters – who are cushioned from market housing costs – have seen a reduction in both their numbers and proportions in poverty, such that 'the traditional association of poverty with social renting no longer holds' (Travers et al, 2016: 11). Social renters remain socioeconomically residualised and relatively disadvantaged compared to the other tenures, but the socioeconomic gap has narrowed especially in relation to private renters.

Social housing, class analysis and socioeconomic groups

London's social housing estates are working-class urban spaces – socio-spatial 'fields' in Bourdieu's terms. Most interviewees and estate residents that I met during fieldwork were sociologically working class given their generally limited resources in terms of both economic and cultural capital.[1] As such, they were grounded within a working-class habitus constituted by the choice of the necessary (Bourdieu, 1984). At the same time, this is not a socially cohesive, homogenous 'traditional working class' of male, white, able manual workers, but rather a 'new working class', which 'is multi-ethnic, of all abilities, and more likely to be female than male, … comprised of people living off low to middle incomes, and likely to be occupied in service sector jobs like catering, social care or retail' (Ainsley, 2018: 2 and 25).

Three broad class-analytic approaches to social renters can be identified. The first is that they are a poor, stigmatised section of the working class (Watt, 2006; McKenzie, 2015). As one woman introduced herself at a housing meeting in central London: "I'm a council tenant and working class – I'm three pay cheques away from destitution, so I know I'm working class." A second approach is that they form a residual non-working class of workless households – or, in more pejorative terms, a workshy 'underclass' (Watt, 2008) – as the residualisation, social exclusion and socio-tenurial polarisation frameworks emphasise. A third approach is that tenants are part of the post-industrial precariat who are not so much *excluded* from paid work as *included* in poor work (Shildrick et al, 2012). Such poor work involves in-work poverty, non-standard labour contracts (part-time, temporary, casual, zero-hours), and endemic job insecurity (Smith, 2005; Standing, 2011; Savage, 2015). This is the approach that Wacquant (2008) adopts in relation to understanding zones of urban marginality, such as social housing estates, where the rising class of the precariat dwells. Wacquant emphasises de-proletarianisation and wage-labour fragmentation involving the decimation of full-time employment alongside the blossoming of fractional part-time and temporary contracts.

Each of the above approaches illuminates *one dimension* of social renters' class position – their working-classness, worklessness and precarity. In reality, these are not either/or perspectives since *all three dimensions* are significant for understanding the socioeconomic complexity of contemporary social housing estates. At this point it's worth methodologically highlighting how official statistics, of the kind that Hamnett (2003) relies upon, can only take one so far in understanding the dynamics and shifting realities of working-class getting by and making ends meet (McKenzie, 2015), not least in London (Watt, 2020b). Therefore, the qualitative interview data shines a dynamic lens on residents' labour market experiences and class position. In the following, the focus is on the three main tenures – social tenants, RTB owners and temporary tenants – while the fourth main tenure, market homeowners, are discussed in Chapter 6.

At the time of the interview, more than half the interviewees were not in paid employment, potentially implying that they constitute a non-working class of those excluded from the labour market. However, nearly half of social tenant and RTB-owner householders were aged over 60 and the majority were retired after having engaged in paid work for much of their lives (Table 4.4). High levels of formal employment were evident prior to interviewees becoming unemployed or economically inactive due to retirement, sickness, disability or caring/looking after the home/family.

Several older interviewees had worked in factories when they were younger, but these jobs disappeared alongside London's deindustrialisation (Watt, 2003). Hence interviewees' employment experiences were very largely service industry based, as characteristic of the new working class (Ainsley, 2018). This includes working in private sector industries such as hospitality, retail and caring, which are noted for their low pay (Tinson et al, 2017), and public sector jobs in local government, education and health. This post-industrial employment is heavily gendered (Watt, 2003, 2020b; Ward et al, 2007). Manual occupations – driving (taxis, vans and buses), skilled trades (plumber, builder, electrician), and unskilled jobs such as labouring – were prevalent among men. Women tended to work in typically female-dominated, low-paid occupations – caring, child-minding, cleaning, shop assistant, teaching assistant, receptionist, waiting and bar work – although a few female interviewees had better-paid, white-collar office jobs.

Employment and socioeconomic groups on London estates

I have devised a typology of the five main socioeconomic groups that can be found on London's estates based upon interviewees' occupation, employment status, economic capital and age. This typology represents a composite of aspects of the work of Savage (2015), notably in relation to the precariat, and the NS-SEC classification system especially in relation to the service class (Cunningham and Savage, 2017). Neither of these two class schemas adequately examine the position of the non-employed, who are especially important in relation to social renters. The five groups and their dominant housing tenures are as follows:[2]

1. precariat – social tenants and temporary tenants;
2. non-working poor – social tenants and temporary tenants;
3. traditional working class – social tenants and RTB owners;
4. retired working class – social tenants and RTB owners;
5. lower professional and managerial service class – social tenants and RTB owners.

The most numerous socioeconomic group (around one third of the total) is the precariat, whose working lives are dominated by in-work poverty and job insecurity (Wacquant, 2008; Standing, 2011; Savage, 2015). They undertook low-paid, 'non-standard' employment in the form of part-time/temporary/casual work, which has become prevalent in London's 21st century post-industrial economy (Smith, 2005; Qureshi et al, 2014). In 2016, over a fifth of all London employees earned less than the London Living Wage (Tinson et al, 2017). Using this measure, female part-time employees formed the biggest group among the low paid – 31 per cent of the total (Tinson et al, 2017). Other groups likely to be in low-paid work include certain BAME groups (Bangladeshi, Pakistani, Black African/Caribbean/British), migrants and young Londoners (Wills et al, 2010; Tinson et al, 2017; Watt, 2020b).

Such London-wide patterns are reflected among the precariat interviewees who ranged in age from twenties to sixties. It was this group for whom the 'low-pay/no-pay cycle' was prevalent – 'a longitudinal pattern of employment instability and movement between low-paid jobs and unemployment, usually accompanied by claiming of welfare benefits' (Shildrick et al, 2012: 18). Female lone parents, such as Whitney (Woodberry Down, temporary tenant), were prominent among the precariat as they juggled paid work with caring responsibilities (Ward et al, 2007). Whitney cleaned offices for 16 hours a week in north London. She had been using a pre-school breakfast club for her daughter but had to give this up because her wages were too low; instead, she dropped her daughter at a friend's house before going on to her early morning shift. Whitney originally became homeless after being evicted from her previous home and job as a live-in carer. Hackney Council moved her around various temporary tenancies across the city ('recurrent displacement'; Watt, 2018a), before she and her daughter were moved to Woodberry Down. Michelle (Northumberland Park, council tenant) – another lone parent – had two part-time jobs, both in the local neighbourhood. One was as an administrator, while "I do cleaning in the evening as well and that's to stretch my money because I couldn't exist, I need that extra £400 a month that I get for that" (Michelle). Michelle was supporting her son and adult grandson who were living with her. They were both unemployed, although neither was able to claim welfare benefits due to labyrinthine bureaucratic restrictions. Michelle's grandson was 'sofa surfing' (sleeping on her sofa) because he was homeless.

Ayla (Woodberry Down, temporary tenant) was a Kurdish migrant whose parents had brought her to London during the 1990s. She lived in a poorly maintained flat in one of the remaining Woodberry Down council blocks with her husband and two young children. After she left school, Ayla worked as a part-time counter clerk, but gave this up after having children and experiencing health problems. Ayla described her husband's working life:

'He works part-time in security on night shifts. He can work anywhere in London, it's not just one place. He has a zero-hours contract which means he can sometimes only work two to three hours at a time, and then other times he has no work at all and stays at home.'

Akmal was in his twenties and lived at his mother's council flat again at one of the old blocks at Woodberry Down. He worked as a part-time security guard but had recently left a part-time hospitality job: "I was pot washing and clearing up customers' trays, I was on my feet the whole day long, so I quit. I do security at weekends but that's rubbish as well, I just do it to get a little money." Akmal was aiming to leave these 'rubbish jobs' behind and work in human relations.

If the precariat constitutes the low-income working poor, the second socioeconomic group is the working-age non-working poor who are financially reliant on increasingly meagre welfare benefits. This group is closest to the notion of social tenants forming a non-working class. Although nearly all had been employed at some point during their lives, they experienced downward work-life social mobility as they exited the labour market due to chronic sickness, disability or long-term unemployment. Choo (West Hendon, temporary tenant) was a single woman aged 42 who had to give up employment in her thirties due to illness and disability. She had done a variety of jobs when she was younger: "I worked in a chemist, I worked in a post office, and I did some caring work for a while. I think my last job was Sainsbury's [supermarket]." Meena lived with her husband and five children in an overcrowded council flat at Woodberry Down. As Meena said, her husband was an unemployed Bangladeshi ex-factory worker: "He was a handbag maker in a factory, but the factory closed nine years ago. It's very difficult for him to get other jobs, he cannot do supermarket jobs, he tries but he cannot get a job, he doesn't have good English."[3] Older Bangladeshi and Pakistani men in London, like Meena's husband, tend to face difficulties in gaining equivalent work following redundancy (Chouhan et al, 2011; Qureshi et al, 2014).

The traditional working class group consists of middle-aged manual and routine non-manual workers in full-time employment. Not only did this group have relatively stable employment, but their earnings tended to be at middle-income rather than low-income levels (unlike the previous two groups) (Ainsley, 2018). Examples include Elaine (West Hendon, RTB owner), who worked as a telecommunications engineer, George (Clapham Park, RTB owner), who was a bus driver, and Monica (Northumberland Park, council tenant), who worked as a local government officer. It also includes self-employed skilled manual workers like Terry (Woodberry Down, council tenant), who was an electrician.

The fourth group is the retired working class – elderly people (sixties and above) who had retired after having worked throughout most of their lives. This group were reliant on state pensions, although some were better off due to having occupational pensions. Many had relatively stable employment histories in that they did the same or equivalent job, often full-time, over long time periods. These were male manual workers, and women employed in the central London white-collar labour market. Before he retired, Ernie (Carpenters, RTB owner) worked for many years as a long-distance lorry driver. Bert (Northumberland Park) worked as a bus driver for a private company and during the interview he proudly showed me his 25 years' long-service certificate which he received before retirement. Bert's wife Janet was a retired NHS administrator who had used her pension lump sum to buy their flat under the RTB; as she said, "we always worked in this house". Several older female tenants had relatively stable careers in central London administrative work during the period when it was characterised by full-time, stable employment. For example, Deirdre (Woodberry Down, housing association tenant) worked for the NHS as a junior administrator in the early 1970s and stayed there in a similar position until she retired in 2001, while Olive (Heygate, council tenant) was a civil service officer for over 20 years until she took early retirement due to ill health.

Most interviewees had working-class occupational profiles characterised by manual and routine non-manual employment (Ainsley, 2018). However, the fifth and smallest socio-economic group (around one tenth of the total) is those employed in lower professional and managerial service-class occupations (Cunningham and Savage, 2017). Several were teachers, but others included nurses, journalists, IT professionals and managers of small organisations. Two thirds were graduates and thus had considerable cultural capital. This lower professional and managerial group are in NS-SEC 2, rather than NS-SEC 1 (the upper 'elite' section of the service class that is so prominent in London; Cunningham and Savage, 2017). In household terms, this group tended to either live alone or with a working class partner; hence they did not comprise 'dual-career households' that are prominent among London gentrifiers (Hamnett, 2003).

One quarter of these lower professionals and managers – such as Oluwakemi, a black African IT consultant at West Hendon – had bought their homes under the RTB. The remainder were social tenants and their non-take-up of the RTB reflects two factors identified in previous research on marginal professional social renters in London (Watt, 2005). First, an ideological opposition to the RTB on the part of politically left-wing professionals, and second is low economic capital resulting from having fragmented rather than stable middle-class careers. Graham was a retired council tenant at the Ocean estate who had a fragmented career involving numerous teaching jobs interspersed with making educational software and taxi-driving – he baulked at the RTB for both ideological and material reasons:

'I could never afford to buy. And I don't know now if I would buy. I mean this [flat] is a great space for someone later on, that should be preserved for the public. This is public land and it's gold dust. Public land and public housing is so invaluable for communities and it's being lost in the commodification of property which has happened now. So it's [RTB] disastrous long-term, nobody's going to have a home.'

Gender and local jobs

As mentioned previously, many female interviewees had to juggle paid work with caring responsibilities. Such gendered responsibilities help explain why female employment was more likely than male employment to be spatially concentrated in the local labour market near the estates where they lived, for example in schools, shops, health and leisure facilities (Watt, 2003). Such local jobs were typically part-time and low-paid, but being able to walk to work helped with costs as well as facilitating childcare and other caring responsibilities: "I did cleaning jobs and worked at a play group, all part-time jobs – it was hard, but they were all walking distance so that helped" (Geraldine, Carpenters estate, council tenant). Before she retired, Mary had worked for over 20 years at her daughter's primary school near her home on the Carpenters estate. Mary started by volunteering at the school before taking a teaching assistant position following encouragement by the head teacher:

'The teaching assistant [position] come along, and the head sent for me and she said, "would you like to do it?" and I said "Oh no! I would be no good at that, my educational background!" You know you get nervous! And she said, "oh don't be silly, put your name down anyway so you'll go in Monday morning!" [laughs] And that's how it took off from there.'

The head teacher boosted Mary's confidence and helped to give her what Humphry (2014) refers to as 'emotional capital'. Mary's long-term local employment was one of the reasons that she felt so passionately about not wanting to have her home and community erased due to demolition (Introduction). Ali (Northumberland Park, RTB owner) was also employed at a local school: "I escort disabled children to school and school to home, and also I work in [the school] lunchtime." Ali took pride in her job and, like Mary, it was one of the local connections that she valued and contributed to her strong objection to the HDV regeneration scheme. Being able to work locally was important for women with caring responsibilities, such as Paz (Northumberland Park, council tenant), who interspersed local employment with looking after her disabled adult son: "he needs me, I need him, that's why I work part time".

BAME and white working-class women – such as Geraldine, Mary, Ali and Paz – who live on London's estates form part of the precariat by working locally in low-paid, part-time jobs. Wacquant's (2008) analysis, which posits such labour market positions as 'marginal', ignores how women themselves *positively valued* these locally based jobs. Not only did such work contribute materially towards working-class getting by and making ends meet (McKenzie, 2015), it also gave the women a sense of 'getting on', as Humphry (2014) highlights in her research on class and social mobility in north London. The women were *included* within the local labour market due to its spatial proximity and their wider engagement with local institutions such as their children's schools. Rather than being socially and spatially excluded by living on council estates – as the 'social exclusion' perspective opines – these women engaged in the local economy as part of a broader process of building their lives and social connections *within* their neighbourhoods (McKenzie, 2015). This forms an important part of how residents create values and establish place belonging (Chapter 6).

Racism, diversity and social inclusion

Council housing was not equally open to all during the early post-war period. Formal access rules favoured long-term residents, especially the 'respectable' white working-class – married couples with children (Harrison and Davis, 2001; Watt, 2001; Hamnett, 2003). Other groups, such as single people and co-habitees, were excluded, as were New Commonwealth and Irish immigrants, female lone parents, the disabled and mentally ill, people with criminal records (the 'rough'), and so on (Jephcott, 1964). Five-year residency rules by the LCC and borough councils meant immigrants were effectively disbarred from council housing (White, 2008). The Bangladeshi population in Tower Hamlets – initially male workers and then later their families – faced institutional racism during the 1970s: 'although the Spitalfields Bangladeshis lived in some of the poorest housing in Britain they had to contend with a local authority that sought not to rehouse them' (Moore, 1992: 374). Migrants, alongside other socially marginal and vulnerable groups, were forced into overcrowded, sub-standard houses in multiple occupation (HMO) properties at the bottom end of the PRS (Jephcott, 1964; Forman, 1989; Carter, 2008) (Chapter 2).

These various marginalised groups began to gain access to council housing from the 1970s onwards. This welfare state inclusion resulted from a combination of top-down policy and bottom-up struggles by the excluded themselves. Although the Housing Act 1977 contributed towards residualisation, as discussed above, it was also socially progressive and *inclusionary* since it facilitated the entry of homeless people into council housing (Sassen, 2014; Fitzpatrick and Pawson, 2016; Watt, 2018a). Anti-racist policy initiatives were significant, especially in London (Jeffers and Hoggett, 1995). Inclusionary struggles also played an important part, for example in the case of the Bangladeshis who squatted and protested about their dire housing circumstances in both Tower Hamlets (Forman, 1989; Glynn, 2014) and Camden (Watt, 2001). These struggles were aided by the rise of the new urban left in local government during the late 1970s and 1980s, part of whose remit was to challenge the institutional racism that infected London council housing allocation (Forman, 1989; Glynn, 2014).

Therefore, London's council housing population became more socially diverse from the 1970s onwards since its base expanded beyond white working-class nuclear families (Watt, 2001; Carter, 2008; Hamnett and Butler, 2010; Gidley, 2013; Rosbrook-Thompson and Armstrong, 2018). This indicates how the Keynesian welfare state was becoming *more* inclusionary and accepting of social difference (Sassen, 2014).[4] Therefore, while council housing might have residualised in socioeconomic terms, it simultaneously became more demographically and ethnically diverse. This shift represents a genuine improvement for many previously excluded groups because of their dreadful experiences in poor-quality PRS housing: 'households renting privately were the most likely to lack or share basic amenities' (Howes and Mullins, 1999: 32; also Forman, 1989). The PRS was – and still is – discriminatory, insecure and unsatisfactory for low-income Londoners.

Late entry into council housing was, however, by no means egalitarian. In Southwark, for example, 'by 1981, the council adopted an overt policy of transferring "problem families" to less attractive estates' (Carter, 2008: 170). BAME groups were often housed in the worst parts of the sector during the 1970s to 1990s including in the oldest properties, upper floors of tower blocks and most rundown estates (Forman, 1989; Jeffers and Hoggett, 1995; Carter, 2008). The latter include several estates in this study such as Aylesbury, Clapham Park, Northumberland Park, Ocean and Woodberry Down. BAME tenants also faced racial harassment from white British tenants at many estates (Forman, 1989; Carter, 2008; White, 2008; Cohen, 2013). Nevertheless, despite the unsatisfactory nature of the inclusionary process and the tensions that arose out of it, entry to council housing represents a 'welcome opening up of the sector' (Hamnett and Randolph, 1987: 48). For BAME tenants – as well as lone parents, the homeless, single people, and so on – obtaining a council property was far preferable to the PRS – as it was for working-class tenants generally, as now discussed.

Tenure preferences

'Tenure preferences' refer to what tenure people would prefer to live in when directly asked. In his landmark study, Saunders (1990) found that most council tenants preferred to be homeowners. It is true that most of the population have a long-term preference for owner-occupation, although this has also declined among social renters since the 1990s linked to the housing market downturn of the late 2000s (Wallace, 2010). However, tenure preferences are not abstract wishes, but are instead rooted in material realities regarding what type and quality of housing is available at what cost: 'tenure preferences are not created in a vacuum and changing preferences reflect individual's interpretations of their own experience in a specific social, economic and policy context' (Forrest and Murie, 1990: 634).

By relying on quantitative indicators, Hamnett's (2003) interpretation of residualisation and socio-tenurial polarisation is deficient at the level of meaning in Weberian terms. His approach smuggles in normative judgements regarding choice and homeownership as 'preferred housing' with insufficient reference to working-class experiences of housing (Allen, 2008). Rather than symbolising a lack of choice and exclusion, council housing was a normal, unremarkable part of working-class Londoners' lives. It was an integral part of the city's housing field in Bourdieu's terms, one that primarily catered to the working class. Elaine's housing history illustrates the socio-spatial fit between this part of the housing field – council renting – and the mid-late 20th century working-class habitus. Her parents had been council tenants and she explained how entering council housing was a normal rite of passage: "if you started a family you are looking at moving into a council property, it was a given thing basically". As she went on to say, being a homeowner was insignificant within the working-class habitus of the time where " 'bettering yourself', that sort of talk didn't exist":

'So, they [homeowners] got their own gaff [slang for house] and we haven't, it was no big deal, I wasn't interested. It would be nice to own your own gaff, but it wasn't important. What was important is how you lived and what you lived in. We had a home and that was good enough.'

For Cathy (Bacton estate), "my only experience of housing is council housing, and my experience growing up in council housing was happy, everyone I knew was in a council house. No one thought of it as a stigma". As well as being ordinary, public housing represented a powerful expression of working-class rights. Norman had lived all his life in council housing in Canning Town. When I asked why he preferred renting from the council, Norman's initial response was couched in economic terms, "there isn't one housing association property around here that's at the same rent as council". However, he expanded with reference to the rights (of succession) and expectations that council tenants had which he saw as being eroded by government policy: "You must have seen family homes, the mother's been in it, the father's been, the daughter's gone in it, the daughter's daughters gone in it. You see that was the way of life wasn't it? That was council housing and that was the way it was." The binary *either* owning *or* council renting tenure preferences model (Saunders, 1990) ignores the key role played by the PRS: 'since many existing council tenants have experienced private renting, ... it is likely that private renting continues to be an important reference point for them when considering their housing position' (Savage et al, 1990: 109). National survey data shows that nearly three quarters of social housing tenants want to remain in the sector and that a mere 2 per cent want to move into the PRS (Wallace, 2010; see Watt, 2001 on Camden council tenants). The real-world alternative for many working-class Londoners – now and then – is between private and council/social renting, as now discussed.

Housing histories: continuity and change

The interviewees are from a wide age range from elderly residents in their seventies to nineties, who obtained council tenancies during the 1950s to 1970s, to those in their twenties and thirties, who entered estates during the austerity 2010s (Appendix B). Unsurprisingly their housing histories are varied and complex. These are first examined from the standpoint of the expansionary 1950s to 1970s period and then the later contractionary period. One thread of continuity is how obtaining a council tenancy was – and remains – far preferable to renting privately which is the *real* tenure of last resort.

Entering council housing: 1950s to 1970s

Many older interviewees who became council tenants during the post-war period up until the 1980s gained their tenancies through being rehoused from the PRS, either due to slum clearance programmes or via the waiting list. In relation to the PRS, Young and Willmott (1957) and Dench and colleagues (2006) positively describe the informal 'speaking for' system – whereby a newly married daughter would initially live with her mum, who would in turn ask if her landlord had a room which the newly-wed couple could rent – as constituting an inherent part of the post-war, east London 'organic' working-class community. This consensus-functionalist perspective on private renting obscures material conflicts of interest between landlords and tenants. Far from being benign, private landlordism was beset by poor maintenance, discrimination and evictions. In a group interview, two elderly female East End tenants from the Ocean estate reminisced about their families' problems with repairs and maintenance in their previous PRS housing:

Gladys: 'I lived there [private house] until the house was condemned. It had cracks in the walls, and the landlord wouldn't sell so the council just took it over. When we moved in, there was no bathrooms, nothing and my dad asked the landlord if he could put a bath in and make a bathroom. So he said, "yes, but I'll have to put your rent up because it's improving the property". My dad had to pay the landlord to have the bathroom done.'

Jean: 'That's what we had, me and my brother done that too to our property we lived in, that's the only way you got anything done.'

Gladys: 'You couldn't get anything done by your landlord.'

Tenants also described evictions. Mariana (Oxley estate, RTB owner) and her family were informally evicted twice during the 1960s because landlords objected to the presence of children: "she [landlord] didn't want children there. No [she didn't give notice], she just hinted all the time, and I didn't want that atmosphere".

By comparison, newly built council housing was viewed positively by the older generation of tenants. Sarah's parents were poor Jewish immigrants who moved to the East End during the 1950s. Initially the family lived in a Jewish shelter before they went to a private flat in Whitechapel, and from there they eventually moved to the Ocean estate during the 1960s. Sarah contrasts the overcrowded private flat with the spacious 'palace' flat at the Ocean in one of the blocks (Tunis House) that was subsequently demolished under the Central Stepney SRB:

> 'The [private] dwelling that we lived in was Victorian style. There was a row of these, a stretch of blocks, but none of them had a bath except us. We had only two bedrooms for four children and parents. When we moved to Tunis House, it was like a palace to us. We had four bedrooms, we had a separate bathroom, separate toilet, big lounge, kitchen was small, but it was like a palace.'

Interviewees trusted 'the council' – the local state – to look after ordinary working-class Londoners like themselves. As Harry explained, inner-London local authority housing was part of the post-war 'social contract'. His parents worked near their home at the Regents Park estate in Camden, and he contrasts their housing experience and his own early experience with that of contemporary working-class Londoners who have to commute in from the suburbs, whereas the 'rich' can now walk to work:

> 'My view it was a social contract – "you [council] build us cheap housing, we'll provide you with cheap labour. And as long as we don't have to spend most of our money travelling to and from [work], and we can still look after the kids because we can walk back home quite quickly, we don't mind being underpaid". That was the social contract. That was why all the estates around central London were built, to provide housing for the workers. Now, I've sat on night buses and I've seen people coming in from Ealing, Harrow, Romford, sitting there at 4 in the morning and they're off to work! They should be living here, whereas now it's almost as if it's turning [unclear]. The proper people are living in the outskirts and commuting in and the rich people are living in the centre, in apartments, so they can walk to work.'

Mary had previously been living in a PRS flat in Custom House, and she recalled her joy at moving to the Carpenters estate: "Oh, I have a house, a house with three bedrooms! [laughs]. Oh god, I felt excited, you know. That's why I kick back, I think nobody's gonna take it from me now." It was Mary's pride in her house which motivated her to 'kick back' (object) against its mooted demolition. Following an eviction from the PRS, Ernie and his wife agreed to temporarily split up and lived at their respective parents' houses. The family were initially allocated an old 'grotty' flat by West Ham Council in the 1960s, but from there they moved into one of the Carpenters tower blocks during the 1970s:

> 'My wife's quite a strong personality and she stepped in the door and burst into tears because it was like "ahh!" Tears of happiness I must say [laughs]. We was more than happy living here. The estate was brand new, I'm saying brand new but probably about eight years old at the maximum. I got three [bedrooms] because I had a boy and girl. At first, I must admit I was "Wow, lovely, brilliant, great!" We didn't know what to do with all the space.'

Obtaining a council flat was by no means always easy or straightforward during the expansionary period (Harrison, 1983; Forman, 1989). Tenancies were more likely to be given to married couples with children, while single people struggled. As mentioned earlier, Mariana and her family fell foul of private landlords, but they had previously been refused a council flat because she and her fiancé were not actually married: "they [council] said 'no' because we wasn't married at the time they came round, though we'd booked the wedding and everything". Mariana eventually obtained a council flat under slum clearance.

Entering council housing: 1980–2010s

Tenancies were still obtained through the waiting list during the contractionary period, but also via the choice-based lettings scheme introduced by New Labour. It was during this later period that the homeless route into council housing became far more significant following the Housing Act 1977. This legislation 'strongly reinforced an ongoing shift from council house allocations based on "desert" (judged by various moral criteria) to ones based more clearly on housing "need"' (Fitzpatrick and Pawson, 2016: 544). As mentioned earlier, this contributed towards the widening of council housing's social base so that it became more inclusionary of marginal and vulnerable groups in need. Being unmarried, a lone parent, single or from a BAME background became less a barrier in obtaining council housing. Danni (black African) and her grandmother rented a maisonette on West Hendon estate during the early 1990s; prior to this, they had been living at Danni's parents' overcrowded council flat elsewhere in Barnet:

> 'I think there must have been mum, dad, me, grandmother and ... seven, eight of us [in a three-bed flat]. We were camping out in the living room, it was small. We were offered this [West Hendon maisonette], and because of the close proximity to my mum and that we took it, because we wanted to stay quite close to the rest of the family unit. So it was our first offer and we just took it.'

Danni thought it was "fairly easy" to get her maisonette: "at those times, there wasn't as much as now problems with housing". Although a few older interviewees repeated the stereotypical belief that 'young girls got pregnant *to* get a council flat' (Daniel, 2016), there was no evidence for this among the female lone parent interviewees themselves.

As with the expansionary period, applying for council housing as a direct result of evictions from the PRS remained significant. Women (with and without partners) were evicted once they became pregnant or gave birth. Kathleen described how she and her husband obtained their council flat at Custom House during the 1980s:

> 'When I first came over here [to London from Ireland] I stayed with relatives at Plaistow and then we got a private rent in Forest Gate. The reason why we moved out of private rent was because the landlord ... one of the specifications was that he didn't want children in the properties. I fell pregnant with my daughter, so we had to move out. We'd already been on the council list for some time and we got offered this place and we took it.'

Pressures within the London PRS became greater from the 1980s onwards. This was due to legislative changes – the Housing Act 1988 which introduced assured shorthold tenancies – combined with rent hikes and evictions resulting from the gentrification which swept through many previously inexpensive and unfashionable working-class neighbourhoods (Butler and Robson, 2003). Being able to enter council/social housing also became more difficult (in terms of lengthening waiting times and more people entering through the homeless route), although not impossible. Shirley (black Caribbean) had been evicted from the PRS during the 1990s and this prompted her to apply to Hackney Council as a single woman:

> 'I was renting in various places and you know what it's like when you are renting from private landlords, they have the ability to give you notice at any point in time. Then when they give you notice, then you have to start looking again for somewhere new to live, and you have to think when you find this place "will it be suitable for you?" Then they [landlords] usually ask for two or three months in advance rent, so all these things you have to take into consideration which could really stress you out. So anyway, I was living not far from here and one day the landlady came to collect the rent, and she said "sorry but I have to give you all notice", and I thought "what?!"'

Shirley moved to another PRS property, but also put her name down on the housing list and eventually obtained her council flat at Woodberry Down:

> 'I jumped for joy. I was *so* happy. The fact I was going to be in a council flat and once as I do everything right, I know the council is not going to kick me out. Whereas when I am renting from private landlord, they can come at any time and say "oh, I am giving notice for you to move out, blah, blah, blah".'

Phil had been renting a room in a dilapidated shared house in a gentrifying area of north London during the early 2000s. He and his housemates were formally evicted because the landlord took advantage of gentrification-related rent hikes: "the builder who was doing all the work was quite open about the fact that he [landlord] wanted to make them into nice studio flats and get people with the ability to pay far more rent than we could, so we all got notice to quit". Phil moved to a studio flat in Hackney, but was subsequently priced out of that area since his new landlord increased the rent by a third: "there was no way that I could pay it, so then I moved to another bedsit in Tottenham because I'd been gentrified out of Hackney". Following his first eviction, Phil applied for council housing in Haringey and began bidding for properties via choice-based lettings. After eight years, Phil was unexpectedly offered a studio flat on Broadwater Farm estate. The poor state of the flat – and probably also this estate's 'notorious' reputation (Power, 1997; Hendry, 2019) – put the other viewing applicants off, which meant that Phil unusually obtained the tenancy as a single man:

> 'The viewing was a joke [laughs], the window was smashed, the door had been burnt by the local youths, there was soot all over it, the corridor had been burnt as well by the local youths. Nobody wanted this flat, but it looked better than where I was living. I thought I was never going to get anywhere else because of my lack of priority so I accepted it.'

Even if interviewees lacked personal experience of the PRS, they knew about it through family and friends' experiences or through its poor reputation. Council/social renting invariably came off well by comparison due to its genuine affordability and greater security. I asked social tenants who had never rented privately whether they had considered doing so: "No, absolutely not, how would I afford it? The private rented sector is nonsense" (Rita, Woodberry Down). If obtaining social housing became more difficult during the 1980s to 2000s, it has subsequently become near-impossible under austerity conditions.

Homelessness: from housing priority to housing precarity

Housing priority

The 1977 Housing Act resulted in an increasing proportion of households gaining council tenancies via the homeless 'priority need' route in London during the 1980s and 1990s (Watt, 2001, 2018a; Fitzpatrick and Pawson, 2016). Typically, this homeless route involved a sojourn in temporary accommodation. It's therefore unsurprising that the sector has increasingly come to house many of London's most marginal, often vulnerable groups – pregnant women, lone parents, women escaping domestic violence, the long-term sick and disabled, people with drug and alcohol dependencies, and so on. These groups were prominent among the interviewees who gained entry to council housing during the later contractionary period. As a migrant, Adela had little knowledge of the British housing system. She described applying to the council as homeless (with her son) following violence by her ex-husband:

> 'I went to Barnet Council and because no one in my family live in a council place, so I didn't have any idea how it works, I don't know. So all I know is I need a roof and I have a little boy. So we run away, we are like in a film. We went to everybody that I know, and, in the end, somebody told me go to the council and I said "what?" So, I just go there, they put us in a hotel for three months, and after that they gave us the choices at that time, it was 19 years ago. I said, "I don't care as long as you give me a place that is on the ground floor". So, one morning they send me a letter and they said to me "there is a vacant place go there", so I came here [West Hendon].'

Adela's Indian neighbour at West Hendon welcomed her to the estate, an inclusionary gesture and indicative of the supportive, non-judgemental social relations on the multi-ethnic estate:

> 'I quickly knock on my neighbour because I don't have anything. I said, "can I just borrow…", and she said to me, "you just move in?" I said, "yes I move in, like 10 minutes ago". She said "welcome, you will like it here, it's a very nice area"'.

Cathy had grown up in Camden council housing. She applied as homeless with her daughter in the early 2000s following a relationship breakup. Camden Council initially moved the family to a hostel in south London where they stayed for 18 months, but then offered them a flat on the estate Cathy had grown up: "I was chuffed to bits with it, I knew the area, I felt safe there, some of the old families – not that I remembered them but they remembered my mum and dad – and the flat was massive."

Adela and Cathy were relatively fortunate compared to others who described lengthy, tortuous journeys through London's homelessness system. Two single BAME interviewees from Clapham Park estate (Isobel and Sylvester) suffered from chronic mental illness, but both had struggled to get into council housing during the 1990s. Isobel became homeless following repossession of her previous home due to her ex-husband's failure to keep up the mortgage payments. She "moved from hostel to hostel" over a total of ten years, first in central London and later in Brixton – recurrent displacement (Watt, 2018a). Despite suffering from mental and physical ill health, Isobel was not classified as being in priority need: "because I haven't got any children, so housing me was not a priority". It was only after Isobel had been sectioned under the Mental Health Act 1983 that a social worker helped with her council housing application. Despite this assistance, it still took another four years before Isobel was allocated a flat at Clapham Park. Isobel's housing history indicates the problems faced by single women in accessing social housing in London but might very well also reflect institutional racism (Watson and Austerberry, 1986).

Housing precarity[5]

If expulsionary logics occurred during the 1980s to 2000s in relation to homelessness, these have dramatically worsened under austerity. The capacity of the homeless to gain social housing has reduced, partly due to cuts in new social housebuilding, but also because of councils using the Localism Act 2011 to reprioritise their allocations (Hodkinson and Robbins, 2013; Inside Housing, 2014). The latter emphasised meeting the housing needs of the deserving poor – those in employment and the ex-armed forces in the case of Newham (Humphry, 2020). The net result is that the homeless route into social housing dramatically tightened. Not only do applicants spend longer periods living in temporary accommodation, they are also more likely to be offered a tenancy in the PRS instead of a social tenancy at the 'end' of the process. Even if they are offered a social tenancy, these are often 'flexible' fixed-term tenancies (Fitzpatrick and Pawson, 2014). Rather than temporary accommodation and the PRS being transitional tenures, they are becoming *tenures of destination*. Consequently, instead of being in housing priority for social renting, the London homeless are facing indefinite *housing precarity* (Watt, 2018a, 2020b).

This section moves forward chronologically to the regeneration period by examining the housing histories of those interviewees who had been located into empty properties at regeneration estates on a temporary 'non-secure tenant' basis (Chapter 4). Many of these temporary tenants are part of London's precariat in employment terms, but they also experience housing precarity involving multiple, coercive and health-damaging logics of expulsion (Introduction; Watt, 2018a). These expulsionary logics include evictions from the PRS and temporary accommodation, recurrent displacement, geographical widening of displacement and expulsion from the homeless support system within the welfare state.

Several of these logics are illustrated by the case of Nita, a young British Asian lone parent. Nita had been working full-time and living with her parents in Hackney until she became pregnant in her early twenties. Once her baby was born, Nita left her family's social rented home, precipitated by overcrowding and a collapsed ceiling. Nita sofa surfed at friends' houses and then unsuccessfully applied to the council as homeless. While Nita's application was being processed, a homeless voluntary sector organisation (VSO) found her a private flat where she lived for two years. This so-called 'flat' – in reality, an illegally converted garage – lacked adequate heating and was unsafe. Nita's son was "always sick, he had a chest infection and was in hospital". Nita moved her son back to live with her mother, but the lack of space in the family home meant that she had to continue living in the garage. It took several years before the council accepted that Nita was homeless and in priority need, and this only happened after an enormous struggle on her part including lobbying councillors. Nita was given emergency accommodation, but in an outer borough several miles from her parents. Although the property was clean, Nita was sharing with five other families and was sleeping in the dining room which had been converted into a bedroom. Eventually Hackney Council offered Nita and her son a flat at Woodberry Down: "it's better because it's near mum and my son's nursery, it was a headache before".

Many temporary tenants had tortuous housing histories similar to Nita's. Some experienced 'revenge evictions': 'complaints about housing conditions can now lead to so-called "revenge evictions" whereby landlords exploit the no-fault repossession route provided by section 21 of the 1988 Housing Act to evict their residents after a six-month tenancy has expired without giving a reason' (Hodkinson, 2019: 46). This happened to Laiba (West Hendon), a single vulnerable woman, who was evicted because she complained about the flat's poor state: "It went to court and he [landlord] evicted me and the bailiff physically removed me and then I end up being homeless."

When they moved to the estates, these temporary tenants had to bid for social rental properties, a process that they described as 'an exercise in futility' (Watt, 2018a: 91):

> 'When I moved in, the woman [official] said I'd be here at least two to three years but might remain for four to five years depending on how many properties I bid for. She said if you bid for like say a high-rise flat on the 10th floor you might get out sooner, but fourth floor or lower is more desirable so bidding would take longer. I've been bidding

for about a year now. Last week I was 55 out of 550 people, but that's because I went for a three-bed property. I need three bedrooms because my children will grow up.' (Ella, Woodberry Down)

The 'alternative' – private renting – was unrealistic, partly because of rising costs and partly because of how Housing Benefit/Local Housing Allowance (LHA) claimants are routinely excluded due to government caps (Cole et al, 2016), as two Woodberry Down temporary tenants described:

'When we came to Hackney eight years ago it was affordable then, but it's not affordable now. Now we couldn't afford private renting. The deposit they ask for is a lot of money and most of them don't take Housing Benefit.' (Rahel)

'Private renting is out of the question because I cannot afford it. I have two children and I'm on a minimum wage, well less than minimum wage, £7.50 an hour. I work as a cleaner in a company, I'm happy I have a job. It's 25 hours per week.' (Petra)

Others were mentally scarred by their evictions: "I am *not* going to go private, with private landlords, it's just that you're at their mercy" (Laiba). New social housing applicants – who increasingly come via the homeless route – are more and more excluded from entering the sector. Instead, they are either forced into ever-lengthening stays in temporary accommodation or into the PRS, both of which exacerbate their displacement chances. We will return to these temporary tenants in later chapters.

Conclusion

This chapter has illustrated how London's council housing has increasingly accommodated a range of deprived and socially marginalised groups since the 1970s, including the poor and unemployed, sick and disabled, lone-parent families, BAME groups and the homeless. This marginalisation has been interpreted in relation to residualisation, social exclusion and socio-tenurial polarisation.

While there is some truth in the residualisation and socio-tenurial polarisation theses in socioeconomic terms, this chapter has suggested that in other ways these three conceptual approaches are deficient. First, in emphasising the notion that council housing is the tenure of the non-working class, these approaches have under-emphasised the dynamic and longitudinal nature of tenants' labour market experiences. When the latter is examined, one finds extensive labour market engagement. In fact, for many social tenants, the problem is not so much one of *exclusion from* paid work, but *inclusion in* poor work. I created a five-fold typology of the main socioeconomic groups that can be found on London's estates, and this demonstrates the range of labour market experiences that exist.

Second, the increasing presence of marginalised groups – BAME groups, lone parents, the sick and disabled – in London public housing from the 1970s onwards means that estates have become more, not less, socially *inclusionary spaces*. Third, council housing was a step away from housing marginality for these groups, rather than towards it, because the PRS is an insecure, unsuitable form of housing for working-class Londoners. It's the PRS, *not* public housing, which has consistently been the 'tenure of last resort' in tenure preference terms for working-class London council tenants (BAME and white). This theme has been developed at length with reference to interviewees' housing histories, which indicate remarkable continuity regarding how the PRS has been and remains inadequate in terms of meeting working-class Londoners' housing needs, because of its poor quality, arbitrary rent hikes and evictions, all of which have been exacerbated under austerity conditions. Housing scholars have inadequately drilled down into the real sociological underpinnings of tenure preferences, which means that that they fall back on – and reinforce – the misleading binary homeownership-positive/council-renting-negative stereotype.

A major problem is how many groups who would have at one time been able to access social housing can no longer do so. Homelessness provided an important route into social housing following the 1977 Housing Act – and thereby helped to broaden out the demographics of social housing. This route has silted up due to austerity and the homeless are now trapped in housing precarity in perpetuity. They are still housed on estates, but on a non-secure temporary basis rather than as social tenants (either council or housing association).

The chapter has identified how female residents, and especially those with caring responsibilities, often do paid work in the locality near their estates. Such employment has contributed towards their social inclusion and sense of local place belonging. We now turn to examine this place belonging in depth.

6

Valued places

This chapter assesses how and why residents came to value their estates as places to live. It begins by considering their attachment to their dwellings as homes. The importance of place belonging is then analysed at the spatial scale of the estate in relation to neighbourliness and community. This leads on to an examination of the intermediate scale – blocks of flats and rows of houses. The next two sections show how estates have been affected by the Right to Buy policy in relation to place belonging, by considering, first, RTB owners and, second, middle-class homeowners who bought their homes on the open market from the original RTB owners. The final section considers whether London's estates form 21st century urban villages.

Homes and home-making

This section focuses on the domestic dwelling space and shows how residents valued their houses and flats as 'homes'. Most secure tenant and leaseholder interviewees expressed place attachment to their dwellings, albeit that owners were more likely to be positive than tenants. The NES found that nearly three quarters of respondents were satisfied with their flats or maisonettes, with satisfaction higher among leaseholders (91 per cent) than tenants (68 per cent) (Watt and Allen, 2018). Homes provided 'ontological security' (Easthope, 2014) and this attachment is related to the dwelling's physical qualities, their own home-making efforts, and sentimental attachments.

In terms of physical qualities, two facets stood out: solidity and generous space standards. The term 'solid' – meaning well-built, structurally sound buildings – was commonly invoked when people described their homes. Frank was a builder and when I asked him about his flat at Northumberland Park estate, he hit the kitchen cupboard wall in order to demonstrate its sturdiness: "this is four inches thick, it's old school, well-built, they're solid and warm flats". In a joint interview with two tenants at West Hendon, neither could see a good reason for demolishing their 'solid' and 'real' homes:

Adela: 'You are going to build a new one, but this for me, this is too strong, it will last another hundred years. Why build a new one? This is brick wall.'

Danni: 'Yes, this is real.'

Adela: 'Solid.'

Danni: 'Solid. I mean just to hang up things. We were talking about it just before you came. Like in my place, my TV is up on the wall and I had to get a man with a *huge drill* just to get through the wall, because they are very strong, the walls that we have.'

In terms of size, many tenants and leaseholders (particularly single people and couples) highlighted their home's spaciousness in relation to room size and storage space. One elderly male tenant stood up at a housing meeting and stated his reasons for opposing demolition: "I've lived for 38 years on the Aylesbury estate and the standards are very good, they were built to Parker Morris standards – much too good for the working class!" Malana moved into her two-bed council flat at Clapham Park during the 1970s. While the flat was basic, she took it because of its generous size: "I have two bedrooms upstairs and all the living amenities down. So I have the bathroom, separate toilet, kitchen, so for me it was liveable." As Malana went onto say – and others noted – "in comparison to some of the properties that are being built today this was spacious". Council flats were rightly seen as offering generous space standards compared to the properties currently being built, including those resulting from estate regeneration.

I entered over 60 interviewees' homes and visited others during the research. Most homes appeared comfortable, well-furnished and well-decorated, indicative of both domestic care and financial investment. Interviewees engaged in what Pahl (1984: 98) refers to as "domestic self-provisioning" whereby they used their labour and money to maintain and improve their domestic space, for example via DIY. Alf had bought his maisonette at West Hendon via the RTB. I interviewed him after he had been displaced and asked whether there was anything structurally wrong with his previous home which might justify its demolition:

'No, it was very liveable, I had a lovely maisonette. I done a lot of work on it - I put new ceilings in, new floors in, wooden floors and I done all the rooms up. I put a lot of work in, I spent a lot of money on it.'

Those workers involved in manual trades took pride in home improvement. As a plasterer, Damo (Northwold) described how he (and his partner) had gradually worked on their shared-ownership flat:

'The decoration and stuff was pretty basic and there was Aertex on the walls and ceilings and everything. But because I work as a plasterer, we thought we can sort all that stuff out over time. We did room by room over about 6–7 years – re-plastered each room, changed some of the electrics, put in new floors, and then a new kitchen and a new bathroom. Every summer we've done one thing.'

In his 'consumption sector theory', Saunders (1990) argued that council tenants are passive 'underclass' recipients of welfare state largesse who take limited personal interest in their housing conditions, unlike 'active' homeowners (see Miller, 1988, and Watt, 2001, for criticisms). Such apathy and passivity were not much evident in my research since tenants, as well as homeowners, routinely undertook DIY and financially invested in their flats to *make them* into homes. Many tenants described having to invest heavily when they first moved in because of the flat's poor state as left by the previous tenant and the council. This even involved them initially living elsewhere while they made their new flat or house into a home that they felt comfortable living in. Monica (Northumberland Park) stayed with relatives for several months while she worked on her house with assistance from friends:

'I was staying with my grandmother because this house needed a lot of work. It's like they [previous tenants] smoked a lot, so there's a lot of painting to be done. I had to take it all back to its natural state. And because the bathroom was from the 1970s and she hadn't done anything with it, I put everything in – I put in a shower and I put the bathroom in that and retiled it. Then we had to re-plaster it and downstairs put the new toilet in. I wasn't going to keep that toilet and bathroom. And the thing is, mine was better quality. I stripped the whole house, working on different areas and it was in a right state!'

Such home-making activities challenge stereotypical notions that social tenants do not value their homes because they are 'merely' tenants and not homeowners (Easthope, 2014). Tenants developed a sense of ontological security which was both expressed and reinforced by their

DIY activities. Such self-provisioning was also partly a reaction to the council's tardiness in undertaking internal works (Chapter 7) – "if I did not do it, they [council] would not do it" (Deirdre).

If most homes that I visited appeared well-cared-for, a few had spartan decoration and furnishing reflecting both poverty and domestic indifference. Such flats had either no or threadbare carpets, and furniture consisted of worn-out armchairs or basic hardback chairs. These homes were typically occupied by single middle-aged/ older male tenants in the non-working poor and retired working-class socioeconomic categories (Chapter 5). This visible domestic laissez faire did not necessarily mean, however, that such tenants did not appreciate their homes. They did so, but relative to their own values and housing histories. Roger rented a dingy council flat in Southwark where it was obvious that DIY and domestic chores were not a priority. Nevertheless, he greatly appreciated the increased security and freedom that being a council tenant gave him relative to private or housing association renting where landlord interference is far more likely:

> 'When I lived in Leeds as a student, I was living in rented accommodation with private landlords so I know what that's like with the landlord coming in. I found with the council, "oh great they don't come in that much do they?" You can do the housework sometimes and not other times, and I needed the time to chill out like that and so that's how I want to keep it.'

Although Graham greatly valued both his home and the Ocean estate as places to live (including living in a multi-ethnic neighbourhood), he admitted that he had done little internally to his sparsely decorated flat since moving in 15 years previously:

> 'I was pleased to have a place to stay. It was quiet, it was safe, the kids on the estate were friendly. And because I'm very mobile in that I immediately sussed out where the nearest swimming pools were, where I could cycle. I also found it easy to integrate with the Sylheti [Bangladeshi] population.'

Graham also appreciated the trees outside his flat, and it was when he found out that these would be removed as part of the NDC stock transfer/demolition proposal that he became involved in the anti-transfer campaign (Photograph 6.1):

Photograph 6.1: Ocean estate – view from Graham's window, 2016

'There was going to be 12 new homes here, the trees were going to be chopped down, I saw it from the plans. I thought, "agh, this is strange!" This was basically the reason for energising me. I saw that this was all going to come down, that these trees were going to go, all the habitation was going to disappear.'

For Graham, the trees outside his window formed part of his home. The fact that London estates have such green spaces at all is part of the latter's attraction, as now discussed.

Place belonging at the neighbourhood scale

Traditional belonging, neighbourliness and sense of community

Fieldwork and interviews revealed extensive place belonging/ attachment to people's estates, an attachment which was deeply felt in some cases. This place belonging took a traditional form based upon residential longevity among both social renters and RTB owners (Table 4.4). Some middle-aged/elderly interviewees felt extremely attached to their estate having lived at it all or nearly all of their lives. Marion had always lived at Woodberry Down: "I am 61 and all my life I have lived in just three different flats." She was adamant that she did not want to move anywhere else in Hackney due to regeneration – for her, that was 'alien territory': "I wanted to stay on the estate, because it's familiar, I still know lots of people here. I did not want to move away, I don't like Dalston, Stoke Newington, I don't like those areas, I don't know them." Beatty was extremely active in community organisations at the Ocean: "I've lived here all my life actually. I lived here before the estate was born and watched it being built." Harry took me on a walking tour of Regents Park estate in Camden, a place that he strongly identified with: "I was born at the hospital and I arrived on the estate a few weeks later in '62." Unlike middle-class incomers who expressed elective belonging based upon *choosing* to live in the area (see later), working-class belonging took a traditional form: "We didn't choose Hackney, Hackney chose us – we've always been here" (Akmal, Woodberry Down). Further aspects of longevity are discussed later.

The combination of residential longevity with restricted spatial mobility – due to old age, sickness, disability, caring responsibilities and poverty (including lack of access to a car) – meant that the estate and its surrounding locality were extremely important for many interviewees' everyday lives and sense of well-being (Atkinson and Kintrea, 2000; Young Foundation, 2010; Frediani et al, 2013; McKenzie, 2015). Salma had lived 18 years on the Aylesbury estate and felt safe walking in the local area, including to her nearby mosque: "at Ramadan you have to pray in the night-time, I walk because I don't have a car". Even though residents weren't hermetically sealed into their local neighbourhood, the latter held a significance for them that it doesn't have for affluent 'busy Londoners' such as those living in new high-rise apartments (Scanlon et al, 2018). People walked to and from local facilities at or near their estates on a routine basis, and this involved bumping into their neighbours and having a chat.

People were enmeshed in local social networks, which revolved around participation in both formal and informal local groups and activities. Formal networks included TRAs, and voluntary groups/clubs for the elderly, youth and homeless. Although TRAs are less prominent on London estates than they once were, several of the research estates had one (or even more on the larger estates).[1] Engagement with the TRA was partly based on it functioning as a pressure group with the council (Chapter 11). Each TRA also provided a meeting place and fulcrum for neighbourhood sociability. Kevin was active in his TRA in Southwark and noted how most of the regular attendees were elderly:

'Many people use the TRA for social reasons. It's partly to give some of their issues, to listen what issues there are. Often the main issue is perhaps their health or something like that. In terms of the problem in their own homes, my experience is that it might have been the outside light or something minor. But they most often go there for the social reason.'

Olive had been active in her TRA on the Heygate estate before she was decanted due to regeneration. The Heygate TRA put on social events and Olive missed this sociability following displacement: "We had our own community hall, our own TRA, and we had Christmas parties and dance functions and all sorts, and it was just taken away from us".

Informal neighbourhood sociability was based on having nearby extended family, neighbouring, using local public space such as playgrounds and parks, shopping, using local public services such as schools and health centres, and working locally (Chapter 5).

As seen in previous chapters, most working-class estate residents have limited economic and cultural capital. However, long-term residents had developed social connections based on knowing people locally, which provided what McKenzie (2012: 471) describes as 'local social capital': 'it is hardly surprising that if there are groups who are stigmatized, and feel unwanted or of no value to the rest of society that they will find value for themselves, families and locality in what is available to them'. Local social capital does not travel far beyond the boundaries of the estates. It lacks the characteristics of social capital more broadly as an exclusionary resource – knowing *the right people* – that Bourdieu emphasises, which allows 'the privileged and powerful to use their connections to help each other and protect their interests' (Savage, 2015: 131). For estate residents, however, local social capital offers crucial benefits which provided ontological security within the estate – they knew who to trust if they needed help, which they often did due to poverty, vulnerability and ill health, both their own and their children's.

Place belonging and local social capital are illustrated in the case of Danni, who had lived at West Hendon for over 20 years. As a lone parent with three children, support networks of nearby family and neighbours provided Danni with a strong sense of place attachment – a ' real community feeling' based on longevity, mutual support, trust and caring. Danni was rooted in the local area because of residing in close proximity to her parents, children's schools and her paid caring job – in other words, the everyday challenging combination of paid work and unpaid caring responsibilities which working-class mothers on low-incomes have to juggle (Gosling, 2008; McKenzie, 2015):

> 'I am alone with the kids, but with the area, the reason why I really like it is because I am also quite close to my parents who help me a lot as well. I'm a carer as well, so the lady I care for is not far from here at all, it's walking distance in fact. And my little one was born with a congenital heart defect and it has meant hospital stays, so with my two older ones they have gone over and grandparents have helped. They have either come over here or the kids have gone over and stayed with their grandparents. So I feel that I have got a real connection with the area because I have lived here for over two decades, don't really want to move anywhere else, because I feel that our area is quite conveniently located as in quite close to so many amenities and so many shops and [train] stations that are all around. The schools are quite close by as well. One thing that I like about is there is a real community feeling, as in for example if I was delayed at a hospital appointment, I trust my neighbours, they could just spend a few minutes with the kids if they [children] didn't have a key.'

Despite being overcrowded, Danni's overriding priority was to remain at West Hendon because of her attachment to the area, and she was very opposed to demolition. Female lone parents, like Danni, found estates to be welcoming, non-judgemental places where it was possible to build support networks, including among others like themselves. Estates are places where residents and especially working-class women *cared* for others – not only their own children but their neighbours' children.

Many people mentioned what Danni describes as a 'real community feeling' – that is, a 'sense of community' (Morris, 2019). At Northwold, 78 per cent of NES respondents felt that they belonged to the neighbourhood, while 51 per cent had a 'very strong' sense of belonging; the latter is much higher than the equivalent 32 per cent in Hackney as a whole (Watt and Allen, 2018). In describing their neighbourhood 'likes', NES respondents routinely mentioned Northwold's neighbourliness, friendliness and sense of community. Residential longevity contributed towards the latter: "I grew up here. It's home for us. I've a lot of friends on the estate especially my block is a good community. Great relationships with neighbours" (R109).[2] This sense of community was even expressed via the telling 'everyone knows everyone' phrase. This phrase is redolent of the close-knit patterns of sociability identified in the classic post-war community studies of working-class urban villages (Young and Willmott, 1957; Gans, 1962). 'Everyone knows everyone' was most heard among residents of the small to medium-sized estates (Chapter 4) – such as Northwold, West Hendon, Cressingham Gardens and Carpenters – rather than the large estates; these quotations are taken from the NES:

> 'Been here all my life. Everyone knows everyone – no prob[lem]s. Best neighbours. Tranquil sense of community. People help out with old people as neighbours should.' (R312)

> 'I really like this estate. It's a community, we all know each other. The estate has been cleaned up in recent years and is generally quiet. Everyone looks out for each other. Very important that people look out for children, the area is safe.' (R366)

When I met Wesley at West Hendon, he was trimming his neighbour's hedge, a chore he had done for years: "I've always been a DIY person since I was a little boy, and it was them that approached me: 'my son doesn't like to do this, can you help?' 'Yeah, I don't mind helping'. Everyone looks out for one another." Most of Wesley's neighbours in his row of terraced houses had lived there for many years, just like himself. Helping neighbours was simply what you did. The small/medium-sized estates engendered a sense of belonging to a singular identifiable and easily walkable neighbourhood, as Eddie described with reference to West Hendon: "I mean you knew everyone from one side of the estate to the other, and you could walk from one side of the estate to the other. It was a fantastic place [before regeneration], absolutely, you couldn't fault it, really couldn't fault it."

A Social Life (2015: 16) report on Cressingham Gardens found that 'sense of belonging and neighbourliness on Cressingham are strong' (Cooper, 2017), as Bill illustrates:

> 'If anyone asked "what's it like living there?", I'd just say, "I love living there", and I've lived in council places most of my life. It's the best place I've lived, and that's the community as well as the architecture. It really is the best.

Everybody knows each other, and they give you as much
as space – or not – as you want.'

Neighbourliness and sense of community were also prominent at
Carpenters estate (Frediani et al, 2013; Watt, 2013). Cassie described
moving in to this estate during the 1980s: "We loved it when we
first came in. We were struck by the sense of community, people say
'hello' to you when you walk around, we felt safe. My kids grew up
locally and turned out well, they went to university and got good jobs."
Cassie was from a black Caribbean background and when I asked
her about the ethnic mix on the estate, she replied: "you could be
Asian, from the Philippines or whatever, we all get on, you can
see the total mix" (compare Gidley, 2013). Cassie was aghast at the
Carpenters prospective demolition: "why would you want to destroy
something so precious". Ernie mentioned how Carpenters' tenants
who had been displaced due to regeneration missed it: "people were
upset at having to leave what was the safest estate in the whole of
Newham, probably the estate that did the most for the community,
and a place where everybody knew everybody, a classic community
spirit". Ria was one of those Carpenters' tenants who had been
forcibly rehoused elsewhere in Newham and who sorely missed
her 'family estate' (see Chapter 10):

> 'It wasn't like you just lived there, the whole of that estate
> [Carpenters] was just like a family thing. Even if you live
> in a block of flats, everybody knows everyone, because the
> shop was there, everything was just there. Even if you'd
> just moved in, you'd know everyone in the space of no
> time, because you see so many different people and they
> said, "hello" and that's how it was. It wasn't like just "on
> an estate", it was like a *family estate*, because everybody
> knew everyone. If you're going to the shop, you can leave
> your door open and run down to the shop, that was the
> kind of environment that it was. That's where my girls
> were brought up, and if they went downstairs I never had
> to worry about them playing downstairs. I miss it, I miss
> it a helluva lot.'

Facilities and location

Aside from neighbourliness, place attachment to the estates was
enhanced by the availability of local facilities and the location. Local

facilities included shops, community centres and green space, which were either located at the estate or nearby. Local shops were well-used and sorely missed post-regeneration at both Woodberry Down and Clapham Park estates (Chapter 12). Many estates had community halls; Carpenters had two at one time. The quality of such halls was variable. Some were sparsely furnished, minimally decorated, and with poor-quality amenities, indicative of inadequate investment by the council. Others were well-kept, for example at the heavily stigmatised Broadwater Farm estate (Power, 1997; Hendry, 2019). Some estates, like Churchill Gardens, ran their own bar. These facilities were not simply granted by the local authority; residents had campaigned for them:

> 'We fought for this bar.' (Female leaseholder, Churchill Gardens, 2014)

> 'We're not against regeneration per se and we want improvements. Most of the improvements have been led by the residents not the local authority, including this community centre.' (Resident, Broadwater Farm meeting, 2015)

Several estates had had negative reputations in the past (Chapter 7). At the same time, their physical appearance belies their 'concrete jungle' image since they all have substantial green space. Even the two iconic brutalist estates in Southwark – Aylesbury and Heygate – had substantial green space in between the blocks (Watt, 2020c). Other research estates are adjacent to parks. Cressingham Gardens, for example, sits next to Brockwell Park (Photograph 4.8).

Working-class tenants and their children *used* the green space at their estates for playing, socialising and dog-walking, rather than it merely providing an aesthetic backdrop along the lines of Savage's elective belonging (Chapter 9). West Hendon had extensive green space (Photograph 6.2) and is also near the West Harp area of natural beauty. Interviewees highlighted how this space was a boon for parents since it functioned as a public/semi-private garden, as Eddie described when his children were growing up:

> 'The kids were out there all the time. You wouldn't let the kids go too far when they were little, so we used the green space that was directly outside the front of the flats. We had the paddling pools down there and there were little parks

Photograph 6.2: West Hendon estate – residents enjoying a summer evening, 2016

there as well dotted around with a few swings and bits and pieces. They were directly underneath your flat so you could keep an eye on the kids very easily. They went to the sailing ... well even I went to the sailing base there. So it was the ideal place. You look back on it now and you'd think, "blimey, you'd be hard pressed to get anywhere like that in London!"'

A second aspect of place attachment was transport connectivity. At Woodberry Down, residents praised their proximity to Manor House underground station plus the multiple buses which run along Seven Sisters Road. Precarous workers, like Akmal, relied on such connectivity, so losing this due to regeneration/demolition was a concern: "They [council] tell us we're going to move, but we don't want to move from here because everything's two minutes for us, the buses, the tube, everywhere's like a two-minute walk. We live at the heart of central London, we've got all of these buses, working-wise we cannot complain." Residents at those estates which were more physically cut off and spatially isolated expressed living in a 'special place'. While such isolation could attract 'outside troublemakers', it also buttressed neighbourliness and sense of community:

'This estate's quite weird because there's basically one bridge into Stratford, so it's a bit of an island, it was a bit of an isolated community. You'd think it would probably be quite white and racist like Isle of Dogs, but it wasn't actually, it's always been really mixed. So as much as it was quite isolated, it was quite mixed, and everyone really got on with each other. Because it was so isolated, everybody knew everybody.' (Lee, Carpenters)

'Everyone just kind of knows everyone, it's a small ... it has a village feel to it up here.' (Sandra, Central Hill)

Large estates

Even the large estates were not anonymous, soulless urban wastelands (Chapter 4). Interviewees reported knowing people locally, which enhanced their sense of security, community and place belonging. This local familiarity could occur due to having grown up in the area. Ahmed and his wife moved into the Ocean estate during the later years of the NDC. Despite having reservations about the quality of the building and the flat (Chapter 7), Ahmed took it because of his familiarity with the local neighbourhood with its strong Bangladeshi presence: "I was sent to Stepney Green school facing Ocean estate and all my friends lived on the Ocean so I kind of knew the area." Nevertheless, residents at the large estates, like the Ocean, were much less likely to use the 'everyone knows everyone' phrase or to frame their place belonging in terms of a singular community. This is not least because of these estates' sheer size in demographic and spatial terms. Knowing 'everyone' in such large estates is unrealistic, as Terry pointed out when I asked whether he was 'involved' in the life of Woodberry Down:

'Well, when you mean involved ... it's a massive council estate, it's probably one of the biggest ones in Europe, so it's not like everybody knows each other. You can live on that estate for 20 years and not know 90 per cent of the people, because most people get up, they go to work, yeah? People work and most of the people worked in that estate.'

Woodberry Down had nearly 2,000 households spread around 57 different blocks and is divided by a major road. As Terry says, you would be unlikely to know even one tenth of the residents, never mind 'everyone', not least since people went out to work. None of this is to say, however, that convivial neighbouring did not exist at Woodberry Down and the other large estates, as oral histories indicate (Woodberry Down Memories Group, 1989; WDCO, 2015), and as discussed later.

The large estates' size and geographical sprawl meant that separate TRAs existed which fostered subdivisions, while distinct micro-geographies and identities also existed. The term 'Clapham Park estate' originally just referred to the eastern part of the estate that was built during the 1930s (Gater, 1937). Audrey highlighted the split between this part and the more recent Clapham Park west built during the post-war period, a subdivision that older residents still identified with: "the west has never seen itself as part of Clapham Park estate. There's always been the 'old estate' and the 'new estate'. The old estate is the east, because those are the ones that were built in the 30s". Residents even queried whether a singular named 'Clapham Park estate' existed prior to the NDC regeneration: "we weren't Clapham Park at that time. You have the south side, this is the east side, then you have the west side down that way, so it's big, in hectare space size it's a big area. Last time in reckoning there was over 7,000 people in the area, now it's more" (Malana).

Intra-estate place belonging

We have thus far examined place attachment at the domestic and neighbourhood scales. What about the intermediate scale – the internal subdivisions within each estate consisting of blocks of flats and rows of terraced houses? Neighbourly relations were often based on spatial propinquity; they were typically strongest with nearby neighbours in the same block or row of houses (Kusenbach, 2008). Harry described growing up at the large Regents Park estate in Camden during the 1960s and 70s:

> 'I can only speak for my block and the blocks that I can see around here, but yeah we used to know all our neighbours. I know it's a stereotypical thing, but we did leave our doors open. We were the one that owned a phone so next door would come in, give us a couple of pennies and use the phone. My aunty was the first person to have colour TV and we would troop over there, and all that. So you knew everyone. When you walk to the shop and you knew, "there's so-and-so", and all that. You knew enough people to feel comfortable as a community.'

While London's estates are stereotypically portrayed as high-rise tower blocks and deck-access blocks (Coleman, 1990), these are atypical. Most London estates comprise stand-alone, low-to-medium rise blocks (2–7 storeys), while some also include terraced houses. Flats in the blocks are typically arranged along externally facing open balconies which look onto a small public area, for example a courtyard. This arrangement means that residents had to pass in front of their neighbours' kitchen windows to access their own flats. In addition, ground-floor flats often have small gardens. Seeing and bumping into neighbours going about their daily routines is a feature of the blocks' design. Photograph 6.3 shows one such balcony in the half-empty seven blocks at Woodberry Down in 2017. It shows how tenants *use* their balconies as an extension of their flat for both laundry and sitting out (chair), but also how they *care* for this space, which they decorate with pot plants – hence it becomes part of *their home*. During the summer, residents either sit on their balconies or take their chairs and sit out in the courtyards as their children play nearby. The sight of children playing out in public space

Photograph 6.3: Woodberry Down estate (seven blocks) – balcony, 2017

Photograph 6.4: Northumberland Park estate – children playing football on balcony, 2016

(Photograph 6.4) – on balconies, in courtyards and green space – is far more likely to occur on London's supposedly 'architecturally illegible' council estates than the valorised Victorian streets (Adonis and Davies, 2015) which are unsafe due to being car-dominated.

Leroy had lived at Northumberland Park estate for nearly 30 years. Although he was aware of the area's problems (Chapters 4 and 7), Leroy was also extremely positive about his neighbours and accumulated local social capital:

'I know *all* of my neighbours [on the landing]. We are on first-name terms. Nothing goes on up here that we don't ... we look after each other. If anybody has a need, we're there for them. *We* are like a *family*. That's what the community should be, like a family. You've got your neighbours, you treat them like your family. They watch your back, you watch theirs, they need help, you're there, they can call you and there's no way you feel shy, whatever, to do that. That's how it should be and that's how it is up here.'

This was not 'just talk', as criticisms of interview-based research have highlighted (Blokland, 2017). I interviewed Leroy for over two hours on the balcony outside his flat. During this time, he had friendly conversations with several passing neighbours and greeted his postal worker by name.

As discussed above, Woodberry Down is a large estate where knowing 'everybody' is impossible. Nevertheless, Terry gradually got to know his neighbours over the 25 years that he lived there: "I just knew loads of people from all different nationalities." This occurred informally in relation to his block:

'I used to sit up on the balcony with the old lady, Kathy, from next door, and we used to speak for hours, she used to tell me all her stories. The other old woman further down the way, if she had a problem, she'd knock on my door and I used to come out and I'd go, "what's the problem?" The Asian guy next to her, I didn't really talk to him too much, night worker. I used to know everyone on my landing and I used to know people underneath. There's a block here and we've got our balcony, and there's another balcony, and there's a block just across there. So you can see *everybody there*, you've seen them for years, you're going to talk to them. That's the reason why they [LCC] had it like that in the first place, so you could see people over the way, and you're standing on your balcony. It was a proper half-decent community.'

Several things are noteworthy in Terry's description of the 'half-decent community' at Woodberry Down. First, the physical layout of the block, with balconies and facing another block, aided neighbour interaction (Photograph 6.3). Second this neighbourly familiarity was gradually built up: "you've seen them for years". Third, convivial neighbouring did not necessarily extend to everyone. Terry did not know his Asian neighbour who worked nights; it's important to note the staggered working patterns of the urban precariat and the sheer number of working hours that many estate residents put in that leave little time for neighbouring. Fourth, 'keeping yourself to yourself' was not easy. Finally, the original landlords – the LCC – had designed the blocks with social interaction in mind, as it did across its estates (Gater, 1937): 'Sitting out space is provided at almost every estate – in the private balcony in the flat, in the estate gardens below or in the private gardens now frequently provided for ground floor flats and maisonettes' (LCC, 1961: 6). Caroline loved the sociability at Northwold, another LCC-built estate in Hackney. Even as a relative newcomer, she knew most of the people in her block:

> 'The balconies facing inwards is absolutely key to the sociability, and that was designed for the community. I can wave at people over there. This is a functional walkway, but it's got a dual purpose, it's also a social space, it's a space to hang out. People do sit out there on the balconies, even though they're walkways really. You know I'm not the only one with a garden on mine, there's a few other people who've got plants and it's an opportunity to … I've had conversations across the angle.'

Photograph 6.5 shows an example of a Northwold block with inward-facing balconies. Caroline went on to contrast this design with modern blocks: "there's nothing sociable about all these new brown and beige horrors that are going up everywhere, it's about keeping people separate

Photograph 6.5: Northwold estate – block, 2017

in their own little world". This separation was precisely what occurred in the redeveloped estates (Chapter 12).

Even at the small-to-medium sized estates like Northwold, where a singular estate identity existed, knowing people was more significant at the block scale. Like Harry's family earlier, Annie used to leave her front door open at West Hendon, a sense of comfort that reflected the tight-knit – and respectable – nature of her block, where she knew everybody on the basis of longevity:

> 'It was the best block of the lot because we'd all been there for 30–40 years, so everything was clean. We kept outside *clean*, we knew *everybody*. You could walk to the front entrance and if you weren't sure where I lived, you could ask the lady downstairs: "do you know where Annie lives?" – "oh yes, is she expecting you?"'

Such day-to-day, mutual neighbouring practices are mundane – chatting on the doorstep, taking in parcels, asking how people are when they're sick, exchanging Christmas cards, looking after neighbours' homes when they are away, and so on. Nevertheless, they are the stuff of local social life for city dwellers and they go a long way towards fostering 'respect in the neighbourhood' (Harris, 2006) and making people feel comfortable and secure.

The Right to Buy as buy to stay

This section focuses on those ex-sitting tenants who bought their homes under the RTB – either as leaseholders of flats or less commonly as freeholders of houses – and who remained living in them as owner-occupiers. Two thirds of these RTB 'owner-stayer' households were middle-aged and elderly couples (Chapter 4). In terms of ethnicity and socioeconomic groups, they were very largely white and BAME retired working class and traditional working class (with stable full-time jobs), plus a few younger black middle-class professionals in their forties. What is most significant about them is their residential longevity (Chapter 4).

Working-class motivations for RTB purchase did not involve 'playing the housing market' game which reflects the middle-class orientation towards housing as a 'space of positions' (Allen, 2008). Instead, as Allen emphasises, the working-class RTB orientation towards housing was primarily as a home, 'a place to live'. William and Gesil were a married black African working-class couple who had bought their flat at the Aylesbury estate. When I interviewed them, they were in the process of challenging the council over the displacement threat due to demolition. They contrasted their homeownership with the white middle classes who had bought nearby ex-council street properties on the open market. The couple were aghast at the rate of household turnover within this gentrifying enclave:

William: 'You know the private houses opposite? They used to be council houses, proper redbrick houses. It's mainly white people coming in, and they are selling and they are moving out.'

Gesil: 'They come in 2–3 years and they are selling, re-selling to…'

William: 'Because they know how to do research, whereas we in the area, we don't know anything about researching the housing market because it's not like we want to be on a property ladder or anything.'

Gesil: 'We just want a home, we just want a home!'

William: 'This street along here is nice houses, people came in and they were buying it Right to Buy, Right to Buy, and it's all now private.'

Gesil: 'We just want a home, a home for our family, that's all. That's what all our neighbours want, they don't want anything, they just want *a home.*'

As Gesil emphasised, they and their neighbours 'just want a home' – a place to live – but not to be 'on a property ladder', which was alien to them (Allen, 2008). If the RTB was not about making a short-term gain and moving on, nor was it about asserting status superiority over tenant neighbours: "it wasn't about social climbing, 'I'm better than you'" (Wesley). Instead, there were four main RTB motivations (which intertwined in individual cases): first, firming up place attachments to homes and neighbourhoods; second, economic cost/benefit advantages; third, enhancing family security; and finally escaping from problems with renting.

The first RTB motivation involved place attachment – buyers wanted to *stay put* in their homes and their neighbourhoods. In other words, the RTB was a way of shoring up their traditional belonging – 'I belong in this neighbourhood because I've lived here for years, and now I'm going to buy my home to enable me to remain in perpetuity'. Mary and her husband were among the first RTB purchasers at the

174

Carpenters estate during the 1980s and their primary motive was to *remain in place*: "I bought because I liked it, and I thought I'm not going anywhere, and so we decided to buy it. I was always going to stay, I would never move from here." RTB ownership therefore functioned as 'buy-to-stay' since it facilitated a deepening of roots and helped to fix them in space. Theresa and her husband bought their maisonette at West Hendon after living there for several years. They shelved plans to return to Ireland and taking up the RTB reinforced this sense of permanency and home:

> 'I said "no I like it here, I'm happy here, we'll put in for the Right to Buy and stay here". I started to make friends here, my child had started to go to school here, I got into the church community and I started to make a life. And once you start putting down your roots, sometimes it's hard then to pull them back up again and move. My plan was to stay here, so here I am 18 years later in this property.'

In addition to enhancing place belonging, Theresa also highlights the second RTB motivation – differential costs: "the mortgage on this place was cheaper than the rent, so it would have been silly not to buy it". Gloria highlighted increasing rents: "We realised that in the end we would be better off [by buying] because the rent was going up and up and up. We wouldn't be still living there if we had to keep paying that high rent." In addition to such immediate cost gains, owners thought that they would make savings over their lifetimes, thus rendering them more financially secure in old age. Although the RTB owner-stayers were generally in stable employment, this did not mean that they were well off, such as single women like Dolores who lived at the Aylesbury estate: "I love my home. I was thinking that maybe one day I don't have a job and how can I pay the rent?" The RTB was Dolores' way of gaining security and staying put. It enabled working-class people to gain spatial control – what Paton (2014) refers to as elective fixity. The first two emphases on place attachment and cost–benefit are illustrated by Ernie, who bought his flat in one of the Carpenters tower blocks during the 1980s, following a failed bid to transfer:

> 'We come to the decision that we're not going anywhere so let's buy it, because long-term we're going to be better off. It wasn't done as an investment, we just saw it as being better for the future for us, because when we get to retire, we don't have to worry about paying rent.'

Beatty had lived at the Ocean estate for several decades and the RTB enabled her to fix herself in place; she also illustrates the third RTB motivation – enhancing her family's long-term security:

> 'It was very attractive to buy, this big percentage you get knocked off, massive percentage. Well I bought that to make sure that my family had security in their tenancy. I mean there was no security in being a tenant, none whatsoever. I didn't buy it to make money, I bought it for security, I wanted my family to have a home. I had no intention of moving, I love it here, I'm not going to move, this is my home, I was born here. So, I wasn't buying as a, you know, get-rich-quick deal, I was buying to make sure that there was a family home there for all of us.'

The RTB helped to secure their family's long-term housing security, as Gesil described: "I thought it was going to be a cushion for us and the children – they will have a home, wherever they go to they come back home in the future when we pass on, it's there for them".

The fourth RTB motivation was the desire to 'exit' (Hirsch, 1970) from the various problems they faced in renting from the council. One problem was being unable to transfer to a more suitable property for their needs (as with Ernie above), while another problem was inadequate council repairs and maintenance. Rose was a black professional who had initially moved into a hard-to-let property in Lambeth during the 1980s, and from there obtained a tenancy at Cressingham Gardens where she later applied for the RTB:

> 'I couldn't bear having Lambeth Council anywhere in my place. Because I'd already had the experience of Lambeth Council from when I was a student, I knew what they were like. And every time they came into my flat as a tenant they managed to bodge something else. I just wanted to have the right to do my own place, be left to get on with it and fix my own windows, fix my own taps.'

Rose 'naively' thought that buying her flat would keep the council out of her home and her life. Much to her annoyance, this did not happen because of the proposed regeneration.

In terms of place belonging, the RTB helped to embed ex-tenants in their homes and estates and thereby operated as a buy-to-stay mechanism. It facilitated roots, residential longevity and traditional belonging by giving ex-tenants a substantial financial stake in their homes. It's therefore unsurprising that such RTB owner-stayers were so against demolition since it threatened the very things that they thought they were enhancing by buying in the first place: attachment to their homes and neighbourhoods, their own and their family's long-term financial security, and having autonomy from the council (see Elliott-Cooper et al, 2020).

Incoming middle-class owner-occupiers

The foregoing has focused on current council/social tenants and RTB owners who had previously been council tenants. This leaves out one socioeconomic group that are increasingly prominent in London's estates – incoming middle-class professionals who buy their homes at market prices from the original RTB owners who sell up and leave. I interviewed nine such people from eight households (one couple); they were mainly middle-aged, and from both white and BAME ethnic backgrounds. These were graduates (several with postgraduate degrees), who worked in a range of professions in the arts, journalism, health, IT, engineering and finance, tended to self-identify as middle class. They were mainly in lower professional and managerial occupations in NS-SEC 2. Although one or two had better-paying occupations, most were not affluent by middle-class London standards (Savage, 2015) – hence their choice of ex-council housing: "all we can afford is a 1-bedroom flat in a council estate" (Allula, Northwold). Caroline worked for a charity: "I'm on £33,000 in my mid-forties and I've got a degree, an MA, a PGCE, and 20 years' experience of doing what I do. And I basically earn just enough to live on. I've got very little disposable income." Three aspects of this group's relationships to housing and place are discussed: their previous housing histories, their arrival on the estate, and estate social relations.

Housing histories

The professionals had spent many years bouncing around the London PRS with gradually diminishing enthusiasm. Insecurity and high rents were significant drawbacks, as with working-class PRS experiences. Unlike the latter, evictions were rare, but forced moves due to rent hikes were commonplace: "I've never been evicted, but I've been priced out of something, that's definitely happened quite a few times" (Allula). Allula and her partner Dylan had a competition as to which of them had moved the most: "It's ridiculous, I think it might be 13 times in 10 years [each]" (Allula).

While some had reasonable quality PRS accommodation, others described overcrowding and subdivided rooms: "I lived in a house with eight people, I was in the dining room. I'm 30, I want to get out of this" (Allula). Several grew tired of flat-sharing: "I couldn't live with people anymore, I'd had so many bad, stressful house-share situations. I was single, so my options were limited" (Caroline). Only one professional (Alan, Woodberry Down, who worked in finance) emphasised that homeownership was a conscious investment strategy: "you do not pay rent, you un-sink and you build up from there". For the others, the relative security of homeownership represented an 'exit' strategy (Hirsch, 1970) from the manifold inadequacies of the London PRS: "I was thinking I was going to stay here for a good long while, I was fed up with renting with other people" (Luke).

Home-buying preferences and strategies varied. A few exercised definite place preferences, as is prominent among the London middle classes (Butler and Robson, 2003): "I wanted some trees outside so I need greenery, otherwise I start getting the jitters, and Brockwell Park is one of the most beautiful parks in London, so I can't imagine ever living elsewhere in London" (Lynsey, Cressingham Gardens). However, the overriding priority for most was economic– what property they could afford on their limited budgets – which meant an ex-council flat. Caroline admitted to having reservations: "I'd never lived on an estate before, so I did have some slight concerns, I didn't know how friendly it would be." Others were unconcerned because of prior familiarity with estates due to work, family or previous residence: "I know these flats well, I worked as a health visitor for a while and I used to say, 'those flats are really nice', compared with some of the other [PRS] flats we were visiting in the big houses that were in a bad way" (Winifred, Northwold). This group did not adhere to commonplace middle-class judgemental discourses regarding 'problem estates and problem people'.

Arrival stories and elective belonging

Early impressions of their new homes and neighbourhoods were extremely positive. They told 'arrival stories' in relation to the aesthetics of place in elective belonging terms (Savage et al, 2005; Savage, 2010), even including a 'wow' response from Cressingham Gardens incomers:

'Seen from the outside, it's not like the Victorian homes where you think that it looks pretty. But when I walked in, there was just this amazing ceiling height, and you're just like "wow". It's the structure of the flat, like there's so much possibility in this flat, it just blew me away so I bought it.' (Lynsey)

'It was the first place I'd seen that had a garden and it was much bigger than any other place I'd seen, and the fact that it was on the park was amazing. I thought it [house] was a really interesting, unexpected kind of space. That was the thing I was most struck by, the sense of light and space you had in it. So I thought, "wow!"' (Luke)

These first impressions do not, however, mean that they moved into pristine show homes; the quality of some properties was poor, which necessitated lengthy DIY: "honestly it was in a horrendous state, like the kitchen was completely falling to bits, it just looked like a squat. We basically spent 10 years just sort of incrementally making it presentable" (Lisa). If aesthetic appeal forms part of Savage's elective belonging, another dimension is how choosing a home and residential neighbourhood involves staking *moral claims* over place; this was very important for these estate incomers (Chapters 10 and 11).

Disaffiliation or mixing?

In sociological terms, this group are gentrifiers who move into a working-class urban area because of its affordability and who invest in their properties to make them into valued – as well as economically valuable – homes. Several were self-conscious of their privileged position and considered themselves to be 'part of the problem' – gentrification – a self-consciousness that has been identified among certain clusters of gentrifiers in the US (Brown-Saracino, 2007):

'I feel awful about it [gentrification] because I'm part of it, I am a gentrifying agent, and I even look like one with my long hair and my university degree, my BMW company car and my good job and all the money I have compared to others my age. I speak the gentrification down, because I know that it can destroy communities and it can evict communities and change the character of a community, and bring prices up and cause all kinds of financial issues for the community, but I am clearly one of those people because I fit the bill.' (Dylan, Northwold)

'Clapton is becoming gentrified, very rapidly, but it's still very real. It's lively, I love the ethnic shops, the Turkish shops. I think I'm one of the first wave of gentrification of the area, because there might have been a time when someone like me would not have bought in this block because it would have been too scary. I do put myself as part of the problem. This should be a council flat, but then I'm not going to beat myself up about it. But I am conscious that I'm a middle-class professional who's come and bought an ex-council flat and I'm part of this.' (Caroline)

Given their high cultural capital/low-moderate economic capital, this middle-class group are close to what Rose (1996: 133) identified as 'marginal gentrifiers' in the context of 1990s Montreal: 'fractions of the new middle class who were highly educated but only tenuously employed or modestly earning professionals'. This group of London marginal gentrifiers are distinct from the affluent super-gentrifiers in banking and finance who are increasingly prominent in the city's gentrification landscape (Butler and Lees, 2006). This distinction reflects the large differences – especially in terms of economic capital – that exist between nominally 'middle-class' groups in London (Introduction; Butler and Robson, 2003; Watt, 2005; Jackson and Butler, 2015; Savage, 2015).

While elective belonging existed among this group of incomers, this did not mean that their appreciation of their homes and neighbourhood was *solely* aesthetic and asocial, as Savage (2010) emphasises is the case with elective belonging. On the contrary, they *interacted* with their working-class/BAME neighbours and can be regarded as 'diversity-liking middle-class households' (Bosch and Ouwehand, 2019: 1818). Luke and Caroline described being introduced to community life at their respective estates soon after their arrival:

'It was amazingly friendly. There were these old ladies who got the nickname of "The Golden Girls" who gave me a really big welcome. They'd knock on the door and say, "we'd like to welcome you to the area". So my initial impression was it was really friendly. My next-door neighbour went and cooked me dinner a few times when

I first moved in, so I was kind of bowled over. You got a sense of a lot of people that know each other around here. I definitely felt a little bit self-conscious being middle class, buying an ex-council property and thinking I'm definitely a bit different to a lot of people round here, but it dissipated quite quickly.' (Luke)

'My neighbours directly downstairs from me came and spoke to me very quickly. I think there was an issue, but she was really friendly. And I quickly got into the habit of saying "hello" to everybody who I met in the block, introducing myself. It seemed friendly, it seemed nice, everyone seemed nice and I'd say I know the names of half the people in this block of 20 flats.' (Caroline)

Such everyday neighbourhood sociability is far more pronounced than at new-build mixed-tenure developments in London (Kilburn, 2013; Awofolaju, 2014; Corcillo, 2020) or new-build private developments (Allen and Watt, Forthcoming). Incomers mentioned helping neighbours with small chores. Luke described bridging the 'class-gap':

'I think the fact that I made things and had tools, I think that became a way of bridging that gap. I do a lot of DIY and making things and I tend to make a lot of stuff outside. So whether it's in my garden or on the garden wall at the front, that was always a really good way of speaking to … So I got known as a person that has a lot of tools and knows how to fix things, so that became a thing to talk about, a common connection. Kids would come and knock on the door saying, "my bike's broken, can you do this?"'

Caroline described mutually supportive neighbouring at Northwold which signified a sense of community:

'There are definitely people who'd look out for each other. If I had any sort of problem, there are doors I can knock on, and people would knock on my door. She [neighbour] was Turkish and her English was pretty poor, so she had low confidence. I helped her in various ways, some paperwork stuff.'

This group did not engage in spatial disaffiliation (Atkinson, 2006) practices such as avoiding working-class neighbourhood facilities, and did not inhabit the local neighbourhood via selective belonging (Watt, 2009b). Selective belonging was in any case difficult from an architectural standpoint because they were not corralled off into separate enclaves, as in many new developments with separate blocks and/or entrances for owners and tenants (Kilburn, 2013; Osborne, 2014; Corcillo, 2020) – as occurred on the post-redevelopment estates (Chapter 12). Instead, the incomers lived in the same blocks and terraces as their working-class tenant and RTB neighbours, whose space this was. These middle-class incomers attempted to *fit into* the working-class-dominated field of the council estate, rather than either *avoid it* (via selective belonging) or *dominate it* (as occurs in new-build mixed-tenure developments; see Chapter 12). It's noteworthy that the class divide in terms of economic capital was not that wide, thereby supporting the argument that 'more interclass contacts tend to be formed in neighbourhoods with relatively smaller socio-economic differences between renters and homeowners' (Bosch and Ouwehand, 2019: 1822). In other words, elements of genuine cross-class mixed communities were being formed via the gradual entry of middle-class professionals buying ex-RTB properties.

Only one person encountered tenure animosity *because* she was a buyer. Jeanette bought her house at Cressingham Gardens in the late 1990s when there were far fewer Right-to-Buyers or incomers: "some tenants refused to speak to me because I bought the property and it should be a place for tenants". However, this tenure-based animosity dissipated, partly because of Jeanette's sociability and because more tenants themselves bought their homes under the RTB. The *gradual form* of gentrification, as represented by Jeanette and the others, is qualitatively different from that which is promised – or threatened – under demolition and state-led gentrification where socio-spatial separation and accentuated class distinctions are the order of the day (Chapter 12). In fact, working-class tenants who were firmly opposed to demolition did not object to the gradual build-up and presence of middle-class incomers, but instead thought that they added to the estates' social diversity, as Sandra described in the case of Central Hill:

> 'The Right to Buy has actually brought those [better-off] people back in, because that's where we get our young professionals from, because they can afford to live on here, especially if they've just started a young family. They're nice people, they want to get involved. I like living in more

mixed communities, I don't want to live with everyone exactly the same, I like to know that we're all different, but we can all live together.'

Except for Alan, these middle-class incomers were strongly opposed to the proposed regeneration and several played prominent roles in the anti-demolition campaigns at their respective estates – Save Cressingham Gardens and Save Northwold. They were against demolition because it threatened their place attachment – both their elective belonging and their evolving sense of community. Being already socially embedded in their estates enabled them to play a significant role in the campaigns.

Estates as 21st century urban villages?

I have presented a view of estates as convivial and relatively cohesive neighbourhoods involving residents from different tenures expressing a sense of community. However, although there are sociological shades of the urban villages of the kind that Young and Willmott (1957) identified in 1950s' east London – everyone knows everyone – 21st-century London estates are complex, dynamic urban neighbourhoods and not seamless, *gemeinschaft*-like, singular communities.

While many residents expressed a sense of place belonging and community, for others the estate was "just somewhere to live" (Gary). Gary had grown up on the Heygate estate but left during the 1990s. He regularly visited his mother and brother, who lived there until they were decanted under regeneration. Although Gary was involved in the campaign to preserve the Heygate, he provided an unsentimental description of the estate which firmly locates it within its metropolitan context:

> 'The Heygate estate was an ordinary south London estate. A lot of people lived on that estate, they just lived their lives. The focus of their social life wasn't necessarily on the estate, mine wasn't even when I was at school. If you live in London, it's not like a village. I'd say there wasn't one community in the Heygate estate, it was just like anywhere else in London. My interpretation of it as a community would be it was like any other council estate in London, any other south London council estate, that kind of community. And within that sort of loose community, there were people whose social life focused more on the estate than others.

Other people just came and went. They just went out in the morning, did their job, went to school or went to university and then just came back in the evening, it was just somewhere to live.'

Estates thus offered neighbourliness and community for some, and privacy for others. Although Maria enjoyed living at Churchill Gardens, she described how it did not have a one-size-fits-all model of neighbouring: "It's a friendly estate, but it's not as intimate as some estates. You can drop in and out of neighbouring, you could have privacy if you wanted it. It don't feel like you're living on top of each other. Some people choose to have a more private option."

Unlike mid-century working-class urban villages in which 'keeping yourself to yourself' was frowned upon as a sign of snobbery (Young and Willmott, 1957; McKibbin, 1998), contemporary estates are less narrowly judgemental places (McKenzie, 2015). For some residents, the estate provided a home, but that was all. It was simply a base that enabled them to get on with their privatised lifestyles which centred around family and work. As noted earlier, the staggered working patterns of the urban precariat mean that many residents have limited time available for developing neighbourhood-based social relationships. Paz only occasionally attended local meetings because her time was taken up with work and the demands of caring for her disabled son: "I don't have too much contact with the neighbours in the same building, apart to say, 'hello' or 'goodnight'". Having intensive neighbourly relations was thus not something that everyone either had time for or even necessarily wanted – hence they 'kept themselves to themselves'. Prior to regeneration, Rose had little contact with her neighbours at Cressingham Gardens. She subsequently became involved in the Save Cressingham Gardens campaign, but the intense sociability involved did not sit comfortably with her: "I never liked the people nipping through the back-door *Coronation Street* style, I don't like that. I like to be left alone. I'm quite private. So, I'm hoping that after this regen is done and dusted everybody'll leave me alone" (group interview – everyone laughs). Sheer residential longevity could also erode misperceptions of snobbery, as Gloria describes:

'There was one [white] English lady who thought I was stuck up. Then as time goes by, she got to know me and got to realise that I wasn't stuck up. I was just minding my own business half the time, looking after the kids and that. She realised I wasn't stuck up [laughs], we became so close!'

Like Gloria, long-term residents had the time to build trust because they saw the same faces over years and even decades.

If many long-term residents expressed a sense of community, several elderly white British working-class interviewees were also nostalgic for past times and expressed 'narratives of urban decline' whereby 'the intimate social relations of yesteryear ("the community") were said to be no more' (Watt, 2006: 782). For example, Rene was in her eighties and had lived at Northumberland Park since it was built nearly 50 years ago. She missed the close-knit neighbourliness from years ago: "We used to go to a little pub up here in Park Lane, we used to go there occasionally. Well it was more neighbourly then, everybody used to go there." Rene's decline narrative can be interpreted as nostalgic in that "recollection of the neighbourhood and neighbours of the past appears to continuously produce a sense of loss and isolation" (Smith, 2009: 144–5). Such narratives of urban decline, incorporating nostalgia for a time gone by, have been identified in studies of housing estates and other post-industrial working-class neighbourhoods (Blokland, 2003; Gest, 2016; Watt, 2020a), including my research on Camden council tenants around 20 years ago (Watt, 2006). Narratives of decline featured in my current research, albeit not to the same extent; deindustrialisation and manual job losses, for example, were less significant, reflecting London's intervening transition to a post-industrial service-based economy (Chapter 5).

Contemporary London estates are socially complex spaces, not least due to their ethnic diversity (Gidley, 2013; Rosbrook-Thompson and Armstrong, 2018). Such complexity reflects London's status as a super-diverse global city (Wessendorf, 2014). However, London's estates are even more demographically diverse than the rest of the city because they disproportionately accommodate poor, marginalised and vulnerable populations (Chapter 5). Such populations are typically priced out of and/or made to feel unwelcome in affluent, generally whiter neighbourhoods which deploy a myriad of socio-spatial practices to exclude these abject urban dwellers – the 'poor and unwashed' (Watt and Smets, 2014; Atkinson and Blandy 2017). By contrast, estates are more inclusive and much less judgemental and conformist places than affluent middle-class neighbourhoods where hanging out your washing, allowing 'noisy children' to play out, and having the 'wrong' external façade is frowned upon (Butler, 2003; Butler and Robson, 2003; Davidson, 2010; Kilburn, 2013; Awofolaju, 2014; Corcillo, 2020).

To reiterate, London's estates are not homogeneous working-class urban villages. Instead, they are concentrated spaces of social heterogeneity – of housing tenures, ethnicities, migrant statuses, classes, and so on (Gidley, 2013; Rosbrook-Thompson and Armstrong, 2018). Such heterogeneity speaks to the *inclusivity* of London's estates, an inclusivity that demolition advocates are oblivious to. My interviewees included Nigerian NHS workers, Ghanaian taxi-drivers, Bangladeshi housing officers, black African professionals, East European cleaners, Turkish students, elderly Jewish people, young Muslims, refugees from the Middle East, as well as people with mental health problems, recovering alcoholics, old hippies, and elderly white Cockneys who had never left the East End – to name just a few. This spatially concentrated 'commonplace diversity' resulted in what Gidley (2013: 367) refers to as a 'sort of low-level quotidian rubbing together'. Notably I came across far fewer overtly racist and xenophobic remarks in this research project than in my previous north London research undertaken during the late 1990s (Watt, 2001, 2006).

Estates' demographic complexity is also reflected in how 'micro-communities' formed around age and family type clusters such as lone parents. Such micro-communities are often informal, but also involve membership of local organisations. The elderly had dedicated clubs at several estates, some of which either emerged from or were enhanced by regeneration programmes as part of their community development remit, as at Clapham Park and Ocean estates due to the NDC.

Conclusion

Both tenants and owner-occupiers expressed place belonging to their homes, their blocks of flats/rows of houses and their estates. These were valued and valuable places where long-term residents developed a sense of community over the decades that they lived there. Ontological security was widespread, rooted at the home scale in solid buildings and domestic self-provisioning, and at the neighbourhood scale in residential longevity and local social capital. Long-term residents 'knew people' at their estates and consequently felt comfortable living there. They had built up trusting and caring relationships with their neighbours, relationships which were especially important for working-class mothers. Everyday sociability was enhanced by physical design features, such as balconies, small courtyards and extensive green space. The small/medium estates emerged as more singular, cohesive spaces than the larger estates – they were places where 'everyone knows everyone'. Both small and large estates are entirely dissimilar from the anonymous, concrete wastelands of the 'sink estate' place myth. In purchasing their homes, RTB owners deepened their long-term roots; the RTB therefore operated as a buy-to-stay mechanism. The incoming middle-class market-homeowners (gentrifiers) expressed elective belonging, rather than traditional belonging based on longevity, although they also began to develop a sense of community based on mutual interaction.

Despite this neighbourhood conviviality, 21st century London estates do not form cohesive, singular urban villages of the post-war period. They are demographically complex places in terms of ethnicity, age and familial differences, and they are also spaces where residents can live privatised lives if they want to. In Bourdieusian terms, the 21st century London estate is a less restrictive, rule-bound socio-spatial field than mid-20th century working-class urban villages like Bethnal Green in London or the West End of Boston (Young and Willmott, 1957; Gans, 1962).

This and the previous chapter have highlighted the positive value that residents derived from their housing, homes and estates. Cynical readers might well object that I have presented a naïve, picture-postcard view of London estates which airbrushes out all their well-known problems. Any Londoner 'knows' these only too well from reading the *Evening Standard*, which routinely carries crime, drugs and gangs' stories about the city's estates. Or, as one critical audience member hearing me speak about my research said, "the south London estate where I grew up was a right shithole".[3] The next chapter explores the problematic aspects of estate life.

7

Devalued places

This chapter illustrates five ways that estates have become devalued places to live in residents' eyes, beginning with the domestic scale in relation to overcrowding and un-homing. Second, it examines the crucial impact of landlord neglect in relation to repairs and maintenance. Third, the RTB is revisited with reference to its acceleration of population transience due to the rise of private landlordism. The fourth devaluation theme is crime and disorder, while the final section discusses symbolic devaluation through territorial and tenurial stigmatisation.

Small places: overcrowding and poor housing

Despite generally positive evaluations of their homes, residents – but especially tenants – also expressed reservations which in some cases spilled over into outright rancour and frustration at the poor housing conditions they were forced to live in. These included overcrowding, poor quality (age, damp, fixtures and fittings) and inadequate landlord repairs and maintenance. One fifth of NES tenants were dissatisfied with their homes, but only 6 per cent of leaseholders (Watt and Allen, 2018). Tenant dissatisfactions at Northwold estate included:

'Old and infested with rodents, bugs and all sorts.' (R242)

'Flat is full of damp, leaks but was covered up by condensation. I've taken further action, hopefully get somewhere this year. Mice problems! Works are not taken seriously. Cheap works!' (R263)

'My family have lived on this estate, in this block for many years and are happy living here. The only issue is the small size of the flat.' (R370)

As R370 highlights, lack of space and overcrowding was a significant problem for some families. Worsening overcrowding is intimately linked to the shrinking aggregate size of the social rental sector since councils and housing associations are unable to transfer their overcrowded families to more suitable, larger properties; this situation has worsened under austerity (Orr, 2018). While single-person and couple household interviewees waxed lyrical about their homes' spaciousness, several nuclear families and lone parents complained about inadequate space. Those worst affected had made transfer applications, but this resulted in years of waiting and frustration, while never-ending overcrowding contributed towards intra-household tensions.

Overcrowding in London impacts most heavily on BAME households, especially Bangladeshi and black African households, and is reflective of deeply embedded racial inequalities (GLA Intelligence, 2014; Elahi and Khan, 2016). While overcrowding was not restricted to BAME households among my interviewees, it was certainly a distressing problem for several BAME families. Omar's family was living in an overcrowded one-bed flat on Northumberland Park estate. I began chatting with Omar when he was fixing his car outside his flat. He had come to London as a refugee from the Middle East in the late 1990s. Initially Omar spent a few years living in hostels and sofa surfing, and then, following a legal struggle with the council, he was eventually placed in temporary accommodation from where he obtained his present flat. Omar had gone to university in London as a mature student and was working 60+ hours per week as an App-based taxi driver – a classic precariat occupation. His family's biggest problem was overcrowding: "we have used every inch of space". Omar invited me to take tea in his extremely neat flat to show me how overcrowded the family were. His wife and two children slept in the bedroom, while he slept on the living room couch, a situation which had persisted for *nine years*. Not only had the family been unable to obtain a transfer to a bigger property, but they also experienced inadequate repairs and maintenance, as well as dust emanating from the nearby Spurs stadium regeneration (Panton and Walters, 2018). Their GP (general practitioner) had told them that the damp and dust was making his wife's asthma worse, while overcrowding was having knock-on effects on their marriage: "small places increase tensions, there's more arguments, it makes me and my wife stressed". Omar showed me a letter from HFH which said that his wife's health conditions weren't severe enough to warrant a transfer, prompting Omar to quip, "maybe someone is dying, maybe they would consider it then". Being 'only overcrowded' is insufficient reason to obtain a housing transfer in London (Orr, 2018). Omar raged against the council – "the worst council in Britain" – and could not understand why some of his neighbours had been able to transfer, but not him. Omar and his family were trapped in a flat that no longer felt like home because it failed to meet their housing needs; as well as being overcrowded, there was damp in the toilet and the kitchen was old and in poor quality. The family were subject to *un-homing*, as highlighted in the Introduction (Atkinson, 2015). Such un-homing is crucial to understanding why some tenants, such as Omar, welcome demolition (Chapters 8 and 10).

Various 'exit' tactics (Hirschman, 1970) are available for overcrowded households, including the RTB (Chapter 6). Another exit option is moving out of social housing to a bigger flat in the PRS and I came across a few people who had done this. However, this was not feasible for Omar due to his limited wages, plus the expense and insecurity of the PRS:

> 'A two-bed flat is impossible for me in the private sector, a one-bed flat is £750. The rent is cheap here, but the private sector is too expensive and then after one year in one place you have to move, then you'd have to change schools and everything.'

Overcrowded tenants, like Omar, projected their understandable frustrations onto the public/social housing bureaucracy which was so blatantly failing to meet their needs. However, some overcrowded female tenants began to *internalise* the stigmatising welfare discourses regarding lone parents and the 'underserving poor' which have proliferated under austerity (Tyler, 2013, 2015). Melissa was a white British lone parent living in a two-bed flat in Newham with her four young children. She felt disadvantaged and stigmatised by the council's reform of its housing application process, which, following the Localism Act 2011, prioritised applicants in paid employment and ex-armed services applicants (Watt, 2018a, 2018b; Humphry, 2020):

> 'Sometimes I have days where I feel this is not on, because it's so small, it's affecting the children and their behaviour and everything, and my four-year-old shouldn't be in a room with his three sisters. They blame the mothers, the single parents for everything. So, they've now completely turned the tables, I'm at the bottom of the tables and they've even admitted that if you're working, you'll go up the list. They [council] actually said to me know that I've made myself overcrowded. I've even started to think, "I don't deserve nowhere", because

obviously I'm not working, "stop complaining, you're not working". I actually started to believe it.'

Although Melissa felt frustrated and resentful at her family's overcrowding, she had also begun to internalise the dominant welfare stigmatising discourses, indicative of symbolic violence in Bourdieu's terms – that as an unemployed lone mother, she was a card-carrying member of the undeserving poor.

Neglected places: landlord disinvestment

Narratives of neglect

The disinvestment identified in previous chapters has resulted in widespread and justifiable complaints by residents that their homes and estates have been run down due to landlord neglect. 'Narratives of neglect' (Karn, 2007) were commonplace among interviewees and in the NES (Watt and Allen, 2018): "Leaking round the living room window from the flat above/top floor balcony. I report it EVERY YEAR!" (R114). Interviewees routinely suggested that outstanding maintenance issues could have been adequately dealt with had their landlords properly invested in and managed their homes and estates, a situation which had worsened under austerity. Rene had lived on Northumberland Park estate since it was built and witnessed a deteriorating maintenance service:

> 'Well, all I know is things have gradually gone downhill. You wait a long time for repairs, if it comes, they [HFH] bodge it up and hopefully it'll be alright. Everything's in really bad condition, but then again I worry because we're leaseholders. It's [maintenance] only changed because they've neglected it. I don't know if you noticed the garages for a start, they're all blocked up because they can't repair them. They've taken the doors off and they're just all dilapidated. Well they haven't got any money.'

Monica was a tenant at Northumberland Park and highlighted inadequate maintenance. Her house was prone to periodic flooding – around 6–7 times in 15 years – linked to the flat roof when there was heavy rainfall. Monica compared the HFH repairs and maintenance services negatively to her sister who lived in council housing outside London:

'The last one happened when I was in Scotland for the weekend in February this year. I came home and it was the worst one because all the floors now separated down there, you can see all the gaps, so ... this [carpet] was put down professionally, so that's ruined. And because the council don't do any maintenance work on this estate ... for 5–6 years I haven't seen them do any maintenance work. Whereas like my sister, where she lives, they paint the window frames and their doors, and they put in new kitchens and bathrooms every 10 years, they do it religiously. Here, no. So, they've [HFH] just left this area to purposefully deteriorate. For the 15 years I've been here they've done no work. I haven't seen them do *any* external improvement work or anything. The only thing they do is cut the grass and clean the rubbish, but generally there's no upkeep here at all.'

Ahmed moved into a block on the Ocean estate near the end of the NDC:

'The building was so rundown and you'd be kind of fearful of coming in, there is always people loitering around, the lifts were really rundown. I mean it broke down at least once a week, so you'd end up climbing six flights of stairs. They'd come and fix the lift and then it would break down because it was so old they literally needed replacing. Like my wife, early morning she'd be scared to go down by herself, so I had to take her down and come back up.'

Ahmed's account indicates gendered differences in relation to the potential dangers of public space. His account also includes how the initial promise of regeneration meant the block would receive wholesale refurbishment, including lift replacement. This never happened because his block was switched to demolition (Chapters 4 and 9).

Stella had previously been a tenant at the East Dulwich estate and described conditions there:

'They're neglected. Like my neighbour, when I moved in one of her kitchen windows was broken and it was filled up with a piece of cardboard. It never got mended the whole time I was there. The council didn't fix it, but I think also they [neighbours] didn't know how sort of to insist that the council came and fix it. And in those days, you used to ring up a neighbourhood office for repairs. Working-class people are basically taught that they are bottom of the pile and that they've just got to put up with rubbish. When it comes to housing, if you're brought up in a place which is rough and grim and unkempt and allowed to decay and be dangerous, you don't matter do you? Definitely there were hazards on it [estate], yeah. There was a set of railings by a children's playground that had been sawn off, iron railings that were just sticking up and [indicating height] they were like that. I rang up and I spoke to the neighbourhood office manager about it and he said, "I don't know about that." "Obviously, you don't walk around the estate because it's fucking obvious!"'

As Stella suggests, neglect reinforces symbolic violence. Unlike elite London neighbourhoods where defending the aesthetics of place is a deeply ingrained part of residents' upper-middle-class habitus (for example, objecting to neighbours' property extensions; Webber and Burrows, 2016), working-class tenants 'put up' with what they've got because they feel that they deserve nothing better – as with Stella's neighbours. Disinvestment in estates is a class issue reflecting wider political disengagement and stigmatisation. Estates don't matter because the people who live there 'don't matter' (Skeggs, 2015; Tyler, 2015), an inhuman logic which led to the Grenfell Tower catastrophe (Hodkinson, 2019). Stella eventually transferred away from East Dulwich, due to a combination of housing and neighbour ASB issues.

Valued/devalued places

Northwold residents expressed extensive place attachment to their homes and estate (Chapter 6). Such positive valuation was threatened by devaluation arising from poor maintenance and repairs services, as well as complaints regarding overcrowding. This valuation/devaluation disjunction can be quantified using NES findings. The NES asked about three aspects of residents' place satisfaction: their homes, blocks and the estate, plus satisfaction with the landlord's maintenance of each. Figure 7.1 shows the comparative results at each scale based on aggregate *dissatisfaction* percentages with the place and landlords' maintenance of same ('very dissatisfied' and 'fairly dissatisfied' combined).

Figure 7.1: Northwold estate – residents' dissatisfaction with homes, blocks and estate, and dissatisfaction with landlord's maintenance of each, 2017 (%)

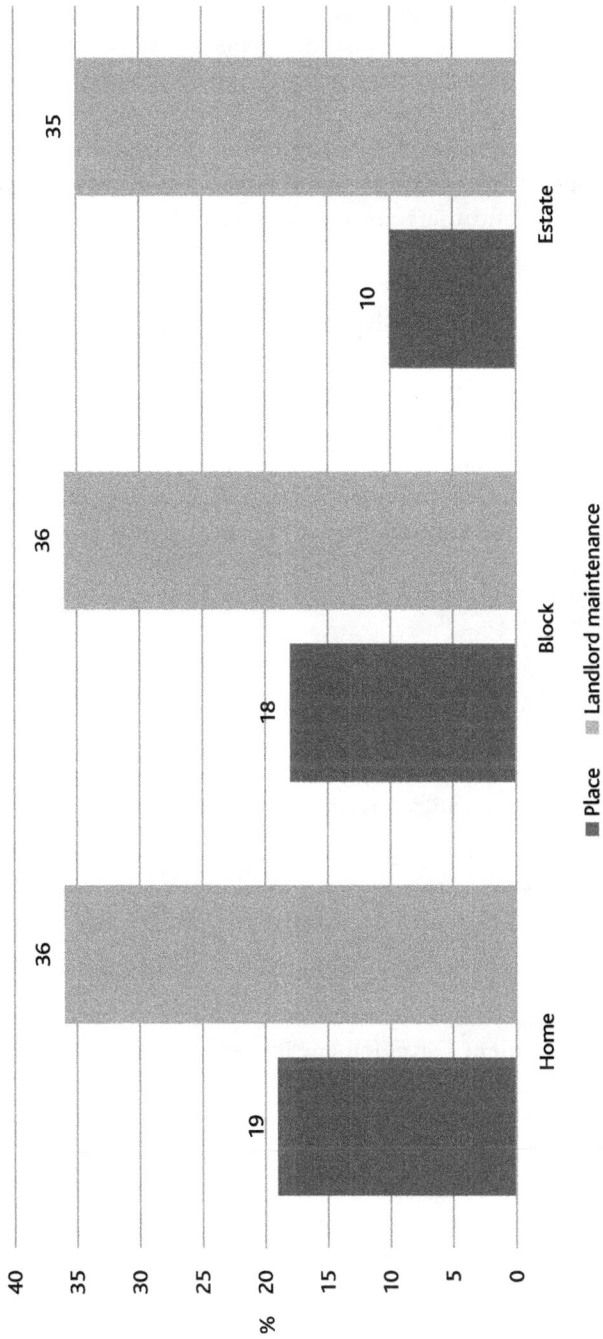

Note: Home data is based on tenants only

Source: Amended from Watt and Allen (2018)

Figure 7.1 shows that around twice as many tenants/residents were dissatisfied with the landlords' maintenance of their homes and blocks than they were with their homes and blocks per se. This differential is even greater – 3.5 times – at the estate scale. The following quotes capture the differential between residents liking their homes/blocks/estate, but having maintenance, repairs and cleaning problems:

'The estate is well-located and generally peaceful. It is not properly maintained by [housing association]. It's in a good location and there are a variety of different people who live here.' (R38)

'It is a good place to live but it could be an excellent place to live if well maintained. Lighting takes ages to be repaired, not cleaned often enough.' (R39, market leaseholder)

'For a long time we have lived here, I am very happy with my neighbours and respect everyone who lives here in the estate. The company doesn't have any care for any houses. They leave the houses without care. Our house has faced a lot of dampness and we've had no help with it.' (R166)

'I love my flat but the maintenance I am very, very upset with.' (R193, RTB leaseholder)

'Lack of maintenance gives the impression it's unloved. (Not by residents who deserve better).' (R478, RTB leaseholder)

Ex-GLC estates

Chapter 3 identified the compulsory transfer of GLC properties to the borough councils during the 1980s. Several official interviewees commented upon how problematic this transfer was. One ex-Senior Local Government Development Professional thought that some of the councils never fully recovered from the GLC transfer, while things deteriorated after the GLC was removed in 1986 since the funding situation worsened even further.

At three of the ex-GLC estates – Woodberry Down, Clapham Park and East Dulwich – I interviewed several long-term tenants who remembered the GLC period and were able to compare it with the borough councils. Narratives of neglect were commonplace – but with the twist that these took a sharp before-and-after binary periodisation – before under the GLC and after under the borough council. The clear consensus was that the GLC maintained the estates in a far better, more proactive manner than the reluctant borough councils, as Towers (2000) argues; see Clapham Film Unit (2010) on Clapham Park. Barbara had lived at one of the seven blocks at Woodberry Down for several decades and was scathing about the current state of her flat and the block generally despite the supposed regeneration (Chapter 12):

> 'It's absolutely awful. The buildings are not maintained properly, they're falling apart, they've just been neglected. When we moved to Hackney Council, that's when the trouble started, it was better when it was the GLC. The plumbing is atrocious. We were told the plumbing was not done properly, it was done in a rush. If it rains, all of the drains come up in the flats. All the flats are damp, I've been flooded out four times just this month where the pipes have gone.'

Barbara was insistent that the buildings themselves were 'solid', but that they had been neglected by Hackney Council:

> 'If these flats were maintained properly, they'd beat anything being put up now. These blocks were really sturdily built, it's a thick wall, but they purposely run it into the ground, the council's not bothered since it went over to the borough. It's not been decorated for 35 years.'

Bob described Hackney Council's poor-quality repairs and maintenance service when he lived in a damp flat at Woodberry Down:

> 'When I went in there [flat], I decorated it all up myself, and three or four months later all the paper in the bedroom come off the wall, and all the ceiling was wet and everything. I kept getting them [Hackney Council] come round and they would look at it and say, "yeah, what can we do?" One bloke looked at it and said, "the pointing needs doing". And he walked away and left it. They [council] never done no repairs.'

Bob gave detailed descriptions of the GLC's and Hackney Council's respective working practices; it was the latter's inefficiency which prompted him to seek out family-based domestic provisioning (Chapter 6):

'When the GLC got disbanded, they made Hackney Council go to court to take it over, cos they didn't want it. And course, as proven, they didn't want it cos they let it go to rack and ruin. They [Hackney Council] never done hardly any repairs and it was always bottom of the list for anything. The GLC, it was a lot better way they worked it. With the GLC you could be in their office, tell them you've got a bit of pipework needs doing or something, and they'd be following you up the road with a little bag and a bit of pipe or whatever. Like "these cupboards, I need a new door, the cover's gone", "I'll send a chippy round". This is Hackney Council – comes round, he's gone [sighs], "that drawer needs a new unit, I can't do that". I said, "I thought you were a chippy?" "I can't make a drawer to go in there." "Fucking hell!" I said, "alright mate, leave it". I was down my brother's, he fucks about with wood, he knocked up a drawer and it worked in there like a treat.'

According to Andrew (Woodberry Down), the GLC "had their act in order" in relation to repairs, maintenance and caretaking services – they "were a good landlord in as far as they had a respect for the properties they managed". By contrast, "Hackney have let the place fall into disrepair". The transfer from the GLC led to neglect which led to regeneration and ultimately to demolition:

'If the GLC had kept going, this [estate] wouldn't have needed that [regeneration], because from day one they [Hackney Council] never done no repair work properly whatsoever, it was all put on the back burner. If they'd have kept the upkeep of this going properly, you wouldn't have needed all this [regeneration].' (Bob)

Long-suffering Clapham Park tenants related an identical before-and-after story vis-à-vis the GLC and Lambeth Council:

'We got central heating, gas fires, new kitchens and bathrooms under the GLC, we were constantly getting repairs done and done again. The estate deteriorated after Lambeth Council took over, we had drugs and prostitution.

Lambeth didn't want to take over our stock, they didn't want to be our landlord, they didn't want to put money into the estate. Lambeth kept saying they hadn't got any money to do maintenance.' (Audrey)

Lambeth did *not* want GLC estates like Clapham Park (Chapter 2). An ex-housing association manager who worked at Clapham Park raised similar concerns to long-term residents:

'It seemed to have suffered from many years of neglect. It had a reputation locally of being heavily squatted. A lot of the squats were let out on short lets, holiday lets, advertised on the continent [laughs]. It had a reputation for that, it had quite a bad reputation as an ex-GLC estate which hadn't had much attention from Lambeth Council. They weren't terribly well geared up for taking over the GLC's estates.'

Bill had lived at Clapham Park during the 1980s. He described how the flats in the west part of the estate were 'high quality' with big rooms, but Lambeth Council "let it go to rack and ruin" after it had taken over from the GLC: "If they'd been looked after they would still be viable. You got a lot of little problems that were allowed to get worse, and if they'd have had a cyclical maintenance programme they wouldn't have half the problems." Sally described the Clapham Park buildings as being "quite sound", but "the whole problem with this estate is pure criminal neglect". Long-term tenants emphasised several aspects of landlord mismanagement which contributed towards Clapham Park becoming in their words, a 'sink estate' by the 1980s-1990s: poor maintenance and cleaning standards, and Lambeth Council's allocations policy: "they dump people here that were real problems from other places" (Sally) – that is, 'problem tenants' (Watt, 2006). Neglect resulted in worsening crime and ASB which was a major factor behind the tenants' groundswell impetus for the NDC (CPP, 2013):

'We were living on an estate that was getting worse and worse and worse. It was a dumping ground for people that nobody else wanted. And that's when we got drug dealers and prostitution. That was when it was Lambeth [council], that was when it was at its worst.' (Audrey)

Of all the estates where I conducted research, it was at Clapham Park that long-term residents were most likely to describe it in negative 'sink estate' terms prior to the arrival of the NDC. Consequently residents initially welcomed this regeneration programme with open arms (Toynbee, 2003; Beaumont, 2006; CPP, 2013), even if the stock transfer and mooted demolition proved highly contentious (Watt, 2009a; Clapham Film Unit, 2010).

Who cares? The diminishing role of caretakers

Long-term tenants pointed to the reduction in caretakers as a factor which both symbolised and enhanced neglect (Woodberry Down Memories Group, 1989; Watt, 2006). Roberts (1988) highlighted the valuable role that caretakers played on estates in terms of routine repairs, cleanliness and maintaining respectability. Older tenants lamented their passing: "When I moved in there were caretakers in more or less every block, now there are none. They kept an eye on what was going on, you know, if kids were causing trouble the caretakers would come out and say 'oy'" (Maggie, East Dulwich). Live-in caretakers were dedicated workers for *their place*, who residents knew and respected, while they disliked the distant bureaucratic replacement system:

> 'You had the porters and the caretakers, and they oversaw things, so you could approach them and ask them, tell them something needed doing. They will either report it to the main office or they would do it for you. Hackney [council] started phasing them out and by then you had nobody on the estate to ask, you had to phone Hackney itself in the borough.' (Marion, Woodberry Down)

While some councils had retained the basic repairs and maintenance services, others had contracted these out to private companies as part of the commercialisation of local authority housing services brought in via Compulsory Competitive Tendering during the 1980s (Cairncross et al, 1997). When I asked an ex-housing officer about outsourcing and erosion of the in-house caretaker service, he replied:

> 'Quite often a caretaker would change a light for an old lady or do some minor repair for someone and not even bother to tell the office. It was really a false economy getting rid of the caretakers. As far as the residents were concerned, they didn't see them as "merely the caretaker", they saw them as "the council person", the person they came to for any kind

of issue. They'd be on first-name terms with residents, very popular with residents. The caretakers generally had more of a conscience doing it, not least because you're going to be going back there next week, unlike the contractor – comes and goes and that's it, they're gone.'

Front-line housing officials

I interviewed six front-line council housing officials whose job was to interface with tenants and their homes.[1] These officials substantiated the housing problems that tenants complained about in their interviews. For example, the dire problems that Southwark tenants had to face (Watt, 2020c), such as infestation and water leaks: "there was a lot of infestation of cockroaches, a lot of bed bugs, a lot of mice, a lot of rats, rodents of all sorts, there was a lot of that in the communal area and also inside the house" (ex-Southwark housing officer). These front-line officials mirrored tenants' views that their flats were inherently solid but had been run down due to inadequate maintenance. When I asked about Northumberland Park, an HFH worker described the quality of the buildings:

'The blocks generally it's all fairly good quality housing in that it's concrete and brick and fairly solid. Some of it has been left, allowed to run down quite a bit. The hallways and some of the roofing stuff, you know the rooves have been allowed to kind of deteriorate, not repaired.'

Photograph 7.1 shows the ceiling of a block of flats at Northumberland Park in 2017 with missing and loose tiles (quite possibly unsafe) indicative of poor maintenance.[2] The worsening service reflects austerity cuts and how preventive work was not being undertaken: "the budget for maintenance has been reduced every year really for the last god knows how long, so it's not so much maintenance as dealing with repairs – firefighting" (HFH worker).

The front-line officials highlighted how their demanding workloads worsened under austerity cuts and restructuring, which impacted on the quality of the service they were able to provide. The HFH worker estimated that his team had been reduced by around half over ten years, while an ex-housing officer complained that the workload "got worse over the years with the outsourcing and the downsizing of staff and the broadening of the patches. With [that number of] properties, you're not going to get around to know everyone". The ex-Southwark

Photograph 7.1: Northumberland Park estate – ceiling in block, 2017

housing officer mentioned earlier was caught in between the Scylla of trying to meet tenants' needs and having repairs and infestation treatment carried out in a timely, efficient manner and the Charybdis of increased workloads:

> 'I was tired of lying as well to the tenants and saying, "I'm logging this problem, I'm saying I'm going to come and get a unit fixed for you and this and that", and it didn't get done. When I come in [to the office], they're pushing it, "yeah we'll do that", and then the big managers don't do anything. And then I'm going back to see this person [tenant] and someone is saying to me, "this is all you do, you come here with your stupid file and you make this note and you bloody go back and drink tea, I don't give a shit, don't come back in my house again" [shouts].'

This worker was extremely frustrated at her incapacity to do a proper caring job for the tenants in her patch:

> 'How then if you're having all these visits, how can you do your work effectively? You couldn't. Because we were understaffed with so much of the flats to visit and when you go

there, I like to treat people with *respect and dignity*. I'm not just going to come into somebody's flat and say "how are you doing, any problems? Okay" [rapidly]. I like to check where the problem, you're telling me what the problem is … they're vulnerable people You have to exercise patience, so you can be in that house with them for maybe 20 or 30 minutes! But they [managers] weren't expecting you to be in the flat for 30 minutes! They wanted you to be in there or five minutes and then run out and go and do another one! How then will you be able to monitor, log the problem? So, it was like a, "are you kidding me?", we didn't have *enough time* to do this.'

Faced by the competing and overwhelming demands, she quit. One of the issues that residents face is high turnover of regeneration staff (Chapter 9).

Contextualising neglect

Narratives of neglect were commonplace, and my own observations confirmed that estates needed maintenance reinvestment and upgrading in terms of homes, facilities (such as community halls), public space and general infrastructure. Nevertheless, their overall physical condition was not at the same appalling level that was prevalent during the 1980s and 1990s, which was also manifested via many thousands of empty 'void' properties including at 'hard-to-let' estates (see inter alia Harrison, 1983; Forman, 1989; Green, 1997; Jacobs, 1999; Watt, 2001). This was the nadir period when London's estates had suffered from nearly two decades of Thatcherite disinvestment (Chapters 2 and 3).

Since then some genuine improvements to the existing social housing stock and to estates have been made, albeit in a laggard, spatially uneven fashion (Chapter 3). Reinvestment has occurred via the DHP, through estate regeneration schemes that incorporated refurbishment, as well as through the extra investment that stock transfers generated (Pawson and Mullins, 2010; Belotti, 2016; Hodkinson, 2019; Tunstall, 2020). Such improvements have genuinely benefited residents who remained in situ. Maggie, for example, appreciated her new boiler, sinks, and bath lift due to internal refurbishment works at East Dulwich:

'When the council officer came and examined the bathroom he noticed that I'd put a handle on the side of the bath, because I found it a little bit difficult getting in and out of the bath, and he got in touch with the occupational

therapy department of Southwark Council and as a result
I have a bath lift – brilliant.'

Previous rounds of regeneration also improved estates' infrastructure, for example at Northumberland Park in Tottenham (Dillon and Fanning, 2011). 'Unpopular', low-demand estates and empty properties are also generally less significant than during the 1990s (Tunstall, 2020).

Domestic self/family provisioning has also made a difference to home interiors (Chapter 6). Tenants have not been passive in the face of widespread public sector disinvestment and landlord neglect. On the contrary, they have strived to improve their homes themselves, either by modernising them or by undertaking the repairs that their landlords either failed to do or only did in a tardy fashion. As Pahl (1984) notes, such DIY is dependent on having the right resources, tools and know-how. By no means all tenants were able to engage in such domestic and familial provisioning; some lacked the necessary equipment, economic capital or requisite social capital – typically poor single people living by themselves. Nevertheless, such domestic and familial provisioning represents one of the great subterranean examples of working-class agency in the face of state inadequacy. This is something that has been inadequately recognised in structural accounts of marginalisation (Wacquant, 2008).

The result of these factors is that estates are generally less physically rundown than they were during the 1980s and 1990s, including the period that I conducted research on Camden council housing (Watt, 2001). This does not however mean that residents' 'narratives of neglect' are exaggerated and bear no relationship to reality (Chapters 2, 3 and 4). The housing stock is also ageing, which requires constant reinvestment to counter it, as with any housing. In addition, the 2012 HRA restructuring means that many councils remain starved of adequate maintenance funding (Swindon Tenants Campaign Group, 2016), such that, all too often, 'fire-fighting' remains the dominant modus operandi.

Transient places: the Right to Buy and private landlordism

London's estates have changed in one important manner since I did my earlier research in Camden during the 1990s – they have become more transient places. The main explanation lies in the ripple effects of the RTB. While the RTB encouraged roots and residential stability by acting as a buy-to-stay mechanism for owner-stayers (Chapter 6), it paradoxically facilitated routes out of the estates as RTB properties have been sold and resold, often to private landlords (Copley, 2014, 2019). Harry perfectly articulates the dual nature of the RTB's impact on estates:

> 'For some people who were the original people, it [RTB] was obviously positive. They were able to buy their homes and they were able to live in their homes and they were able to stop paying rent. But over the years, it has led to its logical conclusion which is people have bought and so it becomes a private thing. If you've a right-to-buy, then you've a right-to-sell, and if you've a right-to-sell you've a right-to-sell to anyone. And so it's become an investment opportunity, which isn't what social housing was all about. I still call it council housing.'

The notion of the RTB as a 'right-to-sell' and 'investment opportunity' has been exacerbated by its commercialisation due to company involvement, but also due to regeneration itself (ALG, 2003), as happened at several research estates (Chapter 4). Such commercialisation feeds through into increased private landlordism. The latter has expanded via several distinct processes:

1. RTB owner remains in situ but sublets rooms;
2. RTB owner retains the property but moves out and becomes an absentee landlord by renting it privately or to family members;
3. RTB owner sells the property to an investor landlord;
4. family members inherit a RTB property upon the death of the owner and then become absentee landlords themselves;
5. family members inherit a RTB property upon the death of the owner and then sell it to an investor landlord.

The net result is the creation of a new 'housing class' (Rex and Moore, 1967) of absentee investor landlords whose sole connection to the properties and estates is one of economic value, as distinct from RTB owner-stayers who have social and psychological valuations and place attachments.

The RTB has therefore been Janus-faced in terms of its effects on place and residential mobility at London estates. This Janus-like quality has received insufficient attention from accounts of the RTB from the anti-gentrification perspective which focuses on owner-stayers who are aggrieved (rightly) at the prospect of demolition and displacement (Hubbard and Lees, 2018; Elliott-Cooper et al, 2020).

Besides enhancing *roots* and residential longevity among owner-stayers, the RTB also encouraged *routes out* by facilitating two sets of spatial mobilities: first suburban out-migration on the part of the original buyers (Watt et al, 2014); and second the rapid comings and goings of private renters and more recently Airbnb guests. Harry estimated that around half the flats in his block at Regents Park estate were sold under the RTB, but that most of the latter were rented out – to students and subcontracting precarious workers – either by the original owners as sublets or by absentee landlords, resulting in greater population churn: "a lot of the leaseholder places, it's not just students that are transient, it's even the workers that are transient. So is there is no nascent community in leaseholder homes. It's becoming one of those high-turnover areas which is what inner cities used to be".

Marion had lived at Woodberry Down all her life and described the RTB impacts there: "You might see people and say 'hello' to them, if you knew them by face, but you didn't know them, know them. Most of them have been bought and sold, bought and sold, bought and sold, so you *lose* the estates." Local social capital diminishes as estates have become more transient, anonymous places: 'there is reason to believe that the Right to Buy has destabilised some council estate neighbourhoods and damaged the capacity of these areas to function as communities' (Jones and Murie, 2006: 214).

Not only has the social fabric of estates changed due to the RTB, but there are two knock-on effects on their physical fabric. The first effect relates to poor maintenance from both leaseholders and absentee landlords, which in turn impacts upon adjacent social tenants. One tenant at the Aylesbury described how she had "water pouring down the wall due to private tenants next door" (meeting, 2015). Housing officials highlighted poor maintenance from cash-strapped leaseholders: "We get an awful lot of cases where they're a leaseholder who have a leak in their flat which then floods the [council tenants] flats below, and the leaseholder is unwilling or incapable of getting that repaired because they don't have the money" (HFH worker). Being unable to liaise with absentee landlords is another issue: "You've got to talk to the people in the flat above to say, 'oh you know you've got a leak', and they say 'well we'll tell the landlord when he comes back from Spain or Torquay or whatever', they may not be even around" (HFH worker). The second RTB knock-on effect is how some absentee landlords modify and subdivide their properties into HMOs. As Maria (Churchill Gardens) said, "flats are being reconfigured from two-bed flats to four bedsits", which caused long-term residents like her to be concerned about health and safety, not least fire safety in post-Grenfell London.

Disorderly places

Crime and anti-social behaviour

In their analysis of housing and the 'disorderly city', Atkinson and Millington (2019: 228) show how "areas of public housing (estates and projects) have long been seen as criminal areas". As they argue, this association is by no means straightforward, given how it is bound up with complex issues of urban poverty, stigmatisation and *perceptions* of crime and disorder, perceptions which are often racialised (Gunter, 2010; Romyn, 2019). Social disorder (vandalism, littering, public drunkenness, noisy neighbours, and so on) – variously termed 'incivilities' or 'anti-social behaviour' – is especially prone to culturally differential signifiers of what is orderly/disorderly, such that "perceptions of incivilities and actual incivilities need not overlap" (Persak and Di Ronco, 2018: 334). Crime rates and fear of crime rates also need not necessarily correlate, as in the case of the Aylesbury estate (Watt, 2020c). The focus in this section is residents' *perceptions* of crime and disorder, rather than statistical crime rates.

Residents expressed concerns about crime and ASB at the research estates, typically in relation to low-level disorder such as youths 'hanging around', neighbour disputes regarding excessive noise and dirt, and fly-tipping. The sight of 'youths hanging around' in estates' public spaces is a perennial London issue, but has worsened under austerity cuts given that 81 youth centres have been closed across the city since 2012 (Perera, 2019). Fly-tipping occurred at Northwold (Watt and Allen, 2018; Photograph 7.2): "mattresses, tyres, bags of rubble, furniture, sofas. But it's not just residents, the tyres wouldn't be residents, that would be a local garage, it's used as a dumping ground by local businesses" (Caroline). As Caroline said, "it can be there for weeks and weeks unless we make a fuss" to the landlord.

Drug taking/dealing in public spaces (stairwells, landings, and so on) was also mentioned at some estates, mainly in relation to 'weed', although occasional reference was made to hard drugs such as crack and heroin: "this is a terrible area for drugs, everything, heroin, crack cocaine round here" (Dave, Northumberland Park). Other long-term Northumberland Park residents, however, thought that the estate's drug problems had diminished:

Photograph 7.2: Northwold estate – fly-tipping next to no fly-tipping sign, 2017

'Twenty years ago this place was full of crackheads, we had cops in riot vans and they used to put their headlight on to the crack house behind ours to try and intimidate them. There was a lot of people with habits, but this place has changed a lot in the last 10–15 years There's been a concerted effort on who's allowed to be a council tenant by Haringey Council. All of that's virtually stopped. There's still kids dealing, but they leave me alone.' (Frank)

While adults mentioned youths 'hanging around', including taking/ dealing drugs, Frank's comment – 'they leave me alone' – was echoed on several estates in the sense that what young people did had limited impact on non-related proximate adults. As an older woman, Winifred felt safe at Northwold due to knowing the local youths and negotiating a mutually beneficial tolerance:

'I mean I can come in and out any time of night, and even if I do see a gang of youths, they're not going to hurt me.

I actually know some of the youths. There was a while they were hanging around outside, and if they were making too much noise I would just say, "guys, can you please turn the noise down". "Oh sorry, sorry!" They were out there dealing. They don't want to upset you because they don't want you calling the police.'

Bilal had grown up at the Ocean estate. Although he had moved away a few years ago, he still worked there, and his parents lived there. He described the gang/civilian, youth/adult divisions regarding whether his parents ever felt afraid:

'My dad's lived here all his life and he still walks around, there's nothing to be afraid of. The only thing that you are afraid of is gang fear. They fight their own, they don't start with civilians, they've got their own groups of gangs, someone's coming into deal in their own area and things like that. But they are not going to go and start fighting with families and residents. They are the dark side of their life, we live our own life.'

Burglaries, robberies and muggings were occasionally referred to, although these were more *heard about* than experienced. Gun and knife crime occurred at some estates, but these were rare events. Gary noted how the Heygate was "nothing out of the ordinary" crime-wise, despite its media-fuelled 'sink estate' reputation:

'There was never any notorious crime on the estate. I mean there are some estates that there's a shooting. There was a notorious shooting in Peckham North estate, it sort of sealed its reputation. The Heygate never had anything like that, as far as I know [laughs]. I can't really remember any really nasty crime. My brother got mugged once walking on to the estate. So we had the usual kinds of London crimes – occasional break-ins, occasional anti-social behaviour, loud music and all that kind of stuff, but nothing out of the ordinary.' (Gary)

As my analysis of the *South London Press* and *Southwark News* indicates, both the Heygate and Aylesbury 'sink estates' were indeed 'nothing out of the ordinary' by the standards of south-east London, an inner-city area with long-term associations with poverty and crime (Robson, 2000; Watt, 2020c).

Crime and ASB were prominent concerns at certain estates such as Northumberland Park and Marlowe Road (PPCR Associates, 2016). As I interviewed Leroy on his balcony at Northumberland Park, he pointed out the young men on motor scooters dealing drugs:

> 'If you come around here in the morning it is so *peaceful*, it is lovely round here. At night it's quiet, but the only problem is, because it's dark and because it's quiet you've got these little babes come around and they do their rubbish on bikes – like that one there [points]. They'll come around on their bikes and do their little crap.'

When Sonia took me for a walking tour of Marlowe Road estate, one of the local shops was boarded up and had been broken into several times. While both Leroy and Sonia considered crime at and near their respective estates to be a genuine problem, they rejected any notion that they lived in a crimogenic, no-go area which warranted a 'sink estate' label that might justify demolition (which both were firmly against). Leroy was adamant that Northumberland Park, and especially his balcony, was well cared for by residents, even if not by officials:

> 'But in reality, round here most people are *decent*. You can see this place is nice and clean, *we* clean out here, we who live up here, we keep it clean. The security doors are supposed to be un-openable except if you've got a fob, but people come up there, they smoke their drugs, they do what they're doing. You tell the police about it, you phone up the councillors and you let them know, but we don't see no changes.'

Leroy (black Caribbean) was annoyed by the estate's 'ghetto' reputation, a reputation with racist connotations:

> 'Bare [slang for "a lot of"] people are saying it's a ghetto. It's not a ghetto! What ghetto do you know that has houses like this? A ghetto by definition is a rundown area that only certain people live in. Yeah, alright, it may have a kind of taste of a ghetto because it's mainly black people down there. But it's not a ghetto, because it's not got that connotation of being run down. This place is not rundown, it just needs a bit of TLC [tender loving care], that's all it needs.'

As we walked around Marlowe Road estate, Sonia joked that "did I know that I was walking on the most dangerous road in the country?" She was referring to a recent story in *The Sun* (2018) newspaper which painted a lurid story regarding the area – "WAR-THAMSTOW …: the UK's most dangerous street" – which bore no relation to her daily life.

If crime remained a live issue at certain estates, others were no longer regarded as 'rough' places to live, reflective of general crime reduction since the 1990s and specific crime-control measures (Tunstall, 2020). During the 1990s, the Carpenters estate had a rough reputation: "it was used by people from outside, kids would come down in stolen cars and stuff and they'd pinch cars on the estate and burn them out" (Lee). Although Ernie generally had a low opinion of Robin Wales (the long-standing Mayor of Newham), he praised him for his crime-control initiatives: "We were a victim on this estate of dumped cars. When Wales became the elected mayor, he promised he would clear this borough of dumped cars and he's done that." Ernie proudly described the Carpenters as "the most crime-free estate in the whole of Newham". Robbie moved into one of the Carpenters tower blocks at the end of the 1990s and had experienced no crime during the intervening 17-year period:

> 'Got stuck in the lift once, but that's about it, no crime. I found out that it had had a bit of a reputation before, but it had really quietened down. It was good, it's okay to live here, it's been a very good estate to live on to be quite honest. Ever since I've been there, no real problems. I think they had a period when there were three burglaries, but that's nothing really.'

Robbie checked with the police regarding his estate's low-crime status and the official crime data also support this view.[3] Mahir had lived on the Carpenters estate for 25 years. He described it as a very friendly place to live and wasn't aware of any crime issues, although there had been "some nuisance from kids of my age [when he was younger], but they've moved away or grown up".

Long-term Cressingham Gardens residents acknowledged that the estate had drug and prostitution issues in the past, but that crime-control measures had removed these – at least from their neighbourhood. Jeanette recollected when she bought her house in the 1990s: "The estate was very rough, there was a murder just before I arrived. Prostitution underneath in the garages, drug dealing, burglaries every five minutes. So it wasn't the best place to be at the time, but obviously now it's all changed." A report by Social Life (2015: 18) found that "there is disproportionately lower crime on Cressingham Gardens than for the rest of Tulse Hill", while fear of crime was also low. Bill mentioned how Cressingham Gardens "was slightly wild" when he moved in around the same time as Jeanette, but that subsequently the TRA had pressurised the council and police to reduce prostitution:

> 'You used to get a lot of prostitutes taking their clients there [car park]. When we managed to get the council to do stuff, it was easy to improve, it was easy to move the prostitutes on. There was a lot of pressure to do it – and most of it was silly little things, the sealing off of the car parks, it took them a day.'

Bill is highlighting the effectiveness of relatively straightforward environmental crime-control measures which made a huge difference to residents' safety and well-being (as with dumped cars at the Carpenters). Such initiatives were also effective at some of the NDC estates such as Clapham Park (CPP, 2013) and the Aylesbury (Watt, 2020c).

In her ethnographic research on a London 'problem estate' with above-average crime levels, Janet Foster (1995: 580) argued that: 'Crime had not reached a point where tenants perceived it as a major factor in reducing their quality of life and did not constitute a "problem" in the way that other issues like the poor housing service and other structural problems on Riverside [estate] did.' Foster's measured conclusion was written during the 1990s, a period when not only did London's estates look much rougher than today (burnt-out cars, graffiti, broken windows, and so on), but one of greater crime overall (Tunstall, 2020). Despite this, Foster's conclusions remain remarkably pertinent to my own findings: that crime and disorder at London estates is not an overwhelming problem and is less of a problem than basic housing services such as repairs and maintenance.

Vulnerable tenants and ASB

London estates are inclusionary social spaces given that they disproportionately house the city's vulnerable populations such as the elderly, disabled, people with chronic physical and mental illnesses, drug and alcohol dependencies, lone parents, and so on (Chapter 5). This inclusion partly stems from the 1977 homeless legislation and the notion of 'priority need'. It also relates to the closure of the mental hospitals and the move towards care in the community. This policy, which took place gradually from the 1960s and then sped up from the mid-1980s onwards, has contributed either directly or indirectly towards more vulnerable people entering social housing (Tomlinson, 1991; Jones, 1996). Interviewees commented on the presence of vulnerable groups on their estates with various mixtures of empathy, tolerance and wariness:

> 'These days, to get housing as a tenant you've got to have one problem or another. So a lot of them on this estate, we've got a high elderly population, we've also got quite a high single mum population, we've got a high population of people with mental health problems, things like that.' (Steve, Cressingham Gardens)

> 'So you get like older people, or people who are unemployed, people who are isolated, there's a lot of people with mental health issues here.' (Michelle, Northumberland Park)

> 'I know one woman who was on very heavy drugs. Quite a few single people living on their own were eccentric, who used to come to tenants' meetings and just be a bit mad – "characters".' (Stella, East Dulwich)

The presence of vulnerable populations (invariably poor) on already deprived estates is socially inclusionary at the urban scale but has had two paradoxical effects. First, it has exacerbated estates' territorial stigmatisation as 'problem places full of problem people' (Johnston and Mooney, 2007), and second it has led to internal neighbourhood tensions between vulnerable 'problem tenants' and other residents (Watt, 2006; Rosbrook-Thompson and Armstrong, 2018). Research suggests that 'perpetrators of ASB are often vulnerable and usually poor, that they often have mental health problems and community care needs and may themselves be victims of ASB' (Jones et al, 2006: 179). Several interviewees mentioned how the placement of ex-mental patients on their estates led to ASB, and they queried how much genuine community care was taking place. Audrey described this situation with reference to pre-NDC Clapham Park, including how vulnerable tenants were exploited by drug dealers:

> 'It [ASB] was also made worse by Maggie [Thatcher] saying she was going to close down all the mental hospitals and everybody was going to be "care in the community", and we had all these poor souls being dumped onto the estate. And that was exactly what they were doing to them, was just *dumping* them and forgetting them. A lot of them were

causing mayhem because they were off the medication. It's not their fault, but nobody was watching them, nobody was coming to see if they were alright. The dealers were taking advantage of them and using their houses as crack houses and dealing from them. This was *extremely* vulnerable people. There was *nothing* in place for them. They were just sent out onto these estates and told to get on with life.'

Similarly at East Dulwich: "[Southwark Council] have a tendency to move in people who have just been let go [discharged] from the Maudsley mental hospital. There were some horrible tales, they never had any support" (Maggie).

Local authorities also have a greater welfare role than either private or housing association landlords. As an ex-housing officer explains, tenants' vulnerability, ASB and local authority caring functions interweave together:

'There is one guy [tenant] that I know, the flat he's in, he's ripped out the electrics on three separate occasions, because he's got schizophrenic delusions about something or other. I mean there was a high threshold of evidence to go down before notice of possession. It has to be very high, so there are people who do get away with a level of anti-social behaviour which you wouldn't see in a housing association or certainly in the private sector. They [specialist staff] try and provide advice, tenancy support. There's a lot of tolerance for it [ASB] that you wouldn't see elsewhere.'

By 'elsewhere', the officer means the PRS and increasingly in the housing association sector where commercial rather than welfare imperatives take precedence.

Stigmatised places

As discussed in the Introduction (and earlier in this chapter), Wacquant's (2008) territorial stigmatisation framework has relevance to UK social housing estates (Hancock and Mooney, 2013; Crossley and Slater, 2014; Kallin and Slater, 2014). Watt (2008: 347) has also highlighted stigmatisation on the basis of housing tenure directed against council tenants: 'the contemporary hegemonic discourse regarding council housing is that its occupants constitute a socially excluded, economically inactive and politically apathetic "underclass"'.

Territorial and tenurial stigmatisation are produced by politicians, non-resident outsiders, and especially the mass media: 'longstanding association between social housing and danger persists in dystopian and apocalyptic fictions and crime dramas. Council estates are never safe' (Sborgi, 2017). These stigmatisations not only reflect and reinforce the symbolic devaluation of estates as working-class spaces, but they also have racist connotations regarding the 'lawless' black inner-city ghetto (Millington, 2011; Romyn, 2019).

Interviewees occasionally remarked on how family, friends and work colleagues made disparaging remarks about where they lived and how they were cautious about visiting them at their homes. Residents' own responses to stigmatisation were complex, even within individuals. Danni objected to territorial/tenure stigmatisation and proudly reeled off her neighbours' educational achievements:

'The image that follows around people who live in council estates is always one of down and outs, people who are not working. I mean we've got neighbours whose children have gone on to do their masters' [degree]. Her son for example is off to university. Tracy's son also went off [to university], my ones will soon be because my daughter is doing her A levels. So we are people who have the same beliefs just like anyone else who owns a property.'

At the same time, Danni internalised the stigma since she had been reluctant to invite work colleagues to her flat because of youths hanging around the estate and smoking "marijuana or whatever they were smoking, that horrible smell". If internalising stigma as a form of shame occurred, others shrugged it off, made fun of it – or even challenged it, as seen in the case of the 'notorious' Aylesbury estate (Watt, 2020c). Stan had lived on Northumberland Park in Tottenham all his life. Although Stan was himself critical of the estate's poor appearance (due to inadequate maintenance) and youths 'hanging around', he was also disdainful of outsiders' snobbery:

'People say "how do you live in Tottenham?", but it's not as bad as it used to be. You had the riots in 1985 and 2011, but things have picked up since then. You get a snobby attitude from people who live outside London or Tottenham. People in Enfield for example say to me, "oh, you live in a Tottenham in a council estate". I take that kind of stuff for granted. This is home for me.'

Long-term experience of living on an estate and thereby developing an insider perspective outweighed outsider stereotypical place images: 'the more profoundly inside you are the stronger is this identity with the place' (Relph, 1976: 49). Bonnie had moved to East Dulwich estate during the 1990s and developed a strong sense of place attachment, despite its reputation:

> 'Everyone said, "oh, you've moved there, bad reputation". But actually I kind of took to it straight away. I loved the space and the people there I thought were generally friendly. Yeah there were some noise issues with my neighbours underneath, domestic issues. But in general, the years I was there I was happy.'

Mass media stigmatisation has intensified under austerity conditions via poverty porn TV programmes such as *Benefits Street* (ITV), which discursively meld social housing estates together with class hatred stereotypes about welfare claimants and 'skivers' (Hancock and Mooney, 2013; Crossley and Slater, 2014; Tyler, 2015). Such media stigmatisation is challenged by tenants (Turner, 2018) and has even led to the creation of *Benefit to Society*, a nationwide campaign that aims to tackle social housing stereotyping: 'The media tends to focus on the female single parent on the council estate, claiming benefits, or on male juvenile criminality. These stereotypes are portrayed on TV, film, journalism and even often by politicians' (Benefit to Society, 2017: 7). As an unemployed lone parent, Natalie was only too aware of the multiple stigmatisations that she was subject to: "you just get branded as 'a single mum on a council estate, on benefits'". As Natalie says, this stigma – encompassing welfare, family type and housing tenure – is just 'automatic' since it reflects the hegemonic nature of estate place myths and media poverty porn.

While Natalie tried to reject stigmatisation, it nevertheless intruded in a twin-pronged manner which managed to taint her own sense of self-worth – reflective of symbolic violence. This occurred not only due to media representation, but also as a result of *media production*, which the academic literature on territorial and tenurial stigmatisation says little about. Natalie lived on West Hendon estate, which has been used as a set for *EastEnders*, the popular BBC TV soap opera. She refers to the gap between outsider place images and her own experiences of living on the estate:

'My kids are saying to me, "mummy, why are *EastEnders* here and the film crew?" I said, "because it's a lovely place" [laughs]. And then my sister who lives in Devon and she's never seen here. I rang her and said, "that's where I live, on *EastEnders*", and she was like, "Oh my god, what a shithole this place is". Because it is from the outside. But they [*EastEnders*] use it for their crime scenes and murder scenes, those sort of scenes. So, it automatically gives out to the nation, "yeah you don't want to live somewhere like that" [laughs] ... that sort of thing because what they're saying is, "yeah it's scummy".'

As Natalie says, "it's advertised the council estate, and they wonder why people have got that vision of a council estate". Not only did the soap opera promote the 'sink estate' place myth, but its physical production threatened to confirm Natalie's devalued social position and location – as living in a 'scummy place'.

TV/film crews were prominent at the Heygate estate, largely because the ITV police drama *The Bill* routinely used it as the location for their shots of police chasing villains (Walker, 2010). Olive lived at the Heygate for over 30 years:

'When we had *The Bill* on our estate they loved coming there and at that time they used to pay us, just the TRA – I mean this was in the early 1980s – £200 every time they came on site. They were very good, they gave us plenty of notice and they apologised.'

If Olive's experience of living on a TV set was benign, others regarded it as intrusive and insulting – and hence indicative of the symbolic devaluation of homes and neighbourhoods. Prior to being displaced, Ria had lived at the Carpenters estate for nearly 40 years. At one point, *The Bill* TV crime programme was being filmed there, although, "no one knew what was going on, they [council] didn't tell us anything, no housing officer came, nobody told us anything" (Ria). I interviewed Ria in the presence of Bridget, a Carpenters neighbour:

Ria: 'Do you remember the one they did with throwing the tellies out [laughs]? I was standing there on the balcony and they were throwing some tellies out the window.'

Bridget: 'The thing is they were filming [*The Bill*], but nobody knew they were filming, and tellies were coming out the windows.'

Ria: 'I was standing on the balcony when all these things come flying down, and I'm hearing the bloke downstairs is shouting, "stand back!", and I'm looking over the balcony and he's going [Ria demonstrates wild gesticulating]. And I'm thinking, "what are you telling me to step back for, this is my flat?" He came up and he said, "Oh we're doing a scene, could you keep off the balcony?", and I'm thinking, "you've got a cheek to tell me to keep off my own balcony!" That was when I realised what was going on. They had the cheek, when they had finished doing that, they came with £20 in an envelope [compensation].'

When I asked whether TVs had ever been thrown out of windows, Ria vociferously replied: "*no, no*, this is it, *nothing* like that has ever happened". The only time in decades that TVs were thrown out of the windows was when a TV programme was being made, a telling illustration of the gap between mass media place myths and residents' lived experiences of place. Ria and Bridget found the filming spatially disruptive since their ability to use their own homes and neighbourhood was neutered. Such a disrespectful approach to a multi-ethnic working-class space would be neither contemplated by TV companies nor tolerated by the residents of London's elite and upper middle-class neighbourhoods where hyper-strict codes of conduct are rigorously enforced (Webber and Burrows, 2016). By contrast, media-orchestrated symbolic devaluation is casual in an east London council estate (Skeggs, 2015). Because of its intrusiveness via the film crews, such stigmatisation is harder to shrug off and more hurtful (as in Natalie's case) than casual remarks from outsiders. The mass media presence on estates and associated territorial stigmatisation escalates once regeneration gets under way (Chapter 9).

Conclusion

This chapter has focused on how estates have become *devalued places,* much of which can be causally attributed to neoliberal and austerity policies (Chapter 13). Material housing conditions form the key component of this devaluation. These have been given insufficient academic attention, either in Wacquant's advanced marginality approach (see Watt, 2020c), or by the anti-gentrification perspective (Kallin and Slater, 2014; Lees, 2014; Lees and Ferreri, 2016). Overcrowded families living in small flats were unable to transfer to larger properties because the social housing sector has silted up, trapping them in dwellings that no longer felt like home. Although their properties and estates generally were physically sound and solid, they had been neglected due to inadequate repairs and maintenance services. Landlord shifts (from the GLC to the reluctant borough councils) and managerialist restructuring (reductions in caretakers and outsourcing) also contributed to tenants feeling that they were living in a deteriorating, more impersonal environment. Interviews with front-line housing officials conformed tenants' housing-related problems, problems, which have been exacerbated by austerity. Due to this, a minority of tenants felt un-homed because they were living in overcrowded and/or poor-quality flats.

The RTB is Janus-faced in its impacts, because the right to buy also grants the right to sell. London estates have become more transient places because of the increasing presence of private tenants and Airbnb guests resulting from the growth in private landlordism due to the RTB. Mobility flows – in and out – have increased and strained estates' social fabric. Crime and disorder were important issues on some estates, less so on others. The presence of vulnerable tenants has contributed to ASB-related issues, although the effectiveness of community care is an important mediating factor. More broadly, basic crime-control measures have made a significant difference to residents' well-being. Finally, estates were symbolically devalued via territorial and tenurial stigmatisation which has been exacerbated by austerity and poverty porn TV programmes.

Despite all these problems, there was no mass desire to exit their homes and estates, unlike in the US projects (Wacquant, 2008). Of the nearly 180 estate interviewees, only around one twelfth had either left their estates prior to regeneration or had made firm plans to do so, and even then, half of these moves/planned moves were housing related. Let us now turn to the beginnings of regeneration when residents are consulted about the future of their estates.

PART III

Living through regeneration

8

Beginnings

This chapter examines the beginnings of regeneration including consultation. It briefly reviews the impetus for regeneration, and then goes on to analyse two examples of early-stage regeneration: the first is the long-running Canning Town/Custom House scheme in Newham, and the second is Northwold estate in Hackney. The consultation process is then examined in depth from the perspective of residents, followed by a briefer analysis of professionals' perspectives. The final lengthy section teases out the complexities of residents' responses to comprehensive redevelopment involving extensive demolition.

Introducing regeneration

Residents are by no means necessarily opposed to regeneration *per se*. Given that their homes and estates had been neglected, unsurprisingly many welcomed regeneration *of some kind* – at least initially, as noticeable at the NDC estates. The immediate impetus for regeneration has primarily originated with councils and housing associations in a top-down manner, either by responding to central government regeneration programmes (for example SRB, NDC, and so on), or by addressing their own regeneration agendas which have latterly involved 'solving' London's housing crisis via estate densification. Somewhat less often, regeneration has been prompted by bottom-up pressure as residents have lobbied the council to do something – anything – to improve the quality of their homes and estates other than merely reactive repairs. For example, in 2003 Carpenters residents formed a protest group called 'Tower Block Action Group' which staged a series of actions to highlight the problems they were having, including an infestation of ants, asbestos, poor repairs and lack of safety (Strauss, 2007). This protest helped to prompt the long-running and still unresolved regeneration scheme at this estate (Chapters 4 and 12). Another example is Bacton estate in Camden, where residents approached an architectural firm to improve their blocks (Wainwright, 2016; Karakusevic Carson Architects, 2017).

A statutory part of estate regeneration in England is consultation, which is theoretically supposed to give residents genuine input into what happens to their homes and neighbourhoods. Having *any* consultation can be considered as progressive given how regeneration can proceed without it in certain countries (Porter and Shaw, 2009; Morris, 2019). International studies have, however, critically noted that consultation regarding estate regeneration has tended to be tokenistic in nature, effectively operating at the lower end of Arnstein's 'ladder of participation' (Teernstra and Pinkster, 2015; Gustavsson and Elander, 2016). Research on the Aylesbury and Heygate estates has exposed the problematic nature of the consultation process (Lees, 2014; Lees and Ferrari, 2016).

Canning Town and Custom House (Newham)

Estate regeneration aims are typically vague and opaque, especially in the early stages when residents are asked to consider planning 'options'. Vagueness and opacity were prominent in the Canning Town/Custom House regeneration project in Newham which began in 2001 and is still ongoing. Disillusionment soon set in, despite initial enthusiasm, as two engaged tenants recounted:

> 'Originally we all agreed with the idea because some of the area did need regenerating.' (Kathleen)

> 'I was all for the regeneration, I've never been against progress. We need the places [homes], but I think it's not so much regeneration as the people who's running it and misleading the people.' (Norman)

The scheme became controversial early on and the Custom House and Canning Town Action Group (CHCTAG) was created, whose chair, Alan Craig, ran a local community centre. Resident opposition to the scheme was not about being anti-regeneration per se; CHCTAG members 'do not oppose the regeneration of our area. We are however concerned about how it is being carried out. ... Our group was formed a year ago to address fears that a large scale decant was about to take place to provide prime land for property speculators.'[1]

Kathleen and Norman became increasingly concerned about whether regeneration would genuinely benefit local council tenants like themselves and their neighbours. Norman's disillusionment was crystallised when a politician visited the area to talk about the regeneration:

'He said that there was a shortage of land to the west [London] for the rich basically, so they had to move further to the east beyond Tower Hill. Well that is what's happening, they are coming from the west to the east but pushing the local community out. They're pushing them out through higher rents in their area, basically making it impossible for the local people to live.'

Residents' concerns at Canning Town/Custom House are typical of those raised at all the research estates – that:

- information is insufficient and unclear;
- the consultation process is top-down;
- existing homes will be demolished;
- the existing community will be broken up and scattered;
- new homes will be prohibitively expensive;
- the result will be housing for property investment rather than meeting current residents' needs.

There were also two further issues at Canning Town/Custom House. First, council tenants were worried that regeneration would involve a change of landlord away from the local authority, and second that they would not get the type of property that they wanted – which was houses, not flats. These concerns are reflected in these two newspaper extracts, the first of which was a report following a consultation attended by 'around 90 people' out of up to 1,900 affected homes (*Newham Recorder*, 2002):

> Despite the council's soothing noises, fury still rages over how the redevelopment area may change. Though protests are not as intense as when the scheme was revealed 13 months ago, locals are frightened of higher rents for refurbished homes that might also be under different landlord control. Residents also fear the neighbourly feel of Canning Town and Custom House will be lost. (*Newham Recorder*, 2002; see also Cattell, 2001)
>
> Nobody is against improving the area. But knowing how the council thinks and builds, we will be a concrete city. It makes me laugh when they pretend to consult the tenants of these areas. What we would like to see is houses or bungalows with gardens and garages, streets and avenues,

not alleyways. But will we get them? […] The area has been
run down through the council's neglect.[2]

Residents' concerns regarding new homes and landlords were
prominent in the results of a 2001 survey of 1,677 households that
Newham Council commissioned (Kwest Research, 2001). Eighty-two
per cent of respondents were council tenants, and 86 per cent lived in
flats or maisonettes. The results confirm that most respondents (81 per
cent) preferred to live in a house or bungalow. When asked what their
first housing tenure choice was if they had to move, 68 per cent wanted
to either remain or become a council tenant, while 6 per cent wanted
to move to a housing association property and just 1 per cent wanted to
rent privately. In fact, 78 per cent of council tenants wanted to remain
as council tenants while none opted for private renting. These figures
reinforce the argument that it's the PRS which is the tenure of last
resort, *not* council renting (Chapter 5). Two thirds of the sample was
willing to consider a home outside the area. However, when asked for
their first choice of area, 51 per cent of council tenants put Canning
Town or Custom House and another 5 per cent put close by; 19 per
cent would move elsewhere in Newham and one quarter wanted to
move away from Newham. These survey findings are in line with the
concerns raised by CHCTAG and my interviewees that:

- most residents wanted to live in a house or bungalow rather than
  a flat;
- most council tenants wanted to remain as such in tenure terms;
- many council tenants wanted to live in or near Canning Town/
  Custom House.

A later smaller survey was undertaken by MORI (2003), which was
more weighted towards homeowners than the earlier Kwest survey.
The MORI survey findings were hailed by the council as indicating
that 'most residents gave their backing to the plans' (*Newham Recorder*,
2004), even though 43 per cent of respondents knew either 'nothing
at all' or 'not very much' about the plans prior to the survey interview
itself (MORI, 2003: 19).

As Norman emphasised, the MORI survey was deficient in many
ways: "the MORI survey wasn't giving the people a clear picture
of what was actually going to happen". Unlike the Kwest survey,
it did not include any questions that tried to find out what tenure
residents preferred, and nor did it include the crucial information that
housing associations – not the council – would be the dominant social

landlords: "when they did the survey on consulting the tenants about housing associations, you find it never happened" (Norman). Whereas the Kwest survey had directly asked respondents what their *preferred tenure choice* was if they had to move, the MORI survey included no such question. In addition, MORI respondents were not asked whether they wanted their homes demolished. In fact, the word 'demolition' is only very briefly mentioned in relation to how a minority of respondents 'feel' they will have to move for this reason: 'one in twenty feel that they will have to move due to their home being demolished', rising to one in eight in the core development areas (MORI, 2003: 11). Not being directly asked about whether one wants one's home demolished demonstrates a lack of transparency (as well as basic respect) on the council's part, and is indicative of a tokenistic approach to participation (Teernstra and Pinkster, 2015; Gustavsson and Elander, 2016). But the D-word – 'demolition' – is an all-too-often absent signifier in consultation exercises, as discussed further below.

The MORI survey included two questions about Robin Wales' (then Leader of the Council) three 'guarantees' to council tenants regarding redevelopment – first whether they had heard of the guarantees, and second how important they thought they were? The guarantees were:

1. Every council tenant who wants to come back to Canning Town can do so.
2. Every council tenant who wants to remain a secure council tenant can do so.
3. Council tenants will be able to move back to a property which has the same number of bedrooms. (MORI, 2003, Appendix: 9)

These guarantees were made as part of the council's engagement with residents and they were reiterated in a newspaper letter Wales wrote challenging critics of the scheme who had complained that they had not been sufficiently consulted.[3] The MORI survey reproduces the mental gymnastics involved in the first and second guarantees above. The first – that every council tenant can return to the original area – is the 'right-to-return'. The second guarantee is a tenurial right that each council tenant can remain as a council tenant. The location of the first two guarantees in the MORI survey and in Wales' letter – one immediately following the other – implies that tenants can have *both guarantees*: return to the area *and* remain as a council tenant. But the guarantees are not additive. They are *either/or* – either the right-to-return, *but* as a housing association tenant – or remain as a council tenant *but* move away from the area. As Norman said: "The council turned around and said 'everyone can come back, everyone can remain a council tenant'. What they didn't say is you can't come back as a council tenant to *here*, there is no council houses." A Newham community worker explained the Orwellian double-speak involved in the guarantees.

> 'Council tenants are loyal to the councils, and they never believed that they were going to be treated in the way they have been. It never crossed their minds – "the council knows best and we've been council tenants all these years, things won't change". It was believed, alright they were told they could return. *But* you can't return as a council tenant, that popped in a little bit later. That last bit of the equation was not explained.'

I struggled with this double-speak myself in an interview with a Newham Officer where I referred to an updated version of these guarantees regarding the Canning Town/Custom House scheme:

Paul: 'So, they [council tenants] have got a right to a council property?'
Officer: 'Yes.'
Paul: 'They've also got the right-to-return?'
Officer: 'Yes.'
Paul: 'What they haven't got is the right-to-return to council property?'
Officer: 'Because they won't. Basically, if you want to stay in the area and be a council tenant then what you would do is you would have to bid for a council property that comes up. That's the way you have to do it. If you want to go back to the site you were in ... and in a sense, I'm not sure why you would other than it being a nice, new place ... you'd have to be an RSL tenant.'

The official could not understand why tenants would 'want' to return to the area. But even if they did, they would not return as council tenants, but as an RSL (housing association) tenant. And yet these are precisely the issues that the Kwest survey, CHCTAG and disgruntled tenants such as Norman and Kathleen highlighted as being of crucial significance.

There was some internal opposition to the Canning Town/Custom House scheme within Newham Council. An ex-Newham Labour councillor – who described himself as being "out of tune with the Wales' administration" – recollected how he objected to the scheme with its council supporters:

> ' "What you are doing is imposing a solution on the people of south Canning Town and determining that there had to be a development-led solution rather than a resident-led solution." They were saying "no, the residents are on board". I said "where's the masterplan that the residents have signed up to, what's the *real* consultation process that's taken place' etc.?" The regeneration [was] top-down rather than bottom-up, giantist rather than localist. It means tower blocks. Well look at what they've built, I just think its ghastly stuff! Look at what Newham has built around Canning Town station [Photograph 8.1]. I think the reason they've done that is ... they've never believed in talking to residents, they've never believed in involving residents really in what's happening on the ground. They [council] wanted to maximise the density and therefore the financial return. I know they sort of ground down the residents. "we're doing this, this is all you're getting, put up or shut-up".'

The ex-councillor's criticisms of the council's approach highlight the deeply entrenched paternalist Labourist politics in Newham (Chapter 4). In fact, the controversy over the Canning Town/Custom House regeneration had seismic political fallout in fostering the success of a party other than the almighty Newham Labour Party. This is the most dramatic electoral change regarding estate regeneration that I have come across in London. Alan Craig was Chair of CHCTAG and went on to stand for the newly formed Christian Peoples Alliance (CPA) in the 2002 local election and gained a council seat in the Canning Town South ward, while all three CPA candidates gained 46 per cent of the votes (Figure 8.1). This was an unprecedented result in a ward which had consistently elected Labour councillors since 1965. As Figure 8.1 shows, the Labour vote went down from 67 per cent in 1998 to 54 per cent in 2002. The CPA momentum was maintained since it gained all three Canning Town South council seats in 2006 with 48 per cent of the vote while Labour slumped to 34 per cent.

Photograph 8.1: Canning Town – new development, 2014

The community worker explains what happened once the previously loyal Labour working-class tenants realised the consequence of the regeneration double-speak: "There was a complete rebellion and rejection of the Labour Party in the ward, *complete*. So they voted, and they were furious when it was all explained to them and they took it out on the Labour Party, which was the party that had betrayed them."

While there were several reasons connected to the rise of the CPA in Canning Town and Custom House, the main spur was how Craig became a local community champion by opposing regeneration:

> 'The reason why we went with him [Craig] is he stood behind us, he agreed with what we were trying to do and a lot of us, that's why we won't vote Labour. He stood behind us, he gave us help with anything we wanted, he was very willing to because the council wouldn't hold meetings with us.' (Kathleen)

Figure 8.1: Canning Town South ward, Newham – local election results, 1998–2010 (%)

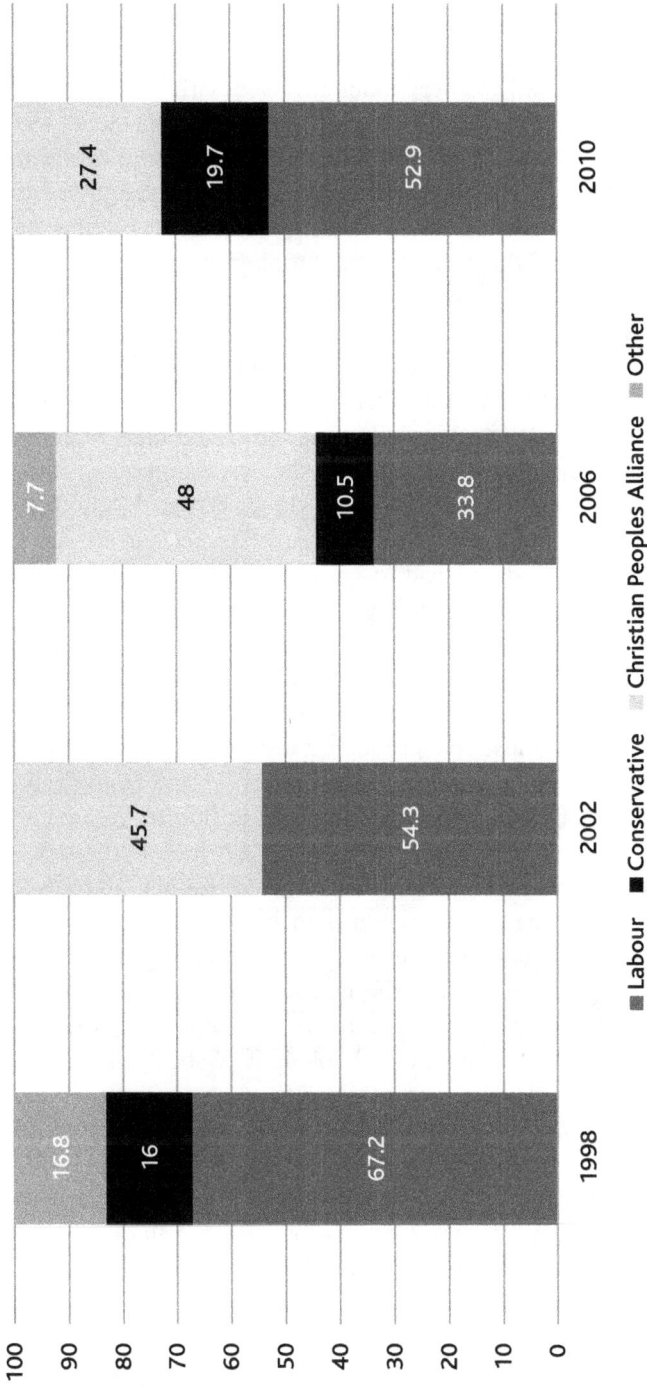

Labour ■ Conservative Christian Peoples Alliance ■ Other

Source: Various

Despite the CPA's efforts, the regeneration-as-demolition scheme went ahead:

> 'He [Craig] was very much involved with local issues and he campaigned, he fought for local people who were being forcefully evicted from their homes to make way for redevelopment. People that had lived here all their lives were actually evicted. I mean he lost. They had to go, and they went, and the redevelopment took place.' (Fred).

The existing population were indeed forced out, as Fred suggests. FOI data suggests that of the 470 council tenants in 2002, less than half (232) remained in Canning Town/Custom House, 186 moved elsewhere in Newham, while another 52 left Newham.[4] As Fred went on to say, "they [CPA] didn't stand a chance, they were overruled" by Labour's electoral dominance in Newham. A 'one party state' (combined with mayoral powers) meant that Newham Council got its way (Leach, 2006) – the residents 'had to go and they went'. Labour retook all three Canning Town South seats in 2010, but the CPA still had 27 per cent of votes while Labour was below its pre-regeneration total with just 53 per cent (Figure 8.1). The CPA also gained substantial numbers of votes in the two adjacent wards of Canning Town North and Custom House, even though it did not gain any council seats.

All of the things that CHCTAG, the CPA and concerned tenants warned about have come to pass: existing homes were demolished; the community has been broken up and scattered; the new private homes are entirely unaffordable for local people; and any council tenant returning to the area had to become a housing association tenant (Chapter 4). I leave the last words to a community worker who eloquently illustrates the notion of the state-induced rent gap with reference to the Canning Town/Custom House scheme and the Labour-run Newham Council's role in it (Watt, 2013):

> 'Two key things have happened, one is political and one is infrastructure. The infrastructure thing was the Jubilee Line station which opened in 1999–2000, which marks the starting gun for the regeneration. Because all of a sudden, the land within 10 minutes' walk of the Jubilee Line station at Canning Town became highly desirable. So that is the trigger for the regeneration, it became speculatively interesting. The second thing that has happened is the

political issue, and that is councils – and one must say Labour councils – have decided that council housing can be pulled down and replaced by other things. And so they have betrayed their origins as a party and have decided that council housing could be removed if the price is right, and that's why the regeneration is taking place. The Jubilee Line appears, changes the value of the land. The only trouble is – the good thing for the council it owns all the land – there is 2,000 council houses on it. They become destroyable, but they couldn't have been destroyed if they were privately owned. It is only possible because it is one big plot that they could do anything they liked with, like Big Brother.'

A Regeneration Consultant who had worked at Canning Town/ Custom House, regarded the councils' regeneration approach as being a de facto state-led gentrification strategy: "I think that the strategy is to change the social mix in the area. It's fairly explicit with Newham. Well, it's very explicit, they are unapologetic about that kind of strategy, so to have a bigger middle class in an area."

Northwold estate (Hackney)[5]

This section examines the much later Northwold housing association estate example of regeneration in Hackney which began in 2016. It illustrates two aspects of the planning phase: the problematic nature of consultation, and residents' scepticism regarding the proposed scheme.

Information and consultation

On one level, regeneration awareness was high at Northwold since 83 per cent of NES respondents had heard about the redevelopment plans. However, two-thirds of respondents did not think they had been given sufficient information:

'I am not clear on why they are redeveloping. They have not stated how many flats will go to residents or Hackney or will be affordable/social, therefore I am not sure what we are consulting on. They have been very unclear on the long-term effects of living on a building site or what will happen with homes/leaseholds.' (R22, market leaseholder)

'They should be more specific and clear of what exactly is going to happen and when, and if what will happen if we are rehoused and if refurbished, are rents going to increase?' (R45)

'Too vague at the moment. People worried about the future. People not being assured. Confusing.' (R81)

'I am concerned about the uncertainty and ambiguity surrounding the proposals – rather like Brexit.' (R366)

Winifred was a market leaseholder (that is, non-RTB) and was shocked to learn about regeneration/demolition via an official who came to her door one day and "started asking me all these questions like 'how many dependants have you got? We just need to know where we would need to house you'. 'What?!' I mean that was the first I heard of it."

Consultation attendance was high at Northwold given that 61 per cent of respondents had attended events. Attendance was correlated with tenure since 94 per cent of leaseholders had attended a consultation event compared to only 53 per cent of tenants. When asked 'how helpful' they found the consultation events, 44 per cent described them as 'unhelpful', 13 per cent as 'very helpful' and 35 per cent as 'fairly helpful'. The following quotations reflect concerns regarding the quality of consultation:

'Their representatives are poorly informed and robot-like. I have experience of consultation as I am an architect. I have written to them, they do not reply.' (R108, market leaseholder)

'Too much going on! It was too much to take in.' (Regarding consultation event, R113)

'Don't agree [with redevelopment], very poorly communicated followed by one sided bombardment of info which is sort of meaningless and stilted – becomes fatiguing.' (R290, market leaseholder)

One female shared owner was aghast at how the professionals at a consultation event seemed to have scant understanding of what their various 'options' might imply for residents:

'It doesn't even enter into their consciousness that it's people's home, and it doesn't really matter that some of those people are going to be displaced and not allowed to continue to live on the estate. So, I think it came as a bit of a shock to her [professional] when I said, "well it's not going to benefit me because we won't be here".'

Attitudes towards redevelopment

The primary result from the closed and open questions in the NES was that there was little support for demolition, and far more support for some form of refurbishment (maybe including infilling) instead. When asked, 'If you had a choice, would you rather see the existing estate improved or demolished?', there was an overwhelmingly 85 per cent preference for improvement; just 10 per cent opted for demolition, and 5 per cent didn't know. A second differently worded question produced greater support (17 per cent) for demolition: 'if you were asked to choose an option for redevelopment of the estate, which one of the following would you most prefer?' Demolition of the whole estate was the least preferred option (8 per cent), with another 9 per cent opting for partial demolition and rebuilding. Infill was supported by 44 per cent, 23 per said 'none of the above', and 16 per cent answered 'don't know'. Most comments in the open questions reflected an emphasis on improving what was already there rather than demolition, for example:

'I think the estate should remain as it is and improved for its residents. More green/garden areas with seating (park benches) would be good. Old, untidy areas need to be tidied and cleaned up. With repairs.' (R188)

'Before thinking about demolishing flats, building higher ones, so more people will be housed, first think about keeping the old residents happy then think bigger. Improve our indoors and outdoors. Listen to us.' (R263)

Many respondents highlighted the social disruption that would result from a major redevelopment programme, including displacement and breaking up the existing community.

'I feel it is highly driven by money, the plan to demolition, which will involve disrupting lives. There are children going to the local schools, in the middle of GCSE, A Levels etc.

235

So prioritising tenants'/leaseholders' needs should have been given stronger thoughts.' (R91)

'It's a nice place. If [the housing association] demolish the estate where are they going to put us? Where will we have to go?' (R111)

'It's not needed, this is the gentrification of the area, and people's lives and communities are not considered. The uprooting of most people will affect children and work communities.' (R346)

When respondents were presented with a binary choice – either improve or demolish the existing estate – there was a large majority in favour of the former by a ratio of over eight to one. Northwold residents had a strong sense of place belonging. They liked their existing homes and the estate, even though they wanted these improved (Chapters 6 and 7).

Consultation: residents' perspectives

Two regeneration schemes under consideration were the subject of a JR brought by tenants: at Cressingham Gardens (Douglas and Parkes, 2016) and in relation to the HDV in Haringey. In each case, the JR case was brought partly on the grounds that the council had not followed due process in relation to consultation. The HDV is examined in relation to Northumberland Park estate later. More generally, interviewees' awareness of consultation was often sketchy, while scepticism and cynicism were widespread regarding regeneration aims and processes.

Information and non-participation

The Northumberland Park consultation involved several private consultancies. One consultancy report from 2015 stated that 'there are few residents that have not been contacted, informed and had the opportunity to express their views on the area and the Key Principles for Change' (FPA and GCA, 2015: 52). This confident statement was contradicted by a later report from a different company which affirmed that 'there is very little sound knowledge of the proposed regeneration in Northumberland Park' (PPCR Associates, 2016: 47). According to this later report, only 14 per cent of survey respondents had taken part in regeneration consultations, while around one third knew 'nothing' about the regeneration proposals and another third didn't know much.

Across the various research estates, some residents described finding out about regeneration in various highly unsatisfactory ways. This included being casually 'informed' that their homes were at risk of demolition. This happened to Joseph when he was told by consultancy agency workers at Westbury estate in Lambeth:

> 'I was leaving home to go to work and I see these young women running around with their clipboard and flyers, "hello, do you want to sign this?" I said, "what am I signing, what's this about?" "We are going to build new homes." And I say "where, across the road?" They said "no, here, this is going to be demolished and we are going to give you new homes and new flats". I thought "where did this come?" They said "we will demolish these and give you new homes and new flowers, and look at these pictures". You know they usually have fancy pictures of people with bikes and holding children [laughs].'

Even if residents were aware of the consultation process, they did not necessarily partake in it for several reasons. First, due to having other demanding commitments (work, caring and generally getting by) which left little time to attend meetings at inconvenient times:

> 'Meetings are too early in the evenings for 9–5 workers.' (R528, Northwold)

> 'Why have the meeting at 7 pm? I've got three kids and they're in bed. It should be in the daytime.' (Natalie, West Hendon)

The second reason for non-participation is distrust of the local state, which could involve outright cynicism: "I just thought it was a waste of time, because like you'd be there listening to a load of crap and then nothing gets done, do you know what I mean?" (Craig, West Hendon). Residents did not necessarily believe the council would do *anything* at all based on previous experiences. Although Eddie had attended consultation meetings, he explained why many of his West Hendon neighbours had not done so because of earlier Barnet Council 'plans' regarding a nearby road which had never happened – so why would regeneration happen?

'You didn't get a whole lot of people going to the meetings for the simple reason that no one believed what the council said, no one's got any trust in the council, they never had. Half the people said, "It won't happen anyway." So, when the council wanted to come out with these ideas, "we're gonna do this, we're gonna do that", people shrugged their shoulders and said, "well who knows, we'll wait and see".'

Similar disbelief existed at Woodberry Down: "when they [council] say something, you think 'oh it's never going to happen'" (Mandy). Gordon had been involved in the TRA at Woodberry Down and the later Estate Development Committee and confirmed fellow residents' scepticism – with some even questioning his sanity![6]

'A lot of people were saying there's nothing going to happen. There were some people who really and truly believed that we were just a bunch of nuts [laughs]. They said it, "they just go into a room and talk with one another about a regeneration that's never going to happen".'

The Independent Residents' Advisor (IRA) at Woodberry Down had previously worked as a consultant at several Hackney estates, and he acknowledged the 'lack of trust' issue that had built up in the borough: "The first thing we had to get over was 'we've heard this all before, it isn't going to get delivered'." Such distrust reflects tenants' learned disbelief in councils' capacity to 'do anything', but is also indicative of tenants' general sense of powerlessness (August, 2016).

A third reason for non-participation was self-confessed apathy, while a fourth reason is how secure tenants were unconcerned because of the rehousing guarantees they received. Sam did not attend any consultation meetings at West Hendon for both these reasons: "I did ask Barnet Council and they said 'yes you'll be rehoused as a secure tenant', so I suppose apathy, not too much worry and stress."

Participation and disillusionment

Those residents who actively participated in consultation made several criticisms of the process. First, that the status and purpose of consultation events was unclear. Elaine queried the shifting status between 'consultation' and 'exhibition' meetings at West

Hendon: "There was no consultations, it was all exhibitions, and it's only after they'd taken place that they changed it to consultation [because] it meant that they was keeping in with the law" – in other words, staying within the statutory remit. Sonia described how she had been *unaware* that she had been attending consultation meetings at Marlowe Road due to their opaque nature:

'We were consulted without knowing we were being consulted. They [council] would have events on the estate and one of them had balloons, popcorn, hot dog stands, candy floss and all that kind of stuff. But when I looked in the document at the very end ... when obviously I was becoming a bit more astute ... they would say all the time that they had done all this extensive consultation. I realised that all these consultations that they were calling them, we didn't know we were being consulted! It needs to literally be the words "consultation" on the doorway, so we know we're being consulted because they did a lot of brain picking where we thought that it was just part of the normal council service.'

Sonia did not realise that 'regeneration' meant demolition: "It was more improvements to the estate. To be fair, I don't think we [tenants] would have rocked up with such enthusiasm [to the meetings] if we thought we were losing our homes." Sonia baulked at having an official at her flat to assist her with completing a questionnaire and became increasingly distrustful: "there's a reason why the first words of consultation start with 'con' – we were conned" (compare Lees, 2014, regarding the Aylesbury estate). Sandra described a similarly opaque process at Central Hill, where "residents were asked to fill in questionnaires and record their thoughts on post-it notes", although the rationale was unclear:

'No one knew why they was holding the event, it wasn't made clear to the residents that it was a consultation to do with regeneration. Most people believed it was a consultation to do with major work and Lambeth housing standards, that we were finally going to be getting our kitchens and bathrooms and maybe some new play areas and things like that. No one understood that it was actually to knock down the estate.'

Photograph 8.2: Central Hill estate – Save Central Hill community banner, 2019

When people found out the real purpose: "they were incredibly angry and that's how Save Central Hill started off" (Sandra) – the estate campaign group (Photograph 8.2).

A second criticism is that the consultation process was being rushed through via poor or non-existent information and was deliberately one-sided. Such issues surfaced at a tense regeneration meeting regarding Westbury estate that I attended in 2015: "As you can see there's a lot of confusion. We're being bulldozed to get a decision. We're being bulldozed into being bulldozed" (female leaseholder). Residents felt they were being steered down the path of approving whatever was presented. Theresa (West Hendon) mentioned how the building models were lowered to make them not look like the 28-storey tower that was eventually developed at the rebranded 'Hendon Waterside':

> 'We didn't know what was happening, and they made sure that they showed the plans where everything looked flat. They did it in a way where you couldn't actually see the height of the buildings that they were building. They are never going to show you the whole land because they don't want to give you a heart attack.'

If models were sanitised, so were consultation surveys, as seen earlier at Canning Town/Custom House. Such sanitisation was apparent vis-à-vis the HDV regeneration programme at Northumberland Park estate in Haringey. Most of the questions in a consultation report involved residents being asked to respond to a series of vague statements about things being made 'better', 'new', 'improved', 'attractive', 'high quality' in a manner which it would be counterintuitive and even perverse to *disagree* with (FPA and GCA, 2015). Unsurprisingly, large percentages agreed to these one-dimensional statements (FPA and GCA, 2015: 5–6):

- 'Northumberland Park should be made up of attractive places with a range of different buildings and open spaces' – 86 per cent agree/strongly agree.
- 'Regeneration should deliver high quality new housing for local people and maximise opportunities for the local community' – 87 per cent agree/strongly agree.
- 'There should be more community, leisure and cultural facilities for all, from young children to old people' – 88 per cent agree/strongly agree.[7]

The report summary emphasises how most Northumberland Park residents wanted 'comprehensive regeneration' – that is, large-scale demolition and rebuilding: 'The view of the majority of residents is that the area needs to be improved and that in order to do so there needs to be comprehensive physical, social and economic regeneration of the area' (FPA and GCA, 2015: 4). What does not appear in any of the 32 statements used by the consultants (FPA and GCA, 2015: 5–7), or the seven statements of principle (FPA and GCA, 2015: 34–40) is the D-word – demolition. However, residents did raise demolition as being a concern:

> Many residents talked about the potential upheaval created by the regeneration process, especially if homes are demolished and it is clear that many residents will need support in the process and with the practical aspects of moving to new accommodation. This is already a concern for a few, mainly elderly residents. (FPA and GCA, 2015: 31)

Despite such hugely important and very legitimate concerns – 'my home is going to be demolished, where will I live?' – the summary statements present an entirely positive spin on residents wanting

241

'comprehensive regeneration' and 'radical re-planning' of the area (FPA and GCA, 2015: 51), indicative of extensive demolition. As with the MORI survey in Canning Town/Custom House, Northumberland Park residents were *not* directly asked what they thought about having their homes and estate demolished. The unsatisfactory nature of consultation was a routine theme at meetings I attended, for example a Northumberland Park Decides meeting in 2017:

> 'No one's been consulted, we need to reinforce that we were never consulted.' (Resident)

> 'There's been no consultation on the estate, just a few comments on anti-social behaviour and a few fluffy comments two years ago. All, "would you like to see your home improved", very general, very broad, the sort of questions no one can object to. At no point has the council given us any clear information as to what they're planning or asked us what we think about it.' (Leaseholder)

> 'We've had no information as to what happens to leaseholders, there's more for the tenants.' (Leaseholder)

Michelle highlighted the sanitised nature of the Northumberland Park consultation, something that she challenged Haringey Council on:

> 'At no point did anybody actually come and say, "you know if you want all this [neighbourhood improvements], it means we are going to knock down your homes, how do you feel about that?" Nobody said that, that was *never ever* put on the table. The only consultation, as they call it, and I sat in a council meeting right and I called X [councillor] on this, because I went as a deputation, and they said "we want you to talk about your experience of consultation, you have 3 minutes". I said, "I'll need 0.01 of a second – zero". X says afterwards "I'm really sorry that you feel that you haven't been consulted because we've had all these meetings". We've had all of this, but what you are saying to people is you are asking the questions to get the answers that you want. So if you say to people "would you like to see more open space?", only a plank would say "no I don't want that".'

As Michelle emphasises, the D-word – demolition – was missing throughout the consultation process. The real opportunity costs of comprehensive redevelopment – 'you can have a "better place", but it's going to mean your existing home will be demolished, the process will be disruptive and might mean that you have to move away from the area temporarily, or even permanently' – were not spelled out. The consultation process was therefore not open, transparent or genuinely dialogic, as a study of the HDV consultation concludes: 'The locals consider that they should have been involved as active participants and contributors since the beginning, but the council did not initially aim much information to the public or organise proper consultation in the early stages of planning' (Viitala, 2018: 31).

A third criticism is that the consultation drawings/maps effaced residents' and community organisations' existing place attachments. Olive described how consultants presented schemes that would provide the services and landscape that the Heygate estate and surrounding area supposedly lacked – in other words, that the estate was a blank space containing *nothing* of any value (Chapter 3):

> 'They were going to make them into lovely little maisonettes, and they were going to make avenues and trees, oh the different things that we were told. And then one of them [consultants] came and he said, "the infrastructure we're going to give you". I said, "what can you give us that we haven't got? We've got at least 13 buses down the Walworth Road, and at that time we had the Euro[star terminal at Waterloo railway station], we've got two or three hospitals, we've got the underground. You're telling me you're going to give us this lovely infrastructure and we've already got it". So he shut up and didn't say any more.'

This illustrates the epistemological gap between the top-down representations of space from regeneration professionals who 'know' about the area's deficits, and the everyday spatial practices of residents which express a working-class habitus rooted in place (Lefebvre, 1991; Allen, 2008). In a later version of the scheme, the main road was erased: "they'd missed out the Walworth Road altogether, it disappeared" (Olive). Being effaced from the 'regeneration map' happened at the Aylesbury estate in relation to a homeless VSO which located there under the NDC. This VSO had been using one of the estate's community halls to support the street homeless, including those who slept rough in nearby Burgess Park. Support took the form of cooked meals, food parcels, as well as help with drug and alcohol dependency. However, the VSO staff described not being invited to consultation events regarding regeneration/demolition after the NDC had finished.

VSO staff 1:   'They've got their little plan and we're not on the plan. All the other organisations, all the other charities are on but we, they erased us out of it. No, they didn't want us at all. They didn't want us to come, we weren't invited. [VSO] can't be at the bottom of one of their little posh houses, we can't be there.'

Staff 2:   'We weren't invited. We're not on the map.'

Staff 1:   'Because we're not going to be included. Homeless people and they don't want their blight on their map. We'll be the dirty mark on their map that they can't get out. They don't want us on.'

The 'dirty mark' of the homeless – signifying disorder and abjection – had to be erased from the neat regeneration map and the 'clean' sanitising redevelopment of the Aylesbury estate.

A fourth criticism is that residents did not feel that they were being asked to engage in a genuinely dialogical and participative process because the key decisions had *already been made*: "We had all of these consultations, but the deal's done. There will be rows and rows of Woodberry Down flats, every inch of it will be covered because they [council] see money so it's going to happen. Consultation is just part of the propaganda" (Frank, Northumberland Park). Such cynicism and distrust regarding regeneration plans reflect a general distrust of officials and politicians, plus a sense of disempowerment resulting from previous frustrating dealings with the council, for example not having their housing needs met (Chapter 7): "People feel that they are being used, or they are receiving lies, or that they don't count" (Paz). 'Being used' meant turning up for events and being presented with a fait accompli. Ben relayed the opacity and 'done deals' at South Kilburn estate regeneration:

'There was consultations coming out of your ears, but our experience of consultation is entirely negative. You go along to these consultations which are like used car lots. They are selling you something and don't really want to know when you raise issues and problems. It's like when they have plans up on the wall, you ask about the scale of the plans – "oh they're not to scale". So how the hell are you supposed to tell anything if the plans aren't to scale? Problems like that, lots of consultations, lots of nice pictures of plans, but all the objections that anybody raised were brushed aside.'

Residents felt that consultation was merely a going-through-the-motions, rubber-stamping exercise – a 'waste of time'. Interviewees initially went along to meetings, only to become disillusioned and subsequently withdraw:

'What's the point going to the meetings, nothing gets done. But they're holding the meetings so it looks good on paper: "we've had a meeting on this day to consult the residents and everything is fine", and that's it. I've stopped [going to meetings]. Waste of time.' (Cheryl, West Hendon)

'You don't get anything from them [council] when you go to meetings, people are fed up with going to meetings. Nothing gets resolved so I don't bother anymore, it's a waste of time.' (Wesley, West Hendon)

'They [council] don't give a damn. I attended two sessions of the Independent Tenants body and it was a waste of time. To be honest, everyone is crying out for their own thing. If you talk, who's going to listen to you?' (Omar, Northumberland Park)

This implies that residents are suffering from 'consultation fatigue', whereby 'prolonged exposure to uncertainty generates consultation fatigue and results in poor levels of engagement' (HTA, 2016: 14). However, residents' cynicism is not merely a weariness of attending meetings, as the term 'fatigue' implies. Luke clarified how the main issue is the *pre-determined nature* of consultation, as it's already been 'sewn-up' by officials and politicians:

'My experience of Cressingham is that it's not so much fatigue, more a realisation of pointless engagement because the whole process is sewn up. Some of us refused to attend any more meetings and concentrated on other strategies to block regen[eration] that have turned out to be more fruitful. That's not fatigue, that's a refusal to participate.'

Dolores went along to a consultation event at the Aylesbury estate, where housing officers suggested she should sell up and move out: "Obviously I wasn't happy about that, what is the point of going to those consultations when they tell me what I have to do, when they are not listening." At West Hendon there had been a 'test of opinion' (that is, ballot; Chapter 9) regarding the initial plans. Charlie had voted against because "I wanted our places [homes] revamped, I don't think you can beat open space". Although the vote was for comprehensive redevelopment, Charlie said that everyone he'd met had voted against, which made him suspicious, while the regeneration stakeholders also changed:

> 'I went to meetings but got fed up because I knew the score would be the same old thing. I lost interest to be honest. I didn't like the way it was going. You knew that whatever we said, nothing was going to happen. Barnet Council had plans and that was it.'

The estate where I came across the most positive residents' comments regarding consultation and planning was Woodberry Down. The active members of the Woodberry Down Community organisation (WDCO) felt that they had made genuine inputs into the planning process: "it wasn't just a tick-box consultation exercise, it was *real power*" (Gerry). WDCO did make a difference in ways that are atypical in the London regeneration context (Chapter 12; WDCO, 2015; Nelson and Lewis, 2019).

Consultation: professionals' perspectives

Consultation is a statutory part of estate regeneration so any scheme will have statistics on how many people attended events, completed forms, agreed/disagreed with the proposals, and so on (see inter alia Social Life, 2013; FPA and GCA, 2015; Local Dialogue, 2016; PPCR Associates, 2016: TCC, 2016). However, as indicated above, questions remain over the *depth and quality* of resident engagement. I interviewed several regeneration and housing professionals, some of whom had positive things to say about consultation and about taking residents' views seriously, while others thought that the process was flawed (Chapter 9).

The most critical professionals I met were a group of idealistic young architects who had formed an anonymous network called 'Architectural Workers' to offer a radical critique of their industry. They had become disillusioned with the existing 'regeneration model' and supported

'No demolition'. As their website says, 'Having worked across leading "regeneration" practices, we've grown to be wary of the socially-led claims made by our bosses, journalists and local councils alike'.[8] They organised a debate on 'What is the Architect's Role in the Housing Crisis?' held at Cressingham Gardens in 2016, at which I was one of the speakers (Architectural Workers, 2017). I conducted a group interview with four members of this network who, for obvious reasons, wanted to remain anonymous – hence they are referred to as A, B, C and D.

During our interview, they evinced a highly sceptical opinion of consultation, one that was not dissimilar to that of cynical residents quoted above. They explained how a tripartite 'regeneration hierarchy' exists which consists of 'clients' at the top – "essentially anyone who has a financial stake" (C), "who's paying you basically" (D) – including the developer, landowner and social housing landlord. Below the clients are the 'stakeholders' – "I guess people, or groups that are using facilities on the site who may not be directly related" (B), such as local businesses or a group which might be using a community centre.

A: 'And there's the residents at the bottom.'

C: 'Yeah. Because they're meant to be represented by the council, I guess.'

A: 'But the council's making the choice to do all this in the first place.'

C: 'They're saying it's in the interests of the residents. They make the decision for them.'

Paul: 'But the residents as independent actors, do they get a seat in this?'

C and D: 'No.'

C: 'Apart from if they're on a steering group.'

B: 'There's a steering panel which is directly employed by the council and generally made up of residents who are supportive of regeneration. For various reasons they've been promised that they will get a good deal out of it.'

The group explained how the consultation process involved working up the preferred option – that is preferred from the standpoint of the client ('who's paying') – to a higher specification than the non-preferred planning options:

'You wouldn't go to consultation with equal weight on all of the options. Because you present something from a few months ago and you don't want those three months of work since the earlier option wasted, so you need to pretend to get the consent of residents. It can only ever go one way.' (D)

I asked whether they thought residents understood the process:

A: 'I think people don't realise the immediacy of the threat posed by these people [regeneration professionals] coming in with biscuits and sausage rolls from Waitrose and what that actually means in real terms on their house. How can you communicate that through ...? How it's formatted is like some nice drawings on the wall, probably some hand-drawn sketches to make it look more friendly. All of the drawings will be communicated in pastel colours.'

D: 'Easy on the eye, and you just think 'no one's got a chance to see through any of this crap.''

B: 'It is very difficult to read as well. Going to consultations as a local person, it's very hard to understand this whole scheme that's presented to you on five boards, after work or whatever.'

When I put to the group what residents had told me – "consultation's a bit pointless because it's already been decided" – they concurred.

A & D: 'Yes, exactly.'

C: 'So why would you go if you think that? You'd go to one consultation and maybe you go to the next and like "you've not addressed any of the issues we've brought up, I'm not going to bother". That's [cynicism] completely justified, that is exactly what has happened.'

What residents think consultation means and what it *really means* are often two quite different things (Chapter 9).

Responding to comprehensive redevelopment

Residents' responses to regeneration and rehousing varied, as adroitly captured by this comment from a private sector regeneration manager:

'I'm not knocking regeneration, it works for some people. With the housing crisis, some families have got an opportunity to move out of a one-bedroom flat into a three-or four-bedroom home and that's great. Regeneration benefits some, some people lose out, and then other people just don't really care.'

The two polar responses I identified were, 'great, how soon can I move?', and 'they'll have to carry me out in my coffin because I'm not going anywhere'. Gerry and Mary (Introduction, Chapter 6) exemplified these. Rather than my question, of 'whether regeneration was a good or a bad thing?', Gerry preferred an alternative question: "The question I was asking, and a lot of people were asking, was 'how soon can I move?' Because the flat was crap, there was water running down the walls a lot of the time, especially in the winter. I mean they were awful bloody places quite frankly." Gerry had been un-homed in his 'crap flat' and was only too happy to see it demolished and to move into a new property (Chapter 10). At the opposite extreme, Mary loved her home and the estate and refused to leave. When I interviewed her, she recollected publicly admonishing Robin Wales (the then Mayor of Newham) at a meeting held at the Carpenters estate: " 'Do you honestly think you're getting my home? Forget it!', and I was pointing my finger at him. 'You're not getting here, you get out'." [laughs]. Across all the estates, I came across far more 'Marys' than 'Gerrys' in fieldwork and interviews.

If people like Mary and Gerry held firm opinions, others were less certain what comprehensive redevelopment would mean in practice. As mentioned above, this is not due to 'ignorance', but rather stems from obfuscatory consultation processes; not having a firm opinion is hardly surprising when key pieces of the regeneration jigsaw puzzle – like the D-word (demolition) – are missing. Leaving aside whether people were 'for or against' comprehensive redevelopment, there were also strong undercurrents of disbelief ('it's all talk, nothing will happen'), and fatalism ('no matter what we say, they will do what they want to'). Such fatalism reflects symbolic violence and the domination that the working class suffers from (Charlesworth, 2001; Skeggs, 2015). Such internalised powerlessness is pronounced among social tenants (August, 2016). Regeneration at Woodberry Down had been going on for nearly 20 years when I interviewed Irmak: "We've given up. If it's going to happen [rehousing], it's going to happen. How many years has it been going on? There's no point in getting worked up about it because there's nothing you can do."

To add to the complexity, the lengthy time scales involved (decades) mean that attitudes can change over time, as Goetz (2013) emphasises in relation to relocation. The main direction of change

I identified was from initial support to growing disillusionment and even outright opposition as regeneration unfolded and was revealed not to have the same form as promised/suggested during consultation – when everything will be better and nobody will be disadvantaged. This change is flagged up in the Canning Town/Custom House case (above). The opposite change occurred in the case of those people who started off being oppositional, but who later became worn down and grudgingly came to accept their rehousing fate (Chapter 10).

As a result of the above, making clear-cut judgements regarding whether residents 'supported' or were 'against' comprehensive redevelopment is fraught with methodological difficulties. Whilst acknowledging this and the necessary caveats, a broad pattern emerged based on the interviews, NES findings and fieldwork.[9] Only a minority of residents welcomed comprehensive redevelopment because they thought they would (or possibly might) get better homes and neighbourhoods (as per the official regeneration discourse). Another minority, especially during the early phases, simply did not know enough about the proposals to make a judgement. The majority, however, were opposed to comprehensive redevelopment, albeit with varying degrees of conviction; they preferred less radical refurbishment/infill alternatives.

This broad pattern was the one that I found at two estates that were in the early phase of regeneration – Northwold (discussed above) and Northumberland Park. At the latter, I interviewed 26 existing residents: 17 council tenants, one housing association tenant, five RTB owners, one owner-occupier and two private tenants.[10] Only two (Omar a council tenant, and Bert a RTB owner) clearly favoured comprehensive redevelopment, while Beverly (housing association tenant) thought it would improve the area but was worried about her own housing circumstances (Chapters 7, 10, and later). One young council tenant was fatalistic, while a young PRS tenant knew little about it. The remaining 21 disapproved of demolition and did not want to move out of their homes or the area, although they wanted to see improvements in relation to existing housing and estate repairs, maintenance and cleaning services, which might involve regeneration in the form of refurbishment.

Three main sets of factors allow us to understand and even explain the overall pattern across the estates as a whole: housing tenure and related rehousing rights, values in relation to homes and place, and material circumstances especially related to housing.

Housing tenure and rehousing rights

Housing tenure – whether people are council/social housing tenants, owner-occupiers or temporary tenants – emerged as a crucial differentiating factor in gauging residents' opinions. Owner-occupiers and temporary tenants were far less likely to support comprehensive redevelopment than social tenants. In fact, there was near-universal antagonism towards demolition among owner-occupier interviewees, both RTB owners and market owners. In the binary 'either improvement or demolition' question in the NES, only 3 per cent of leaseholders preferred demolition compared to 11 per cent of housing association tenants (Watt and Allen, 2018). Temporary tenants were also generally unsupportive of demolition and rebuild, understandably so, because any new homes would not be 'for them'.

Support for demolition and rehousing was greater among council/social tenants than the other two main tenures. Even then, only a minority among both interviewees and NES tenants favoured such a radical surgery approach to regeneration. Most preferred some form of improvement of their existing housing and estates. Even among the minority who favoured comprehensive redevelopment, reservations were also expressed in relation to themselves, their neighbours and the estate. Thus, there were only a few tenants who were positively enthusiastic about comprehensive redevelopment, such as Gerry above.

The significance of tenure is linked to the differential associated rights in relation to the rehousing and financial offers that residents receive, including whether they will be able to return to the redeveloped estate (Table 8.1). While some rights are statutory, others are subject to negotiation and modification in practice, not least following contestation between aggrieved residents and officials. Hence, these are typical rights since they can vary between schemes and even over time at the same regeneration-as-demolition scheme.

Secure council tenants are still the majority at most London council estates, even if they are declining in absolute and relative terms (Chapter 4). As Table 8.1 indicates, they have the most defined and greatest rehousing rights in relation to being decanted from their original home. Legally they must be offered a social tenancy, either on the new development – hence exercising the right-to-return (or right-to-remain) – or elsewhere but usually in the same borough.

Table 8.1: Estate demolition: typical rehousing offers and likely housing outcomes by tenure

Original tenure	Rehousing offer	Financial offer	Right-to-return	Likelihood of returning to redevelopment site	Tenure if returning to redevelopment site	Tenure if moving away from redevelopment site	Likelihood of remaining in borough
Secure council tenant	Social housing either in redevelopment site or same borough	Home Loss and Disturbance payments – £4,900 (2015)	Yes	Zero–high – dependent upon level of replacement social housing	Assured tenancy with housing association or Special Purpose Vehicle	Secure tenancy with local authority	High
Owner-occupier	Shared-equity/shared-ownership property in new development	Market value + 10%	No	Zero–low	Shared-equity/shared-ownership	Owner-occupation or private rented sector	Low–medium
Non-resident owner	None	Market value + 7.5%	No	Not applicable	Not applicable	Same as before regeneration	–
Non-secure tenant	Dependent upon review of homeless application and bidding for social housing	None	No	Negligible	–	Variable: non-secure tenant, flexible social tenancy, private rented sector, homeless	Variable
Private tenant	None	None	No	Negligible	–	private rented sector, homeless	Variable

Secure tenants are also entitled to statutory Home Loss and Disturbance compensation payments:

'Secure tenants who can *afford* to live in the new-build properties, they are most advantaged because they get to live in far nicer homes and get paid to move because the compensation they'll receive – £4,900 – plus disturbance payment which covers costs like carpets, curtains, removal expenses, disconnections, reconnections, mail redirection, a whole swathe of different things.' (Chartered surveyor)

Given that 83 per cent of social renters in England have no savings or investments whatsoever (MHCLG, 2019b), the lure of getting a one-off compensation windfall should not be underestimated, as Eddie noted when demolition was first proposed at West Hendon in 2002:

'You got £1,500 [compensation] for losing your property, which appeals to some people. When that first started, they [tenants] were, "Oh yeah". And they [council] would pay all your removal costs, they would pay for your change of postal address for three months, change your phone line, so people started thinking that way, and thinking "I'm getting a brand new flat and plus I'm getting money". And then you always get some people say, "I don't care what they do, I'll get a bit of money out of it".'

As Table 8.1 shows, the rights and impacts on homeowners vary depending upon whether they are owner-occupiers or non-resident; the latter are investor/absentee landlords who live elsewhere. Owner-occupiers receive market value plus 10 per cent compensation, and can also be offered a new property at the redeveloped site on a shared-equity or shared-ownership basis. Non-resident owners are not offered rehousing, but will receive market value plus 7.5 per cent financial compensation. The chartered surveyor contrasted the different impacts on investor-owners and owner-occupiers:

'The investor-owners generally get a good deal out of it. The reason being is that investor-owners on the whole aren't as sensitive about where they're going to buy as owner-occupiers, so they can afford to buy somewhere in a completely different area because they don't need the same links because they're not living in the properties.

So they can buy something in a different area for the same price, but then they've got their extra 7.5 per cent compensation. If it's an area where there is some other low-quality housing, owner-occupiers may just about be able to afford to remain, they don't do too badly. But if it's an area where their particular estate is the worst of what's around by some distance, then those who are forced further afield can suffer as a result because they are being taken away from their support networks, family, friends, schools, jobs, whatever it maybe.'

RTB owner-stayers and market owners have significant place attachments which tend to make regeneration/demolition unappealing, as discussed in Chapter 6. Two other tenure groups – temporary/non-secure and private tenants – both do very poorly out of regeneration, as the surveyor explains (Table 8.1):

'The insecure [temporary] tenants, quite often they'll just be shunted to anywhere and everywhere, they're very, very much disadvantaged. Those who haven't lived on the estate for very long may not mind that too much, purely because they haven't formed attachments. Insecure tenants don't get [financially] compensated.'
'Private tenants get a very raw deal. They get no compensation, no right to rehousing other than through the council's normal rehousing policy for anyone else in the borough, which effectively means if you present yourself as homeless, we'll put you up in temporary accommodation, most likely a hostel. It's the landlord's duty to secure vacant possession, so the landlord normally has to evict the tenant.'

These rehousing rights provide an important legalistic framework for understanding how the various tenures responded to regeneration-as-demolition. The wider support for demolition and rehousing among council tenants becomes understandable given their greater rehousing rights. By contrast, owner-occupiers, and even more so temporary and private tenants, have far fewer rights.

Mind the value gap – demolishing 'failed places' and 'sink estates'

As the above-mentioned consultation findings illustrate, the things that residents positively valued about their housing, homes and neighbourhoods were inadequately recognised by professionals and politicians (Glucksberg, 2017). In other words, a 'value gap' exists between the official regeneration discourse and residents' home and place belonging. A Regeneration Consultant with a great deal of experience in the industry described one east London area, dominated by social housing, that he had worked on as follows:

> 'Well it was just grim, wasn't it? [laughs]. It had kind of failed really as a place, it seems to me. I mean I wasn't on the inside, so I don't know, I didn't live there. Maybe there was a beautiful kind of community there as long as you were on the inside of it [laughs], but I don't know about that. But I think that it expressed the really serious kind of deprivation of the area. It was basically a rough, poor place.'

As he admitted, he didn't live there so was not 'on the inside'. Residents, especially long-term residents – who are insiders (Relph, 1976) – often did not recognise the 'sink estate' and 'failed place' labels applied to their estates by the regeneration industry and mass media.[11] For example, the dominant place myth of the Aylesbury – as promulgated by local politicians, the regeneration industry and the mass media (John, 2015) – was a 'notorious' 'estate from hell', an outsider image that did not tally with many residents' insider place attachments (Watt, 2020c). A meeting about Southwark council housing was organised by DCH in 2010. One elderly female Aylesbury resident spoke passionately about the NDC and subsequent demolition plan:

> 'I'm not a housing expert but something has gone wrong. I've worked hard on my flat, we've been working on our homes. But we're told by PR campaigns that this is the estate from hell. At the same time, we get these glossy brochures, this costs money and we're paying for it. This money could have repaired two lifts. People used to be apathetic, but word has got out as to what happened on the Heygate. I would love to believe all this, but I don't.'

In Southwark, word did indeed 'get out' about the Heygate, another supposed 'sink estate' whose 'notorious' reputation was undeserved according to residents (Heygate Was Home, 2014; Romyn, 2016). Broadwater Farm is another heavily stigmatised estate (Hendry, 2019) whose media reputation differs from residents' experiences of supportive local social capital;[12] a female Turkish tenant spoke apprehensively about potential demolition: "I've known people there for over 20 years, we're like a family to each other. My daughter was in hospital for four days and my neighbours helped me. What will happen to me? My daughter is crying because of maybe losing her home" (DCH meeting, Tottenham, 2015).

Although less 'notorious' than the above examples, Churchill Gardens estate in Pimlico has also been subject to territorial stigmatisation. The *Evening Standard* (2013) newspaper covered a story about a fatal attack on a young man in the nearby area, but even though the assault did not occur on the estate itself, its 'reputation' was invoked: 'the street … is yards from the gang-plagued Churchill Gardens estate'. In 2014, Westminster Council proposed to regenerate Churchill Gardens including demolishing one block. Residents quickly organised a 'Staying Put – Save the Gardens' public meeting in the estate's community hall. Over 40 residents attended (mainly middle-aged and elderly), and they heard speeches by housing campaigners and words of support from their Labour ward councillors. Several residents spoke passionately and eloquently about their feelings of living on the estate in terms which challenged the outsider place myth:

> 'I've lived on this estate for over 40 years, everyone outside the estate thinks it's a sink estate, but it's not.' (Female)

> 'Churchill Gardens is the finest estate in England and Wales. It's got a mixed community, it's got to be preserved as such.' (Male)

At the end of the meeting, a straw poll was taken regarding who wanted to leave and who wanted to stay. Not a single hand went up for leaving, while everyone's hand went up when asked about staying. The council dropped the regeneration proposal following pressure from residents.

I put the argument that was made by Barnet Council justifying demolition to several West Hendon interviewees – that the estate was an isolated enclave of deprivation (as per the IMD) and was socially and spatially 'cut off' from the rest of the borough. No one agreed with this top-down place mythical perspective. Whatever problems West Hendon had – landlord neglect, stigma, youths hanging around – did not gainsay residents' generally very positive sense of place belonging (Chapter 6). Charlie contrasted pre-regeneration West Hendon with its redeveloped present-day anonymity and isolation (Chapter 12):

'The estate was fantastic, a real multiracial place. It had
a bit of a reputation as a sink estate, but I never had any
problems. Everybody would sit out back in the summer
and the kids would play out. We were all on the balcony
and we'd chat, anyone who went by would stop and have
a chat, and you had your own little spot. But you don't see
as many people now [in the new block].'

The incongruity between regeneration rationales and residents' place
attachments was stark at the Carpenters estate. Regeneration was
supposed to create a mixed community – but residents replied that
they *already had* a mixed community (Watt, 2013). Mary recalled
challenging the then Mayor of Newham who made a speech about
how regeneration would bring about 'decent homes':

'He was telling us what he was going to do for us good folk.
I said, "you're going to make the estate decent by knocking
it down and building it up when it is a decent place! *What
are you on about?*" When he started talking about, "you're
going to live in a decent home", I said "what do you think
I live in, a shack?"'

At a large and stormy meeting held at the Carpenters estate in 2012,
senior managers from UCL, the erstwhile regeneration partner,
presented their vision of the new Stratford campus which would sit
exactly where residents lived.[13] The latter were angry at how their place
attachments – to their homes and neighbourhood – were collateral
damage in the official regeneration-as-demolition rationale:

'We the Carpenters estate community don't want UCL here.
The council or UCL don't seem to care what we think.
What makes the rights of your students take precedence
over our rights, the people who are here?' (Female resident)

'You have seen us, but have you really seen us? Are we
insects, cockroaches, or ants under your feet? I've lived
here 42 years. We know each other, but you don't know
us.' (Female RTB owner)

'We are essentially a working-class community. What you
[UCL] are proposing is social cleansing in the name of your
corporate objectives. That's injustice and we do not intend

to let it happen.' (Carpenters Residents Steering Group – read out at the meeting; cited in Watt, 2013: 110)

The disparagement of their homes and homemaking efforts through the demolition 'solution' created distress, anger and confusion among interviewees. Tenants, as well as leaseholders, engaged in domestic self-provisioning (Chapter 6). Mehmet and his family had been living in temporary accommodation for several years before they moved to Northumberland Park. Although Mehmet was pleased about their newfound secure tenancy, the house itself was rundown when they moved in, which necessitated a great deal of financial investment on his part to make it liveable and comfortable. Mehmet was incredulous that his home might be knocked down as part of the HDV programme:

> 'I don't know why they are changing these buildings. For me, it is not a good idea. If this council is making new houses, it can find some empty place, but why you are breaking one down and making again? This is too much money spending. Why you broken an old one? I think it's all money going to the dustbin. They [council] showed me many houses, but I choose this one, but they didn't tell me the new plan. If they tell me the new plans, I don't choose this house. I've maybe spent £20,000 on the house, because everything was old when we moved here. We changed everything – we put a new floor in, new stairs, a new wall, everything.'

Despite having concerns about ASB in his block at Northumberland Park, Dave was aghast at the HDV demolition plans and did not understand why his block could not be refurbished instead. He proudly showed me around his council flat and demonstrated the extensive internal work he'd done which had cost several thousand pounds: "I knocked the ceiling down and put that up. I did that in the bathroom as well. It's me home. At the end of the day I'm living here, as far as I'm concerned I'm going to be here until the end of my dying days basically. So I want it how I want it" (Photograph 8.3).

If there was a large value gap between the official regeneration discourse and residents' place belonging, they were also resentful at how this gap was *widened* via what can be termed 'demolition propaganda' – distorted official representations of their estates that are used to justify demolition (Kallin and Slater, 2014). Terry recalled how Hackney

Photograph 8.3: Northumberland Park estate – Dave's bathroom, 2016

Council had commissioned a promotional film about the Woodberry Down regeneration:

> 'It started off with really frightening music, and they pan to the worst part of the estate, with just a brick wall. It looked like Hiroshima, 20 years later or something! It was ridiculous, I was just so shocked when I saw it. I just thought, "Is this what you're doing behind our back?" It was a horror movie of the estate, and you wouldn't recognise it if you lived on the estate. If they said that was Woodberry

Down, you wouldn't know it was Woodberry Down. That was a purposely made propaganda film, that's what it was.'

The 'horror movie' represented Woodberry Down as the 'sink estate' that it was unjustly accused of being. Such symbolic devaluation heightens territorial stigmatisation, and this process is exacerbated even further when regeneration proper gets under way (Chapter 9).

Poor housing conditions

If a minority of social tenants supported comprehensive redevelopment, this was largely a response to their own dire housing circumstances. The latter overrode whatever neighbourhood place belonging they might have. As one female tenant passionately expressed at a regeneration meeting held at Broadwater Farm community centre in 2015:

> 'I've lived on the 8th floor of a tower block for 16 years and I'm so desperate. It's not about the estate, it's about individual circumstances. I have three kids in a one-bedroom flat, and they all sleep in one bed. I don't invite people back because I'm so ashamed of the place. Nothing happens, people don't care, I want to move out.'

The tenants who welcomed demolition tended to be those who had been un-homed either due to overcrowding and/or living in poor-quality accommodation.[14] Demolition just might – at some ill-defined point in the future – mean that they could finally leave their *non-home* and move to a more suitable property which could become a *proper home*. Omar's family was un-homed due to overcrowding and their inability to transfer and this underpinned his willingness to go along with demolition (Chapter 7):

> 'I don't mind if they knock it [estate] down tomorrow, I don't care. They've said that they're going to move you to a bigger property, so I think I'm going to get something better than this. The council is saying that I will be okay if I'm a secure tenant, and I'm a secure tenant.' (Omar)

Tiffany had been trying unsuccessfully for many years to transfer from her overcrowded one-bed flat at West Hendon which she shared with her teenage son and young daughter. She was 'only overcrowded' (Orr,

2018) and hence not 'deserving' enough: "we got pushed to the bottom because of other people coming onto the list in worse circumstances". Barnet Homes advised Tiffany to use her front room as a bedroom and she'd done so for 17 years. Although Tiffany acknowledged the negative impacts that demolition had on leaseholders and elderly tenants, she was pleased for her family given that she would be "moving from a one-bed to a three-bed flat, it's fantastic".

Conclusion

In focusing on the early stage of regeneration, this chapter has drawn parallels between Canning Town/Custom House in the early 2000s and the recent case of Northwold estate. Residents raised remarkably similar issues at each regarding demolition: an inadequate one-sided consultation; unclear and inadequate information; that it would lead to the breakup and displacement of the existing community; and the primary beneficiaries would be developers rather than residents.

More generally, residents regarded consultation as a confused and confusing process. This was not due to their 'ignorance', but rather resulted from the obfuscations and sanitisations that are built into the consultation process – models that are not to scale and questionnaires that omit the D-word – demolition. Given the interview with the young architects, it's hardly surprising that so many residents came to cynically regard consultation as a waste of time. What residents and the architects said about consultation makes perfect sense once we apply a Bourdieusian framework. Regeneration constitutes a highly stratified field – one in which the rules of the game are heavily loaded in favour of the clients at the top of the hierarchy (the social landlord and developer), with residents at the bottom. The latter are bit-part players in this field who are brought onto the consultation stage merely to admire and approve the professionals' handiwork.

Residents' responses to demolition are impacted by tenure and associated rehousing rights, with council tenants (with the most rights) being relatively more favourably inclined than either owner-occupiers or temporary tenants. Among council tenants, the minority of demolition supporters tended to be those who were un-homed due to overcrowding or living in otherwise poor-quality housing. The chapter also argued that a profound value gap exists between the regeneration rationales and mass media place myths, and residents' own place attachments to their homes and neighbourhoods. The next chapter analyses what happens once regeneration proper begins.

9

Degeneration

This chapter examines what happens once regeneration-as-demolition begins in earnest. In stark contrast to the official regeneration rationale – creating better places and lives – it argues that residents experience physical, social, symbolic and psychosocial *degeneration*. If regeneration involves spatially targeted reinvestment in and revitalisation of physically rundown and socially deprived areas, degeneration is regeneration's demonic alter ego in the form of financial disinvestment in those areas and their accelerated physical, social and symbolic deterioration *over and above* any original problems they might have. Such degeneration encompasses multiple overlapping strands: enhanced landlord neglect, loss of valued estate facilities, boarded-up properties, increased population transience, living on a building site and heightened stigmatisation. As degeneration takes hold, estate residents' support for and engagement with regeneration dissipates, and trust breaks down. Degeneration/regeneration elongates into the distant future and creates a psychosocial limbo-land in which residents put their lives on indefinite hold.

Enhanced neglect and managed decline

Regeneration ushers in degeneration via heightened landlord disinvestment which is experienced as 'enhanced neglect'. Such enhanced neglect involves 'managed decline', which refers to the notion that 'the area's problems could be solved by allowing the neighbourhood to get worse and worse until it was no longer viable and had to be pulled down' (Davidson et al, 2013: 62). Residents thought managed decline was occurring via the actions and inactions of the official regeneration partners, initially to soften them up for major redevelopment, and then later to pressurise them out of their homes. An exhibition held at a 'Northumberland Park Decides' meeting included photographs of rundown areas and asked, 'Is this managed decline?' (Photograph 9.1) at Northumberland Park estate.

Managed decline was a prominent theme raised by Cressingham Gardens residents (Local Dialogue, 2016; Cooper, 2017). Steve was a Cressingham Gardens tenant and he linked managed decline with the

Photograph 9.1: Northumberland Park Decides meeting – managed decline photographs, 2017

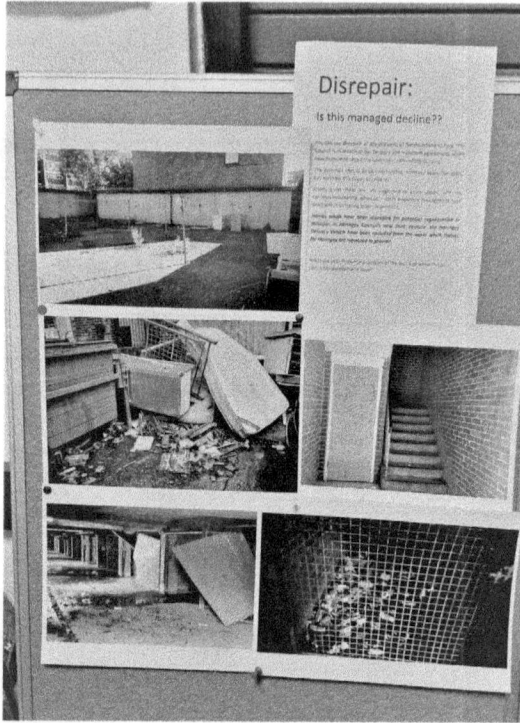

potential redevelopment value that the estate could have – that is, a state-induced rent gap:

> 'Once I heard about the plans, and because of my previous experiences, was knowing that the value of this land must be huge […] so it didn't take much imagination to see with views like that over the park … my own property has got a window view over the park that would be sort of literally a million-pound home on a certain type of development. So, I felt that it's a managed neglect, because if you let a place run down, tenants will get dissatisfied. Then when you look at what they spent on maintenance on our estate, they under-spent compared to other estates because so little maintenance has gone on – managed decline.'

Managed decline took two broad forms: suspension of the DHP, and a deterioration in routine repairs, maintenance and cleaning services.

Suspending Decent Homes

The suspension of DHP works at regeneration estates awaiting demolition was routine. A chartered surveyor, who had worked at many such estates, was aware of its negative impact on residents:

> 'If you've got a large council estate and it's done over let's say a seven, eight, nine-year phasing programme, the people at the very, very end of that are waiting an eternity. But meanwhile councils normally will suspend their Decent Homes Programme, which means they will be spending the minimal amount possible on that estate to maintain the properties – which is understandable because it's public money. But for the people who are living in those properties, they're seeing their quality of life go downhill. Normally councils will do the bare minimum that they're required to under the leases, which is far less than the Decent Homes Programme. So you'll find other estates which are not subject to regeneration will get a lot of money spent on them, but the regeneration estates will get next to no money spent on them, so the difference between the two becomes quite stark.'

Once it was decided that Woodberry Down would be demolished, 'Hackney Council withdrew the estate from its Decent Homes programme and instead adopted a mixed communities approach, which proposed to finance re-provision of all the social housing on the estate through cross-subsidy from private sector development' (Mixed Communities Evaluation Project Team, 2010: 33). Due to delays and rephasing, those Woodberry Down blocks widely considered to be in the worst condition – including the seven blocks – remained standing many years later, but with their unmodernised kitchens, bathrooms and windows (Belotti, 2014). Although Terry had the necessary skills and money to counterbalance the DHP suspension via self-provisioning, many other tenants did not:[1]

> 'I just laid proper flooring all over the place, and I'm a proper builder. I had a parquet floor in there because I wanted it to look good. I'd been there for 20 years and over time it gets done. Then it became a new kitchen because we weren't in no Decent Homes. So I re-done my kitchen, I did the whole thing, just gutted it completely

and ripped it out. I plastered all the walls in the whole flat, even though it's just a rental, and the reason why I done this is because it was in really bad condition. They [council] hadn't touched the flat since the 1970s. The whole flat was stripped so I could live comfortably because I was working. I know that the estates that were due for demolition within the next seven years or something were not going to be Decent Homes. Obviously, they say it's the next seven years, but next year, they go, "oh, we're going to change the phasing". So, it's probably eight years, and then its ten years, and then it's eleven. So, you've got an old, old, old flat. Your quality of life is going down, you know. When they [council] decided to do the regeneration, they were going to make sure it was a horrible place to live.'

Following bitter resident complaints (Belotti, 2014), DHP works were undertaken at Woodberry Down, but only in 2015–17. One family at the seven blocks that I visited in 2017 had a new bathroom and kitchen fitted the previous year, while another interviewee's next-door neighbour was having works done as we spoke on the balcony (Chapter 12).

At the Carpenters estate, a Newham Council report noted that 'the properties at Lund and Dennison Point do not form part of the Decent Homes Programme' (cited in Watt, 2013: 107). In Barnet:

> Most properties on the priority regeneration estates were not included in the wider Decent Homes programme which was successfully completed by Barnet Homes in 2010. This is because these homes are due to be demolished and replaced with new homes over the next 2 to 15 years. (LBB, 2014: 3.2)

As part of this borough-wide strategy, DHP work prematurely ceased at West Hendon, much to the chagrin of residents: "the wood was rotten on the outside of the building, windowsills and everything else" (Alf). At Central Hill, Sandra summarised the estate's changing DHP status:

> 'We're not entitled to Decent Homes because we're being knocked down. No one on this estate has had any Decent Homes. The only reason you'll get something is if it

breaks, they will replace it. We was in the [Decent Homes] programme for year 3, then we got put back to year 4, then we got put back to year 5, and then year 6, and then regen.'

The London NDC estates had manifold housing and physical environment problems at the beginning of the programme and allocated a higher than average proportion of their budgets on this NDC theme (Chapter 3). However, the ten-year NDC programme failed to resolve these problems in the case of the Aylesbury, Clapham Park and Ocean estates, and this was regardless of whether the estate was retained by the council (Aylesbury and Ocean) or transferred to a housing association (Clapham Park) (Watt, 2009a, 2009c, 2020c; Watt and Wallace, 2014). There are several reasons for this lack of progress, but they include the de facto removal of these estates from the DHP.

At the Aylesbury NDC, the 2001 'no vote' against stock transfer effectively led to a hiatus in the housing and built environment aspects of regeneration. Following this, Southwark Council decided it lacked sufficient funding to refurbish the estate, and in 2005 demolition emerged as its preferred option. However, progress on physical housing and estate conditions was glacial, and an evaluation of the programme identified 'the delay in pursuing substantial physical regeneration of community or housing facilities earlier within the programme' (ERS, 2010, cited in Watt, 2020c: 28) as a key failure of the NDC. As Dolores, a long-term resident said, "we have New Deal for Community for ten years, and they say they improve, but the estate looks the same". A housing report showed that 58 per cent of Aylesbury households were living in unsuitable housing and 28 per cent had major disrepair in 2008, compared to equivalent figures for Southwark of 31 and 10 per cent (ORS, 2009, cited in Watt, 2020c: 28). By 2010–11, 44 per cent of Aylesbury homes failed to meet the DHP compared to 31 per cent in Southwark (Luba, 2012), while the estate did not receive any DHP funding until 2015–16 (Watt, 2020c). Interviews and fieldwork from 2014–17 indicate the depths of distress and frustration that Aylesbury tenants experienced as managed decline was ratcheted up: ' "There's no hot water, its freezing sometimes. There's a lot of repairs' issues, there's rats and the heating's messing up. A couple of days ago we had no hot water. I live with my gran [grandmother], she shouldn't have to boil water"' (tenant, cited in Watt, 2020c: 28).

The housing and physical environment aspect of the NDC also ceased at the Ocean estate following the 2005 'no vote' against transfer: "in terms of the housing there was no plan B, there was always just the Sanctuary proposal which was a very generous proposal" (ex-NDC officer). A 2010 planning report found that nearly all – 96 per cent – of the rented properties failed one or more of the DHS criteria: 'there are problems with physical conditions of the blocks including non-operational lifts, inadequate security to both blocks and individual homes, poor thermal and acoustic insulation and poor quality public open space' (GLA, 2010: 2). The massive extent of non-decent stock at the Ocean was nearly double the 56 per cent average for Tower Hamlets local authority housing in 2009–10 (DCLG, 2010). As I noted on site visits in 2007, the estate looked decidedly rundown (Watt, 2009c).

The stalling of physical housing improvements at the Ocean and Aylesbury NDCs could be attributed to the 'no votes' against stock transfer. However, large DHP lags also occurred at the transferred Clapham Park estate. An Audit Commission report (2009: 47) found that 92 per cent of the social housing stock at Clapham Park did not meet the DHS in 2008. This compares to Lambeth and national averages of non-decent local authority homes of 30 per cent and 22 per cent respectively in 2008–09 (DCLG, 2010). I undertook numerous visits to Clapham Park beginning in late 2008. By then, the estate had gone through eight years of regeneration courtesy of the NDC, while it had been three years since the stock transfer ballot. My fieldnotes reflect my consternation at the conditions that I found and the slow pace of change: "There is some evidence of renewal and refurbishment as well as demolition, including vacated buildings. But I am also surprised at the extent of general dilapidation. There are lots of old windows, a few broken windows and peeling paint."

I went into one of the blocks at Clapham Park west and walked up the stairwell, noting a broken and missing window. I recorded my surprise at seeing a flagship NDC estate, one that prominent journalists lauded at the time (Toynbee, 2008), and compared it to the Ocean estate which had a stalled housing programme due to the 'no vote' against transfer:

> I am quite shocked. After eight years of the NDC, it's not that much different from the halted Ocean Estate NDC. There is some evidence of improvements, for example the bike shop, kids' play areas, and some blocks are done up with new windows and paint. But it is not as glossy as the official leaflets, websites and newsletters make it out to be. It still looks like a rundown council estate – there's lots of rubbish outside the communal windows and lots of old,

Photograph 9.2: Clapham Park estate (west) – window frame, 2008

naff windows [Photograph 9.2]. By contrast, the next-door Oakland Estate had new windows.[2]

Deteriorating maintenance, repairs and cleaning services

The second aspect of physical decline is worsening routine maintenance, repairs and cleaning services. Oluwakemi had lived at West Hendon for 20 years and described the deteriorating state of her tower block:

> 'The building wasn't looked after by Barnet [Homes] anymore, once the regeneration was going to start and the [property] guardians came in. You couldn't get them [Barnet Homes] to come and fix the [entry] door downstairs. The building might be coming down, we might be negotiating selling our properties, but the door downstairs should still be locked. Unlike before, in two days' time someone would come out. They didn't clean the corridors, the stairs, nothing got cleaned anymore.'

Enhanced neglect had an un-homing effect on remaining tenants and leaseholders – of making them less likely to think of their dwelling as home – and therefore of *pushing* them out (Huq and Harwood, 2019).

In other words, their homes *became* non-homes. Olive described the deteriorating conditions at the Heygate estate:

> 'The majority of us [residents] didn't want to move, but they [council] gradually let them rundown. We used to have a lovely caretaker – he took such pride – then all of a sudden he was sent somewhere else. And towards the end, the cleaners weren't allowed to go above the third floor. We assumed the council wanted to get us out, because the lifts were often not working. The lifts got dirtier and dirtier, they weren't being cleaned, and I think people gradually thought "let's get out of this dump".'

As Olive went onto say, this forced relocation was "sad because they're still there". The Heygate flats were still standing at the time of our interview in 2013, even though Olive had been decanted several years previously. The managed decline that Olive highlights is illustrated in an interview with an ex-Southwark housing officer who described the later stages of the Heygate:

> 'Very few [landing] lights were working, and one of the two lifts was not working. The one that was working, there was no light and the staircase was very dark. With Heygate estate, every time I went there for a visit, I didn't see them [cleaners] and there was a lot of rubbish stuff which was equally inviting pests, rats and stuff. Every day someone was moving and as they're moving, they're just throwing stuff everywhere, so all of that, so cleaners couldn't really do much. The council were not really monitoring what they were doing or what we were doing, so they just cut down on the number of cleaners that were supposed to be supporting or cleaning that estate.'

This officer reported communal lighting faults but noted how these jobs had not been carried out, even though no one in management had explicitly told her that works were not being undertaken *because* of regeneration:

Officer: 'If there was a faulty bulb here or there, we would give it to the managers. We'd go back the next day and it's still there, two weeks later it's not been fixed.'

Paul: 'So it wouldn't get done?'

Officer:	'No.'
Paul:	'Because it's a regen estate?'
Officer:	'Yes. Why would you want to waste money?'
Paul:	'Did anybody ever say that?'
Officer:	'You don't have to say, but you can *see it* because you've logged the complaint. You put this complaint forward, they say "Okay, we'll get it done". Go back three weeks, it's still there and then the person [tenant] is asking you … I didn't like it, I felt uncomfortable.'

Residents such as Olive mentioned earlier (see Chapter 10) who were reluctant to leave their homes – called "stubborn tenants" (ex-Southwark housing officer) by the council – thought that managed decline was part of a deliberate strategy to pressurise them out (Huq and Harwood, 2019). As leaseholders at the Aylesbury, Gesil and William were challenging their removal and were angry about the managed decline pressures they were experiencing:

Gesil:	'They're [council] leaving it now to rundown, that's what they are doing. They've left *everything*.'
William:	'The boiler goes off every week.'
Gesil:	'We're not getting hot water, we're not getting heating.'
William:	'From January to now [March], I think the hot water's been off for at least 16 times.'
Paul:	'How long does it take for it to come back?'
Gesil:	'Three days sometimes. They just want it to rundown completely, frustrate us and then we move out. It's been like that for more than three years now.'
Paul:	'Before then, was it okay?'
Gesil:	'Yeah. Before, even if they are doing something like they are servicing, they will let you know and then it comes on at the right time for you. If they tell you, "in two hours' time you will get your hot water", it comes on. They just want us out. They want to frustrate us. They want us to throw in the towel so they can get on with whatever they plan to do. But they are not going to get it'.

Such deteriorating conditions only made Gesil and William more determined to stay put – "they're not going to have it [flat] unless I go in my coffin" (Gesil) –although they prompted other Aylesbury residents to seek to move out (Watt, 2020c). Bill commented on maintenance and repairs' deterioration at Cressingham Gardens:

'I think it pretty much started to deteriorate as soon as they mentioned regeneration. I mean all the rubbish that Lambeth [Council] came out with about 'structural faults', there aren't any, there are no structural faults, there are just things caused by the fact that they stopped doing maintenance. When I moved here in 1996, they used to clear the gutters four times, twice in autumn, twice in winter, so you never had gutter overflows. By mid-2000s they came twice, and about five years ago they stopped doing it.'

Tenant satisfaction with the repairs and maintenance service at Clapham Park near the end of the NDC was just 49 per cent compared to a national average of 76 per cent (Audit Commission, 2009: 47). By 2016, while the eastern part of Clapham Park had had considerable refurbishment, the western part (which was due for demolition) looked as rundown as it did in 2008. Malana lives in the east but described walking around the west: "I haven't been down there for a while and I walked around, and I thought, 'my god!' I was shocked and I thought, 'Is this what it's coming to?!' Where humans are actually living in these conditions, boarded-up properties, no sense of ownership, none whatsoever."

I counted over 40 broken/boarded up windows at Clapham Park west on one visit in summer 2016. One of the clearest disjunctions between the official regeneration discourse – onwards towards a bright new future – and reality occurred at the Clapham Park Fun Day in summer 2016 which was held to mark the ten-year anniversary 'success' of the regeneration. The housing association had arranged boards to illustrate aspects of this success and these were located against one of the west blocks. Without a trace of irony, these were placed right next to a broken window (which had been broken for several weeks, if not longer, Photograph 9.3). Clapham Park west was the most consistently rundown-looking part of any estate that I observed during 13 years of research.

Dispossession of estate infrastructure

While neglect increased, residents were simultaneously dispossessed of their valued and valuable facilities. Estates were *made into* less liveable spaces as those features which enhanced residents' place belonging were eroded and eventually removed altogether. This contributed

Photograph 9.3: Clapham Park estate (west) – Fun Day celebrating ten years of regeneration (boards on right and broken window on left), 2016

towards their un-homing well before they were physically displaced. Cheryl was furious about the prospect of losing her valued home at West Hendon, but also about living on a building site and the loss of pre-regeneration community facilities:

'I feel like I've been forced out of my home, and I've been forced over there [new block]. But who wants to prolong it? I'm not well, I don't want to live on a building site. I got to think of my son who's got autism, it's freaking him out, all the noise and everything. He needs to be settled. He's uneasy the fact that's he's moving. He's anxious so he's having a terrible night's sleeping, so sometimes I'm up at 1 in the morning. Sometimes he shouts at the workmen, "shut up, how dare you take away our park?" And next door [children] does. They used to play football out the back there, used to take the kids out the back, Frisbee, and the councillors do like a fun day for the kids, bouncy castle and community thing. They've absolutely smashed the community there, completely *smashed it*. It's absolutely horrible there now.'

Photograph 9.4: West Hendon estate – building over green space, 2014

The loss of green space at West Hendon was a recurrent theme and reflects how the open spaces on the estates – with their opportunities for spontaneous socialising – were built over and destroyed (Photograph 9.4).

At Clapham Park, the potential loss of mature trees was an issue (Watt, 2009a). As at West Hendon, residents *used* the open spaces (Chapter 6). Not only did the green space at Clapham Park west provide the site for the annual summer Fun Day, it also functioned as an informal meeting space during the summer. This included parties – which some residents objected to because of the noise – but also low-key get-togethers. An ethnically mixed group of three young single mothers held a summer barbecue in this space, what one of them – Jasmin (and her mother who also lived at the estate) – called "their garden". Jasmin lamented what was happening because of regeneration:

> 'The green space will all be gone, it's only going to be new blocks and alleyways. Until all this shit [regeneration] happened, we knew our kids could run around. We can have a barbecue here, but it's sad that in a couple of years we won't be able to do this, it will all be gone.'

Other losses included parking spaces and IT connections, as Ben noted at South Kilburn:

'One of the things they have taken away is the [resident] parking spaces, and they have a nice little private parking lot within the site for their managers which I think is really taking the piss. They cut cables on two occasions, cutting off people's cable TV and Broadband and so on. They refused to pay compensation. I mean it was only for a day or so each time, but it's not the point.'

Environmental deterioration and loss of facilities were extreme at the Aylesbury estate, which latterly took on a fortress-like appearance: "we're fenced in, people think it's a prison" (female leaseholder, Aylesbury meeting, 2015). The spikes, wire and large boards surrounding certain blocks meant that the remaining residents became prisoners who had to prove their identity to the security guards to be let into their own homes (Photograph 9.5; Minton, 2017).

A homeless VSO operated at the Aylesbury estate (Chapter 8). However, the post-NDC regeneration organisational setup meant

Photograph 9.5: Aylesbury estate – fortress with anti-demolition slogans, 2015

that it was prevented from using the kitchen and halls so that the homeless were restricted to using the facilities once a month, as VSO staff described: "What they [regeneration officials] said in the meeting, 'these people we are helping, they are giving the area a bad image because they're homeless', and they refused them from using the main entrance to come in" (Staff 2). Not only did the charity's capacity to work effectively decline, but the decanting of tenants shrank their pool of locally available volunteers who used to help them: "They [tenants] used to live upstairs and they would come down and support us, but they [council] have moved them out and put just temporary in" (Staff 1). Thus, the social threads that connected estate residents to local vulnerable groups were eroded. Sandra highlighted the non-engagement of temporary tenants at Central Hill in relation to the loss of collective gardening:

> 'The place has changed. I mean the permanent residents did the gardening, we always did our own gardening, those people have left. You would have residents that would take control of their patch, and they'd keep it clean and plant, and they've left and so those areas are getting slightly more rundown and it just all these little things add to the deprivation of the whole thing. Because the temporary tenants won't do the gardening, why would they? They've got weekly tenancies, and they get no compensation, they get nothing, so they're never going to have that connection to the area that we've got.'

Sandra felt sorry for the temporary tenants, but they lacked the same engagement in the neighbourhood that the secure tenants and leaseholders had, an engagement that was built up over many years of residence.

Transience and boarded-up flats

Demolition has a degenerative impact on neighbourhood social relations because it accelerates population turnover well above normal levels due to deaths, transfers, sales and re-lettings. Consequently, estates become more transient and anomic places to live. Heightened transience results from displacement away from the estate by secure council tenants (decanting) and owner-occupiers (being bought out). The loss of their previous neighbours was unsettling for those left behind: "it's really, really upsetting, you see the removal vans in here every day, and you know that someone else is going and they've gone all across the country. Most people [tenants] are staying in Lambeth, but again they're going all over Lambeth" (Sandra).

Displacement of tenants and leaseholders resulted in empty flats and boarded-up properties. These physical scars on the landscape symbolise the place myth which the estates were falsely accused of in the first place – that they are places where *no one wants to live*. I asked about the boarded-up flats at West Hendon:

'It's nasty for our children to look at.' (Vicky)

'Well it's nasty, it just degrades the area even more.' (Lilly)

Not only did the boarded-up flats exacerbate estates' symbolic devaluation, they contributed towards increased crime, disorder and squatting. There were growing numbers of empty homes at Canning Town/Custom House (Photograph 9.6), some of which were squatted. Norman made a distinction between the initial wave of 'neighbourly' squatters and the later ones who engaged in theft: "then we got a few different lots in where they would break in that property and just nick all the copper". While many residents sympathised with squatters' dire housing circumstances, the empty homes/squatter combination

Photograph 9.6: Canning Town – occupied and boarded-up flats, 2013

also made them feel insecure. Newham Council admitted that empty properties at regeneration sites were problematic in the way that Norman highlights:

> Experience in the past three years in Canning Town is that squatting does impact on crime and disorder and public authority resources to deal with the associated issues. Empty properties are more likely to be and have been subject of illegal occupation (squatting); will and have been broken into and any saleable materials such as copper and other fittings removed. Also premises that are the subject of squatting have resulted in an increase in anti-social behaviour and noise issues, which have a significant impact on local residents/adjoining properties.[3]

Tenants lobbied Newham Council to refill the squatted properties at Canning Town/Custom House, and in 2011 the council contracted a property management company (Tando) to run the empty properties (Newham Recorder, 2017).

> 'We also had a very big problem with the residents that moved out and the properties were boarded up for a number of years, and with squatters and everything like that. Then two years ago we kept screaming at them [council]: "you need to do something, you need to bring back the properties into use". They have brought the properties back into use but they've given them into Tando, who are a private company and they're running it.' (Kathleen)

Other councils were more proactive and routinely used their empty regeneration properties as temporary accommodation. Not only did this help to prevent squatting and break-ins, it also assisted councils struggling to find in-borough temporary accommodation in the PRS due to LHA cuts (Rugg, 2016; Watt, 2018a):

> '[Hackney Council] have got a massive increase in homelessness, they are paying for expensive temporary accommodation that is often largely unsuitable, sometimes out of the borough. So what they are doing is, they are using regeneration stock, not just on Woodberry Down but elsewhere, to house them in better accommodation at a cheaper rate where they'll get the benefit from any

Housing Benefit themselves, before they move them on.'
(Woodberry Down, IRA)

While Newham employed the services of third-party managing agents to rehouse its homeless, Barnet Homes managed the rehousing process itself. It could do so since its large-scale estate regeneration programme meant that many hundreds of homes became available as temporary accommodation (Chapter 4). The same was true at Southwark because of the sheer size of its two main demolition estates – Heygate and Aylesbury. If temporary tenants add to the new faces at estates, they were later expelled themselves as demolition moved closer, and were replaced by property guardians who are even more easily disposable (Ferreri and Vasudevan, 2019).

Heightened transience due to regeneration is filtered through the RTB. The latter has contributed towards population churn due to resales and private landlordism, both of which *accelerate* following regeneration due to increases in investor-owners and sub-letting (Chapter 7). RTB applications increase following demolition proposals, and these are more likely to come from those sitting tenants who wish to either sell or sub-let their properties, as happened at the Ocean estate (ALG, 2003). Beatty identified a decline of community at the Ocean resulting from RTB-connected population churn: "when you're sub-letting, the estate is more of a transient community – they come in, they go out, they come in, they go out". Lee described how the RTB created a "transient population" at the Carpenters estate: "there's a few people that have bought houses and live in them like families. But generally, in the late 90s and 2000s, people were buying to let, so it changed the demographics, so people were renting rooms out".

Regeneration estates become epicentres for speculative RTB resales to investor landlords. This occurs while prospective demolition reduces the capacity of owner-occupiers to sell due to remortgaging difficulties:

'Investor-owners are generally people who will buy in cash or with very large deposits and who may be looking for very attractive yields, rather than capital growth. If you're an investor-owner looking for an attractive yield then your concern is, "how much rent am I going to get?" What's happened over a number of years is that these estates, whilst the market values are being kept low because not many people want to live there, the rents have actually gone rather high compared to those capital values, and the main reason they've gone rather high is because of Local Housing Allowance [Housing Benefit], [such that] the rent you can get is very decent. So what happens is the investor-owners who buy these properties will often focus their efforts on getting people in who are on Housing Benefit. And because there's so few owner-occupiers who can afford to buy properties either in cash or with very large deposits, then investor-owners really dominate these estates.' (Chartered surveyor)

These RTB-related changes result in increased numbers of private tenants. Given the high eviction rates in the London PRS (Rugg, 2016; Watt, 2018a, 2020b), regeneration estates become more transient places.

As far as any remaining council tenants and leaseholders are concerned, the net result of the accelerating population churn is a loss of familiar faces and a proliferation of strangers in the form of squatters, private tenants, temporary tenants and property guardians: "I can't tell you who's temporary and who's permanent now because most of the people that I did know were secure have gone" (Sonia). Joseph regarded Westbury estate as a once-thriving community which was being destroyed by rounds of boarding up and rapid population turnover:

'You move people away saying you're going to demolish, and then you move people back in on short-term whatever. Meaning that originally they wanted to get rid of the person with the secure tenancy, because these ones they can easily do what they want with them. Of course, there's no sense of community, there's no sense of attachment, or care about the community, it's people who are just strangers. That community spirit is destroyed. I've seen them [temporary tenants] for a few months, then I don't see them again and then the thing is boarded up, and then the flat is locked, you don't see any lights. You see the windows are black, then someone else comes in. That's the thing, it destroys the community.'

In a truly tragic sense, degeneration *creates* the physical degradation and social anomie that the estates were originally – unjustifiably – accused of via the 'sink estate' place myth and regeneration rationales. Kathleen estimated there were eight temporary tenants in her block of 30 flats in Custom House whose rapid throughput caused anxiety among existing residents (some of whom were vulnerable):

'It isn't that the people [temporary tenants] are bad, they aren't, they're just ordinary people. But the thing is […] Tando seems to change their residents quite quickly, they're here for six or seven months then they're moved, they're moving another group in. The first house [in the block] has had two lots of Tando residents in. Next door is council tenants, they're older people, they're very vulnerable and so they feel that they don't know who's living next door.'

Each regeneration estate changed from having a stable core population – long-term secure tenants and RTB owner-stayers – into an urban transit camp characterised by constant new faces – a 21st century version of the Chicago School's 'zone of transition'. While existing residents often expressed sympathy for temporary tenants, they also felt their half-empty estate was an all-too-convenient 'dumping ground' for people with challenging vulnerabilities and problems: "the anti-social stuff peaked when they started moving in all these temporary tenants" (Sonia). Sandra thought there were around 50 temporary tenants at Central Hill in 2019 and "many of the residents on this estate complain to me about the tenants that are being put in" because of ASB which "is coming from the temporary tenants". Although Sandra recognised that "everyone deserves a home", she baulked at the increased disorder:

'It's not fair on the existing residents if you turn the whole estate into temporary accommodation. The guy [temporary tenant] we had down there used to beat his wife, and we all had to listen to that and watch the police drag him out. They were only in that property for three weeks. The other temporary tenant over there just gets drunk and abuses everyone around her.'

'Problem' or 'rough' tenants are by no means a new phenomenon on London estates (Chapter 7; Watt, 2006). However, the temporary tenants' greater insecurity and transience means that there is less time and capacity for them to adhere to the respectable working-class habitus that is prominent among long-term estate residents. Furthermore, councils use the regenerated estates as places to put their 'problem tenants':

'Let's say you've got your noisy neighbours next door who have been kicked out because they cause too much trouble, well these are the sort of estates they go to. Quite often you'll find that people go from one estate to another to another, all of which maybe regenerated.' (Chartered surveyor)

The in-movement of temporary tenants at Cressingham Gardens contributed towards greater anonymity: "you've just got new faces that are knocking around, and you get a sense that there's a dwindling old guard" (Luke). Local social capital – knowing people – is an important aspect of long-term residents' relationships based on the slow build-up of familiarity via everyday interactions, largely low-level activities such as passing the time of day and mutual favours (Chapter 6; Harris, 2006). This local social capital evaporates as transience becomes the new normal. Cressingham Gardens residents had negotiated that the council should inform them when new temporary tenants move in as part of the Right-to-Manage process – "so we can welcome them" (Luke) – although Luke said that this had not happened. I did not hear about any social landlords proactively supporting the inclusion of temporary tenants via information exchanges or 'meet-your neighbour' social events with existing residents – the temporary 'non-secures' are just dumped.

Living on a building site[4]

Once physical redevelopment begins, residents found themselves 'living on a building site', as manifested via noise and dust pollution arising from the demolition, building works, lorries and workers. Their ability to lead a normal life deteriorated, as did their mental and physical health. Those who lived closest to the redevelopment sites were badly affected. Ben's block was adjacent to one such site at South Kilburn estate and he described the effects of the lorries entering and leaving:

> 'I just hear their noise all the time, every day, so the sound of "vehicle reversing", that beep, beep, beep, beep, I get all day, every day. Myself and the chair of the tenants' association we reckon that is our theme tune now, that sound of "vehicle reversing", because it's just in our heads all the time.'

Sleep patterns were affected: "bang on 8 o'clock, the noise *dududududu* and I'm like, 'it can't be time to get up – just gone to sleep!'" (Pat, West Hendon). Those who were at home during weekdays (including vulnerable people) – the housebound elderly, sick and disabled, home-workers and unemployed – were worst affected. These include Shiela and Laiba, two vulnerable temporary West Hendon tenants. Not only did the noise disrupt their sleep, but it had acute un-homing effects:

> 'Today we're lucky that they're not drilling something into your brain. I mean it's right here, it's a horrible noise. Two days ago, as soon as they started drilling I left home. I thought let me go to the park and sit there because it's going to take at least five hours.' (Shiela)

> 'I applied to be moved from here because the noise started since last year, I knew that would affect me. You can't sleep there for the noise, I wake up early with that noise.' (Laiba)

Joseph had to physically leave his home at Westbury due to the disruption: "The guy brought a *big* digger and, he's drilling the concrete and I could feel *every vibration*. Now if I could feel it, what about my son? This is a bank holiday and very early in the morning, so I had to get out of the house."

Theresa was not too badly affected by noise at West Hendon because her flat was located away from the building site (Photograph 9.7), but it had driven two of her neighbours 'over the edge', as confirmed in this interview with them:

Lilly: 'We have had it absolutely wicked here, wicked. We've had these 200-foot pilings, like a huge corkscrew, we've had two of them going in at the same time, just here.'
Vicky: 'Just outside my window.'
Lilly: 'And then they are taking the concrete up and they are banging it with these great big diggers that have got these sort of scoops on and they are smashing the scoop and the building shakes and you think, "Christ this is going to drive me mad." It's made people ill.'

Vicky had been on antibiotics because she had breathing problems due to the dust, while Lilly's health was also affected: "never had blood pressure in my life, and my eyes stream, and my throat dies up and it closes up and my ears". Natalie had three small children and was distressed by the noise and dust, but also by the floodlights outside her window. She'd taken to closing her windows, but this exacerbated one of her children's breathing problems:

Photograph 9.7: West Hendon estate – living next to a building site (view from balcony), 2014

'The noise, I've got it here all day or clanging of metal. And then at night when its 5 o'clock and they've got all the floodlights on, you've have to shut your curtain, because all the floodlights are coming in your window. It's just a building site ... months that's been. Yeah, all the dirt from the building site, the windows were black.'

Pat described how she was unable to open her windows in her new flat at West Hendon: "the dust, the noise is *horrendous*!" Joseph related how the drilling at Westbury affected him and his ill elderly neighbour: "It interferes ... the noise and disruption ... of peaceful and quiet enjoyment of people's lives, the health effects. Like that man, the 73-year-old man who's ill, they're drilling in front of his door for weeks."

If noise and dust pollution are bad enough, residents were also distressed by how work went on outside of the stipulated hours: "they've turned up on bank holidays when they shouldn't with heavy machinery drilling in the concrete, we've seen lorries turn up and park there with fumes" (Joseph). They complained about out-of-hours working to on-site managers with mixed results:

'As part of their planning permission they get set hours where they can work, so it's 8 till 6 weekdays and 8 till 1

Saturdays. Over the years they've been doing it, they've continually breached the stuff about deliveries turning up before 8 o'clock, working after 6 o'clock and so on, we have had to continually raise it. So now there is a big sign saying "vehicles turning up before 8 o'clock won't be unloaded". Well that is only there because of our complaints over the years, and it still gets breached. Every time it gets breached, they say "well we're doing this now", and then it's quiet for a week and then it happens again.' (Ben)

A Brent Labour Councillor was very sympathetic to residents' complaints, like those of Ben:

'there are periods when my [email] inbox has been 45 per cent complaints about the construction firms in South Kilburn. That's like a daily 20 email barrage of, "they turned up too early/they're making noise on a Sunday/they park their cars in our car parking space/they're smoking outside our block/they're doing X, Y..." – never ending.'

Even if building work did not formally start until 8 am, noise could still emanate from the workers before then: "in the morning at 7.30 they start walking in group of five from here. They talk loud, they laugh, they shout, you know someone here standing here shouting to someone over there, didn't care that this is your bedroom here" (Shiela). Danni was also disturbed by the workers: "they're very noisy and they have got no consideration for the people that are living here". This lack of consideration included profanities, as one female resident commented with great annoyance at a West Hendon regeneration meeting: "We live in this neighbourhood and we hear them effing and blinding it. We're finishing our school run at 4 pm and they're out there swearing all of the time." Such 'not caring' behaviour symbolised tenants' second-class status, devalued by class and tenure: "they think that this is their own possession and we're their slaves, so they have the right to deal with us as they wish to" (Shiela). Direct complaints to the site office occasionally produced results, as Lilly proudly described:

'You have to even keep an eye on the workmen. Well the other Saturday, I caught them banging and crashing out there at 7.20. So I went outside and I went to him [manager in the Portakabin] and I went [taps watch] and it went dead. The men were stopped, there was a real hoo-ha about it.'

If constant complaining could mitigate negative effects, residents also had to provide evidence to the council which reinforced a general sense of not being taken seriously due to their second-class status: "if we don't take photos it hasn't happened. If we didn't do it [complain], nobody would notice that we had problems" (Ben).

All residents' complaints at West Hendon – the neglect, the noise, the disruption, the illegal out-of-hours working – were graphically summarised by a Barnet Labour Councillor who worked closely with residents in trying to alleviate what they described to her as 'torture':

> 'I just get phone calls [from residents] all the time. I can't even hear the people speaking in their own homes because the noise is so bad outside the window, and they are just desperate. They go to the site managers and say, "please we can't hear ourselves think, I can't hear my television, I can't speak on the phone", and they say "oh yes something will be done", and *nothing* is done. The noise never stops and one time they had these bright lights that were shining into people's rooms from about 6 in the morning. They are living a nightmare and then they are suddenly given the choice of some sort of awful place to move to and if they don't say "yes" then they are out. In fact they have just said recently that "its human torture", that's their own words.'

The mass media: producing urban dystopias

The mass media stigmatise estates and social tenants and contribute towards the symbolic devaluation of both people and places (Chapter 7). Territorial and tenurial stigmatisation *worsen* at estates undergoing regeneration, exacerbating already-existing symbolic devaluation – hence resulting in *symbolic degeneration*. Such degeneration is predicated upon the increased corporeal presence of film and TV crews at estates, as discussed below.

As Clarke (2003) argues, the consumerisation of the urban occurs via 'selling the city'. Urban landscapes are increasingly valorised for their symbolic rather than their utilitarian connotations via urban entrepreneurialism (Harvey, 1989). In Guy Debord's terms, cities become the main sites for the 'society of the spectacle' (Gerrard and Farrugia, 2015: 2219). Consumer capitalism creates safe spaces for consumption – the archetypal shopping mall – against which rough sleepers constitute the "aesthetically spoiled homeless Other" (Gerrard and Farrugia, 2015: 2226; and see Kennelly and Watt, 2011). One of the ironies of consumer capitalism is how spaces of advanced marginality – such as public housing estates – can be symbolically transformed into spaces of valorisation via their insertion into circuits of mediatised capital accumulation. This happened in relation to the siting of the 2012 Olympic Games in Stratford, which saw all three Carpenters estate tower blocks emblazoned with large corporate advertising while the top floors of two blocks became the locations for BBC and Al Jazeera TV film crews covering the Games (Watt, 2013). Residents resented how this additional corporate cash bypassed the estate and went straight into the council's coffers: "none of that revenue, 'we [council] won't actually spend it on the people in Carpenters'" (Abiola).

If the Olympics promoted 'spectacular capitalism' (Kennelly and Watt, 2011), the entrepreneurial sale of cities involves the hyperreal promotion of urban dystopianism, for example via poverty porn TV shows (Tyler, 2013, 2015). What better place to locate such urban dystopias than in the epicentre of the city's abjections: the council estate? TV and filmmakers wish to find a suitable landscape for their dystopian urban imagery: stigma sells. The mediatisation and sale of territorial stigma has occurred via the marketing of estate place myths – that such places are nether-worldly 'sink estates' populated by an unruly 'underclass'. What is less understood is how the selling of territorial stigma is predicated on real-world processes of degeneration as estates empty out and visibly crumble. This section looks at the travelling media circuses that visit the estates and what happens when TV and film production takes place at regeneration estates.

As with so many regeneration issues, the Heygate is emblematic of the intertwining of media and real-world degeneration (Chapter 7). The Heygate was routinely used by *The Bill*, but this TV/film usage intensified as residents were displaced and the estate emptied out (Photograph 9.8). In a *Guardian* article – 'South London's Heygate estate mourned by locals – and Hollywood' – Walker (2010) comments how it was subject to almost two film/TV shoots a month from 2007–10, including *Harry Brown* (2009), 'a drama about a widower who takes on local drug gangs'. Olive said that the TRA received money for the filming, as Walker mentions. Walker notes how Southwark Council only permitted filming provided the Heygate was not identified.

While the filming may have financially benefited Heygate residents, the relentless media representation has helped to cement the 'sink estate' place myth in place, irrespective of whether a specific estate is identified or not. This can be seen in how many of the 126 Heygate film shoots for the March 2007–August 2010 period were crime-related, as in *The Bill* and *Luther*.[5] These are generally within a realist

Photograph 9.8: Heygate estate – empty flats, graffiti and trees, 2012

genre, but others present a dystopian view of a blurred present/near future as in *Attack the Block* (2011), a horror-comedy mash-up which pits London 'hoodies' against aliens, and *Shank* (2010) in which, 'In a dystopic future London in 2015, society has fallen apart, gangs have taken over, and the economy is in complete anarchy'[6].

The dominant narrative arc of the Heygate – from post-war municipal utopianism to present/future dystopianism – has been captured by experimental filmmaker Chris Saunders in his haunting film *Memory Block* (2016). This film juxtaposes dystopian imagery of urban decay taken from films and TV programmes such as *Harry Brown*, *Attack the Block* and *The Bill*, with tenants' home-movie footage and scenes from the 2013 CPO inquiry (35% Campaign, 2013). In *Memory Block*, neighbours cheerfully wave to each other in the blurred home-movie footage, while the CPO filming shows residents protesting at how the regeneration was not being done in their name – it's not for us.

Symbolic degeneration associated with the intrusive presence of TV/film crews has occurred at several estates. At Westbury, "since regeneration was announced, we've had an increase of people filming and they're literally on your doorstep with dogs, music, loudspeakers, barbeques, the whole day strangers" (Joseph). Not only was the TV/film crew presence physically disruptive, but Joseph was aggrieved at what the films were representing: "I think they want to recreate the 'typical rundown environment estate', that's the theme." This 'sink estate' theme is also racialised in that films and TV shows reinforce the racist stereotype of the crime-ridden 'black ghetto' (Romyn, 2019). As a black professional, Joseph was aware of this ghetto stereotype, and was affronted at how it was being produced in his treasured neighbourhood:

> 'This morning I was at the bus stop and I saw these people walking over to Westbury, so I pretended I was just a stranger. So I said, "are you doing a movie?" "Yeah, we're doing a movie." "What is it about?" "Just estates and crime", and they went on Westbury. Basically, what they're recreating is slums and inner-city life, and black stuff and gangsters [laughs]. I live there, so they come there to recreate that! They come there with actors and dogs, music, it's "typical" in their mind, trying to confirm your "typical gangster estate life" [laughs]. And that is authorised by Lambeth [Council], because they have to get a permit for that, but Lambeth doesn't tell us, they don't inform us.'

When I asked Joseph if there was any truth in this 'inner-city' portrayal, he was adamant there was not: "*No!* If it was like that for even a fraction of a second, I would never have lived there for 20 years. It's not like that, it's a very, very quiet decent place, mixed environment, a real community." Or it was until neglect, population transience and ASB worsened via degeneration.

Shifting aims, broken promises and lack of trust

There was often considerable resident support for *some form of regeneration*, especially in the initial stages (Chapter 8). However, support, engagement and trust dissipated as the plans, partners and finance changed, plus due to sheer fatigue as regeneration and its demonic degeneration alter ego drag on interminably. The notion that they'd been misled at best or lied to at worst – as plans changed and early promises were broken – was an all-too-familiar leitmotif: "the original promises were not kept, and I cannot tell you how many different plans you had, it was horrendous" (Barbara, Woodberry Down).

Residents who had supported regeneration in its early stages subsequently became vocal opponents. Kathleen had initially welcomed the Canning Town/Custom House regeneration but changed her mind as the scheme unfolded: "we're not opposed to the regeneration, we're opposed to the way Newham Council have changed their ideas". The latter included the lack of new suitable shops, but also how tenants were unable to return to the new properties as council tenants. The latter represented a "massive difference" for Kathleen because it wasn't what "we were promised originally". The proposal did not offer council housing tenancies to returnees (Chapter 8). However, while 'breaking a promise' may be technically inaccurate, the presentation of the 'three guarantees' was obfuscatory and contributed to residents' lack of trust towards regeneration and the officials and politicians who were driving it, as indicated by the subsequent collapse in the Labour Party vote in Canning Town (Chapter 8).

Lack of trust in councils and housing associations was a prominent theme at many of the meetings I attended. This breakdown in trust is exemplified by residents mounting legal challenges to regeneration (Chapter 11). One example is how the first Cressingham Gardens JR in 2015 found in favour of tenants that they had not been properly consulted because their preferred options (involving refurbishment not large-scale demolition) had been withdrawn by the council (Photograph 9.9; Douglas and Parkes, 2016).

A chartered surveyor explained why there's often a large gap between the consultation and what transpires many years later at the tail-end of

Photograph 9.9: Cressingham Gardens estate – 'Lambeth Council lied to us' protest signs, 2015

the regeneration process when residents bitterly complain, 'this isn't what we were told would happen during the consultation':

> 'It's a huge gap and often because the original process of consultation, the developer's normally not on board and they come in with their own ideas. Or the developer may well change, and they'll come in with their own ideas, or very simply it's taken so many years and the market has changed. Quite often the market changing can be used as justification from councils or developers to change what they originally intended to do. Almost every estate I work on, leaseholders, tenants alike, they rightly harp on about "we want like for like, that's what we were promised". This term, "like for like", I hear everywhere and it's extremely rarely actually offered, apart from during the consultation period. During the consultation, you can offer what you like because years later, when you're actually doing it, it's very easy to get away from previous promises simply by saying, "circumstances have changed, new developer, the market's altered".'

Not getting 'like for like' was one of the key objections raised by residents at the 2015 West Hendon CPO inquiry; in other words, that the plans they were balloted on back in 2002 had not transpired (Hill, 2015). At the 2017 CPO Inquiry, Barnet Council rebutted the notion that there had even been a ballot, and instead described it as a, 'non-statutory test of opinion, … to determine the level of support for the *principle of regenerating the estate*. When the non-statutory test was undertaken it considered only the principles associated with regeneration rather than a developed scheme or masterplan' (Worden, 2017: 53; emphasis added). In other words, the large gap between consultation promises and what occurs in reality is inherent in the process, because of how consultation (even if it includes a 'test of opinion') is merely an in-principle affair that provides *zero legal accountability* for disgruntled residents years later down the lengthy regeneration track.

At West Hendon, tenants objected to how the main social housing block was in the worst section of the redevelopment – in the old car park area behind the busy Hendon Broadway thoroughfare – away from the Welsh Harp where the new private apartments were sited (Chapter 12). As Cheryl angrily recounted, this relocation confirmed tenants' second-class status and ratcheted up feelings of class resentment:

'It's just been prolonged and delayed and then we had them coming around and telling us we could move back into where we are. Then all of a sudden it's changed, and we've all been *crushed* into the car park. I went to the last meeting and I spoke to a guy [from a housing association] who was chairing the meeting, and I said to him, "you just want to change this bit into a private estate and chuck us out", and basically he said "yes". I said to him "why have you gone back on your plans, because we were supposed to go back in Y but now you're putting us in the car park?" He said boldly in the meeting, "who would buy flats over there?" It's built on a car park. You've got a garage there that's been there for donkeys' years. You've got a chicken shop, the smell and the grease that comes out of the back of that, and when it rains the one-way system absolutely gets flooded and drenched. But because I'm not an official person, I'm just an ordinary resident, they've just … you know.' (Cheryl)

Ernie expressed a widely held opinion at Carpenters estate: "The council, as far as I'm concerned – and several people would probably back me up on this – the council have never been truly open in where they want to go" (see also Frediani et al, 2013). At Woodberry Down, a major shift in phasing occurred which had negative effects on residents who had to live in old, unmodernised properties much longer than originally 'promised' (Belotti, 2014). Marion liked her old flat at Woodberry Down and especially its location with views over the reservoir. However, she was swayed by the early regeneration presentations which implied that she would have a new flat in the *same location* – near the reservoir. Marion spoke at length about her own and her fellow tenants' growing disillusionment with regeneration meetings, and she grieved over the fact that her old block remained standing years after she had moved out, and was annoyed that it would eventually be replaced by an expensive apartment block (Chapter 12).

'I think they [tenants] were excited to begin with because what you were told is there was *no threat*, there was *no problem*, you were going to move into a brand new, spanking clean, beautiful flat where you've just moved out of. I think everybody was under the impression that there's nothing to lose but 100 per cent to gain. It felt like a whole new beginning, but I'm going to move in where I am. So literally where I'm sitting now – this chair would be demolished and I would sit in a brand-new chair exactly where I am here. And I think that is what everybody expected. As the meetings changed, people got disillusioned because there were people [officials] standing with a board, and tenants were raising their arms to ask a question and they had no idea how to answer you, they had their own script which they then were telling you. Then I stopped going [to meetings], purely because we [tenants] were all asking questions and they had no answers. We are trying to find out, these are *our homes*. You were beginning to then feel that you were going to be taken away from your home and you had no idea what your future would be. And that's how I feel about [the old block]. I'm taken away from my security, my home that I'd lived in for 51 years, and that is now going to be taken away from me because I was told it was going to be demolished. And it's still there. And when it does get demolished, *if* it gets demolished, it will be a private block of flats.'

During my interview with Gordon, a WDCO stalwart, I referred back to early regeneration documentation which stated: 'A Community Based Housing Association, underwritten by the D [Housing Group], will have resident representation on the management board to enable local people to participate in local management and decision-making' (Woodberry Down Regeneration Team, 2009: 30). As Gordon admitted, the cuddly sounding 'Community Based Housing Association' never happened:

'That didn't go through, and the promises that were made there ... well I think it was a bit of a sweetener really for a lot of residents. You know you live in the fantasy land for a while and then you come back to reality because none of it was going to happen. Yes, that was the idea at that time, but I mean the government didn't come across with the money and that fell through.'

Having residents on the management board did not materialise either: "that's just pie in the sky really. There's a lot of things in that document that when you ask them now, there'll be a silence, because a lot of the staff switch over" (Gordon). While Gordon was phlegmatic about the watering down of the early regeneration promises, other tenants felt cheated: "they really lied to people" (Terry).

If substantial changes and lack of trust are built into the regeneration process – due to fuzzy consultations, shifting partner organisations and changing market conditions – these features are compounded by official staff turnover. At meetings, residents frustratingly referred to earlier verbal guarantees/promises they had received which were no longer valid, while the staff who gave these had long since departed. An architect working with People's Empowerment Alliance for Custom House (PEACH; Sendra and Fitzpatrick, 2020: 51–5) explained what negotiating with the council entailed:

> 'There's a high level of [staff] turnover, because we are constantly in negotiation with the council and, at the beginning we were negotiating with a different person every six months. Because, "now it's so-and-so who's the lead of regeneration, now it's so-and-so". No continuity and that obviously had a massive effect on such a large project.'

At Woodberry Down, some of the staff involved had been working on the scheme for several years (nine for the IRA, six for one Hackney Council officer), and during this period they had built up substantial trust with residents. However, this atypical staff longevity is still *not equivalent* to that of residents who had been in situ since regeneration was first mooted at Woodberry Down nearly 20 years previously. Gordon described how the original staff were no longer involved:

> 'The majority of the people [officials] that started off here are not here at all. The people that were with the council they're not here anymore, and the people with the housing association are not here anymore. I mean you know that was a new [housing association] assistant manager that came in there, the guy with the glasses. He only started a couple of weeks ago and by the looks of it he ain't going to be here long [laughs].'[7]

Residents became the regeneration memory repository. Gordon thought that this might even work to WDCO's advantage in knowing things the other partners did not. The shifting sands of official personnel reflect the inordinate longevity of the schemes, and also the profound chronological and ontological gaps between residents' life-worlds and the official regeneration edifice: "With Lambeth [Council], the officers, they come and go. For example, the original crew, I think it's just M that's there, the rest have gone. So it's a revolving door. But for us, it's where we live, it's our lives" (Joseph).

Waiting for Godot in limbo-land

The temporal, long-term nature of estate regeneration has received scant academic attention, with Davidson and colleagues (2013) being unusual. In fact, one of the major methodological challenges regarding regeneration research is the timescales involved. Programmes are initially projected to take 10–15 years on the larger estates, but the reality is often longer – 20–30 years – for those involving comprehensive redevelopment. Such timescales do not fit into research grant deadlines. An exception is one of the most ambitious UK regeneration evaluations, that of the NDC which was undertaken by the Centre for Regional Economic and Social Research (CRESR) at Sheffield Hallam University from 2002 to 2009 under the leadership of Paul Lawless.[8] Despite its longevity, even eight years is too short because it misses the long-term impacts and ongoing nature of the post-NDC regeneration. This limitation has prompted underfunded lone researchers to return to NDC sites in order to ask, 'what happens to estates and their residents after the multi-million pound regeneration programme has wound up and after the research evaluation teams have packed up their measuring tools?' This section addresses this question by focusing on how the endless nature of regeneration impacts on residents. In so doing, it offers a similar perspective to that of Andrew Wallace, who returned to the Salford NDC several years after it had finished (Wallace, 2010b, 2015).

Regeneration-as-demolition is not simply a matter of 'it'll get worse before it gets better', as Davidson and colleagues (2013) suggest. It's more complex and disturbing than that. All the above mentioned degeneration strands – the deteriorating environment, worsening housing, increased transience and living on a building site – affect residents in real time over years and even decades. Regeneration time-frames elongate by two or even three times. Residents living in London's 'failed' but now 'renewing' estates enter an existential black hole – what Wallace (2015) calls a 'limbo-land'. The psychosocial feeling of being in limbo was a recurrent theme in my research:

'We had been out in limbo so many times when like "this is what's going to happen", blah, blah, blah. And then suddenly "no we can't do this because of …", and you're back in limbo again.' (Ernie, Carpenters)

'We shouldn't be afraid to speak out, but people think if they speak out they won't get rehoused. My children were brought up here. I am now in limbo, I am just a number to them. They [council] don't care if they hurt your feelings.' (Female leaseholder, Aylesbury meeting, 2015)

'I put everything on hold, I don't see my family, I don't see my friends, everything is about regen.' (Rose, Cressingham Gardens)

As regeneration drags on and on, this limbo existence deepens while cynicism and disengagement intensify. People who used to diligently attend regeneration meetings cease doing so. George stopped attending meetings at Clapham Park once the schedule was yet again pushed back:

'In 2006, they said that we would move out and everything would be demolished by 2011. I used to go to meetings and then by 2011 they said they have no money so then I stopped going to meetings, what's the point in going? Then it was going to happen by 2015, then 2017 and now it's 2021! God knows when they're going to do it.'

Audrey had been active in various TRAs at Clapham Park and she remained a community volunteer in the post-NDC period. Like George, she was dismayed at the changing schedules and delays: "The flats I lived in, we were told they would be refurbished in 2010, then we were told were told it would be 2011, then it went up to 2013, then it went back to 2012. It got done last year [2015]." As Alf said, the regeneration at West Hendon was rescheduled as the stakeholders changed:

'They kept putting it off and putting it off and putting it off. "We'll do it next year, oh we'll do it in five years' time, we'll do it, we'll do it in…", you know. First of all, it was the council was going to get involved right, but "oh, we've got no money". So, they brought C [housing association] and D [developer] in on it and they were the first two companies that was involved in it, and of course

it didn't happen. And then D dropped out and that's when
E [developer] took up.'

Residents received different timescales from officials which only added
to their sense of living in limbo. Dolores reported how she and her
fellow Aylesbury residents were confused by the different messages:

'At the moment I know that it's coming down, but we
don't know when, because different people say different
times. They [neighbours] say two years, but when you go
to the council, they tell you, "don't worry it's going to be
at least ten years". My neighbour told me that a housing
officer told her that "it's coming down in two years", so
I don't know why they are giving this information. They
are giving different dates. I don't think it's good for our
health because many people live in limbo, they don't know
what's happening and I think this is no good.'

In such fraught, uncertain and all-encompassing life circumstances –
'when will our homes be demolished, when will I have to leave and
where will I go?' – it's unsurprising that residents talk to each other and
share their snippets of information. Contradictions are built into the
process as officials either attempt to assuage residents' anxieties or simply
don't know themselves. Residents became fatigued and exasperated as
regeneration dragged on interminably:

Lilly: 'We should have been gone from here a long time ago, and
          every time this got near the time, it got put back, it got
          put back and we are still sitting here in 2014.'
Vicky: 'Grinds you down.'

Sheer exhaustion and weariness set in. A male Aylesbury tenant said at
a 2015 regeneration meeting, "I've been living here for 22 years and
I'm tired of this, I just want to get on with my life". As degeneration/
regeneration rolls on and their lives trickle out, people despaired: 'when
will this end?' Like Samuel Beckett's Vladimir and Estragon, residents
were *Waiting for Godot* – but Godot never arrives. They were stranded
in limbo-land in perpetuity (Wallace, 2015). When I interviewed
Kathleen in 2013, she was dumbfounded by the length of time 'regen'
was taking at Custom House: "it was all supposed to be done and
dusted within eight years. Thirteen years down the line we're still …
do you know what I mean? Well the way it's looking, we'll be here for

another nine years at the moment". Given the minimal redevelopment progress at Custom House in the intervening years, nine years is an underestimate. In 2019, the PEACH architect explained what had happened there: "at this point there's still no planning application, there's no tender, nothing's happened, there's no developer. They [council] decanted at least half, probably more, of the original tenants, and nothing's been built, there's been no development partner". The same situation – a half-empty estate, but no development partner and no redevelopment – exists at the Carpenters estate (Chapter 12).

Disinvestment, blight and pushing up daisies

As well as landlord disinvestment discussed above, owner-occupiers and tenants cut back on their domestic self-provisioning under regeneration, making their homes feel less homely: "I mean we've not put a new kitchen in because we just don't know whether it's worth spending two grand to put a kitchen in – you're just in limbo" (Lee). The chartered surveyor described this as routine:

> 'It's always happening, every single estate I ever work on. People tell me, "I was thinking about fitting a new kitchen but I thought I'd be moving out soon so I didn't bother". I hear the same things repeatedly. People don't appreciate that they could be living there for years because they think the regeneration is going to happen a lot quicker.'

As the surveyor explained, "there's less investment by the acquiring authority and less investment by the leaseholders". Decreased self-provisioning, plus landlord disengagement, represents a significant aggregate financial disinvestment in estate properties once demolition is decided upon. Therefore, in addition to the degenerative features discussed above, the financial value of demolition estates drops. They become 'blighted' leaving owner-occupiers trapped in homes they cannot sell on the open market: "No prospective buyer would buy into the estate, since no mortgage company would lend money for a property which is scheduled for demolition" (Belotti, 2016: 13). Lilly (West Hendon) found out that her flat was blighted by trying to sell it via a local estate agent:

> 'They can put your property in the window, but nobody can get a mortgage, had to be cash buyer. I said to them [estate agent], "tell me the truth, do you think there's a chance?"

He said, "I don't think so because it's blighted". It comes up at all the meetings, the word "blighted".'

Farhad's RTB flat was blighted at Woodberry Down due to the rephasing.

> 'They [council] keep changing their mind. The regeneration has been going on since 2003 or something like that. This was supposed to come down in 2017 since we were in Phase 3, but we're in Phase 5 now [in 2017]. We were supposed to move from here two years ago, but now they say it could be another six or seven years. It's annoyed us because we don't know where we stand. We cannot get a mortgage to buy a flat elsewhere, we're stuck here basically.'

The elderly felt trapped in places that were shadows of their former selves. Melissa described her elderly mum's limbo existence on the Carpenters estate:

> 'She obviously loves her home, she's in her 80s now so the last thing she wants to do is move. My dad's not around anymore so she's on her own. Everyone's moved out, but she's bought her house and I don't see why she should be forced out of her home at this time in her life where she should be relaxing. But she doesn't even know whether to do her kitchen or put her gate on her garden door because she's in limbo.'

Elderly residents commented that they might not be alive to see the completion of the regeneration, as sadly happened to three of my interviewees. While I was on a site visit at Clapham Park in 2016, an elderly female tenant said to me, "regeneration is a gimmick, they never do it – all my friends were waiting, but they just died". As people were filing out of a lengthy and acrimonious meeting at West Hendon in 2014, one female resident remarked how she was, "fed up with it, it's been going on since 2002. I was 50 when it started, but I'll be pushing up daisies by the time it's finished". Bob was contacted by people living in the seven blocks at Woodberry Down who were frustrated at being pushed back in the phasing and were struggling living in damp flats: " 'why is it we keep getting changed and changed? I suppose I'll be dead before they decide to do our blocks up!', which is probably right, the way they are [going]". Premature deaths result from physical displacement, but they also occur due to the stress and anxiety caused by waiting for the bulldozer to arrive (Chapter 3; Watt, 2009a; Crookes, 2011; Morris, 2019). Terry thought the uncertainly brought about by rephasing resulted in premature deaths at Woodberry Down:

> ' "Your blocks are in Phase 1, that means it's going to get knocked down in the next three years." "Okay, no problem." "Oh, we've changed the phasing, now your blocks are in Phase 3, that means your blocks won't get knocked down for another ten years." That's ten years, like come on, there's a big difference. That's why I said people might say, "oh, the old people died of normal…", but I don't think so. I think it was exacerbated by the lack of knowledge what they're going to be doing next.'

Conclusion

This chapter has painted a grim and disturbing picture of how regeneration morphs into degeneration: physical, social, symbolic and psychosocial. In *physical* terms, degeneration deepens the estates' rundown status through managed decline/enhanced neglect over and above standard landlord neglect (Chapter 7). Managed decline involves financial disinvestment, suspension of the DHP, depleting maintenance, unresponsive repairs, and worsening cleaning and caretaking services. The result is a downward spiral of housing conditions and estate appearance. Physical degeneration is marked in the landscape by boarded-up properties which symbolise the doxic place myth – 'no one wants to live in these failed places' – and contributes towards symbolic devaluation and degeneration.

Social degeneration occurs via decanting and buying-out of familiar neighbours who leave and are replaced by a shifting gallery of new faces – squatters, temporary tenants, private tenants and property guardians. These are all exemplars of the mobile, rootless 'transients who are here today and gone tomorrow' (Savage et al, 2005: 53). These transients, however, are not globalisation winners, unlike the affluent middle classes and super-rich elite. Instead they are members of London's housing precariat whose fate is to be buffeted around the city's marginal netherworlds, cast adrift and searching for a home, any home. Degenerating estates become transit camps for the housing precariat rather than homes for the relatively stable working-class communities that existed pre-regeneration. Estates become more socially anomic places as mutual neighbourliness and local social capital evaporate and

ASB increases. Physical deterioration and empty properties make these half-empty estates more appealing for urban dystopian TV programmes and films which only adds to the already-existing symbolic devaluation of these working-class people and places – territorial stigmatisation is heightened, and *symbolic degeneration* occurs.

Psychosocial degeneration occurs through the enormous psychological strains that residents are put through – via the stress of living on a building site, the depressive loss of familiar faces, anxiety around when and where they will have to move, and the endless nature of degeneration/regeneration which propels them into a limbo-land of lives put endlessly on hold. A 'why bother?' attitude sets in which manifests in reduced domestic self-provisioning, which in turn contributes towards overall financial disinvestment. Owners are trapped in blighted properties. Degeneration wears people out, mentally and physically, while elderly residents die before 'regen' is completed.

The combined effect of the multiple degeneration strands on remaining residents and what used to be 'their place' is truly tragic. Degeneration narrows the ontological gap between the 'sink estate' place myth and residents' lived experiences. In other words, the physical dilapidation, social anomie and symbolic devaluation that characterises this pervasive place myth becomes *more* – not less – part of residents' everyday lives. As this gap closes, so the stage is set for residents' displacement, the subject of the next chapter.

10

Displacement

This chapter focuses on residents' displacement experiences, both before and after physical relocation.[1] It begins by providing an overview of dispossession with reference to social cleansing. It then analyses displacement among social tenants, the tenure with the greatest rehousing rights, including the right to return, and examines the displacement anxiety theme. The next two sections examine the physical displacement experiences of secure council tenants – those who have returned to new properties in the redeveloped neighbourhood, and those who relocated away from the estate. The displacement experiences of owner-occupiers are then discussed, followed by the temporary tenants. The penultimate section scrutinises what the right to return really means, while the final section discusses agency, control and power in rehousing.

Dispossession

The Introduction summarised the notion that estate regeneration involving demolition forms part of what Harvey (2003) calls accumulation by dispossession. Urban working-class populations are dispossessed of publicly held resources, including land and housing, to make way for new predatory rounds of capital accumulation. In the case of estates, this occurs via the springing of the state-induced rent gap (Watt, 2013). This section presents residents' views on dispossession.

'It's not for us' – social cleansing

Many residents displayed a profound distrust of the official rationale for demolition as expressed by their routine invocation of 'it's not for us' – meaning us (ordinary working-class people) will not be the prime beneficiaries of regeneration, not least since we will be physically displaced away from the area (Watt, 2013). Ali is a Bangladeshi leaseholder at Northumberland Park estate and recalled how she became disillusioned with the official regeneration aims:

> 'I have been to the first meeting, there was a gentleman
> came in and he was talking about regeneration and he was

saying, "regeneration is going to be like this and like that", but there was no mention about the residents of the area. That kind of put me off. I was thinking "this is not for us, this is misleading us". They're going to make new buildings and they're going to have new green areas, new play areas or whatever but for who?! They're not going to be for us.'

Working-class residents like Ali thought demolition would primarily benefit them and not us. 'Them' consists of the social nexus involved in state-led gentrification including local authorities, housing associations, private developers, and the latter's affluent homeowning customers. Residents highlighted the underlying profits that would accrue to the various parties involved:

'When you hear the word "regeneration", that's just a nice way of saying "demolish". I think they want to get rid of council housing altogether and give it in the hands of private individuals who are making a profit out of it. You know it's sad, but true.' (Michelle, Northumberland Park)

RTB owners (like Ali) and tenants (like Michelle) felt that they may well not be living in the post-redevelopment area – that they would be socially cleansed from it. The term 'social cleansing' has become firmly established in London housing activist circles and refers to the displacement of the city's multi-ethnic, working-class residents away from their neighbourhoods due to evictions, demolitions, rent hikes and benefit cuts (Elmer and Dening, 2016; Watt, 2018c). Ordinary people from all tenures explicitly invoked this term. Damo lived in a shared-ownership flat at Northwold:

'When people think there's going to be redevelopment on the estate there's a feeling of "will we be cleansed from it?" People feel under threat generally, that people like us will get pushed out. People do know more and more people who are moving further and further out of London. Lots of people, if they grew up in a council house when they were kids, they don't really see a way that their kids can stay on the estate.'

William was an Aylesbury leaseholder who challenged the council's demolition decision. He had been checking house prices at the nearby Heygate redevelopment – Elephant Park – and concluded that not only would his family lose their beloved flat, but they would also be displaced away from Southwark and most likely from London:

'We found out that they [council] were just social cleansing. Because what was happening was the new ones they built, it was people coming from outside, coming in. When the foundations started [at the Heygate], they start selling it in China and all these places. I go on the computer and check what's happening and then we saw the prices – a one-bedroom [flat] was £488,000 on the new one!'

Given the Heygate leaseholder displacements and the large extent of overseas' investment at Elephant Park, William's social cleansing concerns are entirely realistic (Flynn, 2016; Transparency International UK, 2017). Several of the above-quoted interviewees actively contested estate demolition. What is striking is how 'social cleansing' was also invoked by interviewees who had disengaged from the regeneration process and were not involved in any collective resistance, such as Cheryl from West Hendon: "It's really bad what they've [council] done. And I think it's just social cleansing to be quite honest with you, what they're doing. And they're doing it all over, the councils. But what can you do about it? They don't listen to us. They're not for us at all."

Residents looked across the city with trepidation as they identified the same processes occurring time and time again – state-led gentrification masquerading as regeneration. Frank was adamant that the HDV scheme at Northumberland Park meant social cleansing, and he pointed to the Woodberry Down example, but he also felt that opposition to the HDV was a waste of time (Chapter 11):

'It's not regeneration, it's a mass extermination that's coming. There will be rows and rows of Woodberry Down [redevelopment] flats, every inch of here will be covered. They call it "luxury", but I feel sorry for everyone getting mugged off at Woodberry Down. They're dense buildings, they're squashing people in, smaller rooms, no storage space. The modern architecture cannot hold a candle to the past. There's lots of protests about it [HDV], but it's going to happen. They [council] see money. It's profiteering, they're not going to be putting in Housing Benefit people, they want to put everybody up in Stoke-on-Trent or Manchester. It *is* social cleansing – to think otherwise is naïve, and you haven't got a clue as to what's going on.'

Carpenters residents and ex-residents were only too aware that the Stratford area of Newham, where they were located, was rapidly gentrifying not least due to the 2012 Olympics (Watt, 2013; Corcillo, 2020). Such changes threatened to engulf the estate, a remaining working-class island in a sea of gentrification:

> 'They're lovely homes, but they [council] just don't want to do anything with them, because they want to get rid of that estate [Carpenters]. They're not interested in social housing, that's gone out with the dinosaurs, that's going to be extinct. I was born and bred here, this is my home, but I'm not part of what they want for this estate now. I do get really angry, I go to Westfield and I just feel like I don't belong, I don't fit into it. It's all about money, money, money, money. Carpenters estate doesn't fit in. They'll [council] regenerate it, but it won't be for working–class families.' (Melissa)

The previous fit between Melissa's working-class habitus and neighbourhood was being eroded by 'indirect displacement' (Marcuse, 1986), as it was for other Newham residents (Kennelly and Watt, 2012). Melissa also referred to Newham Council's 'Live, Work and Stay' logo, one which is belied by how homeless people were physically displaced outside London: "go to Hastings and all them places" (Melissa; Watt, 2018b). This interrelated set of losses – class, social housing, the estate, community – became sharply crystallised: "once you take away that community, you're social cleansing aren't you?" (Melissa).

London's social cleansing is also racialised (Perera, 2019). At a housing/regeneration meeting in Tottenham in 2014, the mainly black Londoners in attendance expressed concerns over how areas of the city with established black identities – such as Brixton and Hackney – were becoming whiter due to regeneration and gentrification (Wessendorf, 2014). They were fearful that regeneration would transform Tottenham in the same way, as seen in these quotes from two black female attendees:

> 'We will be forced to go to the outskirts of London, and they want to make inner London posh. It's happening in Dalston and Brixton – the government and council are

pushing this through. It's the regeneration and it will force people out of London.'

'What about our families? It's what we know. Once we move out, we'll never be able to move back. It's our home, we're Londoners.'

Social cleansing the 'others' – clearing out the 'riff raff'

The previous section has illustrated how a social cleansing discourse was invoked based on a socially inclusionary notion of estates as places; that multi-ethnic, working-class people – like us – would be removed by state-led gentrification masquerading as regeneration. However, a few residents drew narrow boundaries around 'us', such that it only included 'respectable' people – like themselves – but not *everyone* in the neighbourhood. For example, Beverly rented a house at Northumberland Park estate and like other social tenants was perturbed at what rehousing would mean in practice. At the same time, Beverly was bothered by drugs and youths in the local area and saw the HDV as providing a good opportunity to remove these disorderly elements: "there's a lot of riff-raff around the area and the regeneration will shift them out. They're trying to build the area up, so they don't want anything to stigmatise it".

Most long-term tenants were sympathetic towards temporary tenants who had the least rehousing rights. However, not everyone was so inclined, and I came across some who thought that these 'undeserving poor' *should be displaced* and not rehoused. I observed a protest at West Hendon and one elderly female council tenant bystander distinguished between council and temporary tenants: "the secures will be okay, it's just the non-secures and I don't care about them – they don't pay their rent anyway, the government pays [via Housing Benefit]".

Comprehensive redevelopment was thus acceptable for some long-term residents because it offered a *surgically precise* form of social cleansing that would cut out the rough and undeserving poor estate elements. Hence the associated devalued elements of estate life – crime and ASB (Chapter 7) – would be erased by demolition. The local abject 'others' (the 'riff raff') would be cleared out, making the redeveloped estate into a more orderly space, while respectable residents, like themselves, would be able to exercise the right to remain or return.

Social housing tenants: pre-relocation

Despite social tenants having better rehousing rights (Chapter 8), the prospect of relocation caused apprehension which is here analysed through the conceptual lenses of displacement anxiety (Watt, 2018a) and un-homing (Atkinson, 2015). The threat of demolition and rehousing undermined ontological security, built around their home and sense of community (Easthope, 2014; Morris, 2019). This was replaced with ontological insecurity and displacement anxiety *prior* to any physical displacement occurring. Displacement anxiety involves stress, worry and confusion over potential relocation and entails endless questioning: "If [housing association] demolish the estate where are they going to put us? Where will we have to go?" (R111, Northwold tenant). Sonia was "very stressed" by her imminent relocation and tried to temporarily escape (by taking breaks away) only to find even worse news when she returned home:

> 'It's almost like the council plan their awful letters for when I return, because every time I've gone away, I come back and there's always bad news waiting for me. This time when I came back it was a Compulsory Purchase Order, before then it was my notice of repossession, it's every single time I come back. I go away because I can't take it, I can't take it.'

Sonia was subject to both displacement anxiety and un-homing *before* she was physically relocated. Vulnerable tenants (due to ill health, disability, old age, and so on) were especially affected by displacement anxiety which can – and does – spill over into clinical anxiety, depression and even premature death (Chapter 3; Morris, 2019). Even though demolition was not imminent at Cressingham Gardens, its prospect had robbed Heather of whatever ontological security her home had once held and affected her already fragile mental health:

> 'I think the level of anxiety I'm having is as if they were demolishing it at the moment. It's pretty hellish really. I mean when I feel really vulnerable, it sort of transfers itself onto the flat, so that I'm in the flat and I don't feel safe in the flat. I think what I have done is kind of internalised a lot of the anxiety so it's in my body, so I am experiencing it physically, and then I am also projecting it onto my surroundings, if that makes any sense?'

Instead of tenants seeing their future, courtesy of regeneration, as a bright new dawn, it brought trepidation, stress and deteriorating health. Although Danni liked her new post-relocation flat, the protracted struggle she had to go through to obtain it (as a lone parent with three children) had health-damaging effects:

> 'I remember seeing my hair, it was just shedding, losing, I was just completely stressed. I think not sleeping, thinking a lot. In that sense I was really unhappy for well over a year, just really worried and afraid of what the future holds. I've got my young family and it's only me that makes the decisions. So really it affected me in a lot of ways.'

Tenants sought assistance with their decanting from official agencies and actors including lawyers, local politicians and health professionals. This was partly for practical assistance, but also to help them cope with the mental stress of forced relocation (Chapter 3). A GP who I interviewed described how tenants came to her practice "in their droves" as they were affected by the nearby estate demolition scheme: "it exacerbates their sense of stress, or any previous thing, mental health problems, and it exacerbates any other illnesses that they have. They are definitely frequent attenders". Not only did this GP see more stressed-out tenants, she also had to write letters of support regarding rehousing: "every surgery we have someone asking for a housing letter, so that would be ten letters a week". She was shocked at the inadequate support tenants had from the regeneration agencies and also at how this social issue had become medicalised: "they [tenants] come here often in frustration and they've been told to come and see their doctor, but the issue is not really about their medicine, it's about housing which I don't control". The GP identified a key issue that the regeneration industry is seemingly oblivious to, regarding tenants as nominal non-homeowners who nevertheless are losing their de facto homes that many have lived in and maintained for years (Chapters 6 and 8):

> 'I think the way it's [regeneration] been done currently is bad for people's health, because I think what you're forgetting is that even if you don't own your home, that *is* your home. I think that's the base that you have to start from. The fact that people might have been here for years, they call it their home.'

Social tenants: returning to the redeveloped estate

This section focuses on rehousing experiences in relation to the *domestic home scale* with reference to 30 social tenants (in 28 households) who were decanted, but who exercised the right to return (or remain) by moving to either new-build (27) or refurbished (1) properties at or near the footprint of the original estate. Twenty-five came from West Hendon and Woodberry Down, and the rest from Clapham Park, Ocean and Carpenters estates. The fact that these tenants remained on their estates, instead of moving away, indicates how most tenants valued their estates as neighbourhoods. Such place attachment is congruent with that identified in the critical displacement literature (Allen, 2008; Crookes, 2011; Slater, 2013; Morris, 2019). These London findings are therefore quite dissimilar from those Glasgow-based studies which have emphasised how tenants were only too keen to leave their areas because they had little place attachment and even felt fearful (Kearns and Mason, 2013; Egan et al, 2015; Lawson et al, 2015).

In focusing on the domestic home scale, this section concentrates on those tenants at the polar ends of the rehousing satisfaction spectrum: those who couldn't wait to move to the new flats, and those who bitterly resented being forced to move. Most tenants were somewhere in between these two polar positions. See Chapter 12 and Watt (Forthcoming) for further discussion, including tenants' displacement at block and estate scales.

Rehousing as liberation

A positive rehousing narrative – the replacement of old, overcrowded, damp and dilapidated council flats with new bigger flats – was prominent among previously un-homed tenants, such as Lorraine. She was a lone parent at West Hendon who opted to move earlier than scheduled due to overcrowding, and was "over the moon" with her new flat:

> 'I wanted to have a new start, especially when it got to the stage that my daughter was old enough to have her own room. My son had his own room, but I was sharing with my daughter, so it turned out perfect in the end. The plusses are that it's a new place, it's big … well mine is. It's double the size of everything that I had before, literally. The kitchen is a lot bigger, my daughter has her own room, my son has a room as well and I have mine. I have a dining table and

I can have guests in my kitchen now, because I didn't have that before.'

Lorraine and a few others like her experienced rehousing as liberation – they were freed from unsatisfactory and even intolerable housing conditions. Gerry's relocation experience at Woodberry Down was unambiguously positive (Chapter 8). He had zero attachment to his old flat because of its poor condition and wanted to leave as soon as possible: "I saw this letter and it says 'we are going to knock down your council flat', and I said 'thank god for that'." Mandy no longer felt "at home" in what had once been the family home. This was due to personal reasons (including the death of her husband), plus how her old Woodberry Down flat was poorly maintained. Like Lorraine, Mandy moved earlier than scheduled:

> 'I was in a four-bedroom flat on my own because my kids are all grown up. They [housing officials] said "would I like to move?", so I said "definitely". I couldn't wait because I thought I was going to have to wait until they knocked us down. Once my kids were grown up, there was nothing, just stuck in one great big flat. It was freezing, they [council] didn't fix the radiators proper, so I didn't see any sense in me staying there. I didn't have to leave but I wanted to.'

At the time of our interview, Mandy had been living in her new two-bed flat for around five years. Despite the housing association block being located on a busy main road, her flat was "one of the best" because of its rear-side location which meant it was relatively quiet. When I visited Mandy, the sun was streaming through the windows and the balcony door was open: "I love it, I used to hate it in the [old] flats, because the noise of it was atrocious."

Another perspective on un-homing is how tenants gave up self-provisioning at their old homes once they knew they were 'under regen' (Chapter 9). This was evident among single, middle-aged/ elderly men such as Sylvester. His old Clapham Park flat was one of the most dilapidated and spartan that I visited; black spores in the toilet, old malfunctioning windows, uncarpeted and hard-back chairs in the living room. Sylvester was long-term sick (part of the non-working poor) and had little money. He had also disinvested in his flat over the many years of regeneration, "because it's going to go in a few years' time". Sylvester later regretted this: "I didn't bother to get a carpet, because it was going to be demolished, so I didn't spend money on it but looking back I should have done." The combination of landlord neglect and his own disinvestment left Sylvester feeling un-homed in his old flat. By contrast, he was happy with his move: "My new flat's great. It's refurbished to a high standard, it has a decent-sized bedroom, a big living room, and a big bathroom and big kitchen. It feels like home now, I want to be here for the rest of my life." Mandy said how the housing officers mentioned how unusual it was for her to want to move: "they said 'my goodness we can't believe that, because a lot of the elderly people they don't want to move out of their flat'". The next section discusses some of those who did not want to move from their old homes.

Rehousing as bereavement

At the opposite end of the rehousing satisfaction spectrum were those tenants (mainly female) who suffered an intense emotional loss which can be termed 'rehousing as bereavement' (Fried, 1966; Marris, 1986). Annie had lived at West Hendon since the 1970s and had moved to a new flat in a purpose-built social housing block two years before our interview: "I appreciate that some people that sort of came from rubbish, they are absolutely over the moon here [new block], but I didn't. I had a lovely flat and they just took everything away from me." This dispossession was traumatic and involved deep feelings of ontological insecurity, un-homing and social injustice. Annie and others like her were not merely 'very dissatisfied' – as in a questionnaire response – they were distraught and furious at how a great social injustice had been committed and that they were suffering as a result. They had no sense of appreciating a brand new flat, because these were 'cheap rubbish' by comparison to the beloved homes they had been dispossessed from:

> 'It's absolutely bloody killing me here. Millions of people are in worse situations, but we didn't have to be in this situation. I didn't *choose* to be here. You [officials] took me from where I lived, and you put me here! And I am not going to be happy here, it doesn't matter what anybody says, this is not my home. My home was full of warmth and love and everything. There is nothing here, absolutely nothing.' (Annie)

Photograph 10.1: West Hendon estate – Annie's photograph of her old view (original 2014)[2]

Annie took photographs of the views looking out from her old and new windows (reproduced in Photographs 10.1 and 10.2) which powerfully express what she had lost through rehousing.

Annie and others like her are proud women – either living alone or with children – who put time, effort, care and love into making their flats *into homes*, and created values beyond value (Skeggs, 2014). We saw earlier how some single men gave up maintaining their domestic space. This was not the case for female tenants and reflects how demolition disadvantages working-class women in a gendered as well as classed manner (Gosling, 2008). These women were traumatised movers who experienced massive psychological loss (Marris, 1986). They mourned their old solid homes and felt betrayed and hurt at having to move to new flimsy, hotel-like, non-homes (Chapters 6 and 12):

'Despite what they [regeneration organisations] said, the rooms are smaller, you feel like you're in a hotel, Premier Inn. We've got X company, we can only have electricity. I left a beautiful gas cooker in my flat to move in there and I had to learn to cook on electric. They were *lovely flats*! They were out of this world! And then they come and give you something like that, made of wood, a piece of balsa wood. On a good day you can put your hand right through the wall. You can hear people upstairs doing it, coming through the vents, you can hear them talking.' (Pat)

Photograph 10.2: West Hendon – Annie's photograph of her new view (original 2017)

Pat highlights the small rooms, lack of choice and control in relation to energy suppliers ('only electricity'), and the thin walls which means she can people talking but also 'doing it' (having sex); she contrasted this to her previous 'lovely flat' which she missed. Similarly, Tina had lived in her old spacious flat with her grown-up children for nearly 30 years at Woodberry Down: "it was a lovely flat and I had done it up the way that I wanted it". By comparison, she disliked the standard kitchen-diner arrangement in her new two-bed flat, a common complaint among middle-aged and elderly female tenants, again reflecting the gendered (and ageist) nature of regeneration discontents (Gosling, 2008):

> 'This place, all of the furniture smells of cooking. They call these "luxury flats", but what's luxury about them I don't know [laughs]. They said they would knock them down in five years, but they're still there five years later. I just want to get my stuff and go back there. At least we had solid walls back there, not like here. Here, if someone's talking next door, you can hear them.'

Like other bereaved movers, Tina could see no good reason why her old 'solid flat' had been slated for demolition. These tenants were indignant at how their old blocks *remained standing* several years after they had moved out, indicating to them how the regeneration rationale – fundamental structural problems – was disingenuous.

Social tenants: moving away from the estate

This section focuses on the experiences of nine council tenants who spatially relocated *away from* their estates. One had left London altogether, but the other eight only moved a few miles away and remained within their boroughs. Six had successfully bid for council properties, while two became housing association tenants. Had regeneration not occurred, seven of the nine would *not* have moved, and hence can be described as 'reluctant movers'. Cathy liked her previous area and "really spacious" flat: "I wouldn't have moved, I was very happy living in Bacton for the rest of my life." Bonnie had similarly felt settled at East Dulwich: "You can now park 16 cars where you used to have 16 flats. That's where I lived and I lived at the top. It was lovely, it was beautiful and I was happy there."

The relocation process proved stressful, even for those who eventually managed to find a home and area that they liked. Olive had lived at the Heygate estate since it was first built. She had been an active member of the TRA (Chapter 6) and liked her home and neighbourhood, as did many other tenants (Heygate Was Home, 2014; Romyn, 2016). She did not want to leave but felt pressurised out by managed decline. Her relocation was protracted, extremely stressful and involved multiple moves – 'recurrent displacement' (Watt, 2018a). Having experienced hardly any crime or ASB at the so-called 'muggers paradise' estate (BBC, 2011), Olive moved to a house with garden but was there less than a year because of neighbour ASB problems: "I found out that he was an alcoholic, drug taker and mentally ill and from then on chaos. He started having screaming sessions and then he had a girlfriend who he would kick out at 3 o'clock in the morning." During the period that she lived at this flat, Olive lost around 20 kilograms in weight due to stress. After a protracted struggle with the council, she transferred to a second flat where she finally felt settled.

Four of the seven reluctant movers eventually managed to obtain a suitable property in an area that they liked. The other three were in worse housing circumstances than originally. Having been heavily involved in the regeneration process at Woodberry Down over many years, Terry became "sick and tired" of it: "they've [council] really consumed a lot of my time and my life with the regeneration, not knowing where you are and then moving out twice". Terry's first move was to another flat on the estate, but the second was away from the area: "moving off the estate, that's what really bothered me because it's a very nice area". Terry moved to a poorly maintained council flat elsewhere in Hackney. Ria remained visibly irate at her forcible rehousing and drew a stark comparison between her old beloved flat at the Carpenters estate – her 'palace' – and the 'crap hole' flat that she had to move to elsewhere in Newham:

> 'The one that I left was my palace, because if you was to see the inside of it, you would think that I had bought the flat because that's how it looked. Where I am now … I don't want to use the word, but that's what it is … a crap hole. When I actually found my way there to the flat, it had a bit of board over a broken glass, all the glass was on the floor in the passage, plus a bit of board nailed on the front door. When I got in, there was no electric, there was no heating!'

Ria's current one-bed flat was in such a poor condition that she could not move in for a month – an example of post-relocation un-homing. It was also much smaller than her Carpenters two-bed flat, which meant that she could not fit all her furniture in: "I was told that 'I need to throw them out and take what I need', the housing officer told me that." Eventually Ria gave her furniture away, a form of wastage (Glucksberg, 2013). The fact that Ria was only offered a one-bed flat also meant that her granddaughter – who had been living with her and provided care – had to move away to a cheaper borough: "they didn't offer her any flat and they didn't give me a two-bedroom flat, and now she's in private accommodation". Ria remained grieving in her new flat and neighbourhood, both of which she disliked intensely. Displacement is a 'hidden injury' of class (Sennett and Cobb, 1973) that still badly affected her: "brutalised actually, because I feel that I wasn't treated fairly, any of it from day one even till this day. It's made me very bitter about it because I didn't get what I was entitled to, and the [financial] compensation I've still never got".

Just two of the nine tenants – Niall and Femi – wanted to relocate, but this was because they had *already decided* that they wanted to do so. This is indicative of how rehousing can involve moving people further along an already decided-upon housing pathway (Kleinhans and Kearns, 2013). However, this was primarily for housing reasons rather than disliking their respective estates. Niall had been living in a "crappy bedsit" at New Kingshold estate and had been unsuccessfully applying to transfer to a larger flat, which became more urgent once he got married; he also did not want to "live on a building site" due to demolition. Femi was living with his family at the Carpenters estate, and as a young man he wanted to live independently. However, both Niall and Femi later came to regret their move from council to housing association tenancies due to inadequate information from officials: "I didn't even realise I was moving from a secure to an insecure [assured] tenancy. We didn't get any help whatsoever" (Niall). Femi also highlighted the "lack of clear advice", and compared his new neighbourhood much less favourably to the far more community-spirited Carpenters estate.

Owner-occupiers

In both fieldwork and interviews, I encountered near-universal antagonism towards demolition among owner-occupiers, plus extensive displacement anxiety. These issues are discussed in relation to RTB owners, and then with reference to incoming market homeowners (see Chapter 6).

Pre-relocation – RTB owners

RTB owner-stayers, like Ernie (Carpenters), felt affronted at being pushed out of homes that they had bought with every intention of remaining in: "I'll be leaving here in a wooden overcoat. The residents that've been here the longest, they just don't want to move, they want to just stay as they are." Residential longevity and age are both pertinent factors in this desire to stay put in the homes and neighbourhoods where they felt ontologically secure. Over 90 per cent of RTB owners had lived at their estates over 20 years; nearly half were aged over 60 and one third were over 70 (Table 4.4). Mary's husband, who was in his seventies, wasn't interested in any financial compensation and just wanted to stay put: "I don't want the money, where would I go at my age?" (Carpenters Against Regeneration Plans (CARP) meeting, Carpenters estate, 2012). Although Stan was critical about Northumberland Park as a place to live (Chapter 7), he liked his 'sound' flat. Stan was the carer for his elderly father (who was the owner): "I don't want to move, my dad's 88 and he doesn't want to move at that time of his life. I don't want to be faced with looking for a new property and dad certainly doesn't. If we'd have wanted to move, we'd have done it years ago."

If age is important, so is race/ethnicity (Cooper et al, 2020). Three BAME RTB owners baulked at having to move from two stigmatised estates – Aylesbury and Northumberland Park. The Aylesbury had been one of Southwark's 'hard-to-let' estates that BAME groups were rehoused from the 1970s (Carter, 2008), while Northumberland Park had a similar reputation in Tottenham. These BAME interviewees had raised their families and put down roots in their areas, as well as done 'the right thing' in terms of entering the property-owning democracy courtesy of the RTB (Chapter 6). The latter promise was literally about to turn to dust due to prospective demolition, as in the case of Gesil and William at the Aylesbury:

Gesil: 'This was bought for the future of our children. We did not buy this to move out, we want to stay in there, the children love the place. When we first move in here, nobody wants to come here, *nobody*. That was 1994, nobody wants to come here.'

William: 'The blocks were all empty.'

Gesil: 'And to take your child out, you are scared ... and now that the place is coming up, they want us to move out. That's when I plugged the corridors and said "no, I am not moving!"'

Now that the "place is coming up" – gentrifying – black working-class homeowners like Gesil and William were being pressurised to leave. Not only was the area near the estate gentrifying, but it was also becoming whiter, as has happened in traditionally black London areas: "It's becoming like Brixton, we used to live in Brixton before we moved there, Brixton is changed, that's what's happening here as well" (Gesil) (see Jackson and Butler, 2015 on Brixton).

Ali (Bangladeshi background) and her family had been placed at Northumberland Park nearly 30 years before when they were homeless. The family subsequently bought their flat under the RTB with the intention of fixing themselves in place:

'This area had a very bad reputation before, and because we were homeless we had no choice where the council put us. Wherever they told us to go, we went. Now we're living in this area for so long we got used to it, we made friends. We are accepted by the community, we are community members and everything. Now we inherited this area, this is our home. I want to die in this area, I want to die in this flat. Why are they taking everything away from us?' (Ali)

When BAME leaseholders – like Gesil, William and Ali – had moved onto their respective estates, the latter's low status signalled that *they themselves* weren't valued; they were just 'put' in hard-to-let estates that white tenants were better able to refuse (Carter, 2008). Now that they had created homes and communities in these areas – and now that the surrounding area was gentrifying and whitening – they were the 'wrong sort' of people – too BAME and too working class. They faced a *double stigmatisation* of being unworthy as both arrivers and potential leavers: being sent to a 'sink estate' in the first place, and then later being threatened with displacement once the area was 'coming up'.

Displacement anxiety featured even among estates which were relatively early on in the regeneration programme, such as Northumberland Park and Northwold. Given the significance of extended family relations among the British South Asian population, Ali was extremely concerned about being displaced away from Tottenham and her relations:

'I feel very bad, like I've been made homeless again. Because at the moment I'm not growing younger, my husband is going to be 60 next year. So to buy a house somewhere else, mortgage is out of question for us because of our age, so we'll have to buy a house with cash and how much cash are we going to get after paying the mortgage? I want to spend my old age surrounded by my friends, my neighbours, my family members. My younger sister lives in W Road, I can see her wall from here. I have one sister living in Wood Green. My husband's sister is living in Seven Sisters, and my daughter recently bought a flat in Tottenham Hale. I want to be close to my relatives when I'm old, and when I need help I want my family to be surrounded by me. I can't just pick up in my old age and go outside London and buy a house with cash money and be there *lonely*.'

As demolition and forced relocation loomed nearer, displacement anxiety heightened. Dolores (Aylesbury) was worried about where she (and her neighbours) would go since the new redevelopment flats were well outside their price range:

'This money [compensation] is not going to have a very spacious flat like this and for us it's going to be very sad when the time comes. It worries me so what am I going to do next. They want to take my home, so where I am going to live after this, this spacious and nice flat?'

Dolores felt sad and confused as to where she might move to. The prospect of *having* to move was psychologically overwhelming, as in her oft-repeated 'I don't know': "I love to stay here, but to be honest with you I don't know, I don't know when my time comes, I don't know what I am going to do, I don't know if I have enough money to hire a solicitor to challenge because they are so expensive."

Elderly homeowners expressed displacement anxiety about losing familiar faces, places and routines – their ontological security – as Gloria (Carpenters), who was in her seventies, commented:

'Where would I move with my husband? He's so used to the house and he's not well. For me to move now, it's all on my back because my husband can't do anything and it'll be all down to me, and I think I've got enough on my plate. Not only that, my neighbour has the key to my house, and I have got a key to my other neighbour's house, and we look out for each other. Where else am I going to go to find a neighbour who's going to look out for me? Christmas time we all exchange cards.'

The worst-case scenario was premature death due to the anxieties arising from prospective displacement – that is, 'death by displacement anxiety' (Chapter 3). Joseph described how two of his neighbours (a brother and sister in their late fifties/early sixties) had bought their property many years ago via the RTB, and how both had died under the strain of regeneration and prospective displacement:

'I know that in the last two years [of their lives] they spent their time distressed about regeneration. They didn't want to move, they didn't want their money, they just wanted peace of mind. They couldn't go anywhere else. It's sad that they spent their last years like that. That is what in a way, the level of severe emotional distress. It's intangible, but it's across many, many, many people. That's "regeneration".'

If displacement anxiety was prominent among RTB owner-stayers, it must also be noted how buying their flats or houses did in fact help them to 'stay put'. At several estates, including the Carpenters, it was the leaseholders and freeholders who were able to remain while most of their council tenant neighbours had been decanted (Chapters 3 and 12).

Pre-relocation – middle-class incomers

If long-term RTB owners felt distressed at the prospect of having their long-term roots and traditional place belonging ripped away, the middle-class incomers felt similarly aggrieved, albeit for somewhat different reasons. They faced the prospect of leaving homes and areas that they felt they had moral claims over via elective belonging (Savage, 2010). It came as a great shock that they were being uprooted from homes and neighbourhoods they had *chosen* to put down roots in:

> 'I remember thinking "oh my god, how stupid I've been". I've been totally conned into thinking I was investing in something that was going to actually amount to something at the end of the day. In terms of CPO, I mean basically it's sling your hook isn't it? I mean it's pretty devastating really to sort of spend ten years making something, putting all your effort into it and then be facing the end, like being totally shafted.' (Lisa)

Caroline highlighted how morally wrong she found the prospect of demolition and rehousing at Northwold, which she pointedly described as 'social cleansing':

> 'We [incomers] all bought somewhere within our means and we are being offered something that isn't within our means. So that isn't an offer, it's a false offer, it's a false option, and that is morally wrong. If I'd wanted to get myself into loads of debt, by buying a shared-ownership flat in an expensive luxury block, I would have done that, but I didn't want to do that, so I didn't and none of us did. We all bought ex-council flats because that was our income, that was what we could afford and we liked our flats.'

The prospect of having their moral claims to place removed was hugely threatening to their sense of wellbeing. This was even so for those who had only recently moved in, like Dylan and Allula at Northwold:

> 'You [Allula] texted me that it was going to be demolished and my heart sunk. I was really upset and we've not even lived here for more than a couple of weeks. You are handed the keys and you just think "I've got a home", and this is wonderful and then the next week it's going to be demolished, I mean that was devastating.' (Dylan)

This couple later found out that their flat was not earmarked for demolition, but this did not reassure them – "I'm petrified that they'll want to do it, they'll change their mind or whatever" (Allula) – indicative of entrenched displacement anxiety. Given the potential loss of their elective belonging as well as their developing sense of community (Chapter 6), it's unsurprising that several middle-class incomers played key roles in their anti-demolition campaigns (Chapter 11).

Relocation

This section focuses on displaced leaseholders from West Hendon and Woodberry Down. In 2019, I interviewed a chartered surveyor who represented 93 leaseholders from West Hendon of whom 43 were owner-occupiers and 50 were landlords. Twenty-one of the 43 owner-occupiers had taken up shared-equity properties at the redeveloped estate; I interviewed two people in this position (Lilly and Theresa). Of the surveyor's 22 remaining clients, only two had remained in Barnet; most had left London because they lacked sufficient economic capital to remain. Of the West Hendon RTB owners, I interviewed Oluwakemi, who became a private tenant elsewhere in Barnet, and Alf, who left London. At Woodberry Down, only three leaseholders had moved into the new flats (Nelson and Lewis, 2019), far fewer than at West Hendon, and I interviewed one of these (Alan).

I interviewed Theresa and Lilly together several months after they had moved into their new flats at West Hendon in 2016. Theresa itemised what she found positive about her new environment:

> 'My list of likes is very small and my list of dislikes is quite large. I like it because it's new and it's clean, but that's not to say that where we lived couldn't have been like that if they [council] hadn't let it fall into disrepair. They let it

fall into disrepair that in a way it's nice to have something clean again. I have a nice view of the Welsh Harp reservoir again; that's another story, I had a big fight for that. And I like the fact that [one stakeholder] is going to appoint someone to look after the wildlife. So that's really the end of the "likes".'

Theresa's list of 'likes' took up less than 90 seconds out of an 85-minute interview. During the rest of the interview, she elaborated on her 'quite large' list of dislikes. Rather than smoothly 'choosing' her new flat according to the official regeneration discourse whereby residents are individual market actors with perfect information, Theresa felt bullied:

'You have no idea what they do to people, what pressure they put you under and the games they play. It's like, "if you don't take this there's three other people to take this flat, make up your mind now!" It's all psychological warfare, you know what I mean? Because they want your home, they want you out quick. So I must have cried my eyes out for a week.'

Theresa expressed a keen loss of status and control over her home by changing from owner-occupation to shared-equity:

'We're not even homeowners anymore – we own a percentage – so that's the major difference. I mean who wants to give up their own home? It's your home, you can rent it out, but you can't rent this out. You've got people telling you what to do. So basically, we've lost having complete control over our lives.'

Despite her flat's novelty, she had already experienced problems: "I can see cracks on my walls coming down and they're telling me, 'that's just the way the cement settles in the building'. Flushing the toilet is a nightmare – someone else's faeces keeps coming up in my toilet." Theresa detailed the expenses she faced, including a higher council tax band, greater car parking charges and additional heating charges: "we weren't aware of half of these bills, they glossed over all that to get us out". The new flats were more expensive and likely to become even more so once the five-year rent and service charge relief was up. Like Theresa, Lilly disliked her shared-equity status, and thought the viewing process was pressurised. At the same time, Lilly was more positive about her new flat: "It's lovely, I'm really happy there. I haven't got a view of the lake like I had before, but they are building at the moment and it's all going to be nicely landscaped." Nevertheless, Lilly would not have moved had it not been for regeneration.

Alan was unusual among the market owner-occupiers in welcoming demolition. Although he liked his old flat, his new flat was "far better" because "it's environmentally friendly, it's warm", and he had a "fantastic" view over the reservoir. Apart from enhanced use-value, Alan also thought his flat "was a good investment". He had a well-paid professional job and obtained another mortgage easily. He acknowledged that he was fortunate in this regard since "some people actually reached the end of careers, getting retirement, so they probably do not have a spare cash for deposits and good salaries for the mortgage". This was indeed the case, as a chartered surveyor explained: "A lot of my clients [on regeneration estates] are quite elderly. They've long since retired and they would struggle to get a mortgage for that very reason."

Oluwakemi and Alf both decided against the shared-equity rehousing 'option'. Neither trusted the council or housing association as a result of their psychologically bruising degeneration/regeneration experiences. Oluwakemi "didn't want to have anything to do with the council ever again. No 'shared' anything, no 'ownership' anything. Just give me my money and I'm gone". She also baulked at potential resale problems with shared-equity flats. Alf was an elderly RTB owner who objected to the rehousing offer due to its insecurity and expense: "I could have had shared-equity, but then the service charge, and they'd charge me £10,000 for a car park space." Alf was aggrieved at being forced to move: "I wouldn't have moved out from there [if regeneration had not occurred], and if they had have given me like for like I would be still there." He moved to a cheaper part of England because he could not afford to buy anywhere in London: "the cheapest property was a dirty dump and that was £260,000. Now I've got a bungalow, four-bedroom, and it's only £173,000". Although Alf had some family where he moved to, he left other close family behind in north London and described the traumatic leaving scene: "it was terrible, all my grandkids were there and my daughter was there and she was crying, and what can you say because she didn't want me to go, but I'd got no options". A group with even less options than the owner-occupiers are the temporary (non-secure) tenants.

Temporary tenants[3]

This section focuses on 14 temporary tenants from West Hendon (9) and Clapham Park (5). They all felt that they should be treated as de facto secure tenants given the lengths of time they had lived at their estates – an average of eight years at West Hendon and nine years at Clapham Park (Brixton Buzz, 2018). These tenants were part of the non-working poor (especially at West Hendon), and precariat (especially at Clapham Park). Over half had BAME backgrounds.

Pre-relocation

Given their histories of housing precarity (Chapter 5), the temporary tenants dreaded having to go through relocation *yet again*. Their longevity at the estates resulted in a strong place belonging which was threatened by the prospect of being unable to remain in the area. Their lack of a defined housing re-offer meant they experienced displacement anxiety: "if it does come to it, what do I do, where do I go?" (Douglas, West Hendon). Several were vulnerable, and displacement anxiety undermined their already fragile mental health, as in the case of Douglas.

> 'It looks like I'm going full circle and coming from being homeless to being homeless again, because there's no guarantee of being a council tenant or a housing association tenant. It has played with my mental health because I'm on anti-depressants because you've got this at the back of your mind, you can't sleep. It's not like you can walk out the door and disappear for a couple of weeks and come back – it's there. And they're building there [outside] from 8 o'clock in the morning till 5 o'clock at night, so there's constant noise and reminding that they're building that and you're not even going to get one. Seeing the place built is like a condemned man watching the gallows being built.'

Unlike those who could afford to take short breaks away from home to relieve their anxiety, Douglas could not do so because he had little money. Choo (West Hendon) was long-term sick and disabled. When she first moved to West Hendon, she had struggled moving into a strange area: "I think the first couple of years I was really scared, I kept my door locked at night." Gradually this changed as Choo began to recognise familiar faces: "I got the confidence, I saw that it was okay, and people started to get to know me." Three of Choo's neighbours had given her their phone numbers in case of emergency: "sometimes I'm ill and because of that I have to have somebody close by." After living in her flat for eight years, "this has become home for me now". Choo's slowly evolving ontological security was threatened by demolition resulting in displacement anxiety:

> 'The council haven't given me any indication as to what's going to happen to me. It's very difficult for me because it's giving me a lot of stress because I don't know where I'm going to be. I don't want to be moved from place to place. I just want to be moved once and that's it.'

Remaining near her current neighbourhood was crucial for Choo's support networks, health and well-being: "It's quite difficult for me to move somewhere else where I don't know. I've got my doctors nearby, I've got a lot of people that I know of around this area and the hospitals are nearby, they've got all my details." Choo's family also lived nearby, including her bother who she relied upon for financial and general support.

Families reported a cavalier attitude on the part of officials regarding moving their children away from the area. Natalie (West Hendon) was worried about where she might be relocated, which exacerbated her mental illness: "if I was stressed or agitated it affects everything else, which is what I said that day, and he [housing officer] said my kids may not be able to go to the same school". Clapham Park tenants realised that it was impossible for them to remain in the same area by renting in the PRS; their wages were insufficient, and they had also encountered landlords/agents who would not take children, even though they would take pets: "so I will change my boys for two dogs and I'm going to move in [laughs]" (Katrina). Being unable to afford anywhere locally meant Katrina would have to move her children's schools, but she had already experienced problems getting them registered where they were:

> 'I have to start everything from the beginning, but I don't know where. Where, I mean in which side of London? Where should I go, what should I do? I don't know. But for them [officials] it doesn't matter if you have kids or if they are in schools, their answer is "we have schools everywhere in London, even in Dover we have schools".'

Katrina's job was also local. She was bewildered with displacement-anxiety questions which meant she had had a "very stressful year" worrying about being evicted, homelessness and where she might end up living (Brixton Buzz, 2018). Not only were temporary tenants badly affected by displacement anxiety, they felt dehumanised during the rehousing process:

'Barnet Homes look at you as if you're not a human being, that's how they treat us.' (Kofi, West Hendon)

'I mean we're not dealt with as human beings here at all. It's as if you're ants on the floor.' (Shiela, West Hendon)

'The council put so much stress on me, that my body actually can't take stress. You know I'm human, I'm not a robot. They just treated me like garbage and still are.' (Kayleigh, West Hendon)

'It's like being in limbo. You're getting moved out in six months' time, but you don't know where you are going. We're getting treated like we're nothing, that's how we're feeling.' (Chris, West Hendon)

'They treated us very bad. We are just numbers for them, we are not people. For them just to make money, this is the most important thing … money, money.' (Katrina, Clapham Park)

Such dehumanisation − of not being treated as human beings with needs − is an inevitable consequence of a failing social housing system. Tenants spoke about housing officers being "hardened and cynical" (Pippin). Such hardening arises from working within a system which is overstretched and rationed to the Nth degree due to austerity cutbacks (Alden, 2015; Orr, 2018). Housing officials − 'street-level bureaucrats' − are themselves pressurised into making fraught gatekeeping decisions which restrict welfare support − social tenancies − to the 'deserving poor'. Temporary tenants are expelled or threatened with expulsion from the housing aspect of the welfare state because they are not deserving enough.

Relocation

All seven West Hendon temporary tenant interviewees whom I contacted after they had been relocated from the estate had managed to remain in Barnet, but only after going through a traumatic eviction process which included several going to court following eviction notices. All had various vulnerabilities (illness, disability) which made eviction even more harmful. Going to court had worsened Kayleigh's illness: "I can't remember everything all the time, so it was very, very, very, very stressful, very tiring, and a waste of time, and a waste of taxpayers' money."

Of the seven relocated interviewees, two were in a worse housing situation because their homeless cases were dismissed by the council following difficult legal battles and, as a result, they wound up in the PRS. Following a "horrible, *hugely, hugely* stressful" court appearance, Pippin (a single woman with a long-term physical illness), was living in a private bedsit in an unsafe, cramped HMO which was regularly broken into: "I live in a hovel, I'm back to living in squalor."

Two other interviewees were moved sideways in housing terms since they were relocated to other Barnet regeneration estates, again as temporary tenants. Kayleigh, for example, was evicted after losing her court case: "They [council] gave me one day to pack my stuff. They bolted my door on the Friday and said I can come and get my stuff on the Monday." She had been living at her new estate for two years but felt bereft since she lost her West Hendon support network:

> 'I'm really, really sick and I don't trust no one, I've got like zero trust. I talked to my neighbours and that, but I don't know them so I can't say, "can you take my daughter?" It's not like West Hendon, I knew everyone there so I could say "look do you mind having Lindsey for a bit".'

Kayleigh did not know where she would be living next and felt trapped in a limbo-land nightmare: "it's impossible, I will end up dying or something because of my disabilities".

Three other relocated West Hendon temporary tenants became either housing association or Barnet Homes' tenants. Objectively they were in better housing positions than previously, but their displacement journey had left them psychologically bruised and battered. I met Douglas and Laiba at Willesden County Court in 2015 and both were visibly shaken by their encounter with the criminal justice system (Chapter 11). Rehousing was far from voluntary or painless: "I still up until today dream about being evicted from Barnet Homes, I always dream about that, I still get frightened about it" (Laiba). Although all three were pleased that they had not been made homeless, their housing precarity and sense of insecurity remained because they were placed on flexible tenancies which included a one-year probationary assessment, leaving them anxious whether they would 'pass': "At the end of this year, we don't know how I'm going to be assessed with all these fights that we have had. God knows whether I'm going to end up on the streets or what. It's not secure, none of these tenancies are secure" (Shiela). Shiela's new flat was in a "very posh" part of Barnet, but as a single woman from a BAME background she "preferred that multicultural place" at West Hendon. Douglas' new flat was located next to a busy main road: "West Hendon was far better than here because we had all that green space."

What kind of right is the right to return?

The right to return was welcomed by tenants and was also promoted as an important part of the official regeneration package at several estates. Having this right is certainly better than not having it, as for example in Sydney (Morris, 2019), while it is also something that London tenants have campaigned for (Glucksberg, 2017). At the same time, there are fundamental problems with the right to return, as this section demonstrates.

Although local authority tenants have a right to be rehoused in social housing, this does not mean they have a right to *secure council tenancies* (Chapter 8). If tenants wish to exercise their right to return, they must accept whichever landlord is there. This means having an assured tenancy, either with a housing association (for example at Canning Town/Custom House), or with an SPV landlord (such as Homes for Lambeth; Local Dialogue, 2016; Beswick and Penny, 2018). Alternatively, if secure tenants want to retain the council as their landlord, they must renounce their right to return by leaving the estate. Whereas stock transfers necessitate a *statutory ballot* of tenants, there is no equivalent ballot where demolition and rebuilding are involved; the best they could expect prior to 2018 was a non-statutory 'test of opinion' (Introduction and Chapter 9). Therefore, council tenants have a new landlord foisted on them, one that they did not vote for – that is, a 'back-door stock transfer'.

This back-door stock transfer led to huge resident concern at Canning Town/Custom House (Chapter 8) and featured at the later regeneration estates. Having a housing association landlord forced upon them troubled council tenants, not least due to the former's higher rents. For example, at the 2015 Aylesbury CPO, one Aylesbury tenant highlighted the same false choice tenure/area scenario that plagued Canning Town/Custom House: "My preference is to remain in location as a council tenant, but this is not an option. I would instead move off to be a council tenant. I would prefer to be a council tenant rather than housing association because the rents are cheaper."

Council tenants were also concerned about differential rights in relation to security of tenure and the RTB. Ahmed noted at meetings how many council tenants, like himself, objected to becoming housing association tenants at the Ocean estate:

> 'I mean we are secure tenants, and then out of no choice of our own we were becoming assured tenants and we are losing a lot of our rights. With assured tenants it's much easier to evict, I mean if you didn't pay your service charge you could get evicted fairly quickly. The right to buy was also quite important to us.'

Moving from secure council to assured Homes for Lambeth tenancies was a major concern for tenants at Cressingham Gardens (Local Dialogue, 2016). As a council tenant from there said at a Lambeth Council meeting in 2016:

> 'All along you [council] claimed nobody would be worse off, but we are set to lose our secure tenancies under the SPV which means we lose the right to buy, the right to manage, and right to succeed. We will become assured tenants which includes a greater right to evict.'

Assured tenancy offers to decanted council tenants could be supplemented by enhanced rights, as suggested at Cressingham Gardens (Local Dialogue, 2016). Council tenants at Woodberry Down "fought very hard" (Andrew) for such rights, including restrictions on rent increases for several years: "here we've got assured tenure; now there is a difference but we've got near enough the same rights" (Andrew). Such enhanced rights are a testimony to the negotiating skills of Woodberry Down tenants and WDCO. Not every Woodberry Down tenant was pleased however: "nobody told us that we would have a new landlord, we don't know nothing about this new landlord" (Tina).

Once the guarantee period is over, rents will very likely increase substantially and this was already prompting concern, especially given the austerity Housing Benefit cap (Cole et al, 2016): "with the capping on benefits, it's going to heavily affect people, I can see an exodus of people being moved out" (Andrew). As Charlie said at West Hendon, "we have a rent reduction for a couple of years, but after that people will struggle". Another related issue is how any enhanced rights only apply to the relocated tenant, *not* to the property. Hence when the original tenant leaves or dies, the property will revert to the standard assured tenancy arrangements as per the rest of the housing association (or SPV) stock. A Brent Labour councillor was concerned about the long-term rental impacts of the back-door stock transfer at South Kilburn estate:

> 'Once somebody is decanted into housing association properties, we [council] have no control over what might happen in that rent in the future. It's might be fear-mongering to say it, but the reality is they could raise the rent and turn round over the next few years and say, "it's not financially viable for us to continue to offer these lower rents, so we're going to raise it to 80/90/100 per cent of market rent", and the council can't do anything about that because now you're in a housing association property.'

Given the increasing commercialisation of the large London housing associations, such rent concerns are entirely apposite (Manzi and Morrison, 2018). Displacement due to rent hikes is highly likely to occur in the future in the housing association properties at the redeveloped estates.

Realistic enactment of the right to return crucially depends on enough replacement social rental properties being available for all the secure tenants that want them. However, the net London-wide reduction in the number of social rental homes (Chapters 3 and 4), renders any right to return contingent and even largely nominal. There were very few replacement social housing properties at the Heygate estate, which "was very, very disappointing because we kept being told everybody's going to have a brand-new place, but we never got them" (Olive). By contrast, at Woodberry Down the relatively large percentage of replacement social housing meant that "everybody got the right to return. The last I heard that 90 per cent of people have opted to stay at Woodberry Down" (Gerry).[4] However, the rephasing at Woodberry Down meant that not enough suitable homes were available for tenants to move into immediately. Hence in some cases tenants' 'return' was filtered through being 'double decanted' – "temporarily rehoused in a refitted void while waiting for the right match to become available" (Belotti, 2014: 32). Bob highlights how such nominal 'temporary' moves became permanent:

> 'The ones [tenants] got moved out had the right to return, because they [council] couldn't find them anywhere here and they was moved out somewhere else, and they were given the letter.[5] Because they was happy thinking "we're all getting new flats up here". "It's only cos there's no empty flats at the moment, we'll bring you back when the next phase is done." But it was taking so long. Someone I knew went out to Essex and I said, "When are you going to move back?" "Can't be bothered [sighs] because the kids are settled in schools out there." It's happened to a few people out there and they said, "it's so long ago now I can't be arsed about moving back now".'

As this example highlights, the sheer length of time that regeneration takes is a crucial issue that affects the right to return. Sandra estimated that over 100 Central Hill residents had relocated by early 2019. However, the ensuing timescales rendered the right to return a notional abstraction entirely disconnected from peoples' real lives:

> 'They're [tenants] supposed to have right to return, but the way this estate's going I very much doubt they'll have anything to return to. I mean Lambeth are now saying five years before they start again. And then by the time they go back in and then it's restarted, you might as well say it's going to be ten years until building. The programme is already supposed to take 10 to 15 years to do the whole project, that's *25 years*. Who is coming back after 25 years? Nobody!' (Sandra)

Joseph raised similar objections at Westbury estate: "We're talking maybe 10–12 years, [so] the reality is that most people move, that's it, they're never going to come back". Some will have died in the meantime, while others will be elderly and will be reluctant to move again later in life. This conundrum – of having the right to return, but being either too old or too dead to exercise that right – was highlighted by Michelle at Northumberland Park:

> 'What they [council] don't say to you is, "alright we are going to give you improved housing but we are going to

knock down your entire estate and we are going to ship you out somewhere else for 10 to 15 years, on the pretext that we are going to give you the right to come back". But in 10 to 15 years you are either going to have built up a community there or you are going to be dead. So, you know, it's an empty promise.'

Given that the private development partner in the HDV was Lendlease, the same one as at the Heygate estate, Michelle's cynicism is well founded.

The so-called 'progress' of regeneration also makes a huge difference to whether the right to return is realistic or not. There are two examples – Custom House and Carpenters (both in Newham) – where the right to return was chimerical because there was *nothing* to return to. Custom House and Carpenters regeneration schemes began in the early-to-mid 2000s, but no redevelopment partner was in place and zero redevelopment had occurred by 2019 (Chapter 12). An architect summarised the Custom House regeneration:

'There was this SPD [Supplementary Planning Document], it was really vague and really inaccurate. That was 2008 and then basically in Custom House nothing at all happened, no repairs on the buildings. At this point [2019], there's still no planning application, there's no tender, nothing's happened, there's no developer.'

Even if a redevelopment partner is found at either Custom House or Carpenters during 2020, it could take another 5–10 years until any new homes are built. This means the decanted tenants will have been waiting over 20 years to exercise their right to return. Having this right and being able to realise it are two entirely different things.

Agency, control and power

Critical urbanists emphasise the coercive nature of physical displacement (Allen, 2008; Crookes, 2011), while others argue that tenants are not passive victims because they can exercise choice and agency within the relocation process (Kearns and Mason, 2013; Kleinhans and Kearns, 2013; Posthumus and Lelevrier, 2013; Posthumus and Kleinhans, 2014). The official regeneration discourse portrays tenants in London as rational individuals who can exercise choice in the quasi-market of social housing tenancies, by either remaining on the estate or moving elsewhere in the borough via 'choice-based lettings'. This begs the question as to how much genuine control people have within the displacement process. As Paton (2014) argues, control is something that working-class residents tend to lack under regeneration and gentrification.

As indicated above, the temporary tenants were thrust into a coercive and stressful legal eviction process over which they had no control. There was not the same overt coercion applied to secure council tenants, even if they often found relocation stressful. Their lack of control tended to take more covert forms within the rehousing process. Among those estates where extensive rehousing had taken place, I heard the most stories about informal coercion (threats, bullying, intimidation) at Carpenters estate: "the council is knocking on doors telling people if they don't go they will be living in a ghost town" (resident, regeneration meeting, 2012). Robbie had managed to remain at one of the Carpenters tower blocks, but many of his fellow tenants had moved out:

> 'They [tenants] have been pressured. It doesn't help when they are being bullied to move. I have spoken to tenants and said "look you need to make a complaint, that you are being bullied to move", and almost some of the wording is threatening as well. But they feel that if they make a complaint, the local authority will come after them in some way. I've run into a few people [ex-residents] who have said to me, "you were right I should never have left". People didn't have to leave. I mean they were never under any jurisdiction to leave, it's just the way Newham [council] went in and said, "look you have to leave".'

Ria did not want to leave her treasured Carpenters flat in one of the tower blocks but, "I kept getting threatening letters, I'm going to be put out on the street if I refuse any [rehousing] offers". She provided a shocking account of what can happen to 'stubborn tenants' like her (Chapter 9). Ria was the last tenant left on her floor which was then sealed off by the council without prior notification. She was literally trapped and had to be freed by the London Fire Brigade: "At one stage I got locked in on the fourth floor [laughs]. According to them [council], they 'didn't know that I was there'. So I had to have the fire people to come and break the things off the back door and the lift." Ria thought that had her fellow block tenants, many of whom were elderly, "stood their ground" they would still be there. Instead they were "threatened" with being made homeless:

> 'The housing officer, she targets the elderly and threatened them, the same way she threatened me, so they all give in. Well yes, no-one wants to know that, "I'm old and the next thing I know is I'm living on the street," because that is what she more-or-less told me, she said that "we can make you homeless." And if that's what she's telling the elderly people that was even older than me – yes they're going to get scared and they will take the first thing that you give them to get out so that they have a roof over their head. It's like they feel that they didn't have a choice, because she told us we're going to be evicted, we're going to be thrown out.'

Carpenters tenants thus felt they had no real choice and no real control. Given Newham Council's 'authoritarian neoliberal' approach to local government (Chapter 4), it's unsurprising that tenants' accounts of informal coercion were most prominent in Newham.[6]

Lack of control was also evident elsewhere in the cases of tenants who challenged official rehousing decisions. Danni and Adela both felt strongly that the initial accommodation offers they received at West Hendon did not meet their family's needs, and they described an unsympathetic response from housing officials:

Adela: 'I have a feeling that we are forced there [new block].'
Danni: 'That is how they came across when they were interviewing us. I remember right at the beginning, I took all my son's medical files with everything and they weren't interested in that.'

Danni had to obtain medical assistance to prove her case and she also engaged a lawyer. All of this took a toll on her own health, as mentioned earlier:

> 'I have had huge bags [under the eyes] and it's was extremely stressful, obviously dealing with the housing and dealing with a young son that's not well. So, I was up a lot. If I wasn't up with him, I'd be thinking, "am I going to end up going to court? What if I lose?" Because even if I've

got a solicitor, there's no guarantee that I would have won,
and this is such a big ... It's the council that I'm up against.'

The power relationship between a social landlord and an individual
tenant is massively unequal (August, 2016). Derya (a student from a
Turkish background) highlighted this lack of control regarding the
rephasing at Woodberry Down which pushed her family's move
down the list: "When the phase moved back, it's not in your control,
you don't have much say, they've [council] got control, it's what they
do. That's the thing about council housing, you have no control." It's
unrealistic for most London tenants to 'exit' (Hirschman, 1970) from
social housing and enter the private housing market due to the latter's
prohibitive costs and their low incomes. This lack of an effective exit
from the sector means the landlord is in a monopolistic position, which
grants enormous power and sets up a dependency among tenants who
need the landlord to treat them fairly. Some council tenants whom
I interviewed contacted me later to say that they did not want me to
include their material in this book because they were worried about
victimisation by the council. The realities of rehousing and exercise of
'choice' by tenants are set within and overdetermined by the structural
parameters of power and control which are built into the redevelopment
and relocation processes. As August (2016) argues, exercising choice
and agency is not the same thing as exercising power.

Nevertheless, a form of tenant choice or agency was evident in
terms of *where* people relocated to and/or *when* they relocated. By
2017, the demolition of Sylvester's block at Clapham Park had been
pushed back another seven years. This prompted Sylvester to move
earlier than planned. Not only was Sylvester able to exercise agency
regarding when he moved, but also choice in where he moved to. He
opted for a refurbished rather than new-build flat because he preferred
the former separate kitchen and dining-room arrangement rather than
the latter's kitchen-diner. Other tenants mentioned exercising agency
with council officials:

> 'I got interviewed about "where would you like to go?"
> I said, "you're building two blocks across the road, I want to
> go into one of those". So, I got offered this one. I thought
> it's nice and light because I got a whole load of windows.
> So, I thought I'll take it.' (Deirdre, Woodberry Down)

Such choices indicate that tenants are not 'passive victims', as
Posthumus and Kleinhans (2014) argue. At the same time, nor are

they truly in charge of their housing destinies or destinations. Even though Deirdre exercised agency, this was within the overall systemic constraints: "I am not going to get offered anything better." These choice/constraint dilemmas are illustrated in the case of Dennis, who was originally very opposed to the demolition of the Aylesbury estate where he lived. However, he shifted towards a pragmatic acceptance of rehousing having been worn down by 'the struggle' over the years. Dennis moved to another Southwark council flat a few miles away from the Aylesbury via the bidding scheme:

> 'I told them [council] what I wanted and where I wanted it and they gave it to me. I got exactly what I wanted, although I would have preferred it to be in Hampstead [laughs]. I did a reconnaissance and wanted to look at the building at night and talked to existing residents before I was officially seeing it. I wasn't so sure because it was a tower block. But the tenants I asked said that when one of the lifts don't work, they [council] fix it in 24 hours, plus you have another lift as well. I love it up there, but I'm single so it might not be so good if you're a family.'

Dennis' overriding priority was to remain a council tenant due to its greater security and his new flat ensured this. Dennis exercised choice via the bidding process and was able to express and realise his preferences including by informally scoping out his new block. At the same time, this agency was operationalised within wider unequal power dynamics over which Dennis had no real control. Despite liking his present flat, he "wouldn't have left had it not been for the regeneration". Furthermore, had Dennis left the Aylesbury any later, the worsening conditions/managed decline would have forced him out as it had done to others: "I'm glad I got out when I did, because I had a friend who stayed on and had a terrible time there, the heating and water went, he said it was a nightmare" (Chapter 9; Watt, 2020c).

If some tenants opted to move earlier than scheduled, others were forced to adjust their relocation timing because the phasing changed for reasons entirely outside of their control, as occurred at Woodberry Down (Belotti, 2014). Another example of changing schemes relates to how three blocks at the Ocean estate were originally due to be refurbished but were later switched to demolition (Chapter 4). Ahmed moved with his family into a rundown flat at one of these blocks: "it was infested with cockroaches, bed bugs" (Ahmed). Ahmed spent around £8,000 to make the flat habitable and during this period the family were physically un-homed since they lived elsewhere while the work was completed. The family only made such a substantial financial investment on the expectation that the block would be refurbished: "they [council] showed us paperwork saying the grant has been agreed, everything is in motion. That is why we kind of invested a lot of money in the property, we thought we were going to be there a long time". Despite such 'guarantees', two years later the family were informed that there had been a change of plans – "they just said it won't happen" because refurbishment was "apparently uneconomical" – and the block would be demolished. Ahmed diligently attended every consultation meeting but was convinced there was no space for disagreement: "There was no other option, it was all "you are moving out", so it's whether you move here or you chose somewhere else in the borough, but ultimately "you are moving out", so you didn't have a say. The choice was made up." The key choice in the demolition and displacement process – whether your home will be demolished – was *not* under residents' control.

Conclusion

This chapter began by examining dispossession and how many residents were opposed to demolition and associated it with social cleansing. It went onto evaluate their displacement experiences, both before and after physical relocation. Housing tenure plays a key role in differentiating these experiences with secure council tenants having the fullest and most defined rehousing rights, notably the right to return. Even then, displacement anxiety was evident in relation to the prospect of forced relocation.

Among those tenants who were able to realise the right to return by moving into new homes in the redeveloped estate, those who had been previously un-homed regarded rehousing as liberation – as a welcome relief from spending years living in unsatisfactory housing conditions. If these tenants moved from un-homing to a new home, others were forced to move in the opposite direction – from their beloved homes to 'cheap rubbish' – hence they experienced rehousing as bereavement. Given that the latter had remained in their former estates, they illustrate Davidson's (2009) argument that displacement concerns what *places mean* as well as spatial relocation. The chapter also considered those secure tenants who had physically been displaced away from their estates. Relocation was stressful, and although some eventually moved to somewhere suitable, others remained bitter at their forcible relocation.

Owner-occupiers, and even more so temporary tenants, were on average more negatively affected by displacement than social tenants. Nearly all the owner-occupiers were against rehousing, and they experienced displacement anxiety as they worried about where they would be living. Displacement anxiety was even worse for the non-secure tenants with very few rights – they experienced rehousing as a traumatic part of their never-ending housing precarity.

The chapter finished with reference to two themes. The first is that while the right to return makes a significant difference to secure tenants, it by no means *guarantees* that they will be able to exercise this right in a realistic and meaningful manner. This is partly due to the elongated nature of the regeneration process, but also due to shortfalls in the numbers of available social tenancies. In other cases, there is *nothing to return to* because no redevelopment has occurred, as at the Carpenters estate (Chapter 12). The second theme is choice and control. Temporary tenants were placed in an overtly coercive process via formal evictions and court appearances. This was less the case among secure tenants, although some described informal coercion. Several social tenants were able to input into decisions regarding where and when they are relocated, indicating how they were not 'passive victims', as Posthumus and Kleinhans (2014) argue. Nevertheless, choice and agency are severely circumscribed by the structural parameters of the demolition process, plus tenants' lack of power and control (Paton, 2014). Regeneration forces residents into procedures and timetables whose parameters are overdetermined by the main stakeholders. This chapter has illustrated individual forms of contestation as residents challenged rehousing decisions. The next chapter examines collective resistance to demolition.

11

Resistance

As Goetz (2016) argues, there is limited research on social housing tenants' resistance to redevelopment and this chapter contributes towards addressing that deficit.[1] It begins by analysing housing activism with reference to council housing, and situates the recent crop of estate-based anti-demolition campaigns in relation to earlier anti-stock-transfer campaigns. The following section highlights campaigners' 'novice' status in terms of housing politics. The impacts of collective resistance are then examined, first under what I have termed the 'paradox of community', and second in relation to non-engagement. The final section assesses how success can be assessed vis-à-vis resisting regeneration-as-demolition.

Housing activism: from pragmatism to contesting neoliberalism

Tenants' struggles against landlord rent hikes and evictions have a long history in both Britain and the US (Madden and Marcuse, 2016). London has been a prominent site of tenant activism: for example, the 1958 Camden rent strike and the campaign against the 1972 Rent Act. There is debate over whether tenant activism is the Marxist class struggle in the sphere of labour reproduction (Glynn, 2009; Gray, 2018) or represents an 'urban social movement' in relation to collective consumption (Lowe, 1986; Bradley, 2014). Lowe (1986: 83) argued that local authority tenant activism in Britain was predicated upon a sense of solidarity arising from its location within an 'overwhelmingly working-class social and cultural milieu' as well as a shared consumption sector position.

Following a sustained period of public housing residualisation, Cole and Furbey (1994) criticised radical analyses (Marxist and urban social movement) as wish-fulfilment on the part of left-wing intellectuals who failed to understand the fundamentally *pragmatic nature* of local authority tenant activism. Much contemporary tenant activism in Britain *is* pragmatic, localist and defensive in orientation as tenants become involved in TRAs to improve their estate facilities and housing conditions (Bradley, 2014). This was highlighted by interviewees who were either current or previous active TRA members. TRAs operate in a trade union capacity by pressurising the council regarding maintenance and facilities. Olive had been active in her TRA at the Heygate estate and noted how most tenant issues related to repairs: "I mean if we had too many complaints [about repairs] then we would ask for someone to come [from the council], and then you would have a full house. And you'd say, 'so and so and so and so, and how long's it going to be?'" Despite such a strong pragmatic emphasis, there is also evidence of ideological tenant activism and this has become more prominent during the period since Cole and Furbey wrote. For example, there have been campaigns against stock transfer (Watt, 2008; Cumbers et al, 2010) and mass media stigmatisation (Benefit to Society, 2017). This upturn can be regarded as a response to neoliberalisation, austerity and state-led gentrification, and anti-demolition campaigns can be placed under this umbrella (Glynn, 2009; Gray, 2018). Such contemporary ideological housing activism is sporadic and spatially uneven, but is prominent in London, reflective of the capital's position at the epicentre of the national housing crisis.

Estate-based campaigns

Council tenants, tenure and place

Opposition to estate regeneration dates to the campaign against HATs during the late 1980s which occurred at several London estates, notably the Ocean (Woodward, 1991). During the New Labour years, the main estate-related housing activism, both nationally and in London, challenged stock transfers. This period saw the creation of the national DCH campaign which was particularly active in the London boroughs of Camden, Lambeth, Southwark and Tower Hamlets. The emphasis was mobilising council tenants to vote against transfer to a housing association, which was regarded as privatisation (Ginsburg, 2005). London anti-stock transfer campaigners also argued that regeneration involving the development of new private housing represented gentrification, for example at the Aylesbury, Ocean and Clapham Park NDC transfer ballots (Watt and Wallace, 2014). In total, one third of London ballots resulted in 'no votes' against transfer compared to one quarter in England, suggesting greater support for council housing and distrust of housing associations in the capital (Watt, 2009c).

Since 2010, anti-regeneration campaigns have mushroomed across London to resist demolition – hence 'anti-demolition'. At the same time, these campaigns are not against the notion that the estates needed improvement, including refurbishment and undertaking the backlog of maintenance works. Belinda, a 'Northumberland Park Decides' campaigner, clarified the policy straitjacket that landlords are increasingly forcing residents into under austerity: "What's counterposed is demolition or not demolition. That you could have either the status quo or you could have demolition, that's what the options are posed as. Whereas really what we need is improvement, which is neither. We don't want the status quo."

Numerous named campaigns have sprung into life, for example CARP at Carpenters estate, Save Cressingham Gardens, Our West Hendon, Save Northwold, as well as Northumberland Park Decides. Others are somewhat looser groupings, such as leaseholders at the Aylesbury. In addition, there are borough-wide groups including the 35% Campaign in Southwark and StopHDV in Haringey, as well as various city-wide networks including Radical Housing Network, Demolition Watch London and London Tenants Federation (LTF). All these campaigns can be considered part of a new politics of housing-related activism that is coalescing around challenging the strictures of neoliberal urbanism and the dispossessions it gives rise to, while advocating the right to the city (Leitner et al, 2007; Harvey, 2012; McKenzie, 2018). This refers to "a 'superior right' concerned with inhabiting the city, rather than owning part of it or being allowed to work or contribute to decisions there" (Millington, 2011: 10).

How does this recent crop of anti-demolition campaigns fit within the recent history of tenant housing activism sketched earlier? The 1980s to 2000s anti-HAT and anti-transfer campaigns were *tenure-based* in that their priority was retaining secure council tenancies and in so doing defending the public housing part of the Keynesian welfare state – as with 'Defend Council Housing'. Place-based issues – preserving existing homes and communities – were of secondary significance. This tenure/place emphasis flips around in the anti-demolition campaigns such that the primary goal becomes *defending place* (existing homes and communities), while public/social housing preservation becomes secondary. Hence rather than mainly tenure/tenant-based, the anti-demolition campaigns are primarily *place-based* (Watt, 2018c).

This tenure/place reprioritisation has occurred for two main reasons. First, despite what the official regeneration discourse opines (Adonis and Davies, 2015), London's council estates are no longer 'mono-tenure' after several decades of the RTB. While council tenants remain the majority at most London estates, there are substantial numbers of homeowners, as well as private and temporary tenants. Gary explained the increased significance of leaseholders at the Heygate estate, most of whom were displaced from Southwark, and with many outside London (Flynn, 2016).

> 'At the beginning [of the regeneration] nobody really bothered about them [leaseholders], they were going to get their compensation, they weren't council tenants anyway [laughs], you know "they bought theirs, they've got nothing to worry about". But that's not the case. I would say now the leaseholders were treated worse than anybody. Everybody was treated badly. Council tenants were treated badly on secure tenancies because they didn't get new homes. Insecure tenants were treated badly because they're really at the mercy of the council depending on their individual circumstances, but leaseholders they've really got to shift for themselves. And most of them have had to move, if not right out of London, to the suburbs.'

The emphasis on council housing and its tenants has therefore become anachronistic, as emerged at several housing/regeneration meetings I attended: " 'Defend council housing' is outdated because estates are more complex than this" (council tenant, regeneration meeting, Churchill Gardens, 2014). The second reason is the rapid growth of housing associations in the city, which is partly linked to stock transfers. Several of these associations have themselves pursued regeneration via demolition (G15, 2016; Watt and Allen, 2018). Therefore, defending the rights of council tenants *alone*, rather than social tenants more broadly, makes less political sense in the anti-demolition context.

Unlike the earlier anti-HAT and anti-transfer tenant-based campaigns – and unlike social housing campaigns elsewhere which are tenant focused (Goetz, 2016) – the anti-demolition campaigns are *cross-tenure* and rooted in the combined efforts of social tenants *and* homeowners. Some campaigns stressed that this was a deliberate strategy – to be socially inclusive and also to deflect the tenure-splitting tactics that councils engage in. Save Cressingham Gardens have explicitly framed their campaign as being based on *residents* rather than tenants or homeowners: "we all pretty much came to the conclusion that if we stick together what they [council] are trying to do won't work" (Bill). CARP was also cross-tenure, as a Carpenters homeowner expressed at a CARP meeting:

'Our core objective is to stress that we want to stay here as residents but failing that as a community. It's not that we're against regeneration and we're not out to have a fight with Newham Council. We're against the plans as they stand. We like our nice houses and we want to stay here as a community.'

Social tenant/homeowner unity is commonplace on London estates challenging demolition, but temporary tenants are generally less evident. Nevertheless, certain campaigns have embraced temporary tenants, for example Our West Hendon and PEACH in Custom House (Sendra and Fitzpatrick, 2020), while temporary tenants have also formed their own campaigns (later in this chapter, and Chapter 12).

If estate campaigns are cross-tenure, they are also cross-class and multi-ethnic. McKenzie (2018) has emphasised the working-class nature and composition of London estate-based campaigns. While this sociological characterisation is broadly apposite, it glosses over the important active role played by middle-class incomers in certain London campaigns, notably Save Northwold and Save Cressingham Gardens. These marginal gentrifiers faced the daunting prospect of displacement away from their neighbourhoods and loss of their elective belonging (Chapters 6 and 10). They had chosen their homes and neighbourhoods, enjoyed living in them, and wanted to preserve the existing social mix, rather than have the forcibly imposed entirely different mix that comprehensive redevelopment would bring about (compare Brown-Saracino, 2007), as Caroline explained at Northwold.

'We bought homes that we liked that we could afford, and that is like fair enough isn't it? So that is our kind of rights, but also *equally* we want to preserve all the social homes that are here and protect the community that is properly mixed. You know all this talk of "mixed communities" normally in development-speak means social cleansing, but in our case the mixture is a *real mixture*. People have been here a long time, it's a very established community. And it's welcoming inasmuch as anywhere in London ever can be, you know if new people move in, people are made to feel part of it.'

Middle-class incomers (like Caroline) played key roles in the Save Northwold and Save Cressingham Gardens anti-demolition campaigns, and this engagement even occurred when their own homes were not directly threatened with being bulldozed.

Tactics and strategies

Estate campaigns have deployed a wide range of tactics in mobilising against demolition. Standard actions include public meetings, demonstrations and protests, leafletting estates, and lobbying the council/landlord/politicians. Lobbying local politicians – councillors and MPs – is undertaken partly to gain political leverage, but also to encourage politicians to support individual residents who are experiencing difficulties, especially in relation to rehousing. Gaining publicity via getting stories in the mass media has been a key strategic goal. We have seen how estates suffer under a weight of stigmatisation, so trying to gain positive publicity is a challenge. Despite this stigmatisation, it's surprising how mainstream media organisations have run several news stories and films which take a broadly sympathetic approach to residents, for example BBC (2012) on the Carpenters estate, and 'The Estate We're in', a BBC documentary about West Hendon (Robertson, 2016). Campaigns have also tapped into existing media stories to publicise their case. CARP successfully linked the fate of the Carpenters estate to the 2012 Olympics and received extensive mass media coverage as a result (Watt, 2013).

In addition, campaigners have engaged in legal action. This includes judicial reviews brought by tenants which challenge the regeneration process, such as the StopHDV campaign at the Royal Courts of Justice (RCJ) in 2017. Although this case was lost, it formed part of the ultimately successful drive to change the Haringey Council leadership, which eventually resulted in the HDV being dropped (Chapter 4). Legal cases have also been brought by leaseholders in the form of CPO public inquiries. The latter were held in relation to the Heygate in 2013 (unsuccessful) and Aylesbury in 2015 (successful) and 2017 (unsuccessful) (Hubbard and Lees, 2018). Three CPO inquiries were held in 2015, 2017 and 2019 in relation to West Hendon, all unsuccessful.

Direct action has been less apparent at estates. Nevertheless, I observed how Our West Hendon campaigners stopped the lorries from entering the building site (Photograph 11.1), while a relative of an elderly West Hendon resident padlocked herself to a gate on the same day. As a result of these actions, building work was stopped for several hours, although two protesters were arrested by the police.

Cressingham Gardens residents (Photograph 11.2) have mounted an energetic, dynamic, and imaginative seven year-long campaign – Save

Photograph 11.1: West Hendon estate – Our West Hendon direct action, 2014

Photograph 11.2: Cressingham Gardens estate – preparing to march to Lambeth Town Hall, 2014

Cressingham Gardens – involving multiple strands (Sendra and Fitzpatrick, 2020):

- mounting two judicial reviews (2015 and 2017);
- devising an alternative 'People's Plan';
- gaining the 'right to manage' the estate;
- applying for the 'right to transfer';
- participation in several Open London weekends;
- attempting to list the estate with English Heritage;
- fielding two Green Party candidates in the 2018 council elections;
- resident-led writing project (Cooper, 2017);
- holding a 'Housing Crisis Question Time' debate in 2014.

Bill explained the rationale behind the Save Cressingham Gardens approach:

> 'We've taken this kind of multi-pronged strategy dealing with them [council] where we don't just have one sphere, we have several all at the same time and they can't deal with it. That's what we've been trying to educate other estates – this is what you've got to do, don't just have a petition, you also pressurise your local councillors if you can. If they're all a particular party, you join the local party and you pressure them there. You have loud protests on the high street, you flier people ... you do all this, and you keep it up over and over and over again, and it works.'

As Bill says, there are interlinkages between the various estates involving campaigners speaking at other estates. Campaigners from Myatts Field North (Hodkinson, 2019) spoke at Cressingham Gardens in the early days of its regeneration, while activists from the Southwark 35% Campaign went to speak at Churchill Gardens (2014) and Northumberland Park (2017). Social media have proved key campaigning tools, as Caroline from Save Northwold says (Photograph 11.3):

> 'Because I run the Twitter, I'm in touch with probably a hundred other housing campaigns. We are mutually supportive of each other in an amazing way. Twitter is incredibly powerful and it's led to a lot of real-life meetings. I've gone and spoken to other campaigners, I've had meetings with a few, I consider some of them my friends

now, although I only know them in that arena, and you learn, everyone learns from each other.'

All of this real-life and social media interaction, mutual learning and support has helped build 'networks of solidarity' (Maeckelbergh, 2012) which have fed into the broader London housing movement (Watt and Minton, 2016; Gillespie et al, 2018; McKenzie, 2018). Thus, while the estate campaigns are focused on defending a specific place, they also involve cross-city coming together, as Caroline explains:

> 'I definitely do feel like part of a [London-wide] community, I feel like it's a movement. It's very fragmented, because everyone is obviously focusing on their own campaign, but there is a serious sense of solidarity which keeps me going. We give each other support, we give each other pep talks, we give each other advice through Twitter.'

For example, campaigners from Our West Hendon and Haringey DCH attended and spoke at the celebratory event following the Focus E15 political occupation of the Carpenters estate in 2014 (Watt, 2016).

Radical outsiders and novice insiders

The official regeneration discourse deploys the following narrative regarding 'opposition': 'residents back demolition and the only people who are against it are established political agitators – in other words, "radical outsiders" who parachute into estates to stir up trouble and who are therefore acting *against* residents' wishes and needs'. I came across variants of this narrative at several estates where local politicians, officials and resident demolition supporters tried to discredit the opposition on behalf of the 'silent majority' of residents who supposedly wanted comprehensive redevelopment. In 2015, most candidates for the Labour Party London mayoral nominations spoke up against estate regeneration via referring to social cleansing and invoked the Heygate as an exemplar. However, one of the candidates mentioned 'outsiders' from already-established campaigns 'coming onto estates' (meeting, University of Westminster).

Far from being radical outsiders, most of the regeneration campaigners that I interviewed and met at meetings were people for whom the world of housing politics was entirely alien. Caroline from Save Northwold described herself as a "novice housing campaigner", albeit one who rapidly had to become an "expert". The core participants in CARP were not the 'usual suspects' – they were all new to housing activism and most to activism of any kind. These were not radical outsiders but instead 'novice insiders' who became engaged due to the direct threat that regeneration posed to *their* homes and communities. Alf had taken part in various actions at West Hendon including demonstrations: "I'd never been involved in anything like that. It's my home ... it was. So I had to get involved." Campaigning was effectively forced upon them (McKenzie, 2018): "the fact that it's our house is a really big ... because you're forced to engage with it" (Luke, Save Cressingham Gardens).

> 'When I turned to activism, forced activism because it was never really my thing – I never thought of myself as being capable of advancing change in that way. If I hadn't been losing my home and I hadn't been feeling injustices that what was going on was not right. That's what I mean about forced activism.' (Sonia, Marlowe Road)

Joseph had no prior interest in housing and explained how his engagement happened at Westbury estate: "it's just something that ends up in your bedroom, and then boom! your home is going to be demolished". At a Lambeth housing meeting, Joseph captured the unusual nature of his involvement: "usually on a Sunday I'm relaxing or going to church. I didn't think that I'd find myself sitting in a pub in Tulse Hill discussing housing [laughs]". With one exception, most Cressingham Gardens interviewees had zero prior involvement in housing activism, although some had taken part in various political and community campaigns:

Rose: 'I obviously did single-handedly free Nelson Mandela back
            in the 80s but haven't really done much since then [laughs].'
Jeanette: 'Within my local community yes, not Cressingham,
            but I was part of doing a lot of voluntary work for local
            nurseries and for local charities.'
Lisa: 'But no this has completely politicised me, like I was not
            politically minded particularly. Everything was just quite
            quietly ticking along. I mean unless you're under threat
            you kind of ... I stopped the war march, twice [laughs].'

The estate campaigns are not formal organisations. Instead, they consist of several 'core' resident activists who play an organisational role in relation to meetings, petitions, emails, liaison with official regeneration organisations, and so on. In addition, there are larger numbers of residents who are supportive, but whose engagement is sporadic – they attend meetings, go on demonstrations, and suchlike. The latter by no means necessarily identified as 'activists', even though they felt strongly about the issues: "I don't class myself an activist, but I think where I'm concerned, I hate injustice and I hate unfairness" (Lilly). They were thrust into a role that did not always sit comfortably with them: "all this protesting it's all new to me, I've never done it before, I've never been interested in it, but now it's happening to me" (Chris).

If most estate activists were novice insiders, this is not to say that outsiders from established housing and community campaigns played no part whatsoever. Southwark and Haringey both had functioning borough-wide DCH groups who played an effective role in estate campaigns in their respective boroughs, notably at the Aylesbury and Northumberland Park estates. The Focus E15 campaign's political occupation of the half-empty Carpenters estate not only spotlighted Newham Council's manifold housing and regeneration policy failures, but also energised the London housing movement more generally (Watt, 2016; Gillespie et al, 2018). The Aylesbury estate was also politically occupied for several weeks during 2015 and the occupiers became involved in the residents' campaign against demolition. Two London-wide organisations – LTF and Just Space – helped to devise the Greater Carpenters Neighbourhood Forum (GCNF) on the Carpenters estate (Sendra and Fitzpatrick, 2020). The Coalition Government's community organiser scheme (Mayo, 2017) ironically also helped to energise estate-based campaigns, for example at West Hendon, and Custom House via PEACH (Sendra and Fitzpatrick, 2020). The role of these outsider organisations and campaigners was primarily supportive of residents who were *already* challenging demolition, for example in relation to providing information, relevant contacts, and so on. Without some internal mobilisation on the part of estate residents, it's extremely doubtful whether outsiders alone would have much or even any impact.

The paradox of community

Neighbourhood-based social relations and identities can emerge out of residents' reactions to urban governance and policy. As Mayo (2017: 134) argues, 'communities have been forming and re-forming themselves, in response to the threat of dispersal from development pressures' – as with demolition. This section argues that regeneration has paradoxical community effects – it pushes residents apart due to top-down pressures, while it also brings them together.

Pushing apart

One major effect of regeneration is that legalistic tenure differences morph into social distinctions. Whereas housing tenure differences between long-term social tenants and RTB owners are sublimated by residential longevity, they are spotlighted under regeneration:

> 'We didn't know who was a leaseholder or not until this came up, the regeneration.' (Oluwakemi, RTB owner)

> 'It is only when all this started [regeneration] that you get to know who bought, who didn't, who was up in arms, because then you knew who the leaseholders were and the tenants.' (Annie, council tenant)

Rather than simply neighbours who have known each other for years, tenure suddenly becomes significant for local social identities as neighbours become 'A the secure tenant' and 'B the leaseholder'.

Such tenure distinctions were highlighted by officials, for example by holding separate meetings for tenants and leaseholders which tried to force residents into tenure-based silos, a separation that campaigners felt was deliberately divisive:

> 'We know the whole divide and rule thing. Lambeth [council] have played off the leaseholders against the tenants and vice versa. So you've had "consultation", in inverted commas, where they spoke to the leaseholders first, got their view – which is often quite understandably concerned with the value of their property. And then attempted to sell that to the tenants on the strength of "but the leaseholders agree with this, why don't you?" Here we just decided the best thing for everybody is to fight together, that we've got to be united or they're just going to walk all over us and of course they tried very hard to split [us].' (Bill, Cressingham Gardens)

I spoke at a 'Question Time' panel debate about Cressingham Gardens in 2014 (Single Aspect, 2014), held in a nearby church, alongside two Labour councillors. One of the latter mentioned how it was 'only the leaseholders' who opposed demolition, which prompted a tenant to stand up and angrily say that she was opposed to demolition and knew many other tenants like her. In addition to such top-down divisive pressures, residents could also disagree over 'what, if anything, should be done?' Such disagreement is seen in the split votes for and against stock transfer at the Aylesbury, Ocean and Clapham Park NDC estates (Watt and Wallace, 2014).

Coming together

A sense of community is often strengthened by the presence of an external threat, especially at the neighbourhood scale (Somerville, 2016; Mayo, 2017). The threat of demolition can therefore bring residents together. For example, it provides a common concern – a talking point – irrespective of people's actual views. This concern was expressed via multiple questions: 'did you go to the consultation meeting?', 'when is our block supposed to come down?', 'have you heard when we will be moved?':

> 'Since this Northumberland Park Decides has taken off, I've met an awful lot of people that live in the area and now I've

got a way to talk to them because you've got something in common, so it's broken down a lot of barriers. So, you know, I mean people that I've probably walked past for years, they will now say to me, "hi, how are you doing?" and I'll say to them "hi, how you doing, have you heard anything?" and we chat about that.' (Michelle)

'Regen' provided a mutual talking point and strengthened local social capital via people attending meetings. This strengthening could be enhanced via the formation of oppositional groups and campaigns, as Caroline described:

'Every time we [Save Northwold] do a stall, an event, we chat to people and I've got to know loads more people. We did a lot of door knocking last year, putting leaflets through, and getting people to come along to our meetings and I've spoken at meetings. So, they know me and now when I'm walking around people say "hello" to me that I wouldn't have known before. I like that. It's made the community stronger, definitely, and that is ironic. We've got something to talk about, we've got something in common to discuss that we might not have had otherwise.'

Existing neighbourly relations became stronger, while entirely new relations were forged between people who hardly knew each other before regeneration began. Such mutual coming together helps to form a 'community of resistance' in bell hooks' terms (cited in Keith and Pile, 1993: 5), as these quotes from two long-term Carpenters residents' illustrate:

'What I would say is, the people that have been here the longest now, all the to-ing and froing with the council has galvanised us, made us a more solid group.' (Ernie)

'The good thing about it – the few of us who know each other – the fighting has brought us together. One lady said she would die fighting, she had bowel cancer. And she said, "I am not leaving, they will have to take me out of there", and they did because she died.' (Gloria)

Not only did resistance bring long-term residents closer, it helped to bond old-timers and newcomers together, which was prominent at West

Hendon. As a temporary tenant, Douglas knew few of his neighbours, but this changed once he participated in the Our West Hendon campaign. Such connections spanned the tenure spectrum: "we're sort of mixing a bit more now we've all got one common goal" (Douglas). When I asked Theresa (RTB owner) whether there were any tenure divisions at West Hendon, she rejected this because all tenures were involved in campaigning against the redevelopment.

Collective action enhanced this 'community of resistance'. I attended the first day of the JR hearing for the HDV at the RCJ in October 2017 Photograph 11.4). On the bus travelling to the RCJ, I met two female Northumberland Park residents who had come down together to attend the hearing. Over a hundred Tottenham residents and assorted campaigners went to the RCJ. Because of the unprecedented numbers involved, the hearing had to be moved to a larger court and attendees spent nearly an hour wandering around the corridors in search of justice. Michelle reflected on this collective solidarity: "what some people were saying after the court case, and so many people turned up,

Photograph 11.4: Royal Courts of Justice – anti-HDV protest sign, 2017

was that it actually gave them a feeling of being part of the community, where I think we've lost that quite a lot".

Housing struggles and non-engagement

The earlier discussion illustrates how the tenants' movement emphasis on defending homes and communities has had a 21st century makeover via resistance to demolition and associated state-led gentrification of London estates. This resistance reflects a David versus Goliath struggle whereby social housing residents have stood up to neoliberal state/corporate interests in the cause of promoting social justice and preserving existing homes and communities. It therefore falls within the longue durée of housing struggles that David Madden and Peter Marcuse (2016) discuss in *Defense of Housing*, their brilliant neo-Marxist account of how struggles from below have created a more socially just housing landscape and have realised values beyond value. Madden and Marcuse's radical interpretation reflects the critical urbanist notion of praxis – that a socially just housing world is possible and achievable. Many of the campaigners I met and interviewed subscribe to this vision, the novice insiders as well as the established activists.

At the same time, we also need to consider the mundane realities of collective struggle, including tenants' *non-engagement* in resistance to redevelopment. This has received little academic attention, with August's (2016) study of the Regent Park estate in Toronto being an exception. Although resistance was widespread and long-term in London, one grumble I heard from campaigners was that *not enough* of their fellow residents were similarly engaged, despite how people routinely complained about their appalling degeneration and rehousing experiences.

Reasons for non-engagement mirrored those discussed in Chapter 8 regarding why residents did not partake in the official consultation: they had other commitments (work and caring) and therefore were unable to make the meeting or action times; that the decisions had already been made; and that the power struggle was highly unequal and only had one outcome – that which 'they' have pre-decided. This scepticism is reflected in these comments from estate residents who attended Northumberland Park Decides meetings held at St Pauls Church:

'Money and power, how can you stop it?'

'I moved from Hackney, it's worse there. You cannot stop it, it's happening everywhere in the UK.'

'They've not consulted any of us. Do we have a chance? Is the campaign going to be a wasted effort if they've done this in different boroughs?'

Thus, for some tenants, contestation, just like consultation, was a waste of time – 'they' have the power and have already decided the outcome. August (2016: 25) attributes such non-engagement to 'an internalized sense of powerlessness and un-deservingness among tenants'. This internalised powerlessness was evident in London, reflective of symbolic violence among the subordinated working class.

Non-engagement is also linked to differential rehousing rights (Chapter 8). Secure tenants have a right to rehousing, unlike leaseholders or temporary tenants, which means that they will probably remain in their existing borough and *might* even be able to return to the estate (provided enough social homes are built). Therefore why aggravate the council by involving yourself in a collective struggle with an uncertain outcome?

'Some people don't want to get involved in estates, largely tenants because they've got a lot to lose. There are people who say, "we support you", but they don't want to put their name down to anything. They don't want to annoy the council over rehousing. We have 80 registered CARP members, but we're lucky if we get 15 to 20 at meetings.' (Activist, CARP meeting, 2012)

As August (2016: 30) says, tenants have a fear of reprisal: 'Given the power imbalance between tenants and their landlord, many were convinced that speaking out would work against them.' As an RTB owner, the CARP activist was not *complaining* about tenants, but merely acknowledging the all-too-real power imbalance; council tenants are beholden to their landlord who has monopolistic power to make decisions vis-à-vis rehousing. At the end of one estate regeneration meeting at South Kilburn, tenants surrounded the council's housing officer to discuss their individual reallocation cases. By contrast, homeowners have no equivalent rehousing guarantee, and are dependent upon the vagaries of the market, which means they have less to lose by resistance.

If class-based symbolic violence and tenants' fears of reprisals are prominent factors in prohibiting resistance, racism is also a significant factor. As a black African male, Otis was against demolition at Northumberland Park in Tottenham, but was also wary of displaying opposition:

> 'People want to stay, but when it comes to the law, if the council says, "we have to break this down", it's nearly impossible for me to stop them. What can I do as a citizen, as an individual person, do you follow me? I cannot fight the council can I? If I start fighting the council, they will bring the police and get rid of me.'

Black Londoners, such as Otis, not only experience symbolic violence but also *physical violence* from the police, especially in deprived areas of the city with a strong BAME presence like Tottenham (Dillon and Fanning, 2015; Perera, 2019). Migrant status was also significant. At West Hendon, Kofi was engaged in combatting the appalling housing conditions and minimal rehousing rights the temporary tenants had to endure (Chapter 12). However, his fellow temporary tenants' engagement was muted by their wider fears: "some of them are refugees from places like Iraq and Iran and they don't come to meetings because they are scared, but they talk one-on-one" (Kofi).

Due to these factors, many temporary tenants (who are often from BAME backgrounds) were understandably wary about getting involved in campaigning. At the same time, they have 'nothing to lose' by engaging in collective action because they have nothing to begin with in terms of defined rehousing rights. The temporary tenants at Clapham Park (most of whom were from BAME backgrounds) mounted a vigorous campaign against evictions and threatened displacement (Brixton Buzz, 2018). This included demonstrating outside the housing association offices near the estate on a cold winter morning in November 2018. As one of them said, the demonstration was an expression of frustration and anger at how they were being treated (Chapter 10): "people are angry you know, we never knew there was so many of us that was going through the same problem" (James).

The short and sharp anti-transfer campaigns lasted a few months and "focused around a relatively narrow set of tenure issues and moreover hinged around a ballot at a single point in time which determined a clear 'winner' and 'loser'" (Watt, 2018c: 124). By contrast, anti-demolition campaigns reflect the longevity and complexity of comprehensive redevelopment itself. Inevitably activism was more intense at certain periods than at others. Residents modulated their engagement by focusing on the *immediate* threats to their homes and communities.

Others, such as Dennis from the Aylesbury (Chapter 10), shifted over the years from active opposition to weary pragmatic acceptance. They 'threw in the towel' and tried to get the best deal for themselves in what is ultimately a very unequal power struggle (August, 2016). Pippin was a temporary tenant at West Hendon who had not been engaged with Our West Hendon but later attended a CPO (where I met her) and there witnessed the full range of forces – including expensive, high-profile lawyers – ranged against residents:

> 'The struggle is quite difficult – the mountain is too high and too difficult to climb over, to try and battle this behemoth of an institution which has QCs [Queen's Counsel] and money for days. After a while, people don't have the energy, the want to carry on and they don't believe anything will change. I don't blame them. The CPO that I went to was really depressing, highly depressing, seeing what we're against and thinking, "money really does run things".'

Resistance successes

If money really does run things, does this mean that resistance is futile? This section illustrates how resistance can and does makes a positive difference with estate regeneration.

Big wins

How can the success or failure of regeneration contestation be assessed? One obvious metric is whether demolition is stopped. At four of the research estates that were subject to full or partial demolition, the campaigns contributed towards the halting (Carpenters and Northumberland Park) or radical downgrading of demolition (to just two homes at Northwold and to one block at East Dulwich). These successes represent inspirational 'big wins'.

Although the official explanation for the UCL withdrawal at Carpenters estate is that it was due to financial differences, it's extremely likely that the negative publicity UCL received due to the CARP campaign (plus opposition from UCL academics and students), played a part in the collapse of this scheme (Photograph 11.5). Residents were thrilled. They had seen 'them' off – the demolition forces – and celebrated with a BBQ on the weekend after UCL withdrew in May 2013. They breathed a collective sigh of relief, and their previous

Photograph 11.5 UCL Bloomsbury campus – protest about Carpenters estate by residents, students and academics, 2012

activism tailed off, even though a few soldiered on through the GCNF (Chapter 12; Sendra and Fitzpatrick, 2020).

The StopHDV campaign – which included Northumberland Park Decides supporters – managed to do what it its name suggested since the HDV scheme was withdrawn in 2018. The latter was intimately bound up with the change in Haringey Council leadership away from being Progress-dominated to one more sympathetic to the Corbynite wing of the Labour Party (Inside Housing, 2017, 2019). The cancellation of the HDV meant that Northumberland Park estate was preserved.

Save Northwold succeeded in having partial demolition taken off the planning table following 18 months' intensive campaigning (Hackney Citizen, 2018). After this positive result, the campaigners were relieved but also exhausted from the struggle. Caroline was scathing about the endless hours that regeneration takes up: "it robs people of their time and their lives, it's one of the most evil things about it".

If success is measured solely by a binary win-or-lose stopping demolition, then the logical corollary is that other campaigns which have either atrophied (Our West Hendon) or are still active (Save Cressingham Gardens) have failed. As McKenzie (2018) has argued, this binary judgement is flawed since activism can involve both successes *and* setbacks, as occurred at the New Era campaign in Hackney. Most

London estate campaigns are akin to the grim business of First World War trench warfare where a few yards are gained one day, only to be lost the next. In the case of Save Cressingham Gardens, there have been multiple wins (the first JR and the right to manage; Douglas and Parkes, 2016), *and* losses (the second JR and listing). Save Cressingham Gardens has been going since 2013, while the various campaigns in and around the Aylesbury estate been in existence since 2001. A simple binary 'win-or-lose' distinction in such lengthy campaigns is too crude because of their incremental nature, given that 'they are forced to operate on the terrain of a seemingly endless war of attrition' (Watt, 2018c: 125).

Little victories

This still does not provide an adequate account of success and failure because it focuses on major set-piece battles and thus elides the incremental gains that are made. As a South Kilburn tenant said at a Brent Housing Action meeting, "we need to celebrate every little victory" – four of these are illustrated here. The first little victory relates to the therapeutic benefits of collectivisation. The potential forced loss of a home is so intimate and the organisations pushing for demolition are so powerful that it's unsurprising that residents often feel isolated, worthless and powerless – all depressive reactions to something that appears to be beyond any one individual's control (August, 2016). Simple acts of meeting together and sharing concerns can make a huge psychological difference, as people gain mutual strength and hence counter such depressive reactions. Damo and his wife had been worried about regeneration at Northwold, but they felt empowered by attending a residents' meeting.

> 'We were doing nothing, we were just sitting at home talking about it … a real frustration, feeling of powerlessness. Once you meet a few other people and think, "Oh hold on, we can do something here – we can get a letter out, we could produce a leaflet, talk to the people", you know.'

A second example is that tenure-inclusivity is not necessarily spontaneous, but has to be actively constructed, especially in the face of official divide-and-rule tactics. Sandra described a regeneration meeting held at Central Hill:

> 'We don't have that divide between leaseholders and tenants that some other estates definitely suffer from. In fact, the

council tried at the beginning to drive a wedge between us. We had to elect ten residents to form the group that would work with the council. There was probably about 150 residents at the meeting, and you was asked whether you was a tenant or a leaseholder, and a tenant got a pink slip and the leaseholder got a yellow slip. And then leaseholders were only allowed to vote for leaseholders and tenants were only allowed to vote for tenants. And we said "no, we're going to vote for exactly who we want to, we don't *care* if they're a leaseholder or a tenant", and we threw their slips back at them and held the vote the way we wanted to.'

Bill explains how the council tried to have separate meetings at Cressingham Gardens: "what basically happened is people wouldn't attend the meetings or one would attend and say, 'well you know why no one's turned up?' and eventually they started doing joint meetings, only under pressure".

A third little victory operates at the scale of interactions with officialdom (housing officers, courts, and so on). Residents described not having their concerns taken seriously during the rehousing process. Collectivising strengthened their hand in such interactions, for example by gaining a psychological advantage over housing officers, who preferred to see people individually: "they didn't like that, that we are together and going in a group" (Katrina, Clapham Park). Many social and temporary tenants are vulnerable due to illness, old age caring responsibilities, and suchlike. Receiving support from others helped those tenants who felt intimidated going to official meetings or to court by themselves. Danni mentioned how the housing officials did not appear to care about her health concerns regarding her children (Chapter 10). However, at subsequent meetings Danni was accompanied by Elaine (a leaseholder), who acted as mentor. During a joint interview, Danni and Adela (both from BAME backgrounds) thought that the tone and speed of their rehousing meetings changed dramatically once they brought a mentor along: "they were in a hurry before" (Adela):

'Their mannerism, the way they were talking with us was *completely different*. They were more polite when they saw someone was present with us, whereas the first meeting they didn't want to know, they just wanted to "right sign here, this is what's going to happen". I just thought, "you know this is the way they are treating people who have lived here all these years". I mean god knows how they are treating the temporary people who don't really have that much rights as we are being told, at least as a secure tenancy you have a bit more rights. Yes, definitely a lot more polite that day [with mentor].' (Danni)

Elaine's presence helped to ensure their cases were heard with adequate time and respect, which they felt they had not thus far received. Danni was surprised at how she was treated, but also wondered whether it might be even worse for temporary tenants. Several West Hendon temporary tenants went to court, where, as I observed, having the support of empathetic campaigners was hugely important for their sense of well-being (Chapter 10). Campaigners also helped to obtain legal representation. Laiba panicked when she received the eviction notice, but the presence of Elaine and the solicitor helped enormously: "I was very frightened. You see when I went to court, luckily I got the support from Elaine. Do you remember she came in the court, and then I had a solicitor? I couldn't even make the journey by bus [due to stress], I had to get a taxi."

Without legal support, the temporary tenants, alongside those secure tenants who challenged the rehousing decisions, were convinced that they would have been made homeless. Elaine worked tirelessly on behalf of the many West Hendon tenants with rehousing problems, including helping them get legal assistance. At our last interview in 2019, Elaine mentioned how the council/ALMO had no initial interest in rehousing the temporary tenants: "they said, 'we've got no responsibility to them whatsoever'". But the Our West Hendon campaign provided the necessary 'clout' for Elaine to be taken seriously by the council/ALMO. This, in combination with legal representation, assisted in getting better rehousing results, including social tenancies, for the temporary tenants than they would have otherwise got:

'I was the negotiating arm and I had the knowledge but I didn't have the clout. Until Our West Hendon started up and we had the physical clout to be able to carry out actions – which included blockading the works, putting picket lines basically across stopping them from doing it – we would never have gained what we gained without it.'

All three of the above-mentioned victories illustrates enhanced social values of solidarity and caring, as well as supporting people's health and well-being. The fourth little victory illustrates improved economic value. Leaseholders' statutory rights revolve around levels of financial compensation (Chapters 8 and 10). The valuation of leaseholder properties at regeneration estates is hardly an exact science, as I learnt by following the West Hendon rehousing and CPO inquiry. The buy-back offer for one-bedroom flats was £90–95,000 in 2014, while the two-bed flats and maisonettes were offered around £130,000. Through Our West Hendon campaigners' efforts – forcing the first CPO Inquiry in 2015, and hiring surveyors who negotiated on behalf of leaseholders – these amounts were later doubled. A chartered surveyor thought that the negative publicity generated by campaigners (2014–15) helped to lift the compensation:

> 'The balance of power is very, very much with the local authority and the developer. Now what's happened recently, particularly in the last year or so, is that there's such a wave of housing activism against this entire process … the "us against them" … that councils and developers are getting such bad publicity in the press and on the TV, that they're sometimes taking the attitude of "okay, now we will have actually have some kind of fair process in to be able to give people fair figures because we want to avoid this negative publicity".'

Tilting the balance of power in such unequal struggles represents a significant achievement by anti-demolition campaigns.

Conclusion

This chapter has examined the socio-spatial, organisational and ideological nature of resistance to demolition. Unlike the earlier anti-stock transfer campaigns, these anti-demolition campaigns are not solely based on council tenants via a *politics of tenure*. Instead they embrace owner-occupiers and illustrate a defensive *politics of place* based upon maintaining existing homes and communities. These campaigns have become prominent and are in the front line of London's struggles over the right to the city. Despite official accusations that estate campaigners are radical outsiders – politically motivated, socially disconnected housing activists – they are mainly novices to the world of housing politics.

The chapter examined how regeneration pushes residents apart socially (via top-down emphases on tenure distinctions), while it paradoxically also brings them closer together via shared concerns and actions including resistance. Such collective resistance was widespread, as seen in the slew of campaigns at London's threatened estates. At the same time, lack of engagement was also evident as some people felt that resistance was a waste of time, because 'they' have already decided that demolition will happen – an expression of class and tenant powerlessness. Contestation is often long-term – a form of trench warfare – reflecting the interminable nature of regeneration itself. The final section assessed what success might mean in these long-running campaigns, and illustrated this with reference to big wins and little victories. One major win was how Carpenters campaigners saw off UCL in 2013. The next chapter follows up on what subsequently happened at this estate, plus two redeveloped estates.

12

Aftermaths

This chapter examines the aftermaths of regeneration at three estates – West Hendon, Woodberry Down and Carpenters – and analyses what kinds of new places and inequalities are being produced. Regeneration has been going on for 15–20 years at these estates. Not only is this timescale much longer than the 1990s' CEI and SRB schemes (Chapter 3), but these later work-in-progress schemes are unlikely to be completed within the next decade, if then; hence any aftermaths are provisional. I encourage readers to refer to Chapters 3 and 4 for details regarding housing tenure and rehousing provision at the three estates, which are distinct from one another in relation to tenure patterns, governance and finance. This chapter provides an experiential socio-spatial perspective on the emergent new places. As such, the chapter does not assess the estates' respective micro-political economies à la Hodkinson (2019), although brief comments are made about governance in the next chapter.

The West Hendon and Woodberry Down cases illustrate how the long-term, incomplete and dualistic nature of degeneration/regeneration means that *two places* are in symbiotic tension: the old estate which is undergoing degeneration, displacement and demolition, and the redevelopment which is under construction and receiving new tenants and owners. West Hendon and Woodberry Down represent hybrid schemes comprising elements of both places. Four aspects of these hybrid places are analysed: the old part of the estate as a residential area; residents' views on new homes and new landlords; the new redevelopment as a neighbourhood; and whether 'mixed communities' are being created. The final section returns to the Carpenters estate, where regeneration has hardly begun despite having been under 'regen' for 15 years.

West Hendon/Hendon Waterside (Barnet)

By 2019, West Hendon had morphed into a mishmash of the remainder of the old estate and the new rebranded 'Hendon Waterside' development. The latter is physically dominated by a 28-storey private tower block; there are also other private blocks, mixed-tenure blocks, plus a dedicated social housing block with 71 units. West Hendon/

Hendon Waterside has a bewildering set of governance arrangements involving a housing association, private developer, property management company,[1] utility company, as well as the council and the ALMO (Barnet Homes). The West Hendon Partnership Board monitors the regeneration and includes stakeholder and resident representatives. Responsibility for the social tenants is divided between the housing association and the ALMO, while the latter is the landlord for the temporary tenants.

Living in the old place

Over the course of the research period at West Hendon (2014–19), the original estate physically shrank due to demolition. The proportion of temporary tenants increased from over one third of all households in 2013 to the majority by 2019, at which point they lived alongside a diminishing pool of owner-occupiers and secure tenants (Watt, 2018a; Brown, 2019). As seen in Chapter 9, residents living in the 'old estate' were struggling with multiple aspects of degeneration. In addition to the noise and dust emanating from the building work, the estate became increasingly rundown and shabby-looking due to fly tipping, overflowing dustbins, and poorly cleaned and maintained public areas. Conditions worsened as regeneration stretched out, as seen in the crumbling walls at one of the walkways in 2019 (Photograph 12.1). Female temporary tenants were concerned about the estate's deteriorating appearance and official managed (aka mismanaged) decline:

> 'Because they're going to demolish everything, they think that well it's already demolished. They don't even clean, this is not clean enough this area. We've been forgotten. These dustbins are always stacked full, it's horrible, it's always like this. Because they know they're going to demolish it, they don't do much. They don't think they need enough dustbins.' (Shiela)

The cleaning service in Pippin's block got so bad that she offered to do it herself but was turned down by the ALMO:

> 'It just wasn't done frequently enough. I don't blame the cleaners because Barnet Homes had reduced the cleaners. One man cleaning this whole block and then that whole block, so he'd never get around to doing all of it. They

Photograph 12.1: West Hendon estate (remaining block) – walkway, 2019

didn't have enough man/woman/human power. So, I was like, "look, this isn't a criticism of the cleaners, I just want to clean my block because it's always gross and nasty". They wouldn't agree to it.'

Social relations between long-term residents and temporary (non-secure) tenants were generally amicable, as seen during fieldwork where I witnessed convivial interaction between the two groups. This conviviality was underpinned by how many of the nominal 'temporary' tenants had lived at West Hendon for several years, long enough for them to be accepted by the established residents, as Oluwakemi (RTB-leaseholder) explains: "The non-secure tenants, some of them have been there for 10 to 15 years, so they are more-or-less secure tenants, it's just that they don't have a secure tenancy. So many of us had lived there for so long, we just looked after things."

The nominal non-secure tenants had therefore gained a de facto 'more-or-less' secure tenant status due to residential longevity. They became 'one of us' – established residents – provided that they didn't engage in ASB. Long-term residents spoke sympathetically about how their temporary neighbours, who they had known for years, were badly treated regarding rehousing:

> 'The sadness with the regeneration I feel is that it sort of disperses the community, because not everyone has secure tenancy, some people are leaseholders, some people are non-secure. I know a [non-secure] lady downstairs she has lived here *ten years* and she doesn't know what is going to happen to her.' (Danni)

The temporary tenants themselves had developed a sense of belonging (Chapter 10), while female secure and temporary lone parents bonded over mutual childcare support. Natalie was a temporary tenant who got on well with Cheryl, her council tenant next-door neighbour: "If I'm not feeling right, then Cheryl will get the boys for me, or I'll get Jay [son] for her from school – everybody helps each other." The inclusion of temporary tenants was also predicated on their adherence to established respectable estate norms regarding ASB and not making a noise or mess. Temporary tenants' integration was also assisted by how several became involved in the Our West Hendon campaign (Chapter 11). Not all long-term residents were pleased, however. Some regarded the temporary tenants as an additional burden on an already stressed neighbourhood and associated their presence with increased ASB: "everyone that they've moved in so far has brought it down, windows are smashed, doors are kicked in" (Wesley). If there was a good deal of support for the temporary tenants, their replacements – short-term property guardians – were regarded with far more suspicion: "But with the new people [guardians] coming in, I think because they don't have that sense of "let me keep things tidy", the place was just a tip, a mess. So you had people leaving trash out on their front doors and it would smell" (Oluwakemi).

The original West Hendon estate had its share of youths occasionally smoking 'weed' in public spaces. However, as the estate emptied out and physically deteriorated, drug problems worsened as hard drug dealers/users congregated in the half-empty blocks: "they just come in because they know these blocks are empty" (Elaine). Danni was one of the last tenants to leave her old block. She described how all the old familiar faces had disappeared as the block emptied out, and that it became "very eerie" and unsafe due to the visible drug dealing:

'Especially when the council let it run down, there were people there selling drugs and whatever. And I remember I used to meet my kids, they were in secondary school, and I used to stand downstairs to escort them up. I climbed up to my flat and that's what I noticed, there were more people that I knew that didn't live there, because I'd known everyone that lived there because I'd lived there over 20 years.'

The previous informal social control mechanisms which relied on familiarity and trust had broken down and social disorder flourished. Elaine had not insured her flat for over 20 years because she "knew everybody", but was reconsidering this because of the proliferation of "new people". In the past, the established estate youth also acted as control agents: "basically years ago when we had dealers coming over onto the estate, the youngsters kicked them off – 'you can't come on our estate, sod off!'" (Elaine). By 2019, increasing insecurity and visible drug dealing/taking had become a pressing issue for the remaining temporary tenants living in the Marsh Drive block (BBC, 2019; Brown, 2019): "they do drugs in the blocks, they know the estate is not secure, so they come in" (Kofi).

When the cash-poor temporary tenants moved into their flats, several had to undertake emergency self-provisioning in order to make them habitable: "I had to buy a carpet when I moved here, because it was just a bare floor" (Kofi). Pippin spent around £1,000 on repainting and laminating the floor. Shiela described how around ten people went to view her flat; all of them, bar her, turned it down:

'Everyone said "no" to it because these walls looked horrible. There were stains on the walls, and it was terribly, terribly dirty as if no one had lived here for two to three years. They [ALMO] gave us a budget of £150 to redecorate it, but on your own. They don't do anything to it. I painted it with three friends of mine, it took us five to six months.'

Over the years, the temporary tenants' flats deteriorated due to inadequate maintenance; they mentioned cockroach and vermin infestation, damp, mould, leaks and water pouring down the walls due to lack of tiles (BBC, 2019). Natalie had problems opening her windows due to the dust from the building works. She showed me a litany of poor housing conditions that she had reported, but to no avail because her flat was 'on the regen':

'Their [children's] wallpaper lifted in their bedroom off the wall, there's not enough ventilation in their room, and the kitchen windows have rotted. It's all been reported, like the tiles in the bathroom that fell off on the boys. They still haven't done those because they're "on the regen" they won't. When the boys or myself are having a shower, it's [water] running down. The tiles just peeled off the wall. Yeah it's come through on top of the other kitchen cupboards ... you can see where it's peeling.' (Photograph 12.2)

Being 'on the regen' equalled managed decline and enhanced neglect: "If you say ask them [ALMO], which I did, for a load of kitchen cupboards, they say, 'oh no, no, no, you're not getting anything, this is a regeneration estate, it's going to be pulled down'" (Douglas). After getting nowhere with their individual complaints to Barnet Homes, in 2019 the temporary tenants collectivised by forming a campaign group – 'West Hendon Warriors' – with the assistance of

Photograph 12.2: West Hendon estate – Natalie's bathroom with missing tiles, 2014

community organisers from the local Labour Party (Brown, 2019). As Kofi said, "if you complain as an individual, you haven't got a chance". They went to see one of their Conservative councillors to "force him to come and look at the conditions, we were so full of anger and we wanted to see him together because we're in the same conditions and they want to divide and rule" (Kofi). The temporary tenants' case gained national publicity by appearing on the 'Victoria Derbyshire Programme' (BBC, 2019) on TV. The tenants gained some traction with Barnet Council due to this publicity and collective action (Brown, 2019).

As a result of the multiple degeneration processes, a Labour councillor (2015) who worked closely with residents described how West Hendon had become a parody of an estate, due to the worsening physical conditions, new people (especially guardians) and ASB, all of which distressed long-term residents:

> 'Living there is not easy and especially as they have had all these new people coming on … apart from the mice and the rats and the damp and the dust and the mould, and it's really bad, *really bad*. They have also got this sort of like anti-social behaviour now. I think it's sort of a council estate now that people have parodied as a council estate, and its turned into that. People [long-term residents] have remarked about how very different it is now.'

The old remaining part of West Hendon became a distorted parody of a council estate. In other words, the 'sink estate' *place myth* – which West Hendon was unjustly accused of being and was used to justify its demolition – *became reality* because of that very same regeneration that was supposed to make West Hendon a 'better' place to live.

New homes, new landlord

West Hendon council tenants had the option of returning to their new homes either as tenants of the ALMO or the housing association. All the post-relocation tenants I interviewed opted to remain with the ALMO because they trusted the council ('the devil you know'), and also wanting to preserve their existing rights: "a council tenancy is good as gold" (Sam). Although this appears to be a 'real choice' of post-relocation landlord, its de facto significance was minimal because the major landlord functions were no longer undertaken by the ALMO but by the housing association: "I'm a Barnet Homes tenant, but because we're in a housing association building, all the repairs and everything else is with them now" (Lorraine).

Around half of the 12 tenant and owner-occupier interviewees who moved into new flats in the redeveloped part of the estate appreciated their new flats, with some saying they were 'much better'. Those who were previously un-homed due to overcrowding or poor maintenance were especially pleased (Chapter 10). Eva compared her new flat favourably with the old one:

> 'Inside the flat was terrible, it was very old. Barnet Council didn't want to repair, they repaired once because it was flooded, but they didn't want to know. My son paid for a new carpet and he painted everything because it was flooded. It was the same when I moved in, it was terrible. Here I don't complain because everything is new, it's a nice lovely flat, all new, I have no problem.'

Despite her long and painful rehousing journey, Danni was pleased with her new flat: "it's a lot larger so there is a bedroom for all of us now, it's really a family home". Others were ambivalent. Sam liked his spacious 'modern' new flat, but not the kitchen-diner arrangement, while his flat was in a worse location: "I didn't really want to leave, I mean because I'm losing that fantastic location overlooking the reservoir, the parkland, it's very quiet. Now I'm facing all these other flats, and cars are literally using it like a racetrack" (Sam's old block and view, Photograph 12.3). Five of the 12 were much more critical about their new flats; these had experienced rehousing as bereavement and identified numerous faults with their new flats – thin walls, poor sound insulation and inadequate storage space (Chapter 10; Watt, Forthcoming).

Some West Hendon tenants had either no problem with their new flats which required repairs or were satisfied with the landlord's response. Others, however, were displeased: "There was a leak in the casing where the wastewater pipe goes. All the mould had gone along the skirting at the back of the kitchen. And it stinks, I can't even cook there anymore. They were meant to come around and fix it up, never did" (Craig).

Complaints had to be made to the housing association by telephone, which could be frustrating: "They don't pick up the phone so sometimes you can be holding 20 minutes, half an hour. Then when you do get through, you can't speak to a housing officer, you can't have their direct line, you've always got to go through

Photograph 12.3: West Hendon estate – Welsh Harp (foreground), Franklyn House (background), 2014

customer service" (Cheryl). What residents also found frustrating and bewildering was establishing *organisational responsibility* for repairs and maintenance. Hodkinson (2019) has highlighted this opacity in his research on PFI estate regeneration schemes where multiple organisations are involved and where legal responsibilities are encoded and enforced by dense thickets of contracts. Although Lorraine was "over the moon" with her new flat, she experienced several months with no heating or hot water and described the Kafkaesque situation she found herself in:

'Finding out who's responsible was a *major* problem and it took a long while to get sorted. It was a very, very long, drawn-out process. I had to wait for parts to be ordered, and then various calls in the night to come and have a look at what's going on. I'm constantly calling and no one seems to have figured out what the problem was. It was like three different ones [organisations], and it just didn't make any sense. One would say, "oh no, it's a plumber that's needed", "no, it's an electrician that's needed", "oh no…". So, it was like different people would turn up, sometimes after midnight, and I'm having to wait up/cancel my work/swap my days around, just to be there for someone to come and have a look and they didn't do anything, they just looked [laughs], it was really annoying. In the end they found some industrial guy to come and do something. I can't remember what organisation he worked for, but he managed to fix it there and then.'

Cheryl had problems with her heating but was bounced between the various housing and utility organisations: "You're constantly to-ing and fro-ing, you just want to pull your hair out half the time. They've made it so difficult so you just say, 'I can't be bothered'."

New blocks, new neighbourhood

Several interviewees considered the new blocks of flats to be an improvement, at least in relation to cleanliness and security:

'It's clean, it's secure, it's carpeted when you approach your front door. I'm situated in a nice little place of that building, I can go downstairs, I don't have to leave the building, beautifully landscaped – which I do enjoy – it's clean and it's well-kept. They have a team that cleans all the time.' (Lilly)

Despite the new blocks' cleaner appearance, they lacked the old blocks' informal conviviality. While Lilly was personally pleased with her flat and block, she appreciated (along with Theresa) how the elderly and disabled tenants felt isolated:

Theresa: 'I'm talking about the elderly people, like Vera who's depressed, closed in in a building.'
Lilly: 'Isolated...'
Theresa: '...like a hotel which they cannot...'
Lilly: '...because they shut their doors.'
Theresa: 'They shut their doors, they're seeing nobody. Before you could walk along the balcony, you know the open balconies along the top? We all stepped out onto the balconies to talk, lean over, shout up, shout down.'

As Theresa indicates, such isolation is connected to the differential physical layout of the blocks. Instead of the old blocks' external balconies (Photograph 12.4), the new blocks have internal corridors

Photograph 12.4: West Hendon estate (remaining block) – balcony, 2019

which give them a hotel-like appearance (Photograph 12.5). These are anonymous 'non-places' (Auge, 1995), which inhibit routine social interaction. Theresa felt that she was on holiday in her new 'hotel' rather than at home:

> 'The [old] maisonettes are open onto the street, but now we're enclosed. Ours is like a hotel foyer, with no reception but with two doors you have to go through to get to the lifts. You come in the front door and you have to go through another door to get into the corridor where the lifts are. I feel that we're in a hotel, we're on our holiday, when do we go home [laughs]?'

Theresa highlights the amusing side of her hotel-like existence but, as she acknowledged, she had a job and went out of her flat most days unlike the elderly and disabled. Even though Eva (aged 80) appreciated her new flat, she felt lonely in the block:

Photograph 12.5: Hendon Waterside (new social housing block) – 'hotel corridor', 2017

'This flat is like a prison believe me, no one knocks on the door to see how you are, if you're alive or dead. It was better in the [old block], there were neighbours to ask how you are. Because it was a ground floor flat, I could go out to have my coffee and a cigarette. Now it's difficult for me to take a lift and sometimes it doesn't work so it's not easy.'

Charlie accepted that the "old flats needed doing up" (because they'd been neglected) and appreciated the design of his new flat. At the same time, he also felt the loss of everyday informal conviviality and concomitant decline in local social capital at the block scale:

'It's funny, but I don't see anyone anymore. The place is nice, but I don't see people, I just go to work in the morning and come home. Whereas before we used to congregate outside, but there's nowhere to sit outside now. I see my next-door neighbour when we're both on our balconies, but all that sort of thing has gone. You might meet people in the lift sometimes. Before we were all on the balcony [Photograph 12.4] and we'd chat, anyone who'd walk by would stop and chat, and you had your own little spot.'

The old blocks, the abundant green space and residential longevity contributed towards the general opinion that the original West Hendon estate had a good community feeling (Chapter 6). Equally widespread was the notion that this sense of community had been broken *because* of regeneration. Thus, despite only physically moving a few metres from their old homes, West Hendon residents *felt* displaced at both the block and neighbourhood scales (Davidson, 2009; Pull and Richard, 2019). Pat summarises this loss of a way of life, sense of community and human warmth as she contrasts the everyday conversations she used to have in her old block with the current 'dead' space of her current block as budget hotel (Chapter 10; Photograph 12.5):

'When they break down council estates, they break down families, they break down people, they break down a way of life. That way of life is you can always go to your next door neighbour and say to them, "The gas man's coming, he needs to read my meter, are you in or are you going to be at work, can you do it for me?" Because I used to do that. Now it's not like that because you *don't know* your neighbour. It's not the same, there's no love, there's no feeling there … it's just *dead*! You lose the sense of community feeling, of knowing the people that are around you, you lose the sense of love, you lose the sense of my next-door neighbour, "Jenny, you alright my love, how are you darling?" "I'm fine." It's not like that, it's changed so randomly, it's changed for the worst, I don't think for the best.'

Not only were the new blocks socially anomic, they were also far more controlled, rule-bound spaces, as has been identified in new-build, mixed-tenure developments elsewhere in London (Kilburn, 2013; Corcillo, 2020). After our interview, Annie and I stood in what she described as the "antiseptic hospital corridor" outside her flat. She explained how personalisation of this space was impossible: "You're not allowed to put things on the wall. I wanted to put a pot plant outside but was told 'no' because of health and safety". This is indicative of the subtle, but very real shifting power relations between council tenants living in the old estate – where they controlled the immediate space outside their flats – and the new blocks where control of the equivalent space is ceded to the various housing organisations.

Residents used their balconies at their old blocks as an extension and integral part of their domestic space: for socialising, hanging out washing, and to leave toys, bicycles and chairs outside (Photograph 12.4; Chapter 6). This reflects how council/social tenants exercise control within the working-class-dominated space or Bourdieusian field of the estate. By contrast this control is lost in the new socio-spatial field of the redevelopment, since none of their old practices were allowed in their new blocks. One of the housing organisations issued a long list of 'regulations for use of balcony' (2018) which included the following 'DO NOT' instructions: store items on them including children's toys and bikes; put out washing; play music; display flags or bunting. Vicky reeled off this list and laughed – "I just ignore them". Cheryl, on the other hand, found it intimidatory: "We're getting threatening letters, 'not to have this on our balcony, that on our balcony' and if we do, they'll take action against us. You can't have a flag, like when the World Cup was on." According to one official leaflet I came across, the rationale for the new rules was 'numerous complaints' about the 'poor appearance of the properties' due to some residents' 'inappropriate use' of the balconies. It was clear to Vicky, Cheryl and Cheryl's neighbour (who had received a letter warning her about hanging out laundry) *who* was doing the complaining – and it wasn't social tenants like us: "the private people don't want to walk past there and see the laundry" (Cheryl). Similar complaints about 'disrespectful conduct' have been levelled against social renters by private owners/ renters in other London mixed-tenure developments (Kilburn, 2013; Awofolaju, 2014; Corcillo, 2020). This suggests that tenure mixing is far less harmonious than planned or anticipated within the official regeneration rationale.

Mixed communities or new inequalities?

The West Hendon scheme aimed to: 'contribute to the creation of a vibrant and sustainable mixed tenure neighbourhood', which 'will make this part of the Borough a better place to live, leading to improved community cohesion in an area with a highly diverse population' (LBB, 2012: 4.1, 8.1). This fits into the 'mixed-tenure/ communities' approach to regeneration whereby remaining social tenants supposedly benefit from the presence of the incoming private owners and tenants (Bridge et al, 2012). As the use of balcony rules suggest, this is not how the social tenants experienced their redeveloped mixed-tenure neighbourhood.

Social mixing can occur in two main ways: informally and spontaneously via day-to-day neighbouring activities; or formally via organised community development. The latter includes staged large-scale events such as fun days, and small-scale events, classes and clubs at local community centres. West Hendon had a new community hub at the bottom of the social housing block which put on a variety of classes. Tenants participated in such activities, with the yoga classes being popular with middle-aged females. However, as far as both social and temporary tenants were concerned, interaction with residents of the private blocks was virtually non-existent:

> 'You see people at the weekends going in and out. Maybe they're Airbnb? I've never met anyone in the new blocks and they've never said, "let's have a BBQ". It's meant to be mixed, but it's not really mixing between the blocks.' (Charlie)

> 'You started to see more suited people coming into the estate, but they would just walk straight through and go straight to where they lived. Any community event I've been to at the new community hub, there's no private rented people there ever, not that I've seen.' (Pippin)

Such absence of tenure mixing partly reflects the spatial configuration of the Hendon Waterside development. Although several blocks in the middle are mixed-tenure, those at the extreme ends are not; the private blocks are located near the waterside location, whereas the main social housing block is near the busy Hendon Broadway road. Lack of cross-tenure interaction was reinforced by the enclosed and securitised nature of the private blocks, as Sam explained:

> 'I've not seen much [interaction] no. But the nature of the blocks themselves, they're not conducive to community. You don't see children playing outside any more. Because before at least children could play outside almost unsupervised but they can't do that now, there's nowhere really for them to play. I don't see a lot of the [new] residents, I think a lot of them, they go to work, they're coming back, crash out and go back to work, they're not really mixing with anybody. But it's not conducive

to a community atmosphere. What I see is you having increasingly gated communities, and you know getting into buildings, there's no access. If you know somebody then you can get in, but you can't just walk in there now, there's a concierge there.'

The everyday social porosity promoted by the old estate's design had disappeared as the new blocks are isolated, securitised inward-looking islands protected from outsiders via gates and concierges (Atkinson and Blandy, 2017; Photograph 12.6). Sam's quote alludes to how the new residents are typical middle-class 'busy Londoners' – off to work in the morning and then back in the evening but with relatively little time for locally based social interaction: "Most of the private ones, you see the ones that live in the big blocks, they're going out work in the morning and coming home at night, and that's it. There's no interaction because you don't see anyone" (Eddie).

Instead of producing a mixed community, long-term residents felt that regeneration had brought about 'them and us' class/tenure divides. Whereas previous ex-RTB leaseholders like Theresa had previously lived *alongside tenants*, she now felt cut off from the latter – she was in her block, they were in theirs:

Photograph 12.6: Hendon Waterside – gated mixed-tenure block, 2016

'There's only one tenant block that's been built – that's in the old car park – so they're all corralled over there. We were all mixed, tenants, non-secure tenants, leaseholders, but now they've divided us. They've put the leaseholders in with the private tenants and they've divided them across the way. So we're thinking now of "them and us". We're walking into the lovely new block down more by the river and they're up in the car park area. It's a terrible feeling, you feel you've been divided.'

Tenants living in the dedicated social housing block experienced a *heightened* rather than reduced awareness of class inequalities. Craig scoffed at the idea that there was a mixed community because the people buying the new flats were the same kind of people that live in Hampstead – London's super-rich elite: "It's rich and poor mate. You've got the rich people buying the flats over there overlooking the views of Wembley and the Welsh Harp and all that green space. You don't see that unless you live up in Hampstead when you get that sort of view."

Annie had no interaction with the private newcomers and did not expect there would be: "No [mixing], I don't think so at all. But they've got a porter there or concierge or something, we've got nothing here". Class inequalities – them and us – were highlighted by the looming presence of the private apartment blocks with their concierge, plus the gym which social tenants were not allowed to use. When I asked Pat whether some of the new blocks were gated, she replied angrily:

'Yeah, *them* and us. The gated ones are the private people, aren't they? They're the ones with the flowers, we're the ones with the bush, because we're council tenants. But the people in the private ones, they've got lovely little flowers and things like that. That's how you know that they're private ones – the council are bush, they're flowers. Why can't we have flowers? Are we not worthy? How come they've got a gardener and a concierge? Are we not worthy? Them and us! So then it does make you very angry, it makes you look at things differently, and it's not fair. But a concierge because you own your flat. Can't we have that privilege?'

Such spatially proximate symbolic devaluation made the social tenants *feel* like second-class citizens – 'are we not worthy?' As noted earlier,

Photograph 12.7 Hendon Waterside – billboard, 2017

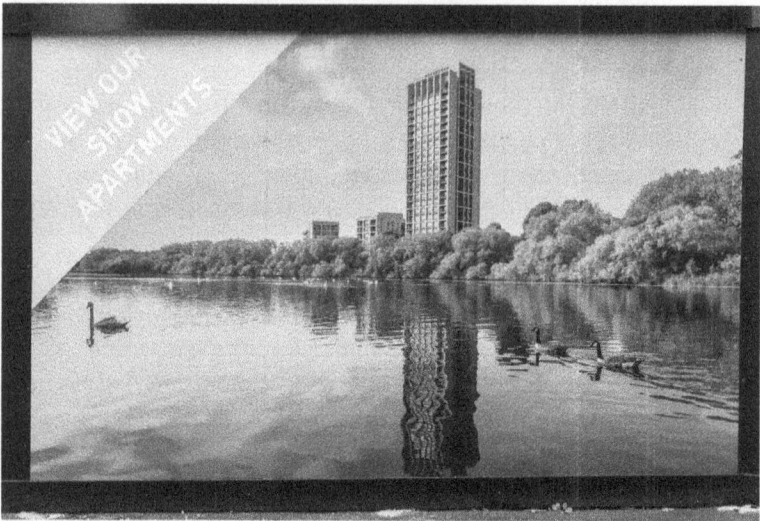

Sam lost his previous views of the Welsh Harp (Photograph 12.3) – but these views were the prime selling point for the new private blocks (Photograph 12.7).

The old residents made efforts to reach out to the new. Female tenants bid for funding from the regeneration partners to put on an evening get-together at the community hub in autumn 2017. At this event, there was food, alcohol, raffles, prizes and music (African drumming) and generally it was a very lively, friendly atmosphere. There was a pronounced demographic and ethnic mix (BAME and white) among the 50+ residents who attended. Adults chatted together at tables alongside children and a few youths (albeit the latter were mainly on their mobiles). It was a largely female event, indicative of the gendered nature of local informal community activities (Gosling, 2008). As one of the organisers said at the start of the evening, "we don't know our neighbours so much, so this is a way of getting to meet people". Lorraine had helped to organise the event and she thought that there was little community feeling in the main new social housing block compared to the previous estate and how elderly tenants were isolated: "the building that they're in is like an old people's home, because the majority of the people who are in that building are actually elderly people that don't go outside". In addition to trying to recreate the now lost community among long-term residents, Lorraine wanted to attract people from the private blocks and so bridge the old/new divide:

'It was really to try and reach out to people, because there's that little divide now. You've got people who've bought their own property, they don't feel like they're part of this whole thing, whereas people that have been here for years and years feel like they've lost that sense of community, whereas new people don't really care as such. Maybe they do, but they haven't sort of made an effort to merge with the old. I haven't seen that happening.'

No private residents attended. As one female attendee said, "they'd leafleted all over including the private blocks here, but it's all the old-timers who already know each other". The event's ethnic and demographic mix was therefore not replicated by a tenure or class mix. The attendees were predominantly social tenants plus a few shared-equity owners from the old estate. In class terms, they were retired working class, traditional working class and precariat (Chapter 5). Lorraine admitted that she did not think the new residents would cross the class/tenure divide due to stigmatising stereotypes about social tenants:

'That's basically what was going through my mind, that I doubt if they will come. So I did try to put things in there that were an incentive, like the first five will get a prize. But obviously that wouldn't appeal to these people that are paying half a million [£] for their property. I went to the designer outlets and I got hampers made up, and some of the prizes were donated from neighbours. It's [mixing] difficult, because you've got people who are there from the old building that I suppose people from the new buildings will perceive as social housing – that they're poor, or they're scrounging or they don't want to mix with that kind of people.'

If there was little social interaction between the different tenures within the new Hendon Waterside section, there was a massive socio-spatial and environmental chasm between the 21st century squalor of the degenerated old estate which accommodated the temporary tenants and the new shiny private blocks. The temporary tenants were struggling to get by as either part of the non-working poor or precariat. Living as he was under the constant threat of displacement, Kofi described the so-called mixed community that was being created: "what it is, they [council] want middle-class young guys to move in and then move out the non-secure tenants completely so you get a different mixture altogether". Hendon Waterside is a *fragmented* not mixed community.

Social housing has even been symbolically erased from Hendon Waterside since the main social housing block names do not appear on the developer's website map (Barratt London, 2020).

Woodberry Down (Hackney)

Woodberry Down is much larger and more spatially spread out than the relatively compact West Hendon (Table 4.1). Somewhat over half-way through its comprehensive redevelopment, Woodberry Down is divided between the remnants of the public estate, managed by Hackney Council, and the new development which is managed jointly by a housing association and private developer. This new development includes numerous blocks: some are for social tenants, the new tower blocks are for private owners/tenants, while others are mixed tenure. All the major stakeholders, plus residents, have representatives on the WDCO board which acts as an overview body for the regeneration (Nelson and Lewis, 2019). Unlike at West Hendon/Hendon Waterside, WDCO successfully challenged the rebranding of the redeveloped area to 'Woodberry Park' in 2012, an important symbolic victory (Nelson and Lewis, 2019).

Living in the old place

The old blocks which are still standing straddle the Seven Sisters Road and include the seven blocks which were rephased back in the schedule (Chapters 7 and 9). The occupied properties accommodate the remaining council tenants and leaseholders together with a floating pool of temporary tenants. This part of Woodberry Down is dominated by degeneration signs: boarded-up properties, rundown appearance, crime and ASB, a transient population and an atmosphere of social anomie – where no one knows anyone anymore (Chapters 7 and 9).

In November 2017, I counted 32 boarded-up and 34 empty flats at the seven blocks; a void total of 66 or 30 per cent of the entire 220 flats (Photograph 12.8). The Woodberry Down IRA summarised the associated issues: "You get problems with people feeling isolated, you get problems about break-ins, you get increased levels of anti-social behaviour, so you've got all of those issues." As Ella, a temporary tenant, said: "It just doesn't look very nice to have these boarded up, it doesn't give a good image, it makes it a stigma." Wayne (council tenant) was dismayed by the physical deterioration and population churn: "There's still old-school people here from back in the day when my mum was alive, but now there's lots of new people. Also, there's a guy sleeping on the balcony in one of those

Photograph 12.8: Woodberry Down estate (seven blocks) – occupied and boarded-up flats, 2017

boarded-up flats around the back, and there's fucking syringes and drug paraphernalia all over."

Several long-term and temporary tenants felt that their part of the estate was unsafe. They commented on visible drug dealing which occurred in the lifts and stairwells: "We can see drugs being done in front of our eyes, but we've given up complaining. The council says it's the police [responsibility] and the police say it's the council's responsibility because it's a local authority estate" (Irmak).

At Woodberry Down, as at West Hendon and the other degenerating/ regenerating estates, local social capital dissipated as old neighbours moved out and new faces constantly appeared, as two long-term council tenants described:

'I don't know who lives here anymore, I just see new faces. Before I used to know people, I had friends in the area. My neighbour upstairs, she moved.' (Grace)

'I went [on holiday] Sunday and was back Tuesday and oh my god, everyone had gone. I was on my own in this block apart from three other people for ages, for about three years. It was creepy in this block at that time. I felt a bit frightened especially coming up the stairs and if you get stuck who's going to come and get you out? The block looked terrible and then they started putting people [temporary tenants] back into the empty flats about a year and a half ago. They're moving in from hostels and they could be here six months or two years. I might say "hello" to the people next door, she's only just moved in. But you don't get to know anybody anymore.' (Barbara)

Long-term residents were propelled into an anomic world full of strangers – temporary tenants and itinerant drug dealers/takers. The IRA estimated that the non-secure tenants began moving in around 2013. Unlike at West Hendon where the temporary tenants stayed for several years, Hackney Council was more proactive in clarifying how they had to bid for properties (as a Regeneration Officer mentioned). The IRA was explicit that the temporary tenants would not be included in the rehousing scheme: "They won't be, they are not going to be part of Woodberry Down, it's made very clear to them that only the existing residents of Woodberry Down will be rehoused." There was, however, an official underestimation of the length of time the temporary tenants were at Woodberry Down – 'several months' – compared to my interview data. The seven interviewees had lived there for periods ranging from two months to four years with a mean period of 18 months.

Compared to their West Hendon equivalents, the Woodberry Down temporary tenants were much less well integrated into the existing estate community. All seven of the Woodberry Down temporary tenant interviewees had young children and four were lone parents. Most knew a couple of neighbours to say 'hello' to, but little beyond that. Local social capital had not been built up and some thought the estate was unfriendly. Whitney had been in her flat for nearly two years: "I don't really know any neighbours, only one lady. I'm just in and out working and picking up my daughter from school. The kids are not making friends. Some of the people are not friendly here, and I've been here two years." The limited neighbourliness was partly a function of how they expected to be only for there a short time since they had been officially told that this was the case:

'I've not had any problem with anyone in the area, the neighbours seem pleasant enough – there's two mums either side of me. Next door is temporary as well. Even then I don't invest in the neighbours because I know we won't be here for long. It's just a friendly "hello" when we meet.' (Ella)

The IRA acknowledged that his work was limited to "the existing council tenants, existing leaseholders, and looking to get integration with the new residents [private owners and renters]". If the temporary tenants were not part of his remit, they did not appear to be part of any organisation's remit regarding the *quality* of their sojourn. Although they were not disbarred from participating in WDCO and estate-wide events, the impression given from nearly everyone I spoke to who was part of the established 'Woodberry Down community' (residents and officials) was that it was up to the temporary tenants to 'make the effort'. Among the temporary tenant interviewees, knowledge of WDCO was virtually non-existent and they were only vaguely aware of the fun days. The temporary tenants were de facto socially excluded from the mixed community that was supposedly being created.

One issue which was repeatedly mentioned by both long-term and temporary residents was the dire quality of their housing. As at West Hendon, poor temporary tenants had to spend their extremely limited money on making their flats habitable when they moved in. Ella moved into her flat during winter and there was just a concrete floor: "I asked the council for flooring, but they said it was for emergency only." She spent £400 on the "cheapest laminate" (all she could afford) and her family members put it down for free: "it was cold and because of the children, I had to get it done". Rahel's flat was in a similarly spartan state when she and her family moved in and they spent several thousand pounds to bring it up scratch. As she pointed out, they would not be financially compensated for any of this self-provisioning when they moved out, unlike the secure tenants (Chapter 8).

Despite the old part of the estate eventually having DHP work undertaken, there was a sense of desperation regarding the chronically poor housing conditions in terms of damp, overcrowding, cold and non-existent/poor-quality repairs. Several residents of the seven blocks ushered me into their homes to highlight the appalling conditions they had to live in. Meena lived in an overcrowded four-bed flat with her husband, four grown-up daughters and young son. Meena was thrilled at recently having a new kitchen put in under the DHP, although it took the council 20 years to replace the old kitchen: "it was so bad, the sink was blocked". The flat was damp, and water had leaked into one of the bedrooms. Two of her adult daughters, who were in their early thirties, shared a room and slept in a bunk bed. The family had not received any suitable rehousing offers. One daughter was "begging the council to give me the empty flat next to my mum, but the council didn't listen". Meena and her daughters were dumbfounded at why they weren't allowed to have one of the many empty flats in their block: "why not open up the flats to us?" (Meena, council tenant).

Ayla (temporary tenant) had not had a light in her bathroom for over six months and was forced to either bath her children during the daytime or at night using the torch on her mobile phone. The light was broken due to a water leak: "they [council] came and fixed it, but then it went off again after two days because the water is still coming through". Her children were "always coughing" because of the damp in their bedroom. Claudia was a lone parent council tenant who lived with her four children in an overcrowded two-bedroom flat. As well as being a mum, Claudia was a proud member of the London precariat, working shifts in a local fast-food restaurant, which she enjoyed. Claudia had complained to the council about the cold and mould, but "nothing happened about it". Last year, she had not had a functioning boiler, hot water or heating for seven months and had to go to her mum's flat to have a wash: "we slept with the blanket all together to keep warm". All this is highly ironic – or rather tragic for those so badly affected – given how the seven blocks were supposed to be redeveloped much earlier due to their original poor condition as identified in the original regeneration rationale (Chapter 4).[2] To conclude this section, the old remaining part of Woodberry Down has taken on the visible appearance of a 'sink estate', in much the same manner as happened at West Hendon.

New homes, new landlord

A greater proportion of Woodberry Down residents – compared to their West Hendon equivalents – thought that their new flats were an improvement on their previous ones: they were new and did not suffer from problems of damp, and so on, while some had impressive views over the reservoir which they greatly appreciated (Photograph 12.9). This difference reflects the worse physical state of the buildings at Woodberry Down relative to West Hendon, and how WDCO negotiated that the new social rental homes are at a larger Parker Morris plus 10 per cent standard (Belotti, 2014; WDCO, 2015).

Photograph 12.9: Woodberry Down (redevelopment) – view from housing association tenant's window, 2017

Despite widespread appreciation of having better flats, this does not necessarily mean that tenants thought that their old homes had *no value*, especially their solidity as buildings, while a few interviewees even preferred their old flats (Chapters 6 and 10). Furthermore, while some tenants benefited from having views over the reservoir, others lost *those very same views* as they were relocated to blocks next to the busy main road (Photograph 12.10). The latter suffered from noisy traffic and Jack had not used his roadside balcony for two years because of this:

> 'It quietens down a bit maybe about 2 am when it slows down a bit, but up until then it's all day, sirens, police cars, fire engines, ambulances, it's all there. One day I had a piece of paper and I ticked how many sirens went past … there was 19.'

As with West Hendon, another source of dissatisfaction was their new housing association landlord. This emerged at the three WDCO meetings that I attended and was also a running sore in interviews in relation to repairs (timing and quality), cleaning, service charges and remote communication. Tipp thought that the regeneration was "definitely a good thing, and I mean personally I'm delighted with

Photograph 12.10: Woodberry Down (redevelopment) – new social housing blocks, 2018

it, I'm very grateful for that superior accommodation". At the same time, he was highly critical of the housing association:

> 'I mean the council never did a great deal, but the thing is, [the housing association] aren't much better. You know they've caused an awful lot of dissatisfaction from the residents' point of view. My opinion is that they essentially lack communication skills. If you've got a problem, they will give you a phone number. They are not staffed here, there's no interface with them. I don't know now who to complain to. They won't even answer the phone and when they do, you talk to a bloody machine. It's all at arm's length instead of hand's on.'

Even once they managed to get workers to come out, several tenants reported being dissatisfied with the service. Shirley had wanted to leave her old flat because it was old and tired looking. Although Shirley felt comfortable in her new flat, she was "fed up" with the recurrent, unresolved problems that she had with the central heating; the previous winter, she had no heating and hot water for over two weeks. Shirley even compared her new landlord unfavourably with Hackney Council:

"I'll be honest with you, and it's just not me who will be saying that it will be everybody – the council was much better, as regards to complaints. Things did not used to go bad in the old flats like it goes here. These are modern, they use cheaper things".

These are, it must be emphasised, newly-built flats.

New blocks, new neighbourhood

In terms of the redeveloped neighbourhood, the dominant regeneration narrative is unremittingly positive:

> People are very happy with the Woodberry Down redevelopment to date. (LBH, 2014: 4.9)

> the consensus, borne out by resident surveys, is that Woodberry Down is generally a much better place to live, a place where fear is not a daily emotion. (*Evening Standard*, 2014)

> What makes Woodberry Down special is its sense of community. It's a place where people know their neighbours, actively join local interest groups and invest culturally in the area. (Totality UK, 2015: 92)

This positive narrative is buttressed by case studies of entirely contented residents, as featured in *Source Magazine* (Totality UK, 2015), a magazine by a place marketing company commissioned by the developer (see also Quod, 2014). The implication of such post-redevelopment 'assessments' is that homes and sense of community were entirely deficient prior to regeneration, which is not the case, as seen in previous chapters.

Despite some interviewees feeling more secure in the new blocks, the dominant resident discourse was the same as at West Hendon – that these were anonymous, hotel-like places which lacked the openness and conviviality of the old blocks:

> 'There's something about it that whenever my mum and my sister [have] ever visited me and they come up, they've never met anybody. And they say it's got a hotel-feel about it when you walk in the door and you come up the lift and you go along the corridor, its door, door, door, door, door, carpet, but you don't see anyone. I've never met anyone on that landing for about five years. I've seen them outside,

but you never meet anyone. I couldn't tell you who lives here, honestly.' (Jack)

Jack contrasted this soulless anonymity with what used to happen in his old block: "It's different from over there, because it was more open. The flats were open and you had balconies, and you'd go, hello Bill!'." In fact, rather than the gushingly positive media and official spin, many residents expressed a lost sense of community, for example, as related to the closure of the previous shops (Belotti, 2014; Nelson and Lewis, 2019):

> 'It [regeneration] doesn't seem to be going like it should be, I don't think. It's just I think they've killed the community quite a lot. The community isn't there as such now, I don't think so. You used to have quite a good one. That's why when the old shops was on that side, it was a *proper* community. You went down there, there was the café, the fish and chip shop, the barbers, hairdressers, bakers, everything was there. Now you go in Sainsbury's, I don't like that Sainsbury's anyway. Anyway, it's not the same, you know.' (Jane)

Long-term tenants, like Jane, felt regeneration had eroded their sense of community and that the neighbourhood wasn't 'the same', and this was despite the efforts to create a mixed community, as now discussed.

Mixed communities or new inequalities?

Like West Hendon, one of the main aims of the Woodberry Down regeneration was to create a mixed community out of the different housing tenures. WDCO (2015: 2) consistently pushed for this aim in terms of building a "balanced and integrated community", one that the regeneration partners had signed up to. Additional community facilities had been provided, such as the Redmond Centre, which puts on a wide range of neighbourhood activities. WDCO has also made dedicated attempts to find the holy grail of a mixed community via extensive formal community development efforts, such as the annual summer fun days (Nelson and Lewis, 2019). The fun days are funded by the developer and are popular affairs with several hundred people enjoying the sun and various games and activities.

Despite these efforts, the dominant view among resident interviewees was that Woodberry Down was going 'upmarket' (gentrifying), that the new shops and eating facilities were prohibitively expensive, and that there was little tenure/class intermixing. Marion described the new facilities "over the other side" (across the main Seven Sisters road) as catering for a "different clientele, they're aiming for the private owner", *not* social tenants like herself: "I've been in there [café] twice, I loved it but it's very expensive. And the new restaurant, I've never been in there and I don't know anybody who has." Shirley described how the people living in the private blocks across the main road were "middle-class people who walk like this" – she demonstrated their rapid strides with her two fingers – the standard morning and evening walk of London busy professionals. Shirley was a gregarious older social tenant who knew no one in the private blocks:

> 'These are middle-class people working in the city. They just go home, then they go to work and then they go to Sainsbury's, they don't mix, they don't come to no meetings, they don't come to the fun day and all that. They're from a different rank maybe. There's no mixing there [between social tenants and private]. I know nobody there at all. It feels cut off [over there]. That is the way people [social tenants] feel.'

When I asked an ex-regeneration officer about how much social interaction occurred between the social tenants and new private owners/renters, he replied:

> 'There's definitely not that much interaction. And okay there are these events that get done, and people do get to meet each other. I mean for example in school, people do get to talk in school. But if you ask me whether someone in the private unit would invite a social rented tenant into their home, or vice versa, I don't see that happening, I've never seen that happening. I think it's just two different worlds, to be honest.'

Rita, the organiser of a thriving community garden project, mentioned how she had an ethnically diverse group of 30 residents signed up, but these were nearly all social tenants. As with West Hendon, the lack of tenure/class mixing partly stemmed from the securitised and class-distinctive design features of the private blocks, as Bob highlighted:

> 'You only have to walk round there and you can see where it's private and what's not. Because private blocks have all

Photograph 12.11: Woodberry Down (private block) – lobby, 2017

got concierges on the door, so you see that cos you've got to buzz into someone who's sitting there at a desk to let you in. And the others you ain't, you've just got a fob to get in the door. And a couple of them have got swimming pools.'

Gordon was active in WDCO and supported its 'balanced and integrated community' aspiration. However, he acknowledged that this aspiration had not yet been realised due to the exclusionary upmarket features of the private blocks (Photograph 12.11), although "we [WDCO] have got in bits of it", for example in gaining views for social tenants over the reservoir:

'So far we haven't been successful [in creating a balanced and integrated community]. In the sense that there's swimming pools in some of the blocks, in the sense that concierges and all that. We all live in the same Woodbury Down, regardless of what we try to hide behind when we go through the door we live in Woodbury Down. I'm speaking entirely for myself here – no matter how much money I have, I would never go and hide behind a 20-millimetre glass door with a concierge guy doing the talking for me. We haven't been successful there.'

Gordon's reference to 'hiding' and the concierge is reflected in my own failed attempt to gain access to one of the private blocks to undertake interviews. It was clear from the response by the concierge and manager (who rapidly appeared to check me out) that these blocks are highly securitised spaces in which security and the protection of their affluent clients is paramount (Atkinson and Blandy, 2017). Entering the private blocks and informal 'passing by' without knowing someone beforehand is impossible. Unlike most interviewees, Andrew thought that the blocks were 'blended' together, "But, having said that, private people are very snobbish and they won't walk along outside this block, they cross over, it's kind of weird you know".

Long-term tenants criticised how the private flats appeared to be mainly rental with high tenant turnover and limited local engagement:

> 'I've got an issue with the private blocks not being owned by the people that bought them, they're on a continuous loop of rental, those people are not invested in the community. One question is how much they actually spend locally, because my feeling is they go to work, they spend their money in town, they come back to sleep. Their shopping is done online because I see all the supermarket vans every day, there's dozens of them doing the rounds, delivering food.' (Rita)

Social tenants also referred to how the new private blocks were owned by overseas investors. At Woodberry Down, 42 per cent of the private properties had been sold to overseas buyers (Hackney Citizen, 2019), indicative of how the city's residential space is being remade for a global super-rich elite (Atkinson, 2020). This new space is by no means convivial (Photograph 12.11). A survey of buy-to-let private tenants in the new blocks at Woodberry Down found that nearly one third knew *no one* in the new development, while half knew 1–3 people (Scanlon et al, 2018: 53). Such lack of sociability *within* the new affluent and securitised enclaves strongly suggests that there is likely to be very little cross-tenure social mixing across the estate as a whole, and none at all between the occupants of the private blocks and the council and temporary tenants who live 'on the wrong side of the tracks' (Cohen, 2013) in the remaining dilapidated council blocks (Photographs 12.8 and 12.12).

If socio-spatial segregation was highlighted by those social tenants who lived in the new housing association blocks, it was even more

Photograph 12.12: Woodberry Down (estate/ redevelopment) – old blocks in foreground; new private blocks 'over the other side', 2017

starkly felt by residents of the remaining council blocks. Ayla was a temporary tenant and had not heard about the fun days in the four years she'd lived there. She compared the two areas either side of the main road: "it's like heaven and hell, they've got all of the nice stuff over there, they've got the walkway, the post office, Sainsbury's, a nice supermarket, this is heaven. But as you can see, this side is hell, it's really bad this side". She was desperate to leave due to the poor condition of her flat (noted earlier), and felt unsafe due to nearby drug dealing/ taking which had worsened in the period she'd been living there: "I feel scared here with my children, most of the time I won't open the door." Rahel made a similar contrast between the 'two worlds': "It's a nice area over the other side [laughs]. We live in the other world, they live in the planet and we live somewhere else, that's how it feels." Ella had been over 'the other side' to use the play area with her children: "it's nice, lovely, it's lucky for the people who live there". She highlighted the class/tenure divisions between the two sides of the road.

'There's no young professionals this side of the road, it's mainly older tenants or people being put here due to homelessness or young families. Judging from the cars on that side, they're doing okay for themselves. At the reservoir, there's a lot of people going for early morning jogging. They own their flats over there.'

Although Ella occasionally used the supermarket over the 'other side', she tended to shop 'at this side' because it was cheaper; "I need to be really careful with money".

Rather than being a 'balanced and integrated community', the regenerated Woodberry Down is a highly fragmented, unequal place, both physically and socially. A recent survey found that 69 per cent of secure tenants and 90 per cent of temporary tenants had annual incomes of less than £14,000 (Social Life, 2020: 26). By contrast, 46 per cent of owners and 40 per cent of private renters had annual incomes over £62,000. Scanlon and colleagues (2018: 29) cite a private tenant who mentioned their 'sense of [the] fragmented nature of previous/historic tenants of the area and the new "posh" people'. By contrast, the old rundown blocks are populated by London's post-industrial precariat, the non-working poor and retired working class of the elderly, sick and disabled. They are also predominantly from BAME backgrounds – black, South Asian and Turkish. My observations over the 'other side' suggest that the incomers tended to be mainly white, young/middle-aged professionals.

Carpenters estate (Newham)[3]

The Carpenters estate is the only one of the three in this chapter that remains an entirely state-owned council estate. Since no redevelopment partner has been found for it, Newham Council is the main organisation involved, although the London Legacy Development Corporation became the planning authority in October 2012 (Sendra and Fitzpatrick, 2020). After 15 years of 'regeneration', the Carpenters estate remains stuck within the degeneration side of the degeneration/regeneration duality. It is characterised by empty homes, a sense of lost community, heightened population transience and enhanced stigmatisation, with regeneration still somewhere over the horizon.

Never-ending degeneration

Degeneration is never-ending at the half-empty Carpenters estate. Photograph 12.13 shows the near-empty Dennison Point in 2019, one of the three tower blocks. Although long-term residents praised the estate for its one-time strong sense of community (Chapters 6, 8 and 10), this was dissipating due to displacement – especially of the council tenants – and degeneration. Ernie greatly valued the estate as a place to live, but he acknowledged that it was changing: "it's sad that that's [community spirit] gonna ... I think I've got to be realistic ... that's going to go eventually". The sense of community was becoming lost as the estate depopulated and existing local social capital thinned out, creating an increasingly empty space:

> 'It was a good community, but the tenants are out already and there's only leaseholders and freeholders like us left.' (RTB owner-occupier, CARP estate tour, 2012)

Photograph 12.13: Carpenters estate at night – near-empty Dennison Point, 2019

'We know some of the neighbours, but it's not like years ago when you used to know everyone. All the children used to play out, but you hardly see any children anymore, just apart from one or two with their parents.' (Vera)

'The estate is not as nice as is used to be. For a start you can't hear children's voices because the people with the children have gone. People have left, many have died, and it's very, very quiet.' (Gloria)

My numerous visits to the Carpenters estate from 2012 to 2019 confirmed that it was indeed 'very quiet', as Gloria says. The high-rise tower blocks were particularly depopulated, going down from 434 occupied properties in 2005 to just 95 in 2011 (LBN, 2012). In 2012, James Riley Point had just four leasehold occupiers remaining. By 2018, 56 per cent of all the homes on the estate were empty (Chapter 4). Cassie was visibly distressed by the changes: "I see people, we stop, we chat, people will greet you, but it's all being dismantled now. Seeing all of the boarded-up houses made me really upset [she cries], because I remember who lived there." Darren described how his mother (a RTB freeholder) lamented the changes: "the estate became a ghost town, my mum missed the community".

Extended family relations, which are especially important for Londoners from South Asian ethnic backgrounds, were disrupted. Mahir was from a Bangladeshi background and lived with his mother, wife and daughter in a house that his parents had bought under the RTB. He lamented how his sister (a tenant) had been decanted against her will, which had split their family support network up: "My sister used to live in one of the high-rise blocks and she got moved towards West Ham. She didn't want to move. It was ideal for us – we have kids, she has kids, but when your hands are twisted there's very little you can do."

Community facilities shrank back. The Carpenters and Docklands Centre hosted a popular long-running weekend computer fair since 1998. The owners described to me how they had run an annual outing for older residents, but that ceased, indicative of the estate's declining local social capital: "we done trips to the seaside for 10–12 years and we used to pay for a pint and fish and chips. This is the first year [2012] we've not done it. We cannot finance it and people don't live here anymore". In addition, the long-running TMO was controversially closed down in 2016.

Degeneration in the form of managed decline, physical deterioration and increased transience was prominent. Empty homes became a magnet for squatters and the latter's presence made residents feel insecure, even if they were also sympathetic. Lee illustrates the intertwining of empty homes and squatting:

> 'There's all these empty properties on the estate. Next door to me the guy sold the house and the council bought it. It was just left empty, wasn't boarded up or anything, so it just had normal windows. So, like four in the morning, I'd be woken up by the sound of banging, like four guys trying to break in next door. So we had to all get together again to get the council's properties boarded up.'

Following complaints to the local MP and Newham Council, "they [council] started boarding all the houses up" (Lee). Even though boarding up properties might solve the empty homes problem, it heightened territorial stigmatisation: "Well it's depressing innit – someone said to me when the first of the Sitex [security screens] went up, 'we're turning into the Bronx!'" (Ernie) (Photograph 12.14).

Photograph 12.14: Carpenters estate – occupied and boarded-up flats, 2012

As territorial stigmatisation increased, Carpenters became a site for dystopian films (Chapter 9). As well as being filmed at the Heygate, *Attack the Block* was also set at James Riley Point, one of the near-empty tower blocks. Ernie had fond memories of the filming since he and fellow residents got paid extra work on the film:

'I never got to see myself [laughs], but I was in there somewhere. We spent most of the night outside in a coffee wagon cos it was absolutely freezing. One or two griped [about the filming], but they're the sort of people who find fault with everything. As I say, several of the residents took part, cashing in, what's wrong with that?'

Ria was one of those residents who griped. She had been evicted from her flat at James Riley Point after living there for nearly four decades (Chapter 10), and she thought that one of the reasons for her eviction was *because* the film was being made. She returned to her beloved flat to collect some belongings and found the film crew sitting inside.

'When I went back to the flat to pick up some bits, there were some blokes sitting, leaning back in the chair with cups of teas in their hands. I just looked at them and I said, "oh, you look comfortable!" And he said, "yeah, whoever this flat was, it's really nice, that's why we wanted this one because it was the best one out of the whole block". So I looked at him and I went, "to do what?" And he said, "for the movie". I said, "so it's because of you lot that I got chucked out?" He looked at me and he went, "is this your flat?" So I said, "yes!" "Oh, you haven't bought the flat?" I said, "no!" He said, "we thought it was somebody that had bought this flat was living here because of the way that it's been decorated".'

Not only had Ria been dispossessed of the use value of her previous home, but the film crew added a layer of tenurial stigmatisation onto this dispossession via their assumption that Ria had bought her flat based upon the stereotype that council tenants, unlike homeowners, 'don't care' about their domestic space (Chapters 6 and 7).

Private renters became more prevalent due to increased private landlordism, which was itself accelerated by regeneration. Ernie noticed a change between the early years of the RTB (1980s and 1990s) and later following the regeneration decision. The former period was dominated by RTB owner-stayers like himself aiming to enhance their roots: "the first thing you did was put in a new bathroom and you put in a new kitchen, I think everybody did that" (Ernie). From initially enhancing roots, RTB sales subsequently enhanced routes out following regeneration: "when the decision was taken regarding James Riley, that's when we started to see people selling and moving on" (Ernie). Regeneration increased the numbers of private tenants such that mutual, 'knowing people' relationships – based upon the slow accretion of local social capital based upon neighbourly interactions (passing the time of day, small-scale favours, and so on) – declined as old faces disappeared and new faces constantly arrived:

> 'People have moved in, but you don't really know them, you don't see who they are.' (Gloria)

> 'Some of the houses are still council, but a lot have been sold and now are rented privately, so you know people less.' (Vera)

> 'The neighbours are all renting rooms, new people stay and go, no community there.' (Darren)

The Focus E15 campaign staged a highly publicised occupation of the empty flats at the Carpenters estate in 2014 (Introduction and Chapter 11). The campaigners deliberately connected with residents, who were generally supportive; some of the latter assisted the occupation by repairing and decorating the empty flats (Gillespie et al, 2018):

> 'I even went up into the house that they were staying. How they got up into the houses I don't know! I thought they did a great job and I commended them for doing that. Because the houses, they should be open. Maybe they should come back again [laughs]!' (Gloria)

In response to the occupation, the council refilled around 40 of the empty low-rise flats with temporary tenants, some of whom were vulnerable. By 2018, 55 properties were occupied by non-secure tenants (Table 4.3). However, this repopulation was a "pyrrhic victory" (Gillespie et al, 2018: 820), partly because these tenants have no tenure security, but also because they added to the sense of neighbourhood flux, transience and anomie: "Newham Council gave the empty flats to people with mental health problems and that made it worse" (male tenant, housing meeting, 2019). This rapid influx of new faces (with little support) proved problematic for existing residents:

> 'There's no continuity [unlike previously] because they've [council] en masse moved people in there with problems. You can try and be nice and friendly like, because that's the way we've always been. Problem is, people with drug problems and stuff, they're just out to get their next fiver ain't they?' (Lee)

Melissa queried what care support vulnerable temporary tenants were receiving and whether their relocation was part of a calculated managed decline strategy on the part of the council – to make the estate look rough and so reinforce their demolition rationale:

> 'They've put a lot of vulnerable people in and some of them are causing a lot of problems for residents, a lot of undesirable behaviour. Is there a reason behind this, so the estate looks very rough? You know, "make it look very like what we believe estates are like, make it look run down and then we've got a good excuse to pull it down".'

Even if established residents regarded the temporary tenants sympathetically as 'ordinary people' (like them), their rapid turnover led to greater anomie: "they don't stay long, you don't get to know them. You might go to the shop, say 'hello' to somebody, and a few weeks later you think, 'oh they're gone'" (Mary).

If the Carpenters estate was depopulating, the 2012 Olympic Games 'legacy' involved a bi-monthly refilling of this emptying space. This resulted from the 2016 controversial relocation of West Ham United from its former Boleyn Ground to the new Olympic Stadium (Fawbert, 2017). The latter is near the estate which now has an influx of football fans every match-day who drink at the local pubs. As a fan, Ernie was eagerly looking forward to the arrival of West Ham, while Ted considered the fans' presence benign: "now the Carpenters Arms is a West Ham pub and they [fans] all congregate in the square in a match-day, but you get no trouble from them". Other residents, however, were dismayed by the associated heightened ASB, as they mentioned in 2016:

'I've got nothing against football, but they leave all of their empty bottles all over the place and we that live there have to go and pick them up.' (Gloria)

'With West Ham, when that's on there's thousands of people walking down the street. And they actually urinate up against the wall that is the back door to the police station.' (Lee)

Residents were unimpressed by the official response to these new arrivals: "we have no police on the estate managing these people, the only policing is on the Olympic Park" (Lee). When I asked if the council cleared up the mess, Gloria replied, "no they don't clean our estate" – indicative of how residents regarded their supposedly regenerating estate as neglected and degenerating. According to the Carpenters Destination Steering Group (CDSG), resident concerns regarding football fans remained prominent in 2019: "West Ham supporters were continuing to urinate and litter around the estate" (LBN, 2019d: 1).

Never-beginning regeneration

Regeneration supposedly began at the Carpenters estate in 2005. However, the only redevelopment partner was UCL, which became involved in 2011 but then pulled out in 2013, much to residents' delight (Chapter 11). Ernie described the after-effects: "When UCL pulled the plug, wow! Back to the old phrase of 'headless chickens'. They [council] did not have a Plan B and they still haven't come up with a Plan B. Well, it'll be Plan A now won't it when it does arrive [laughs]!" Neither Plan A nor Plan B ever materialised. Since UCL, there has been *no* redevelopment partner. Newham Council unsuccessfully advertised for one in 2017 (Marrs, 2017), 12 years after the first tenants were decanted. The GCNF was created in 2013 and devised a neighbourhood plan which was still under review in 2019 (Sendra and Fitzpatrick, 2020). While a few residents, including CARP stalwarts, took part in the GCNF, residents' cynicism and disengagement have generally intensified as 'regen' has stretched into never-never-land.

'I used to be out canvassing neighbours, but I've had to switch off from what's going on in the estate because I don't have the emotional energy really.' (Lee)

'It's not a bad place, but people are exhausted and cannot fight anymore.' (Male tenant, housing meeting, 2019)

Where do the displaced council tenants move to? LBN (2015) data shows that 70 per cent of the 267 decanted tenants remained within the E15/E20 Stratford postcodes, while another 24 per cent went elsewhere in Newham, leaving only 6 per cent who moved out of borough. In terms of tenure, 21 per cent of decanted tenants went into housing association property. Geraldine was one of these and she remained living in Stratford near the estate. Despite not being displaced from the area, Geraldine was distressed by seeing her old block: "If there was anything wrong with the block, why is it that it's still standing? It makes me feel terrible [rolls eyes], it's still standing." The displaced tenants so-called right to return disappeared over the horizon alongside the never-beginning regeneration. Cassie mentioned how decanted tenants "were told they had the right to return, but right to return to what, what are they coming back to?" Tenants themselves said:

'I was a secure council tenant and they told us we will be back. The way they treated us is unfair. Now Stratford is booming, we cannot come back, we just had to move.' (Female tenant, regeneration meeting, 2012)

'That was the whole idea that we would come back to the Carpenters estate, but it's not happening is it?' (Geraldine)

By the end of 2018, Rokhsana Fiaz, the new Newham Mayor, recognised that the Carpenters regeneration had stalled and that the authoritarian top-down approach from the previous mayoral regime had badly failed (*Newham Recorder*, 2019). She initiated a series of meetings and described the results: "it's clear that residents were let down and previously ignored by the Council" (Fiaz, 2019). The result of this renewed engagement has been further consultation on 'regen'. The approach taken by Fiaz — no presumption that comprehensive redevelopment involving wholesale demolition is the only game in town, a firmer commitment to new social rental homes, and a consultation process including tenants who have been moved off the estate (LBN, 2019c) — is certainly an improvement given the previous council leadership's approach. At the same time, the GCNF feel side-lined (Sendra and Fitzpatrick, 2020), while Focus E15 (2020) continue to campaign for the half-empty estate to be repopulated and used for social housing – given Newham's acute housing problems, this is a pressing and reasonable demand.

The new Mayor established a new residents' forum – the CDSG – in June 2019 comprising current estate residents and those who had moved away but still had the nominal right to return. Four workshops were held during 2019, but non-participation emerged as a problem:

> The CDSG felt that although the attendance was higher than the first workshop, there is still evidence of consultation fatigue and a lack of trust in the Council. XX reported that they had met with another returning tenant and they had been cynical about the Council's intentions and how meaningful the consultation actually is. (LBN, 2019b: 2)

On my last visit to the Carpenters estate, there were notices on lampposts advertising the third workshop: "Shape the future, have your say" (Newham Council notice, August 2019). Ted and Vera – an elderly married couple who had lived on the estate since it was built – had had enough of 'having their say'; "the meeting was on Wednesday, but we didn't go because you get no answers, it's a waste of time going" (Ted). A residents' survey identified issues including consultation fatigue and concerns over whether their views were going to be listened to (LBN, 2019a). Having lived through many years of 'regeneration', Lee had few illusions as to what it meant:

> 'At the time [start] regeneration didn't really have a negative connotation. People didn't really realise that "regeneration" is about taking assets from poor people and giving it to wealthy people – and that's what regeneration is. It's still spun as being a beneficial thing for the area. But I don't know if it's that easy now with regeneration, I think people have got quite shrewd to what it really means.'

Darren left the estate several years ago, although his mother remained there. Although he didn't want to leave, Darren eventually resigned himself to doing so because many of his neighbours had already been decanted. He remained bitter at the non-existent regeneration: "It's a scam, no regeneration has taken place. Newham Council should be sued for what they have done to all those people on the estate, kicked off needlessly."

Conclusion

My last visits to these estates were in May 2018 at Woodberry Down and August 2019 at West Hendon and Carpenters. Walking around the estates revealed one obvious difference – both West Hendon/Hendon Waterside and Woodberry Down contain new imposing blocks of flats, some with concierges, as well as new facilities (community centres, gyms), whereas Carpenters remains an east London council estate. Unlike the other two examples, Carpenters has witnessed no redevelopment and is still waiting for regeneration to begin. Whereas Carpenters lies solely within the degeneration half of the degeneration/regeneration duality, West Hendon/Hendon Waterside and Woodberry Down are hybrid neighbourhoods which contain elements of both the old place which is being broken down and the new place which is being formed.

Despite these differences, the chapter shows remarkable congruence between the three schemes in relation to 'living in the old place' – which forms part of West Hendon/Hendon Waterside and Woodberry Down, and all of Carpenters. These are degenerating places where remaining long-term residents' place belonging, local social capital and sense of community have atrophied in the wake of their neighbours' and family's displacement, numerous empty and boarded-up properties, a plethora of new faces and rise in ASB. These degenerating neighbourhoods look like *parodies* of council estates – 'sink estates'. Homes are in a poor and declining state, suggestive of enhanced neglect and managed decline. The temporary tenants and remaining long-term residents are squeezed together in estates whose place image and everyday reality have become congruent with the 'sink estate' place myth.

The socio-spatial position of temporary tenants is somewhat different between West Hendon and Woodberry Down. They are better integrated at the former, and greater residential longevity is a major reason for this. Its striking how the poor housing conditions have prompted collective resistance among the temporary tenants at West Hendon. Their equivalents at Woodberry Down are far more isolated – including from each other – and displayed seemingly little potential for collective organising to challenge their poor housing conditions.

In terms of living in the new place, West Hendon/Hendon Waterside and Woodberry Down residents shared certain similarities, but also had some differences. At the domestic scale, some people experienced better homes, but others did not. Positive appreciation of new flats was more pronounced at Woodberry Down than West Hendon, which largely reflects the former's worse physical conditions to begin with. At both estates, however, there was considerable dismay with their new housing association landlords in terms of repairs and maintenance.

Despite the formal attempts made to enhance community development, there was a common lament at both redeveloped estates – that their previous neighbourliness and sense of community had been lost. At the intermediate spatial scale, although some people appreciated the enhanced security in the new gated blocks, the latter were described in remarkably similar terms at each redevelopment – as soulless, hotel-like non-places (Auge, 1995). Residents' previous informal neighbourly conviviality in the old blocks, enhanced by their open landings, had disappeared along their new anonymous hotel corridors. Local social capital had been eroded (Watt, Forthcoming).

One of the great ironies is how council housing has been lambasted for its uniform appearance. Nothing could be further from the truth. Council tenants individualise the space outside their flats by their pot plants, children's toys and hanging out their laundry in all its colours. Such displays of individuality were not allowed at Hendon Waterside, where outside space had to be regimented and controlled. In this new mixed-tenure development, the middle classes are trying to dominate and control their social tenant neighbours by *making them* fit into the new socio-spatial field which is being created – a field where middle-class notions of 'tasteful domestic appearances' predominate (Edensor and Millington, 2009; Kilburn, 2013; Corcillo, 2020).

One major aim at both West Hendon and Woodberry Down was to create mixed-tenure communities, an aim that was strenuously pursued at Woodberry Down by WDCO (WDCO, 2015; Nelson and Lewis, 2019). At neither estate had this been achieved, at least as far as the old residents were concerned. There was little evidence of class/tenure mixing, and that is even just between the rehoused social tenants in the new blocks and the private tenants in their luxury apartments. Socio-spatial polarisation was wider and deeper between the old parts of the degenerating estates and the new private blocks. These unstable hybrid neighbourhoods are *fragmented communities* rather than mixed communities. Instead of a benign mixing of classes and tenures, the presence of affluent gentrifiers in their sealed-off apartment blocks (with concierge and gym) heightened tenants' awareness of class inequalities and made them feel like second-class citizens.

The Carpenters estate has experienced never-ending degeneration and never-beginning regeneration. It has been degenerating for 15 long years, such that by 2019 it was a half-empty shell of a previous perfectly functioning, multi-ethnic, working-class east London neighbourhood, a place with a genuine sense of community. The remaining residents, mainly homeowners, were far from enthusiastic about going through yet *another* round of consultation, a theme I return to in the concluding chapter.

13

Conclusion

Having outlined the multiple discontents that estate regeneration involving demolition gives rise to, I hope that the question raised in the Introduction – 'why do London estate residents pray that regeneration won't be coming to their neighbourhood anytime soon?' – has been answered. This concluding chapter summarises the key findings and makes various policy recommendations.

Policy and estate regeneration

Chapter 2 examined the rise and fall of public housing in London. The expansionary period involved local government initiatives up until the 1940s, and then reached its apogee under the post-war Keynesian welfare state. The development of public housing in the capital was enabled by the Labour Party's unbroken 30-year control of the LCC which embedded council estates into the physical landscape of the city – municipal socialism in action. The expansionary period allowed hundreds of thousands of working-class Londoners to escape from the manifold inadequacies of the PRS via the decommodification that public housing facilitated.

In challenging notions of a Butskellite consensus in post-war housing policy, I identified how Conservative local government interventions in London began to undermine housing decommodification during the 1960s and 1970s via a series of proto-Thatcherite reforms, including encouraging discretionary sales of council housing. During this period, Labour councils consistently reversed these reforms. Wholesale housing recommodification was then initiated by 1980s' Thatcherite privatisation and demunicipalisation policies, notably the RTB, which brought about the neoliberal decoupling of public housing from the UK welfare state. New Labour continued this decoupling, albeit in a less damaging form. It was more generous in terms of overall public spending on local authority housing, notably via the DHP which helped to redress the Conservative government's disinvestment and the national £19 billion backlog of repairs. However, New Labour's interlinkage of the DHP with its demunicipalisation governance agenda rendered it cumbersome and over-complex, resulting in delays and lack of universal coverage in London. Austerity policies have further intensified the city's social housing depletion. Chapter 2 outlined the reasons for the contraction of public/social housing in London, with estate demolitions resulting in an estimated gross loss of between 17,000 and 37,000 social rental properties from 2002 to 2017, and net loss of over 8,000 such homes from 2004 to 2014 (Chapter 3).

Chapter 3 traced the development of urban policy in London with reference to estate regeneration via an early–contemporary binary periodisation from the 1980s to 2010s. This periodisation means that the neat equation that is often made – between regeneration and gentrification (for example by the anti-gentrification perspective; see Smith, 2002; Lees, 2014; Hubbard and Lees, 2018) – requires qualification and nuance. The early regeneration/demolition period (1980s to 1990s) included relatively generous public subsidies. The results at the Hackney CEI and Peckham SRB included a reduction in density and genuine housing improvements for tenants, even though demolition, degeneration and displacement also proved disruptive. The post-redevelopment aftermath for these early schemes was mixed-tenure neighbourhoods in which social tenants (renting from a housing association) remained in *the majority*, alongside a minority of private owners/renters – in other words, housing improvements for tenants alongside limited gentrification.

Contemporary regeneration/demolition schemes (late 1990s to 2010s) – the book's primary focus – have been far more socially disruptive and have radically changed urban space in a way that the early schemes did not. Not only does later regeneration take much longer – prolonging degeneration effects – but the reliance upon large-scale private funding means that *qualitatively different* mixed-tenure neighbourhoods are created. Returning/remaining social tenants are shoe-horned into upmarket luxury developments in which there is a class chasm between 'them and us'. The result is extensive and intensive state-led gentrification, as has occurred at the Heygate, West Hendon and Woodberry Down redevelopments.

The above housing policy/urban policy periodisation seems contradictory. On the one hand, I have identified a long-term neoliberal decline of public housing beginning in the 1980s (Chapter 2), while the urban policy analysis identifies a public funding peak for estate regeneration during the 1980s and 1990s (under Thatcherism), and then a subsequent tailing off under New Labour as the private sector was expected to do more heavy lifting in terms of funding (Chapter 3). This apparent contradiction can be resolved by understanding the shifting roles of housing policy and urban policy. Under the 1979–97 Conservative governments, deep funding cuts were made in public housing across the board, but these were *partially* plugged at a few targeted 'worst estates' by relatively generous public funding via urban regeneration (as with the CEI, Peckham Partnership SRB and Central Stepney SRB).

By 1997, the physical fabric of London's estates had crumbled even more during the long years of general under-investment in public housing. Most of the research estates in the book not only suffered from the general shortfall in maintenance under roll-back neoliberalism, but they were also not targeted under the 1980s and 1990s regeneration schemes and had to wait for New Labour's raft of ABIs for any substantial reinvestment. In the intervening years, they had deteriorated further – that is, been left to rot. Local government restructuring and the transfer of the GLC stock to the borough councils during the 1980s increased landlord neglect. By the late 1990s, London's council estates were in a parlous state, both physically – as seen in the appalling conditions at the large London NDC estates, including Aylesbury, Ocean and Clapham Park – and socially in terms of deprivation.

If the Conservatives prioritised urban policy at the expense of housing policy, New Labour had far more ambitious aims for *both* sets of policies – housing policy included the DHP, while regeneration was expected to cover more estates but with intensive communitarian goals (as with the NDC) – that is, roll-out neoliberalism. Despite the greater need for reinvestment in London's estates and its own ambitious aims, the fact remains that New Labour was politically unprepared to spend too much (in other words, enough) public money on this non-aspirational and allegedly 'unpopular' part of the welfare state, unlike the NHS or school education. New Labour also distrusted local councils to spend taxpayers' money wisely. In a few cases, such as Hackney, this was justified (Jacobs, 1999; Raynsford, 2016), but reading off local government policy from the most dysfunctional councils was extremely blinkered. The result was that New Labour used both the DHP and estate regeneration as tools in its demunicipalisation strategy whereby public housing became 'social housing', owned and managed by housing associations rather than local authorities. Much of the finance for New Labour's ambitious estate regeneration programme was expected to come either directly or indirectly from the private sector through PPPs.

If New Labour began the journey towards greater private sector involvement in estate regeneration, this was exacerbated under austerity as central government regeneration funding has collapsed, pressurising councils and housing associations to go to market via increasingly private sector-dominated PPPs. The result has been the dominant role that private sector funding plays in contemporary estate regeneration.

The latter plus New Labour's enduring obsession with promoting 'mixed communities' – which remains policy orthodoxy – has resulted in mixed-tenure neighbourhoods consisting of large numbers of affluent incomers alongside a diminishing pool of social renters – wholesale state-led gentrification, as seen in the examples in this book.

Over the last 20 years, London local governments became increasingly concerned to 'solve the housing crisis' by building more homes. One way to achieve this is demolition, which facilitates estate densification (Hanna et al, 2016). Therefore, regeneration-as-demolition has increasingly *become* housing policy in the sense that the emphasis shifts away from improving estates residents' lives (as in the early schemes) and towards meeting borough housing targets. But this is only half of the pincer trap that London estates are caught in which 'justifies' their demolition. The other half is how they stand in the way of councils' entrepreneurial borough strategies as part of their urban renaissance goals for their town centres – for example Elephant and Castle in Southwark, Stratford and Canning Town in Newham, and Tottenham in Haringey. Estates do not fit into these entrepreneurial borough strategies and must be bulldozed – neo-Haussmannisation style (Merrifield, 2014) – for urban renaissance goals to be met. From the standpoint of housing policy (build more homes) and urban policy (renew town centres), 'failed' social housing estates stand in the way of progress. Knocking them down not only promises to release their enormous potential rent gap value, but also removes their abject stain on London's emerging Alpha City landscape (Atkinson, 2020).

Valuing estates before regeneration

The official regeneration discourse justifies demolition via the notion that estates are failed places with decrepit housing and populated by a narrow group of the socially excluded. There are linkages between this policy discourse and certain academic analyses – residualisation and socio-tenurial polarisation – in which council housing was said to accommodate a residual non-working class rump too impoverished to afford homeownership. However, by focusing on council estates as *only* consisting of crucibles of spatially concentrated poverty and deprivation, the social exclusion policy narrative and related academic perspectives elide tenants' housing experiences and place attachments. Estates are often deprived places, but this isn't the *only way* that residents view and experience them. Part II examined residents' experiences of living at estates *before regeneration*.

Chapter 5 developed a three-pronged critique of how social housing estates and their populations have been analysed in terms of marginalisation, residualisation, social exclusion and socio-tenurial polarisation. First, by emphasising the notion that council housing is the tenure of the non-working class, these approaches have down-played the dynamic and longitudinal nature of tenants' labour market experiences. This led to my development of a typology of the main socioeconomic groups on London's estates: the precariat, non-working poor, traditional working class, retired working class and lower service class. Rather than being permanently excluded from paid work, many tenants *are* included but in precarious, poorly paid work, while older residents used to be in employment before retirement. London's social housing estates are not workless ghettos and are quite dissimilar from the US hyper-ghetto of advanced marginality where formal employment is a rarity.

Second, the increasing presence of marginalised groups – BAME groups, lone parents, the homeless, sick and disabled – in London public housing from the 1970s onwards has meant that estates have become *more* socially inclusionary and diverse spaces. Third, entering council housing was a step away from housing marginality for these groups once one factors in the role played by the PRS in London. Tenure preferences are not framed by an abstract binary choice between homeownership and public/social housing, but instead by *real-world alternatives*, notably between social and private renting. Given the inherent problems of the London PRS, working-class council tenants valued their existing housing for its far better security and generally better quality. Hence, council housing (or social housing) in London is *not* the tenure of last resort, as the residualisation thesis opines. For working-class Londoners, private renting is the *real* tenure of last resort.

Interviewees' housing histories showed remarkable continuity across the generations regarding the inadequacies of the PRS in meeting housing needs. Housing scholars have inadequately drilled down into the sociological underpinnings of tenure preferences, which means that that they fall back upon – and reinforce – the misleading binary 'homeownership positive/council-renting negative' stereotype. The main and increasing housing problem for working-class Londoners under austerity is not the fear of being located on a 'problem estate', but instead that they cannot access public/social renting *at all*. Instead, they are trapped in *housing precarity* in perpetuity, either as homeless in temporary accommodation or within the netherworld zones of the PRS – HMOs, beds in sheds, and so on (Chapters 5 and 10).

Chapter 6 examined how and why London council estates are valued as places and illustrates Skeggs' (2014) notion of 'values beyond value'. In stark contrast to estate place myths ('sink estate') used to justify demolition, tenants and owner-occupiers expressed multi-scalar place attachments to their dwellings as homes, to their blocks of flats/rows of houses at the intermediate scale, and to their estates as neighbourhoods. Homemaking was achieved via domestic self-provisioning by tenants as well as owners. Working-class women especially took pride ('beyond value') in making their dwellings *into homes*.

At the intermediate and neighbourhood spatial scales, residents expressed *traditional place belonging* based upon residential longevity and historical rootedness, as characteristic of working-class place attachments. Rather than familiarity breeding contempt, it bred trust, mutuality and caring neighbourly relationships, especially among female tenants with children. Local social capital based upon knowing people had been built up through living in the same space with others 'like them' for years. Longevity was facilitated by the security gained from having *secure* council tenancies – 'as good as gold'. Such secure tenancies enabled London council tenants to develop strong elective fixity (Paton, 2014). With the exception of evictions due to rent arrears or ASB, this security meant that the vast majority of tenants who did not want to move have been under little pressure to do so – that is until they are displaced due to demolition.

Many long-term residents mentioned having a sense of community, with some expressing 'everyone-knows-everyone' comments redolent of post-war urban villages. Local social capital, neighbourliness and having a sense of community were facilitated by the design features of the estates (open balconies, small courtyards), where bumping into neighbours was an everyday occurrence. The rubbing-alongness of London's estates – assisted by the relatively porous physical layout of landings and blocks – means that interaction occurs across the city's manifold social and ethnic differences. This is one of the reasons why London's estates are valued by their long-term residents and recent incomers.

Two groups of homeowners were analysed, the first being RTB owners. Buying their homes deepened ex-tenants' roots by operating as a buy-to-stay mechanism – fixing them in place. RTB owner-stayers also bought to enhance their own and their families' financial security. The sixth main estate socioeconomic group – incoming middle-class market homeowners (gentrifiers) – also valued estates as places. Their place attachment took the form of elective belonging (Savage, 2010), rather than traditional belonging, although they also began to integrate into the existing community. Their relationship to the working-class-dominated field (in Bourdieusian terms) of the council/social housing estate was one of *immersion*, rather than spatial disaffiliation or selective belonging prominent in middle-class residential oases or bubbles where social housing is avoided (Watt, 2009b; Corcillo, 2020).

The emphasis placed on values in Chapter 6 reflects the critique of Bourdieusian deficit-accounts of the working class outlined in the Introduction. As Flint (2011: 87; emphasis added), says about such accounts, they 'underestimate how *a sense of value* and esteem and orientations towards dwelling and neighbourhood are constructed within households, families and communities independently from more powerful narratives'. In the light of this, Chapters 5 and 6 cast a sociological gaze not only at how working-class lives and spaces are materially deprived and symbolically devalued by external powerful forces (the subject of Chapter 7), but also at how such lives and spaces become *valued and valuable*. Estates are places where people (especially women) *care* – about their homes, their children, their relatives, their neighbours and their neighbours' children. They know who to trust – and who not to trust – because they have seen the same faces for years. Such values beyond value are enacted via mundane everyday rounds of working-class getting along and getting by.

This sociological emphasis on positive values, as captured via qualitative research, is a vital corrective to those policy perspectives that predominantly view estates through the lens of area-based deprivation indices. This lens distorts, as well as illuminates, poor places. Supposedly objective quantitative indices, like the IMD, present one-dimensional deficit models of estates. Qualitative studies have demonstrated the wide gap which can exist between place images informed by these indices, and residents' insider perceptions of their neighbourhoods (Whitley and Prince, 2005; Matthews, 2010, 2012). Deprivation indices offer thin sociological portraits of deprived neighbourhoods and, if not used sensitively, contribute toward their symbolic devaluation and territorial stigmatisation. They can also be dangerous in the hands of zealous local politicians who use them to coercively iron out spatial inequalities. Hence, area-based deprivation indices are governmental tools which simultaneously *identify and justify* the flattening of estates – the IMD as a WMD (Chapter 4).

Devaluing estates before regeneration

If estates are valued and valuable spaces, they are also subject to devaluation processes, particularly resulting from neoliberalisation and austerity

(Chapter 7). I identified five devaluation dimensions: overcrowding, neglect, transience, disorder and stigmatisation. These illustrate what Manzo (2014a: 178) refers to as 'a "shadow side" of place attachments that involves negative and ambivalent feelings and experiences of place, and suggest that place attachments can involve a dynamic tension between phenomena such as belonging and exclusion, and positive and negative affect'. Manzo (2014a, 2014b) illustrates this 'shadow side' ambivalence towards place in her research on HOPE VI public housing renewal sites in the USA.

First, the aggregate shrinkage of public/social housing in London has resulted in worsening overcrowding, something that especially affects BAME tenants. Being overcrowded is not enough of a housing needs indicator, so overcrowded tenants cannot transfer to a larger property (Orr, 2018). Being stuck in overcrowded housing for years on end causes immense psychological pressures on families with children, who are also often struggling on low incomes. Lack of domestic space makes living a normal family life difficult, if not impossible – hence families become un-homed. It's therefore unsurprising that some overcrowded tenants welcome demolition as a way out of their non-homes since the existing transfer mechanisms have so palpably failed.

Second, 'the buildings are solid but neglected' was an all too common resident complaint. Some public investment has occurred – due to the DHP, stock transfers and regeneration/refurbishment programmes – while residents also engaged in self-provisioning. However, this investment has taken place from such a low base (following years of under-investment during the 1980s and 1990s) and has also not kept pace with improved domestic living standards. The housing/regeneration professionals' interviews indicate that tenants' concerns were entirely legitimate – that homes and estates were fundamentally sound but had been badly neglected due to years of insufficient investment and inadequate maintenance (Chapters 2 and 7). Estates have also been subject to managerial restructuring (for example, reduction in caretakers, outsourcing) whose net effect has been detrimental to residents' well-being.

Third, RTB privatisation has had a Janus-faced impact on residential longevity and mobilities – enhancing roots for RTB owner-stayers and routes out for others. The RTB facilitated the right to sell, which in turn has increased private landlordism and renting, and thereby population transience. Even prior to regeneration, London's estates were beginning to lose aspects of their stability and local social capital because of RTB-linked transient private and Airbnb tenants. The anti-gentrification perspective has focused on owner-stayers who are aggrieved (rightly) at the prospect of losing their homes and communities due to demolition and displacement, but it has also downplayed the long-term negative impacts of the RTB on estates more generally (Hubbard and Lees, 2018; Elliott-Cooper et al, 2020).

Fourth, certain London estates have suffered from disorder in terms of crime and ASB. As far as residents were concerned, most of this disorder relates to low-level neighbour disputes/youths hanging around. Interviewees spoke favourably about how mundane crime prevention measures by the police and councils made estates feel safer places to live than they were during the 1980 and 1990s. Some ASB stems from what can be termed the 'paradox of social inclusion'. Because estates are among the most socially inclusionary spaces in the city, they also disproportionately accommodate vulnerable groups. Although progressive, this inclusion has paradoxically led to internal neighbourhood tensions between vulnerable 'problem tenants' and other residents. Some ASB issues have been exacerbated due to austerity cuts since vulnerable tenants do not receive adequate community care, while dozens of youth centres have been closed (Perera, 2019).

The fifth aspect of estates' devaluation is symbolic. They have been stigmatised as 'sink estates', a place myth which has been exacerbated by austerity and poverty porn, and also one with racist connotations (Romyn, 2019). Territorial stigmatisation, in Wacquant's (2008) terms, has worsened as cash-strapped London councils rent out their estates as locations for film and TV companies. The resulting crime-laden films and TV shows *advertise estates* as crimogenic places. Hence there is a symbiotic relationship between neoliberalisation and increased territorial stigma. Stigma sells, and local authorities are only too willing to sell their 'notorious estates' to the highest bidder.

As I have recently argued, studies of stigmatised estates have not adequately calibrated what the *relative significance* of territorial stigmatisation is to other problems and devaluations such as poor housing conditions (Watt, 2020c). What is the relative weighting of the above-mentioned five devaluations? For estate residents, especially tenants, the most widespread and frustrating problem is maintenance and repairs; getting this right would greatly improve their everyday quality of life. Overcrowding affects a smaller group of tenants than maintenance – generally families with children – although its negative effects (family stress and discord) are deeply felt. Crime and ASB are variable across the estates, with several having relatively few issues while others were more affected. Even among the latter, there is considerable intra-estate variation in awareness and sensitivity to such issues. It's worth stressing that most long-term residents regarded their estates as essentially safe places to live, as Foster (1995) noted during the more crime-prone 1990s. Transience due to private landlordism is also a variable problem, with those estates which are in central areas and/or near universities (for example Ocean and Regents Park) being most affected.

Despite the substantial academic literature that territorial stigmatisation has generated, stigmatisation is the least-worst problem from the perspective of London social tenants' everyday place belonging. Many did not internalise such stigma and instead joked about it or resisted it. This does not mean, however, that it's not extremely hurtful for those who have internalised it, notably female lone parents who are already heavily stigmatised via austerity as the undeserving poor. Territorial and tenure stigmatisation certainly add unwelcome layers of symbolic devaluation and symbolic violence to the material deprivations that estate residents face. Nevertheless, stigmatisation is not their most pressing everyday concern relative to the grinding housing problems they have to struggle with – overcrowding, infestation, no tiles in the bathroom, tardy repairs, and so on – problems that Wacquant's advanced marginality approach has largely ignored (Watt, 2020c).

Various ethnographic studies have provided sociologically rich and nuanced accounts of British council/social housing estates, accounts which avoid sentimentality and negative stereotypes, while at the same time acknowledging the difficult 'getting by' struggles that working-class residents face (see inter alia Smith, 2005; Gunter, 2010; Wallace, 2010b; Paton, 2014; McKenzie, 2015). This book has similarly acknowledged the ambivalent and sometimes problematic aspects of estates – their 'shadow side'. By contrast, the anti-gentrification perspective has tended to draw a one-dimensional picture which emphasises residents' positive place attachments to homes and communities rather than acknowledging estates as contradictory places (see Slater, 2013a; Kallin and Lees, 2014; Lees, 2014; Hubbard and Lees, 2018). This is because its epistemological focus is on how residents are forced to *leave estates* rather than on their long-term experiences of *living on estates*. By focusing so heavily on displacement, the anti-gentrification perspective elides the problems that estate residents (especially tenants) sometimes can and do face, notably overcrowding and poor housing conditions. It is only by teasing out the above-mentioned devaluations that one can fully understand why a section of tenants (the un-homed) are quite happy to see their homes and those of their neighbours bulldozed (Chapter 10).

In comparative terms, London estates remain a considerable distance from being the anomic, dangerous urban wastelands that characterise Wacquant's US hyper-ghettos or European anti-ghettos of advanced marginality. For one thing, London estates have far less crime and disorder than the US projects (Vale, 2013). Unlike the projects of the South Side Chicago hyper-ghetto, where most residents could see no option but to leave (Wacquant, 2008), I did not come across a single London estate where residents' predominant place image took the form of 'this is a dangerous, soulless concrete jungle and I am desperate to get out'. London tenants and RTB owner-stayers had lived in the same home at the same estate *for decades*. This reflects levels of place attachment and residential stability which fly in the face of the stereotype that residents are desperate to escape their 'estates from hell'. While London's estates have a 'shadow side', in Manzo's terms, this is by no means as pronounced as US public housing, although this is clearly an area for future comparative research.

Part II showed how most social tenants and owner-occupiers positively valued their existing homes and neighbourhoods, even if such valuation was neither unqualified nor universal. Many long-term residents expressed deep ontological security. They had made their homes as they wanted them via self-provisioning, and they felt comfortable living alongside people like themselves whom they had known for many years. Place has not 'dissolved' at London's estates. Or at least it had not done so until regeneration came along.

Living through estate regeneration

Part III focused on residents' experiences of living through regeneration. It demonstrates how the valuation/devaluation duality tilts around in terms of place belonging. Regeneration in the form of comprehensive redevelopment diminishes the valued aspects of estates, while the devalued aspects are heightened and eventually come to dominate. It's only at the latter point that many residents want to leave their homes, *not* in the pre-regeneration period.

In examining the early phase of regeneration, Chapter 8 illustrated how residents routinely considered consultation to be a confused and confusing process which many regarded as a waste of time – as *con*-sultation – a con trick. Disillusioned young architects concurred with and even explained this cynical view from the 'other side' of the regeneration field. Consultation is not only sanitised – for example the missing 'D-word' (demolition) – but it has a chimerical quality given that it's merely an in-principle affair that provides zero legal accountability for disgruntled residents years later down the lengthy regeneration track (Chapter 9). These sobering findings support that literature which argues that consultation regarding estate regeneration has a tokenistic quality (Teernstra and Pinkster, 2015; Gustavsson and Elander, 2016).

Chapter 8 highlighted how gauging residents' responses to comprehensive redevelopment is not easy, especially given how consultation is sanitised. By and large, social tenants (with the most rehousing rights) tended to be more favourably inclined to comprehensive redevelopment than either owner-occupiers or temporary tenants, who were nearly all opposed to demolition. Even so, only a minority of social tenants among interviewees and NES respondents preferred demolition, mainly those who were already un-homed due to overcrowding or poor-quality housing. I identified a profound 'value gap' between the outsider place myths promulgated by official regeneration rationales and mass media imagery, and residents' insider place attachments to their homes and neighbourhoods.

Chapter 9 argued that rather than its promised metaphors of renewal and revitalisation, regeneration brings *degeneration* in the form of disinvestment, enhanced physical decay and social anomie. All the devalued aspects of estate life (Chapter 7) are magnified and eventually take over such that these degenerated estates became gross parodies of the 'worst' council estates. Degeneration takes physical, socio-spatial, symbolic and psychosocial forms. These include increased landlord neglect, disruption in terms of noise and dust pollution, increased transience, insecurity and blight. Homes were removed from the DHP, while managed decline occurred. In the case of the three large NDC estates – Aylesbury, Ocean and Clapham Park – little housing-related progress had occurred by the end of the ten-year programme, as seen by above-average levels of non-DHS properties. *Not* being designated a flagship NDC estate would have been more advantageous for those tenants trapped in chronically poor housing conditions. Even by the mid-late 2010s, there were still severe housing problems on parts of the Aylesbury and Clapham Park estates, although more housing progress had been made at the Ocean estate.

Residents' place attachment deteriorated in relation to the quality of the physical environment and social relations. Those features of estates that they enjoyed – for example green space – were removed, while they also had to endure the misery of living on a building site. The numbers of empty properties increased, as did population churn. Previous local social capital based on knowing people evaporated. Degeneration narrows the ontological gap between the 'sink estate' place myth and residents' lived reality. As this gap closes, estates became sets for film and TV urban dystopian imagery (Saunders, 2016). Symbolic devaluation and territorial stigmatisation are enhanced, contributing towards the class-based sense that they 'don't matter', and to racist stereotypes regarding the crime-ridden 'black ghetto'. In terms of psychosocial degeneration, the remaining residents enter a limbo-land where their lives are put endlessly on hold (see Wallace, 2015). They wait in vain for 'regen' to finish, while elderly residents die off, some undoubtedly prematurely (Chapter 3).

Chapter 10 examined displacement. Many residents invoked the notion of social cleansing, which they could see was happening all over London. They identified demolition and rehousing with the removal of ordinary multi-ethnic, working-class people like themselves via predatory accumulation by dispossession processes – it's not for us (Watt, 2013). They looked across the city with mounting trepidation as they identified the same processes occurring again and again – state-led gentrification masquerading as regeneration. Black Londoners were also concerned about the racialised nature of this city-wide social cleansing (Perera, 2019).

Displacement anxiety – a feeling of dread, apprehension and loss of place linked to imminent forced relocation – was significant (Chapter 10; Watt, 2018a). Displacement anxiety was prevalent among owner-occupiers and temporary tenants, but was also experienced by council tenants despite their greater rights. Owner-occupiers were generally dissatisfied with both the prospect and reality of rehousing, while temporary non-secure tenants experienced rehousing as a traumatic part of their ongoing, never-ending housing precarity.

Those secure tenants who exercised the right to return by moving to new homes in the redevelopment represent the official 'winners' of regeneration. A few experienced rehousing as liberation – a welcome relief from years living in overcrowded and unsatisfactory housing conditions. This group of eager movers could not wait to move from their old 'crap flats' and experienced no sense of home loss because they had *already* been un-homed years before.

At the other extreme were those working-class tenants (mainly women) who experienced rehousing as bereavement – a traumatic rupture as they were forced to move from their beloved old homes to 'cheap rubbish' new flats. Deeply held ontological security was shattered and replaced by ontological insecurity. One of the most surprising and distressing research findings was how tenants expressed such a profound sense of loss, even though they had only physically moved 100 metres from their old flats and not hundreds of miles away. Although I expected disgruntlement, I was taken aback as female interviewees cried and shouted at what had been taken from them against their will. This represents a traumatic and profound psychosocial scarring, redolent of 'root shock' (Fullilove, 2016) and 'slow violence' (Pain, 2019). Such 'grieving for lost homes' (Fried, 1966; Marris, 1986) also illustrates Davidson's (2009) argument that displacement is about what *places mean* to people as well as spatial relocation. Displacement can be emotionally devastating even if it just means moving across the road (Watt, Forthcoming).

The right to return (or remain) makes a significant difference to secure tenants, and it is better to have this right than not. Nevertheless, my analysis explains why this right is very far from a cast-iron guarantee that tenants will realistically be able to exercise. Indeed the only *certainty* with the right to return is that it provides a right to leave. In relation to debates on whether rehousing is coerced or voluntary, there was evidence of tenants exercising agency in relation to the timing and location of moves (Posthumus and Kleinhans, 2014). Ultimately, however, they were *forced* to move whether they wanted to or not, indicative of their lack of control and power, and the erosion of their previously established elective fixity (Paton, 2014).

Chapters 9 and 10 illustrate the health-damaging impacts of degeneration and displacement, the latter both in its displacement anxiety and physical rehousing forms, while Chapter 3 began to quantify these impacts. Poor health and premature death are indicative of the slow-burn destructive and potentially traumatic impacts of estate demolition, as captured by notions of root shock (Fullilove, 2016), slow violence and chronic urban trauma (Pain, 2019). Worse health, increased anxiety and depression, and even early death arising from demolition and displacement inevitably results in extra demands on GPs and the NHS. Thus the health-related costs arising from estate demolition are borne by the NHS, but do not appear on the regeneration partners' (developers, councils and housing associations) balance sheets. In Esping-Andersen's (1990) terms, the decommodified, universalistic part of the welfare state – the NHS – is paying the price of the increased ill health and human misery that the recommodification of London's public/social housing – via comprehensive redevelopment – brings about.

Chapter 11 analysed how residents banded together to challenge and resist demolition. Unlike earlier anti-HAT and anti-transfer campaigns which were *tenure-based* (council tenants), anti-demolition campaigns were multi-tenurial – involving alliances between social tenants and owner-occupiers – and focused around a defensive politics of place at the estate scale (Watt, 2018c). Most campaigners were novices, new to housing activism, but prompted into it by the direct threat that demolition posed to their homes and communities. 'Networks of solidarity' (Maeckelbergh, 2012) were forged across the city between the various estate campaigns which have fed into the broader London housing movement (Watt and Minton, 2016; Gillespie et al, 2018). Estate campaigns are thus linked to struggles over the right to the city. Such extensive and intensive housing activism at London's estates also challenges the structural approach from Wacquant (2008) whereby any collective contestation is, according to him, rendered near-impossible in anomic zones of advanced marginality.

While London's estate-based campaigns are primarily working-class struggles, as McKenzie (2018) emphasises, some encompass cross-class alliances involving middle-class homeowners who have bought ex-RTB properties on estates. Not only is social cleansing a threat to working-class tenants, it also threatens the place belonging of these marginal gentrifiers. This is indicative of how 21st century state-led gentrification is not so much occurring at the middle levels of London's class structure, as with early 1960s-70s gentrification. Instead, state-led gentrification forms a constitutive part of the elite remaking of the city for the benefit of an assemblage of upmarket property developers, overseas' investors, the super-rich and upper middle class – those dominant class groups who are the prime drivers behind London's top-down property machine (Glucksberg, 2016; Transparency International UK; 2017; Atkinson, 2020).

New places, new inequalities

Chapter 12 focused on the aftermaths of estate regeneration with reference to three estates: West Hendon, Woodberry Down and Carpenters. By the mid-to-late 2010s, the first two were hybrid places. The dualistic nature of degeneration/regeneration is captured by how *two places* are simultaneously being deformed/formed: the old degenerated estate which is undergoing decanting and demolition, and the new development which is being built. The latter is the location for the new homeowners and private renters, and enables (some) estate residents to return to newly built homes, as at Hendon Waterside (the rebranded West Hendon) and Woodberry Down.

The domestic scale of the dwelling/home was the most positive aspect of redevelopment at both West Hendon and Woodberry Down. New flats were often regarded as an improvement on old, rundown and overcrowded properties, albeit more so at Woodberry Down where previous housing conditions were generally worse. At the same time, the new flats and housing association landlords did not receive blanket approval ratings. The new flats lacked the solidity of the old flats, while tenants reported frustrating repair and maintenance problems, problems that were exacerbated at West Hendon by unfathomable layers of labyrinthine organisational responsibility.

By comparison to the domestic scale, the sense of place belonging at both the neighbourhood and intra-neighbourhood scales was far more negative. Despite enhanced security features in the new gated blocks, these were described in remarkably similar terms at West Hendon and Woodberry Down – as soulless, hotel-like non-places (Auge, 1995). Residents' previous informal conviviality in the old blocks, enhanced by their open balconies, had disappeared along the new, anonymous internal hotel corridors. Previous neighbourhood facilities – shops, cafes and green space – were sorely missed. Despite their shiny new homes, many residents felt a declining sense of community. This felt loss was not based on rose-tinted nostalgia but was rooted in the rupturing of informal daily routines, long-term neighbourly familiarity and local social capital (Chapter 6; Watt, Forthcoming).

There is widespread scepticism among academics regarding how much post-regeneration mixing – social interaction across tenure/class divides – occurs (see inter alia Bridge et al, 2012; Kilburn, 2013; Paton, 2014; Watt and Smets, 2017; Jeffery, 2018; Corcillo, 2020). In fact, rather than mixed communities, West Hendon/Hendon Waterside and Woodberry Down are socio-spatially *fragmented communities*. Comprehensive redevelopment is a class game-changer on steroids since the symbolic, socio-spatial aspects of inequality are accentuated rather than neutered. The previous working-class-dominated field of the council estate retains a marginal, ghostly presence ('over there'), while an entirely new type of socio-spatial field is in the ascendancy, one dominated by securitised apartment blocks, upmarket facilities and an affluent demographic. Low-income tenants lack the economic capital to socialise in the new local eateries and shops at Woodberry Down, even if they wanted to. They feel out of place in their new place – Marcuse's (1986) displacement pressure. As a study of regeneration in Sweden argues, 'material and symbolic changes in place might so radically alter the everyday lives of occupants that they feel themselves dis*placed* even when staying put' (Pull and Richard, 2019: 5; original emphasis). The design emphasis of new developments is one of securitisation and separation, with a concierge checking who goes in and out of the building (Atkinson and Blandy, 2017). Such segregated, cordoned-off spaces *actively discourage* the kind of informal chance encounters that routinely occur on council estates and which form such a key part of everyday working-class getting along.

I did not interview any private residents in the redeveloped blocks. However, existing research on similar developments suggests that their dominant mode of place belonging is very likely to be one of selective belonging (Watt, 2009b) – sticking within their affluent oasis or bubble and avoiding nearby working-class facilities and areas (Davidson, 2010; Kilburn, 2013; Jeffery, 2018; Corcillo, 2020). This is not just a result of interpersonal class snobbery, although this exists, as tenants noted. It also results from how the private blocks' securitised design and their residents' metropolitan lifestyle (working as busy professionals in the city, going to expensive restaurants in town, and so on), is hardly conducive to meeting people *within* their own block (Scanlon et al, 2018; Allen and Watt, Forthcoming), never mind working-class social tenants who live on the wrong side of the tracks. Such middle-class selective belonging and spatial disaffiliation (Atkinson, 2006) is qualitative different from the place belonging of those middle-class incomers who bought their homes from ex-RTB owners and were living alongside working-class tenants (Chapter 6). Both latter groups were on the wrong side of the tracks – or rather both were enmeshed within the working-class-dominated field of the social housing estate.

Compared to West Hendon and the Heygate, the Woodberry Down regeneration scheme has produced more resident beneficiaries (Chapters 3 and 12), something that has not been adequately acknowledged in critical commentaries on Woodberry Down (Chakrabortty and Robinson-Tillett, 2014; ASH, 2017). This can be largely attributed to the efforts of WDCO and especially the group of highly committed residents (many of whom are social tenants) who play such an active part in it. I witnessed the resident stalwarts of WDCO supporting tenants individually, and battling the council, housing association and developer to get a good deal – or at least a better deal – for the remaining social tenants. WDCO provides a robust and in many ways effective internal critique of how regeneration has been undertaken at Woodberry Down (WDCO, 2015; Nelson and Lewis, 2019). Far more ex-council tenants have returned to new homes at Woodberry Down than either West Hendon or Heygate (Chapters 3, 4 and 12). WDCO prevented the rebranding of Woodberry Down, and has also ensured a commitment to 41 per cent affordable housing, despite increased density. WDCO exercised greater leverage regarding the shape of redevelopment compared to the equivalent body at West Hendon (the West Hendon Partnership Board), and at the other research estates.

Even if regeneration/demolition at Woodberry Down has produced more resident 'winners' than at many other London schemes, its discontents remain manifold (Chakrabortty and Robinson-Tillett, 2014; Belotti, 2014; Nelson and Lewis, 2019). These discontents include: the many leaseholders who have been displaced away from the area; remaining housing association tenants disgruntled with repairs and maintenance; the loss of a sense of community; and council and temporary tenants living in appalling housing conditions in the old blocks. It must also be remembered that one of the council's original aims at Woodberry Down was to rehouse homeless families resulting from the expected additional social housing (Chapter 4). In 2019, there were 269 empty properties at Woodberry Down, at the same time that Hackney Council had 3,133 households living in temporary accommodation and 12,766 households on its housing waiting list.[1] As with Carpenters estate in Newham, something has gone seriously wrong with estate regeneration if it means that social housing properties are standing empty while the homeless have no homes to live in and overcrowded families cannot transfer to a larger council property. WDCO has undoubtedly made a difference, as Nelson and Lewis (2019) argue. But its successes are relative ones and must be put within the context of what remains a state-led gentrification project.

One of the most troubling policy aspects of degenerating/ regenerating estates is how they have become transit camps for London's burgeoning housing precariat (Chapter 5; Watt, 2018a). In class terms the latter consist of temporary tenants who are employed in precarious positions plus the non-working poor. Many temporary tenants were from BAME backgrounds, and hence the fragmented nature of the hybrid estates takes a racialised as well as class form. These transit camps form 21st century 'new urban zones of transition', analogous to the early 20th century Chicago School's zone of transition.

Chapter 12 concluded with reference to the Carpenters estate. In what is an admittedly crowded field, this is the worst example of estate regeneration in this book (with the possible exception of Custom House, also in Newham). When UCL pulled out in 2013, it was blatantly obvious that residents were opposed to the council's scorched earth demolition vision of regeneration. Instead, this vision was pursued for another five wasted years. Such single-mindedness is linked to Newham's status as a one-party local state which for over 20 years, up until 2018, pursued an authoritarian version of neoliberalism (Chapters 4 and 8). In 2018, the new Mayor, Rokhsana Fiaz, acknowledged the manifold previous policy failings and the 'utter breakdown of trust' that occurred at the Carpenters estate (Fiaz, cited in New London Architecture, 2019), and instituted a new regeneration pathway. Importantly a much-needed dose of democracy has been introduced since the long-suffering Carpenters residents are promised a ballot on any future regeneration options. Had a ballot been organised sooner, residents would not have wasted so much time fretting about rehousing or spent so many fruitless hours being consulted about a regeneration that has never arrived. Ballots are certainly not a panacea in the dangerous game of estate regeneration, but they provide a welcome shift towards greater transparency and accountability (Mayor of London, 2018).

Comprehensive redevelopment versus refurbishment

It must be reiterated that this book has focused on those regeneration schemes that involve comprehensive redevelopment – large-scale demolition and rebuilding. However, estate regeneration is a broad church which encompasses a range of physical interventions, such as refurbishment and infilling as well as demolition. Given that many estates need upgrading in various ways – which residents themselves want to see – I am not arguing that such reinvestment should not occur. Several reports highlight the beneficial impacts that refurbishment-only regeneration schemes can have for residents, while managing to avoid the degeneration, massive social disruption and environmental damage that demolition brings in its wake (Crawford et al, 2014; Belotti, 2016; Provan et al, 2016; ASH, 2018).

If London estates need physical upgrading, many residents also need support in terms of health, education, employment and training, and fear of crime. Therefore, the NDC's *aims* were laudable in some ways, even if their *realisation* – especially in London – was highly problematic. Even though all three NDC estates (Aylesbury, Ocean and Clapham Park) experienced degeneration effects (Chapter 9), this does not mean that the multimillion-pound NDC schemes failed to make *any* *improvements* to the estates and to residents' lives. Interviewees and fieldwork revealed support for the refurbishment undertaken in the retained parts of the Ocean and Clapham Park estates (albeit with qualifications at the latter), while all three NDCs saw progress in relation to community development and other social themes including fear of crime (CPP, 2013; Social Life, 2017; Watt, 2020c). The Ocean estate certainly looked much less rundown when I last visited in 2018 compared to when I first visited in 2007, and residents commented on this improvement (Watt, 2009a, 2009c).

To summarise, refurbishment-only schemes have the *potential* to improve estates and residents' lives; although see Hodkinson (2019) on the hazards associated with outsourced refurbishment, including the Grenfell Tower disaster. But if estate regeneration involves major demolition and redevelopment – which in turn entails substantial reliance upon private sector funding – then it will inevitably turn into a state-led gentrification project, albeit at variable intensities. This is especially the case in a city like London that is so unequal and so dominated by a super-rich elite in terms of residential property development (Atkinson, 2020). Comprehensive redevelopment will involve all the degeneration effects – physical, social, symbolic and psychosocial – that have been outlined in this book. It will result in displacement, a felt loss of community for any remaining residents, as well as fragmented rather than mixed communities. The following suggests how this can be avoided.

Policy, politics and research

Public housing in London is a shadow of its 1970s self. At the same time, resorting to end-of-times rhetoric – 'death/end of council housing' – is hyperbolic, especially when placed in comparative perspective. Despite decades of privatisation and demunicipalisation, public housing still has immense significance in London, which has nearly 400,000 local authority homes, around a quarter of the England 1,592,000 total (MHCLG, 2019a). If one adds the over 400,000 housing association properties in London, public/social housing remains a very prominent feature of the city's physical and social landscapes. Even after 40 years of the RTB, London's public housing stock remains over double the New York City Housing Authority's stock of nearly 180,000.

If London's public/social housing stock remains extensive by national and international standards, this should not lead to complacency either (Berry, 2018), as the many anti-demolition campaigns attest (Sendra and Fitzpatrick, 2020). Part of London's problem is that the value of the land on which council estates are built is at such high levels that realising the state-induced rent gap via demolition and rebuilding is far too appealing for cash-strapped local authorities – even if, as in the case of Barnet and West Hendon, the land value was never realised (Chapter 4). This prospect necessitates a sustained defensive politics based around the recognition and preservation of the estates' unique *social value* – not only to their residents but to the city. The anti-demolition campaigns have mobilised around this defensive politics and have achieved many notable successes, big and little. They form a vital part of the city-wide and global movement for socially just housing (Madden and Marcuse, 2016).

Comprehensive redevelopment – knocking down and starting again – should only be the very, very, very last policy resort because of the massive degeneration effects that it brings in its wake. Refurbishment, rather than redevelopment, is the humane *and* cost-effective way forward. By the end of the 2010s, it became obvious to several prominent London politicians that the 'knock 'em down' approach had resulted in a massive erosion of trust between themselves and residents (New London Architecture, 2019). For trust to be rebuilt on firm foundations, I urge politicians and professionals who are in the regeneration industry to do the following:

- acknowledge that you are an outsider and hence that your perceptions of estates are partial and one-sided;
- appreciate that although the estates and the homes within them might look shabby to you, they will be valued and even loved by residents;
- recognise that you are dealing with people's homes – even if they are 'just tenants';
- stop materially and symbolically running estates down;
- move away from 'consulting' residents towards treating them as experts through a genuinely dialogic form of participation – which takes time;
- stop pretending that comprehensive redevelopment is relatively quick and pain-free;
- don't be shy about the D-word – demolition – in consultation;
- publicise how demolition and rehousing are extremely stressful processes which will result in ill-health and premature death;
- stop making bland 'promises' or 'guarantees' that you know deep down are unlikely to be fulfilled;
- emphasise that regeneration will take years and even decades, and that some elderly residents probably won't be alive to see the results;
- acknowledge that you won't be around to see the programme to its conclusion – that you will have moved on to 'better things', while residents will still be living with the consequences of your decisions;
- make sure that the properties that you locate temporary tenants into on demolition estates are of a genuinely decent standard when they move in;
- take proactive steps to socially integrate temporary tenants into estates;
- improve temporary tenants' rehousing and financial compensation rights along the lines of secure tenants;

- stop producing bland, one-sided evaluation reports which are little better than marketing tools.

In terms of housing policy, building more public housing (or social housing at second best), ending the right to buy, and redistributing domestic space away from those with too much of it (the super-rich) to those with too little of it (the urban poor) are all essential (Dorling, 2014; Bowie, 2017; Hodkinson, 2019; Shelter, 2019). However, the thorny issue is not one of inventing good policies, but rather of inventing good politics to implement such policies. This requires a brief consideration of the role of the Labour Party. On the one hand, the Labour Party built many of London's council estates to begin with. On the other hand, by working *within* rather than challenging the Conservative housing neoliberalisation agenda, the New Labour governments cut public housing adrift from the rest of the welfare state. It's hardly surprising that the Conservative Party, for whom public housing is anathema, set about weakening it (and social housing generally) still further via austerity.

There will be little major change in social housing and regeneration unless there is a reversal of the neoliberal policies of the last 40 years. The Corbyn-led Labour Party recognised the damage that neoliberalism has done to the country as a whole and specifically in terms of housing and estate regeneration. Corbyn himself slammed the latter: '"After Grenfell we must think again about what are called regeneration schemes. [… The result is] forced gentrification and social cleansing, as private developers move in and tenants and leaseholders are moved out"' (quoted in Chakrabortty, 2017). However, as Aditya Chakrabortty says, 'He could have added: as tenants and leaseholders of Labour councils are turfed out by the party many of them have voted for all their lives'. Rather than seeing London's social housing estates as a precious resource to be preserved, too many Labour councils have come to regard them as failed places which have to be erased.

The Corbynite drive against the neoliberalisation of housing culminated in the Labour Party Manifesto 2019, which recognised the scale of the housing challenge and proposed radical policy solutions to meet this challenge. These solutions included ending the RTB and delivering a new social housebuilding programme, 'with council housing at its heart', including 'building at an annual rate of at least 150,000 council and social homes, with 100,000 of these built by councils for social rent' (Labour Party, 2019). Tragically for London and the country as a whole, Labour lost the 2019 general election.

By emphasising the discontents produced by comprehensive redevelopment, critics will respond that the book is one-sided, and maybe even based on 'anecdotal evidence' (as suggested at one presentation I gave). I have emphasised the discontents because it's precisely these that have been airbrushed out of the official regeneration discourse, which only shows 'winners'. In methodological terms, the interviewees are not statistically representative of estate residents; for example, the social tenant and RTB interviewees are disproportionately long-term and elderly. But that does not invalidate their experiences, which are real enough. Furthermore, themes from the interviews are in line with the quantitative NES findings (Watt and Allen, 2018).

In terms of future research, an obvious project is examining the role played by local party politics in how estate regeneration has been enacted in London. For example, why have Islington and Newham – both Labour councils – done things so differently? A second research gap is understanding the views of young people vis-à-vis social housing and regeneration (see Telemaque, 2015). The book has focused on estates which have been 'spaces of contestation' (Mayer, 2007), therefore, a third research direction is examining regeneration at estates where there has been little or no resistance; why and with what consequences? A fourth research area is comparing different governance regimes at post-redevelopment estates (as in the case of Woodberry Down; Nelson and Lewis, 2019). A fifth area is much needed cross-national research, for example on teasing out the relative nature and extent of the 'shadow side' in different national contexts (Manzo, 2014a).

Finally, I want to return to what estate regeneration in the form of demolition and rebuilding *does to people*. I have stressed throughout how some people genuinely benefited from it, especially those who were able to escape from overcrowded or otherwise 'crap' housing conditions. For many more, however, comprehensive redevelopment is either disappointing at best ('this isn't what we were told we would get in the consultation'), or devastating at worst. Those people who valued their *existing* homes and neighbourhoods, many of whom are elderly, had their long-held ontological security shattered. In Sennett and Cobb's terms (1973), this is a 'hidden injury of class' – albeit one that never appears in the official regeneration discourse. This is an injury that those who are so affected are unlikely ever to fully recover from:

'1979 I moved there [old flat], extremely happy. The community, that's what I miss, because here [new flat] you are just cut off, you are isolated. Whereas there you only had to open your door and somebody would always pop out – "are you alright?" We all looked out for each other, the people downstairs in the maisonettes, the houses, because we all grew together. I mean to move people at … most of us are elderly, so it was a *big, big* upheaval. I felt it, I mean I haven't been right since I've been here. I think a lot of people it affected them, and I think a big move at a late stage in your life can upset you. And really and truly, mentally you feel isolated. I haven't stopped crying since I've come here.' (Annie, West Hendon)

APPENDIX A

Methodology

The research and resulting book is informed by my ethical and political commitment to the social value of public housing. Since my youth, I have believed that public housing is an extremely positive feature of contemporary society which should be both preserved and expanded. This dates to when my family moved to a council estate on the outskirts of Halifax in West Yorkshire when I was 12. I am eternally grateful to the post-war welfare state that we were able to make this move at a time of need due to my dad's illness.

The book's academic roots lay in research that Mike Savage, Sara Arber and I undertook on Guildford council housing during the 1980s (Savage et al, 1990). This was followed up with research on Camden council housing during the 1990s (Watt, 1996), which was extended into a PhD – 'The Dynamics of Social Class and Housing: A Study of Local Authority Tenants in the London Borough of Camden' (Watt, 2001; see Watt, 2003, 2005, 2006). The book refers to this Camden research, and also draws upon (and updates) my various publications on specific London estates and on the city's housing generally:

- Aylesbury estate – territorial stigmatisation and poor housing conditions (Watt, 2020c);
- Carpenters estate – regeneration and the 2012 Olympic Games (Watt, 2013; see also Frediani et al, 2013); housing activism (Watt, 2016; Gillespie et al, 2018);
- Clapham Park and Ocean estates – the NDC and stock transfers (Watt, 2009a, 2009c);
- Northwold estate – regeneration (Watt and Allen, 2018);
- West Hendon estate – displacement of temporary tenants (Watt, 2018a);
- London housing crisis (Watt and Minton, 2016), housing activism (Watt, 2018c), and homelessness (Watt, 2018a, 2018b, 2020b).

My interest in regeneration developed out of the PhD research, but was spurred by my political involvement in a campaign against stock transfer in Buckinghamshire during the early 2000s (Watt, 2008). Subsequently I have acted in a scholar-activist capacity in various London housing and regeneration campaigns, the main ones being Demolition Watch

London, Focus E15 and DCH (Watt, 2016; Gillespie et al, 2018). This scholar-activism crossed over into book-related fieldwork at the Carpenters estate (Watt, 2013; Gillespie et al, 2018), and to a lesser extent at the Aylesbury, Cressingham Gardens and Northumberland Park estates. In addition, I undertook the NES in liaison with the Save Northwold campaign (Chapter 4; Watt and Allen, 2018). I have presented work-in-progress findings from this book at numerous housing and political meetings, including the 2017 Labour Party annual conference in Brighton.

The research for the book has not been governed by the strictures of grants and their deadlines, because it did not receive any external funding (despite three separate applications). I greatly appreciate the internal funding from Birkbeck, University of London, which paid for interview transcription costs.

The research involved a lengthy and idiosyncratic ethnographic journey through London's estate regeneration landscape, undertaken from 2007 to 2019. As noted in the Introduction, the shape of this journey and its accompanying roster of estates was not based upon a rigid predetermined rationale, but instead emerged out of the numerous fieldwork encounters that I had with estate residents who were experiencing regeneration. My research journey was therefore partly driven by the happenstances of ethnography – who one happens to meet in the field. Having said that, one broad guiding principle was that I wanted to capture residents' experiences on estates that were at different stages of the lengthy regeneration process in order to fully understand the dynamic, shifting nature of estate regeneration.

Resident interviews

One hundred and seventy-eight social housing estate residents and ex-residents were interviewed, plus four owner-occupiers who participated in estate life near their homes. Appendix B provides a demographic summary of quoted resident interviewees. The selection of interviewees is not statistically representative. I accessed them through several routes:

1. approaching people at estate-based meetings/events (regeneration meetings, older persons' clubs, fun days) and London housing/regeneration meetings;
2. talking to people in estate public spaces;
3. being put in touch with interviewees by fieldwork key informants;
4. snowballing from interviewees;
5. wider social contacts including my Birkbeck students;

6. sending out letters and door knocking at three estates which were at different regeneration stages: Northumberland Park (early stages), West Hendon and Woodberry Down (both in the mid–later stages).

Several interviewees had a broad involvement in their respective estates, for example as active members of TRAs. Most interviews took an in-depth, semi-structured format with individuals, although there were also a few joint and group interviews. Over 60 per cent of interviews lasted over an hour; the shortest was 20 minutes, while the longest was with a tenant who was interviewed for four and a half hours (over three sessions). I had the privilege of gaining interviewees' trust such that I was able to interview 18 of them several times over several years, including ten from West Hendon. Nine people were interviewed both before and after they were displaced (eight from West Hendon); this allowed me to track regeneration and relocation longitudinally (Goetz, 2013). Because of the depth gained from these repeat interviewees, I have referred to them several times in the book.

Over 70 per cent of interviews were tape recorded and transcribed (amounting to several hundred thousand words), while the remainder involved written notes for those who objected to taping. Thematic coding was used on the interview data. Most interviews were conducted face-to-face at people's homes (mainly inside, but with a few on the doorstep), in community centres, cafés, pubs, restaurants, parks, and in my office. Eight people were interviewed by telephone. The interviews focused on housing, regeneration and place themes. They included a 'housing history' element (Watt, 2001, 2005), looking at people's housing experiences over their lifetimes, and I also asked about employment. In addition to these interviews, I conducted around 40 shorter interviews at the following estates: Aylesbury, Carpenters, Clapham Park, Northwold, West Hendon and Woodberry Down.

The fact that I conducted all the interviews myself proved invaluable for understanding the depth of people's place attachments, including their affective dimension. The latter cannot be gleaned by merely reading transcripts or even just listening to tapes, but was an important aspect of the interview as a socially embodied experience. I was surprised at how people literally poured their hearts out to a total stranger. This affective dimension was prominent among those BAME and white working-class women who had been displaced against their will and who had not recovered from the trauma – and probably never will (Marris, 1986).

Official interviews

Over 50 officials were interviewed including local politicians, housing and regeneration professionals and workers, community workers and volunteers. Most were employed at the time of the interview, although several had retired or otherwise left their positions. The officials tended to work within a specific borough and even on specific estates, but some had more London-wide roles. Several wanted their boroughs/ organisations to remain anonymous. The politicians were a mixture of current and ex-councillors (all Labour Party). I approached several other local politicians and professionals who either did not reply or refused a formal interview, even though they sometimes spoke to me informally 'off the record'. Although the official interviews are referred to throughout the book, I have not used them as much as originally intended (Introduction) – so apologies to these interviewees if they think that I wasted their time. I have particularly drawn on those interviews with officials who worked closely with residents.

Fieldwork

Fieldwork consisted of estate visits and participant observation. I made numerous solo visits to the estates, but also carried out 33 walking tours with residents, officials, ex-officials, voluntary organisation members and academics. These tours often took a 'go-along' interview format (Kusenbach, 2003). They were undertaken at the following estates/ areas (with number of times in brackets) – see Chapter 4 for the relevant boroughs:

- Aylesbury and Heygate (1)
- Canning Town/Custom House (5)
- Carpenters (3)
- Central Hill (2)
- Churchill Gardens (2)
- Clapham Park (1)
- Cressingham Gardens (3)
- Maiden Lane, Camden (1)
- Marlowe Road (1)
- Northumberland Park (2)
- Ocean (3)
- Regents Park (1)
- Somers Town (1)
- South Kilburn (4)

- West Hendon (2)
- Woodberry Down (1).

Participant observation was undertaken at informal gatherings, but also at the following meetings and events (mostly housing/ regeneration related):

- 67 officially organised council, public and Labour Party meetings, exhibitions, and consultations – for example, Community Links (Canning Town), WDCO, West Hendon Partnership Board, 2017 Labour Party Conference.
- three fun days at Clapham Park and Woodberry Down;
- 215 resident-led meetings, events, community clubs, demonstrations and occupations – for example, CARP, Clapham Park Over 50s, Demolition Watch London, Focus E15, Haringey DCH, Northumberland Park Decides, Ocean Estate Senior Citizen Club, Our West Hendon, Radical Housing Network, Southwark DCH, Southwark Group of Tenants Organisations.

I attended the following legal proceedings over a total of 17 days:

- evictions of West Hendon temporary tenants – Willesden County Court (December 2014–January 2015);
- West Hendon CPO1 inquiry – Holiday Inn, Barnet, and Hendon Town Hall (January 2015);
- Aylesbury CPO inquiry – The Den, Millwall Football Club (April–October 2015);
- Cressingham Gardens JR – RCJ (November 2016);
- West Hendon CPO2 inquiry – RAF Museum, Colindale (March 2017);
- HDV JR – RCJ (October 2017);
- Aylesbury CPO inquiry – Southwark Town Hall (January 2018);
- West Hendon CPO3 inquiry – RAF Museum, Colindale (July 2019).

Documentary and photographic research

I took hundreds of photographs, some of which are used in the book. Secondary data sources include the Census, the Ministry of Housing, Communities and Local Government (MHCLG), local government, qualitative interview data from the Open University and Wendy Charlton (Broadwater Farm), housing surveys, council minutes, regeneration plans. I obtained data (demolition, rehousing and DHP) from the following councils using FOI requests: Barnet, Hackney, Newham and Southwark. What stands out in trying to use this method is the paucity of data that councils hold on owner-occupiers' rehousing. Finally, several local newspapers were consulted:

- East End Advertiser
- Hackney Citizen
- Hendon & Finchley Times
- Newham Recorder
- South London Press
- Southwark News
- Waltham Forest Echo.

APPENDIX B

Profile of interviewees

Table B.1 Profile of quoted social housing tenant/resident interviewees

Borough – Estate (total number of interviewees at each estate, N) Pseudonym	Housing tenure	Gender	Age	Ethnic identity	Years at estate, N	Employment status
Barnet – West Hendon (30)						
Adela	LA	Female	55	Asian	19	PTE
Annie	LA	Female	75	White British	38	Retired
Charlie	LA	Male	60	White British	37	FTE
Cheryl	LA	Female	53	Black British	46	Unemployed
Craig	LA	Male	38	White British	37	Unemployed
Danni	LA	Female	46	Black African	27	PTE
Eddie	LA	Male	62	White British	47	Disabled
Eva	LA	Female	80	White South European	25	Retired
Lorraine	LA	Female	43	Black mixed	17	PTE
Pat	LA	Female	51	Black British	33	FTE
Sam	LA	Male	49	Indian	23	Self-employed
Tiffany	LA	Female	38	White British	20	Unemployed
Vicky	LA	Female	65	White British	35	Retired

(continued)

Table B.1 Profile of quoted social housing tenant/resident interviewees (continued)

Alf*	RTB owner	Male	74	White Irish	40	Retired
Elaine	RTB owner	Female	55	White British	35	FTE
Lilly	RTB owner	Female	65	White British	34	Retired
Oluwakemi*	RTB owner	Female	43	Black African	20	Self-employed
Theresa	RTB owner	Female	55	White Irish	20	PTE
Wesley	RTB owner	Male	55	Black British	41	FTE
Choo	NST	Female	42	British Asian	11	Disabled
Chris	NST	Male	38	White British	11	Unemployed
Douglas	NST	Male	55	White British	9	Long-term sick
Kayleigh*	NST	Female	34	Black British	6	Parent (sick)
Kofi	NST	Male	52	Black African	8	FTE
Laiba	NST	Female	45	British Asian	5	Long-term sick
Natalie	NST	Female	34	White British	6	Parent (disabled)
Pippin*	NST	Female	40	Black British	8	Disabled
Shiela	NST	Female	46	Middle Eastern	5	Long-term sick

Table B.1 Profile of quoted social housing tenant/resident interviewees (continued)

Hackney – Woodberry Down (34)						
Akmal	LA (mother's flat)	Male	20	Arabic	20	PTE
Andrew	LA > HA	Male	68	White British	58	Retired
Barbara	LA	Female	75	White British	68	Retired
Bob	LA > HA	Male	54	White British	36	Long-term sick
Claudia	LA	Female	30	Black African	14	PTE
Deirdre	LA > HA	Female	78	White British	65	Retired
Derya	LA (mother's flat)	Female	20	Turkish	20	Student
Gerry	LA > HA	Male	65	White Irish	40	Retired
Gordon	LA > HA	Male	60	White Irish	20	Disabled
Grace	LA	Female	56	Black Caribbean	22	Unemployed
Irmak	LA (mother's flat)	Female	31	Turkish	18	Parent (unemployed)
Jack	LA > HA	Male	63	White British	34	FTE
Jane (& Brian)	LA > HA	Female	80	White British	45	Retired
Brian (& Jane)	LA > HA	Male	90	White British	45	Retired
Mandy	LA > HA	Female	68	White British	44	Retired
Marion	LA > HA	Female	61	White British	61	Unemployed
Meena	LA	Female	55	Bangladeshi	34	Parent (unemployed)
Rita	HA	Female	50	White British	13	Unemployed
Shirley	LA > HA	Female	70	Black Caribbean	25	Retired
Terry*	LA	Male	50	Black British	24	Self-employed
Tipp	LA > HA	Male	62	White Irish	22	Unemployed
Tina	LA > HA	Female	53	North African	34	Disabled
Wayne	LA	Male	40	White British	20	Unemployed
Farhad	RTB owner	Male	61	Bangladeshi	37	Long-term sick
Ayla	NST	Female	28	Kurdish	4	Parent (unemployed)
Ella	NST	Female	30	Turkish	1	Parent (unemployed)

(continued)

Table B.1 Profile of quoted social housing tenant/resident interviewees (continued)

Hackney – Woodberry Down (34)						
Petra	NST	Female	29	White East European	<1	PTE
Rahel	NST	Female	40	Black African	1	PTE/Student
Nita	NST	Female	25	British Asian	<1	Parent (unemployed)
Whitney	NST	Female	44	Black British	2	PTE
Alan	Owner-occupier	Male	43	Asian	11	FTE
Hackney – Northwold (5)						
Damo	Shared owner	Male	45	White British	13	FTE
Caroline	Owner-occupier (shared equity)	Female	46	White British	8	FTE
Allula (& Dylan)	Owner-occupier	Female	30	White Mixed	<1	Unemployed
Dylan (& Allula)	Owner-occupier	Male	37	Mixed	<1	FTE
Winifred	Owner-occupier	Female	70	White British	5	Retired
Hackney – New Kingshold (1)						
Niall*	LA > HA	Male	60	White Irish	8	FTE

Table B.1 Profile of quoted social housing tenant/resident interviewees (continued)

Haringey – Northumberland Park (27)						
Beverly	HA	Female	45	Black British	19	Self-employed
Dave	LA	Male	52	White British	14	Disabled
Frank	LA	Male	60	White British	20	FTE
Leroy	LA	Male	55	Black Caribbean	29	Self-employed
Mehmet	LA	Male	45	Turkish	3	Self-employed
Michael	LA	Male	50	Black Caribbean	15	Unemployed
Michelle	LA	Female	60	White British	32	PTE
Monica	LA	Female	41	Black Caribbean	15	FTE
Omar	LA	Male	42	Middle Eastern	15	FTE
Otis	LA	Male	40	Black African	5	Not answered
Paz	LA	Female	65	South American	12	PTE
Ali	RTB owner	Female	55	Bangladeshi	29	PTE
Janet (& Bert)	RTB owner	Female	65	White British	42	Retired
Bert (& Janet)	RTB owner	Male	68	Black British	42	Retired
Rene	RTB owner	Female	80	White British	47	Retired
Stan	RTB (father's flat)	Male	50	White British	48	FTE
Belinda**	Owner-occupier	Female	52	White British	Not applicable	PTE
Broadwater Farm (1)						
Phil	LA	Male	45	White British	8	FTE

(continued)

Table B.1 Profile of quoted social housing tenant/resident interviewees (continued)

Lambeth – Clapham Park (18)						
Audrey	LA > HA	Female	64	White British	39	Retired
Isobel	LA > HA	Female	61	Black Caribbean	17	Long-term sick
Malana	LA > HA	Female	62	Black British	43	Unemployed
Sally	LA > HA	Female	70	White British	37	Retired
Sylvester	LA > HA	Male	56	Mixed race	16	Long-term sick
George	RTB owner	Male	52	Black African	27	FTE
Jasmin	NST	Female	25	White British	4	Parent (unemployed)
James	NST	Male	40	Black African	16	FTE
Katrina	NST	Female	47	White East European	8	PTE
Lambeth – Cressingham Gardens (8)						
Bill	LA	Male	60	White British	22	Retired
Heather	LA	Female	52	White British	2	Unemployed
Steve	LA	Male	50	White British	2	Disabled
Rose	RTB owner	Female	44	Black British	17	Unemployed
Lynsey	Owner-occupier	Female	40	White Other	3	Self-employed
Jeanette	Owner-occupier	Female	40	Mixed	15	FTE
Lisa	Owner-occupier	Female	34	White British	10	Unemployed
Luke	Owner-occupier	Male	43	White British	12	Self-employed
Lambeth – Central Hill (1)						
Sandra	LA	Female	50	White British	17	Disabled
Lambeth – Westbury (1)						
Joseph	RTB owner	Male	40	Black African	20	FTE

Table B.1 Profile of quoted social housing tenant/resident interviewees (continued)

Newham – Carpenters (15)						
Darren*	LA	Male	45	White British	41	Employed
Femi*	LA > HA	Male	32	Black African	10	FTE
Geraldine*	LA	Female	74	Black Caribbean	40	Retired
Melissa*	LA	Female	46	White British	27	Parent (unemployed)
Ria*	LA	Female	64	Black Caribbean	39	Retired
Robbie	LA	Male	45	Black British	17	FTE
Abiola	RTB owner	Male	45	Black British	15	FTE
Ernie	RTB owner	Male	72	White British	40	Retired
Gloria	RTB owner	Female	74	Black Caribbean	46	Retired
Lee	RTB (parents' house)	Male	45	White British	45	FTE
Mahir	RTB (parents' flat)	Male	35	Bangladeshi	14	FTE
Mary***	RTB owner	Female	76	White Irish	45	Retired
Ted (& Vera)	RTB owner	Male	84	White British	51	Retired
Vera (& Ted)	RTB owner	Female	82	White British	51	Retired
Cassie	Owner-occupier	Female	50	Black Caribbean	16	PTE
Newham – Canning Town/ Custom House (3)						
Fred*	LA	Male	66	White British	30	Retired
Kathleen	LA	Female	55	White Irish	32	PTE
Norman	LA	Male	65	White British	44	Retired

(continued)

Table B.1 Profile of quoted social housing tenant/resident interviewees (continued)

Southwark – Aylesbury (5)						
Dennis*	LA	Male	52	White British	20	FTE
Salma	LA	Female	42	Black African	18	PTE
Dolores	RTB owner	Female	50	South American	20	Employed
Gesil (& William)	RTB owner	Female	53	Black African	23	PTE
William (& Gesil)	RTB owner	Male	55	Black African	23	PTE
Southwark – Heygate (2)						
Gary*	LA	Male	57	White Irish	7	Self-employed
Olive*	LA	Female	65	White British	32	Retired
Southwark – East Dulwich (3)						
Bonnie*	LA	Female	52	White Canadian	5	Self-employed
Maggie	LA	Female	78	White British	31	Retired
Stella*	LA	Female	50	White British	14	Self-employed
Southwark – Other (2)						
Kevin	LA	Male	60	White British	19	FTE
Roger	LA	Male	55	White British	15	Unemployed

Table B.1 Profile of quoted social housing tenant/resident interviewees (continued)

Tower Hamlets – Ocean (10)						
Ahmed	LA > HA	Male	32	Bangladeshi	9	FTE
Gladys	LA	Female	90	White British	42	Retired
Graham	LA	Male	67	White British	16	Retired
Jean	LA	Female	90	White British	Unsure	Retired
Sarah	LA > HA	Female	62	White British	49	Retired
Beatty	RTB owner	Female	70	White British	65	PTE
Bilal*	Owner-occupier	Male	47	Bangladeshi	35	FTE
Tower Hamlets – Other (3)						
Mariana	RTB owner	Female	76	White British	41	Retired

Supplementary boroughs						
Brent – South Kilburn (1) – Ben	LA	Male	62	White British	27	Retired
Camden – Bacton (1) – Cathy*	LA	Female	45	White British	14	PTE
Camden – Regents Park (1) – Harry	LA	Male	54	White British	54	Unemployed
Waltham Forest – Marlowe Road (1) – Sonia	LA	Female	40	Black African	15	Self-employed
Westminster – Churchill Gardens (2) – Maria	RTB owner	Female	55	White British	28	FTE

* Ex-resident of estate at time of interview

** Lives near estate

*** Actual name

Notes: LA – local authority tenant; HA – housing association tenant; LA > HA – moved from local authority to housing association renting; NST – non-secure tenant; FTE – full-time employed; PTE – part-time employed. Married couples/partners in brackets. In a few cases, minor details have been changed to protect anonymity.

Notes

Chapter 1

[1] 'Decanting' is the process whereby a social landlord moves tenants from their homes to facilitate demolition or major refurbishment.

[2] 'The term "housing estate" is usually used to refer to a physical cluster group of homes which was originally built as a single project with a common design and contracted by a single organisation' (Tunstall, 2020: 27).

[3] These households include 88,560 children. Data for 1st quarter 2018. Available from Shelter Databank: https://england.shelter.org.uk/professional_resources/ housing_databank. This hypothetical projection is based on the assumption that every household currently living in temporary accommodation would be able to have their housing needs met in the public housing sector.

[4] See Watt (2017).

[5] I recommend some excellent books (Boughton, 2018; Hodkinson, 2019; Sendra and Fitzpatrick, 2020; Tunstall, 2020) and reports (Ambrose, 1996, 2002; Belotti, 2016) on this topic.

[6] 'Symbolic devaluation' occurs irrespective of whether working-class people internalise such devaluations or not; if they do, this is 'symbolic violence' in Bourdieusian terms.

Chapter 2

[1] Percentages are rounded up throughout the text.

[2] During fieldwork, I heard four prominent Labour MPs (two of whom served in the New Labour governments), make speeches about how these governments made a mistake in not building enough council housing; several Labour councillors made similar comments.

[3] See Watt (2009c) and Watt and Minton (2016).

[4] Auctioning high-value local authority stock onto the private market is a fifth relatively minor causal factor.

Chapter 3

[1] See Watt (2017) and Watt and Smets (2017).

[2] Glucksberg (2017) argues that between 1,000 and 2,000 people moved out of the Peckham SRB area and did not return, far more than Arbaci and Rae (2013) suggest. Given the net reduction of 838 units, Glucksberg's approximation seems reasonable.

[3] See Watt (2009a, 2009c, 2020c), and Watt and Wallace (2014).

[4] This does not mean that public funding was necessarily sufficient under HATs, as Hull (2006) discusses, but they were more generous per area than the more socially ambitious NDC.

[5] This section is distilled from various estate regeneration plans and interviews, plus the following reports: Adonis and Davies (2015), McLaughlin (2015), Derbyshire et al (2016), Hanna et al (2016), G15 (2016), Karakusevic and Batchelor (2017), London First (2017).

[6] I conducted a secondary data analysis on 35 regenerated London estates now owned by one of the G15 housing associations (G15, 2016: 46–51). These estates include

six featured in this book: Aylesbury, Clapham Park, Ocean, South Kilburn, West Hendon and Woodberry Down. My analysis shows an increase in total affordable units of 9 per cent, but a 25 per cent decline in social rental homes within that. The number of market properties at these G15 sites will increase by over four times. These patterns are broadly in line with the LAHC data.

Chapter 4

[1] See Frediani et al (2013), Watt (2013, 2016), and Gillespie et al (2018).

[2] Data supplied by LBN – FOI request by Paul Watt, reference FOI/E33456, 11 October 2019.

[3] Data supplied by LBN – FOI request by Paul Watt, reference FOI/E31811, 3 December 2018.

[4] See Watt (2018a).

[5] Metropolitan is one of the increasingly market-oriented G15 group of large London housing associations (Manzi and Morrison, 2018).

[6] Data supplied by LBB – FOI request by Paul Watt, reference 5625500, 30 September 2019.

[7] Email from Hackney Council, 5 March 2018.

[8] Data supplied by LBH – FOI request by Paul Watt, reference FOI-000034, 20 June 2018.

[9] Thanks to Wendy Charlton for letting me read the transcripts of her interviews undertaken at Broadwater Farm.

[10] See Watt (2009a).

[11] I also undertook participant observation at Knights Walk (a small section within Cotton Gardens estate) which was also included in Lambeth's regeneration programme (LBL, 2015b).

[12] See Watt (2020c).

[13] See Watt (2009a, 2009c, 2018c).

[14] Fitzrovia YouthInAction, 'HS2 in Camden', YouTube, 15 February 2018: www.youtube.com/watch?v=3z0S_CLVRhc

[15] The following interviewees are omitted from Table 4.4: younger people living in the family home, PRS tenants, shared owners, and owner-occupiers not living on estates.

[16] These are not strictly comparable since the interview data is for length of time on estate, whereas the GLA (2019a) 2015–18 survey data is for length of time in current home. Nevertheless, most social rental and RTB owner interviewees lived in just one home at their estate.

Chapter 5

[1] A few had first degrees, often ones they obtained later in life as mature students.

[2] This typology is a Weberian ideal type, which clusters the main socioeconomic groups alongside their main tenures. There are individual interviewees who do not fit into the five types. A sixth group is the middle-class homeowning incomers, discussed in Chapter 6.

[3] Although Meena's husband was present during our interview, he felt unconfident speaking to me in English.

[4] See Dench et al (2006) for an alternative controversial view.

[5] See Watt (2018a, 2018b, 2020b).

Chapter 6

[1] Southwark is well served in this regard; it also has the borough-wide Southwark Group of Tenants Organisations.

[2] NES quotations are identified by 'R' for respondent and their survey number. Unless otherwise indicated, all respondents are housing association tenants.

[3] Presentation to Tower Hamlets Renters, 20 October 2015.

Chapter 7

[1] Some were no longer employed in this role at the time of the interview.

[2] I took this photograph in October 2017, but I have an earlier one from June 2016 which shows the ceiling in the same state, suggesting that this had not been fixed for over a year. Photograph 7.1 is unexceptional; I have many similar photographs of other ceilings at Northumberland Park estate.

[3] Metropolitan Police crime and ASB mapping data for Stratford and New Town ward during December 2014 (accessed 30 June 2015; www.police.uk/metropolitan/ 00BB03N/crime/2014-12/anti-social-behaviour/). Of the 642 crimes for the ward, just 14 occurred in the footprint of the Carpenters estate, while no burglaries or vehicle crimes occurred on the estate during this period.

Chapter 8

[1] 'Shed a little light please!', letter, *Newham Recorder*, 13 March 2002.

[2] 'Watching too much telly Tom', letter, *Newham Recorder*, 27 February 2002.

[3] 'Right moves keep residents informed', letter, Councillor Robin Wales, *Newham Recorder*, 3 April 2002.

[4] Data supplied by LBN – FOI request by Paul Watt, reference FOI/E32002, 10 January 2019 (also FOI request by Paul Watt, reference FOI/E31811, 3 December 2018). The council's data on rehoused tenants is incomplete. Of the 767 council properties at January 2002 which were demolished, data appears to be only available on the 470 rehoused tenants, but there was also a "high number of empty properties" as of that date (my calculation is 297). Therefore, one cannot establish what happened to the latter nearly 300 already decanted tenants.

[5] See Watt and Allen (2018). Unless otherwise stated, all R (respondent) quotations are housing association tenants.

[6] The Estate Development Committee was the forerunner of WDCO.

[7] Disagreeing with these bland statements would mean supporting the following – that the estate should not be made up of attractive places, that regeneration should not deliver high-quality housing, and that there should be fewer community facilities!

[8] https://architecturalworkers.wordpress.com/about/

[9] I am not making claims regarding statistical reliability vis-à-vis the interviews (Appendix A). However, the NES findings provide more robust generalisability, albeit only for Northwold estate itself (Watt and Allen, 2018).

[10] Fourteen were obtained via door-knocking (Appendix A). Although the sample is not statistically representative, it is indicative of residents' views.

[11] As discussed in Chapter 7, Clapham Park is exceptional since it's long-term residents themselves used 'sink estate' and other pejorative terms when referring to the pre-NDC estate during the 1980s and 1990s (cf. Beaumont, 2006; CPP, 2013).

[12] Wendy Charlton's transcripts based on her interviews undertaken at Broadwater Farm also show this disjunction.

[13] UCL is an elite Russell Group university whose student body is more privileged in class terms than the already existing University of East London which can trace its roots in Stratford back to 1970.

[14] For example, residents' testimonies at Cressingham Gardens support this interpretation (Local Dialogue, 2016).

Chapter 9

[1] Eastlondonlines YouTube video, Woodberry Down Estate, 11 April 2010: www.youtube.com/watch?v=K3ki1L4jw8Q

[2] I have photographs of a nearby estate; this work was presumably done by the council under DHP.

[3] LBN – FOI request, reference FOI/12476, 24 April 2012.

[4] I wrote the final draft of the book during the first COVID-19 lockdown period in 2020. During the whole of this period, my family and I had noisy construction work going on a few metres from our flat every weekday. My interviewees are not exaggerating the daily misery – sheer hell – of living next to a building site, or the exasperation involved in making complaints to self-titled 'considerate contractors'.

[5] Thanks to Chris Saunders who allowed me to examine the data (supplied to him by Southwark Council); my calculation.

[6] https://en.wikipedia.org/wiki/Shank_(2010_film).

[7] Gordon's assumption was correct; this manager was at one of the three WDCO meetings that I attended, but had been replaced by the next meeting.

[8] https://extra.shu.ac.uk/ndc//ndc_evaluation.htm#

Chapter 10

[1] Tracking displacees is methodologically difficult, especially in the case of those who have physically moved away from a neighbourhood (Atkinson, 2000, 2015). However, I managed to interview 51 people (from 49 households) who had been displaced away from their homes. Of the 51, 34 had returned to (or remained in) the original neighbourhood (33 in new-build or refurbished properties), 15 relocated elsewhere in the same borough, and two left London altogether (see Watt, Forthcoming).

[2] Photographs 10.1 and 10.2 are my photographs of Annie's originals, used with her permission.

[3] See Watt (2018a) on West Hendon temporary tenants.

[4] When Gerry says 'people', he means 'secure council tenants' since only three leaseholders returned.

[5] Bob mentioned that some tenants who moved away were denied the right to return because the council had apparently lost the paperwork.

[6] This assessment refers to the period before Rokhsana Fiaz was elected as Mayor in 2018.

Chapter 11

[1] The chapter draws upon the following publications: London housing activism (Watt and Minton, 2016; Watt, 2018c), anti-transfer campaigns (Watt, 2009a, 2009c), and Carpenters estate (Watt, 2013, 2016; Gillespie et al, 2018).

Chapter 12

[1] This company changed during the short time that the redevelopment has been in existence.

[2] Although the recent Social Life (2020) report contains extensive survey data on numerous neighbourhood indicators (satisfaction, crime, deprivation, and so on), bizarrely it hardly mentions housing conditions, which were such a prominent part of the original Woodberry Down regeneration rationale.

[3] See Frediani et al (2013), Watt (2013, 2016), and Gillespie et al (2018).

Chapter 13

[1] Temporary accommodation data for 1st quarter 2019, and waiting list data for 2018. Available from Shelter Databank: https://england.shelter.org.uk/professional_resources/housing_databank

References

35% Campaign (2013) 'Regeneration branded "miserable failure" at CPO Public Inquiry' (http://35percent.org/2013-07-18-regeneration-branded-miserable-failure-at-cpo-public-inquiry/).

35% Campaign (2018) 'Heygate estate regeneration' (http://35percent.org/heygate-regeneration-faq/).

Adonis, A. (2015) 'City villages', in A. Adonis and B. Davies (eds), *City Villages: More Homes, Better Communities*, London: IPPR, pp 5–20.

Adonis, A. and Davies, B. (2015) *City Villages: More Homes, Better Communities*, London: IPPR.

Ainsley, C. (2018) *The New Working Class*, Bristol: Policy Press.

Alden, S. (2015) 'Discretion on the frontline: the street level bureaucrat in English statutory homelessness services', *Social Policy & Society*, 14(1): 63–77.

ALG (Association of London Government) (2003) *The Impact of the Right to Buy*, London: ALG.

Allen, C. (2008) *Housing Market Renewal and Social Class*, Abingdon: Routledge.

Allen, D. and Watt, P. (Forthcoming) 'Place attachment in non-place spaces? Community, belonging and mobilities in post-suburban South East England', in P.J. Maginn and K.B. Anacker (eds), *Suburbia in the 21st Century: From Dreamscape to Nightmare?*, London: Routledge.

Alston, P. (2019) *Report of the Special Rapporteur on Extreme Poverty and Human Rights on His Visit to the United Kingdom of Great Britain and Northern Ireland*, Geneva: United Nations.

Ambrose, P. (1996) *I Mustn't Laugh Too Much: Housing and Health on the Limehouse Fields and Ocean Estates in Stepney*, Brighton: University of Sussex.

Ambrose, P. (2002) *Second Best Value: The Central Stepney SRB*, Brighton: University of Brighton.

Arbaci, S. and Rae, I. (2013) 'Mixed-tenure neighbourhoods in London: policy myth or effective device to alleviate deprivation?', *International Journal of Urban and Regional Research*, 37(2): 451–79.

Architectural Workers (2017) *What Is the Architect's Role in the Housing Crisis?* (https://architecturalworkers.wordpress.com/events/).

ASH (Architects for Social Housing) (2017) 'Class war on Woodberry Down: a national strategy' (https://architectsforsocialhousing.co.uk/2017/05/12/class-war-on-woodberry-down-a-national-strategy/).

459

ASH (2018) *Central Hill: A Case Study in Estate Regeneration* (https://architectsforsocialhousing.co.uk/2018/04/10/central-hill-a-case-study-in-estate-regeneration/).

Atkinson, R. (2000) 'The hidden costs of gentrification: displacement in central London', *Journal of Housing and the Built Environment*, 15: 307–26.

Atkinson, R. (2006) 'Padding the bunker: strategies of middle-class disaffiliation and colonisation in the city', *Urban Studies*, 43(4): 819–32.

Atkinson, R. (2015) 'Losing one's place: narratives of neighbourhood change, market injustice and symbolic displacement', *Housing, Theory and Society*, 32(4): 373–88.

Atkinson, R. (2020) *Alpha City: How the Super-Rich Captured London*, London: Verso.

Atkinson, R. and Kintrea, K. (2000) 'Owner-occupation, social mix and neighbourhood impacts', *Policy and Politics*, 28(1): 93–108.

Atkinson, R. and Blandy, S. (2017) *Domestic Fortress: Fear and the New Home Front*, Manchester: Manchester University Press.

Atkinson, R. and Millington, G. (2019) *Urban Criminology: The City, Disorder, Harm and Social Control*, London: Routledge.

Attenburrow, J.J., Murphy, A.R. and Simms, A.G. (1978) *The Problems of Some Large Local Authority Estates: An Exploratory Study*, London: DOE.

Audit Commission (2009) *Housing Management Service: Clapham Park Homes*, London: Audit Commission.

Auge, M. (1995) *Non-places: Introduction to an Anthropology of Supermodernity*, London: Verso.

August, M. (2016) ' "It's all about power and you have none": the marginalization of tenant resistance to mixed-income social housing redevelopment in Toronto, Canada', *Cities*, 57: 25–32.

Awofolaju, T. (2014) *Making High Density Work in Mixed-tenure Schemes*, London: The Building Futures Group.

Back, L. (2015) 'Why everyday life matters: class, community and making life livable', *Sociology*, 49(5): 820–36.

Backwith, D. (1995) *The Death of Municipal Socialism: The Politics of Council Housing in Sheffield and Bristol, 1919–1939*, PhD thesis, University of Bristol.

Balchin, P. (1995) *Housing Policy: An Introduction* (3rd edn), London: Routledge.

Balchin, P. (1996) *Housing Policy in Europe*, London: Routledge.

Banting, K.G. (1979) *Poverty, Politics, and Policy: Britain in the 1960s*, London: Macmillan.

Barke, K. (2017) 'Interview', in P. Karakusevic and A. Batchelor (eds), *Social Housing: Definitions and Design Exemplars*, Newcastle upon Tyne: RIBA Publishing, pp 22–5.

Barratt London (2020) 'Hendon Waterside' (www.barratthomes.co.uk/new-homes/greater-london/h441801-hendon-waterside/).

Baxter, R. and Brickell, K. (2014) 'For home *un*making', *Home Cultures*, 11(2): 133–44.

BBC (2011) ' "Muggers' paradise" the Heygate Estate is demolished', *BBC News*, 15 April (www.bbc.co.uk/news/uk-england-london-13092349).

BBC (2012) 'Carpenters Estate residents "face uncertain future"', *BBC News*, 18 December (www.bbc.co.uk/news/uk-england-london-20762286).

BBC (2015) 'The price of the knock down', *BBC News*, 22 December (www.bbc.co.uk/news/uk-35124545).

BBC (2019) 'Council tenant: "Cockroaches bit my baby's face"', *Victoria Derbyshire*, 29 October (www.bbc.co.uk/news/uk-england-50183259).

Beaumont, J. (2006) 'London: deprivation, social isolation and regeneration', in S. Musterd, A. Murie and C. Kesteloot (eds), *Neighbourhoods of Poverty*, Basingstoke: Palgrave Macmillan, pp 139–61.

Belotti, A. (2014) *The Effects of Large-scale Demolition and Decanting on Residents and Local Businesses: The Case of Woodberry Down Estate*, MSc dissertation, LSE.

Belotti, A. (2016) *Estate Regeneration and Community Impacts* (Case Report 99), London: LSE Housing and Communities, LSE.

Benefit to Society (2017) Benefit to Society Fair Press Guide (http://benefittosociety.co.uk/).

Bennington, J., Fordham, T. and Robinson, D. (2004) *Housing in London NDCs: Situations, Challenges and Opportunities* (Research Report 59), Sheffield: CRESR, Sheffield Hallam University.

Bernstock, P. (2014) *Olympic Housing: A Critical Review of London 2012's Legacy*, Farnham: Ashgate.

Berry, S. (2018) 'Loss of council homes in "regeneration" speeds up under Mayor Khan' (www.sianberry.london/news/housing/2018_09_03_net_loss-of-council-homes-regeneration/).

Beswick, J. and Penny, J. (2018) 'Demolishing the present to sell off the future? The emergence of financialized municipal entrepreneurialism in London', *International Journal of Urban and Regional Research*, 42(4): 612–32.

Blokland, T. (2003) *Urban Bonds*, Cambridge: Polity Press.

Blokland, T. (2017) *Community as Urban Practice*, Cambridge: Polity Press.

Bosch, E.M. and Ouwehand, A.L. (2019) 'At home in the oasis: middle-class newcomers' affiliation to their deprived Rotterdam neighbourhood', *Urban Studies*, 56(9): 1818–34.

Boughton, J. (2018) *Municipal Dreams: The Rise and Fall of Council Housing,* London: Verso.

Bourdieu, P. (1984) *Distinction*, London: Routledge.

Bourdieu, P. and Wacquant, L. (1992) *An Invitation to Reflexive Sociology*, Cambridge: Polity Press.

Bourdieu, P. et al (1999) *The Weight of the World*, Cambridge: Polity Press.

Bowie, D. (2010) *Politics, Planning and Homes in a World City*, London: Routledge.

Bowie, D. (2017) *Radical Solutions to the Housing Supply Crisis*, Bristol: Policy Press.

Bowley, M. (1944) *Housing and the State, 1919–1944*, London: George Allen & Unwin.

Bradley, Q. (2014) *The Tenants' Movement*, London: Routledge.

Brearley, M. (2017) 'An attitude about cities', in P. Karakusevic and A. Batchelor (eds), *Social Housing: Definitions and Design Exemplars*, Newcastle upon Tyne: RIBA Publishing, pp 90–5.

Brenner, N. (2009) 'What is critical urban theory?', *City*, 13(2–3): 198–207.

Bridge, G., Butler, T. and Lees, L. (2012) *Mixed Communities: Gentrification by Stealth?*, Bristol: Policy Press.

Brixton Buzz (2018) 'Sixty families in Clapham Park estate to be made homeless as Metropolitan's demolition plans go ahead', 28 November (www.brixtonbuzz.com/2018/11/sixty-families-in-clapham-park-estate-to-be-made-homeless-as-metropolitans-demolition-plans-go-ahead/).

Brown, J. (2019) '"Back in Africa you all slept in one room together": the London council making life hell for social tenants', *Medium*, 14 November (https://medium.com/@jessica_e_brown/back-in-africa-you-all-slept-in-one-room-together-the-london-council-stripping-social-tenants-a097241eb19d).

Brown-Saracino, J. (2007) 'Virtuous marginality: social preservationists and the selection of the old-timer', *Theory and Society*, 36: 437–68.

Butler, T. (2003) 'Living in the bubble: Gentrification and its "others" in north London', *Urban Studies*, 40(12): 2469–86.

Butler, T. and Robson, G. (2003) *London Calling: The Middle Classes and the Re-making of Inner London*, Oxford: Berg.

Butler, T. and Lees, L. (2006) 'Super-gentrification in Barnsbury, London: globalization and gentrifying global elites at the neighbourhood level', *Transactions of the Institute of British Geographers NS*, 31: 467–87.

Butler, T. and Watt, P. (2007) *Understanding Social Inequality*, London: Sage.

Cairncross, L., Clapham, D. and Goodlad, R. (1997) *Housing Management, Consumers and Citizens*, London: Routledge.

Campkin, B. (2013) *Regenerating London: Decline and Regeneration in Urban Culture*, London: I.B. Tauris.

Carter, H. (2008) 'Building the divided city: race, class and social housing in Southwark, 1945–1995', *London Journal*, 33(2): 155–85.

Cattell, V. (2001) 'Poor people, poor places, and poor health: the mediating role of social networks and social capital', *Social Science & Medicine*, 52: 1501–16.

CDP (Community Development Project) (1976) *Whatever Happened to Council Housing?*, London: CDP.

Chakrabortty, A. (2017) 'Jeremy Corbyn has declared war on Labour councils over housing', *The Guardian*, 27 September.

Chakrabortty, A. and Robinson-Tillett, S. (2014) 'The truth about gentrification: regeneration or con trick?', *The Guardian*, 18 May.

Chaloner, J., Colquhoun, G. and Pragnell, M. (2019) *Increasing Investment in Social Housing*, London: Capital Economics.

Charlesworth, S. (2001) 'Bourdieu, social suffering and working-class life', *Sociological Review*, 49(1): 49–64.

Chouhan, K., Speeden, S. and Qazi, U. (2011) *Experience of Poverty and Ethnicity in London*, York: Joseph Rowntree Foundation.

Clapham Film Unit (2010) *Brink of Change* (video), London: Clapham Film Unit.

Clarke, D.B. (2003) *The Consumer Society and the Postmodern City*, London: Routledge.

Cohen, P. (2013) *On the Wrong Side of the Track: East London and the Post-Olympics*, London: Lawrence and Wishart.

Cohen, P. and Watt, P. (2017) *London 2012 and the Post-Olympics City: A Hollow Legacy?*, Basingstoke: Palgrave Macmillan.

Cole, I. and Furbey, R. (1994) *The Eclipse of Council Housing*, London: Routledge.

Cole, I., Powell, R. and Sanderson, E. (2016) 'Putting the squeeze on "generation rent": housing benefit claimants in the private rented sector', *Sociological Research Online*, 21(2) (www.socresonline.org.uk/21/2/9.html).

Cole, I., Foden, M., Robinson, D. and Wilson, I. (2010) *Interventions in Housing and the Physical Environment in Deprived Neighbourhoods: Evidence from the New Deal for Communities Programme*, London: DCLG.

Coleman, A. (1990) *Utopia on Trial* (2nd edn), London: Hilary Shipman.

Colomb, C. (2007) 'Unpacking New Labour's "Urban Renaissance" agenda: towards a socially sustainable reurbanization of British cities', *Planning Practice and Research*, 22(1): 1–24.

Colomb, C. (2011) 'Urban regeneration and policies of "social mixing" in British cities: a critical assessment', *ACE: Architecture, City and Environment*, 6(17): 223–44.

Cooper, A.E. (2017) *306: Living Under the Shadow of Regeneration*, London: Devotion Press.

Copley, T. (2014) *From Right to Buy to Buy to Let*, London: GLA.

Copley, T. (2019) *Right to Buy: Wrong for London*, London: GLA.

Corcillo, P. (2020) *Social Mixing and the London East Village: Exclusion, Habitus and Belonging in a Post-Olympics Neighbourhood*, PhD thesis, Birkbeck, University of London.

CPP (Clapham Park Project) (2013) *Clapham Park Project: Ten Years of Change*, London: CPP.

Crawford, K., Johnson, C., Davies, F., Joo, S. and Bell, S. (2014) *Demolition or Refurbishment of Social Housing? A Review of the Evidence*, London: UCL Urban Lab and Engineering Exchange.

CRESR (Centre for Regional Economic and Social Research) (2015) *New Deal for Communities National Evaluation Phase 2: Technical Report*, London: DCLG.

Cresswell, T. (2004) *Place: A Short Introduction*, Oxford: Blackwell.

Crookes, L. (2011) *The Making of Space and the Losing of Place: A Critical Geography of Gentrification-by-Bulldozer in the North of England*, PhD thesis, University of Sheffield.

Crossley, T. and Slater, T. (2014) 'Benefits Street: territorial stigmatisation and the realization of a "(tele)vision of divisions"' (www.academia. edu/8563084/Benefits_Street_Territorial_Stigmatisation_and_the_ realization_of_a_tele_vision_of_divisions?auto=download).

Cumbers, A., Helms, G. and Swanson, K. (2010) 'Class, agency and resistance in the old industrial city', *Antipode*, 42(1): 46–73.

Cunningham, N. and Savage, M. (2017) 'An intensifying and elite city', *City*, 21(1): 25–46.

Daniel, R. (2016) 'How to get a council house – an unfair representation', Researching Sociology @ LSE (http://blogs.lse. ac.uk/researchingsociology/2016/05/10/howtogetacouncilhouse- an-unfair-representation/).

Darcy, M. (2013) 'From high-rise projects to suburban estates: public tenants and the globalised discourse of deconcentration', *Cities*, 35: 365–72.

Davidson, G., McGuinness, D., Greenhalgh, P., Braidford, P. and Robinson, F. (2013) ' "It'll get worse before it gets better": local experiences of living in a regeneration area', *Journal of Urban Regeneration and Renewal*, 7(1): 55–66.

Davidson, M. (2008) 'Spoiled mixture: where does state-led "positive" gentrification end?', *Urban Studies*, 45(12): 2385–405.

Davidson, M. (2009) 'Displacement, space and dwelling: placing gentrification debate', *Ethics, Place & Environment: A Journal of Philosophy & Geography*, 12(2): 219–34.

Davidson, M. (2010) 'Love thy neighbour? Social mixing in London's gentrification frontier', *Environment and Planning A*, 42: 524–44.

Davidson, M. and Martin, D. (2014) *Urban Politics: Critical Approaches*, London: Sage.

Davis, C. (2013) *Finance for Housing: An Introduction*, Bristol: Policy Press.

DCLG (Department for Communities and Local Government) (2010) *Data Interchange Hub – Data download, October 2010* (NI 158 – Percentage of local authority-owned non-decent dwellings), London: DCLG.

Dench, G., Gavron, K. and Young, M. (2006) *The New East End: Kinship, Race and Conflict*, London: Profile Books.

Derbyshire, B., Goulcher, M., Beharrell, A. and von Bradsky, A. (2016) *Altered Estates: Meeting the Challenge of Urban Renewal*, London: HTA, Levitt Bernstein, Pollard Thomas Edwards and PRP.

Desmond, M. (2016) *Evicted: Poverty and Profit in the American City*, London: Penguin Books.

DETR (Department of the Environment, Transport and the Regions) (1998) *1998 Index of Local Deprivation: A Summary of Results*, London: DETR.

Dillon, D. and Fanning, B. (2011) *Lessons for the Big Society: Planning, Regeneration and the Politics of Community Participation*, London: Ashgate.

Dillon, D. and Fanning, B. (2015) 'Tottenham after the riots: the chimera of community and the property-led regeneration of "broken Britain"', *Critical Social Policy*, 35(2): 188–206.

Dinham, A. (2005) 'Empowered or overpowered? The real experiences of participation in the New Deal for Communities', *Community Development Journal*, 40(3): 301–12.

DOE (Department of the Environment) (1981) *An Investigation of Difficult to Let Housing. Volume 1: General Findings*, London: HMSO.

Dorling, D. (2014) *All That Is Solid: The Great Housing Disaster*, London: Penguin Books.

Douglas, P. and Parkes, J. (2016) ' "Regeneration" and "consultation" at a Lambeth council estate', *City*, 20: 287–91.

Dunleavy, P. (1981) *The Politics of Mass Housing in Britain, 1945–1975*, Oxford: Clarendon Press.

East Thames (2016) 'The Ocean Estate, Tower Hamlets', East Thames, accessed 22 July 2017 (www.east-thames.co.uk/ocean-estate-tower-hamlets).

East Thames (2017) *Demonstration Project, Ocean Estate, Stepney Green*, London: East Thames.

Easthope, H. (2014) 'Making a rental property home', *Housing Studies*, 29(5): 579–96.

Edensor, T. and Millington, S. (2009) 'Illuminations, class identities and the contested landscapes of Christmas', *Sociology*, 43(1): 103–21.

Edwards, M., Florio, S., Karadimitriou, N. and de Magalhães, C. (2003) *Central Stepney SRB: Final Evaluation*, London: Bartlett School of Planning, UCL.

Egan, M., Lawson, L, Kearns, A., Conway, E. and Neary, J. (2015) 'Neighbourhood demolition, relocation and health: a qualitative study of housing-led urban regeneration in Glasgow, UK', *Health & Place*, 33: 101–08.

Elahi, F. and Khan, O. (2016) *Ethnic Inequalities in London*, London: Runnymede Trust.

Eldridge, J.E.T. (1971) *Max Weber: Interpretation of Social Reality*, London: Michael Joseph.

Elliott-Cooper, A., Hubbard, P. and Lees, L. (2020) 'Sold out? The right-to-buy, gentrification and working-class displacements in London', *Sociological Review*, 68(6): 1354–69.

Elmer, S. and Dening, G. (2016) 'The London clearances', *City*, 20: 271–7.

Esping-Andersen, G. (1990) *The Three Worlds of Welfare Capitalism*, Cambridge: Polity.

Evening Standard (2013) 'Pimlico stabbing', 28 January (https://www.standard.co.uk/news/crime/pimlico-stabbing-sword-mob-killed-teen-named-as-hani-abou-el-kheir-and-jogged-off-like-nothing-had-8469106.html).

Evening Standard (2014) 'Building for the future: new homes for first-time buyers from £70,875 on a Hackney estate with a regeneration agenda', Homes & Property, 3 December (www.homesandproperty.co.uk/property-news/buying/new-homes/building-for-the-future-new-homes-for-firsttime-buyers-from-70875-on-a-hackney-estate-with-a-40076.html).

Fawbert, J. (2017) 'West Ham United in the Olympic Stadium: a Gramscian analysis of the rocky road to Stratford', in P. Cohen and P. Watt (eds), *London 2012 and the Post-Olympics City: A Hollow Legacy?*, Basingstoke: Palgrave Macmillan, pp 259–86.

Feldman, R.M. and Stall, S. (2004) *The Dignity of Resistance: Women Residents' Activism in Chicago Public Housing*, Cambridge: Cambridge University Press.

Fenton, A., Lupton, R., Arrundale, R. and Tunstall, R. (2012) 'Public housing, commodification, and rights to the city: the US and England compared', *Cities*, 35: 373–8.

Ferreri, M. and Vasudevan, A. (2019) 'Vacancy at the edges of the precarious city', *Geoforum*, 101: 165–73.

Fiaz, R. (2019) 'Carpenters estate progress', letter, June 2019, London: LBN.

Fitzpatrick, S. and Pawson, H. (2014) 'Ending security of tenure for social renters: transitioning to "ambulance service" social housing?', *Housing Studies*, 29: 597–615.

Fitzpatrick, S. and Pawson, H. (2016) 'Fifty years since *Cathy Come Home*: critical reflections on the UK homelessness safety net', *International Journal of Housing Policy*, 16: 543–55.

Flint, J. (2011) 'Housing studies, social class and being towards dwelling', *Housing, Theory and Society*, 28(1): 75–91.

Flint, J. and Powell, R. (2019) *Class, Ethnicity and State in the Polarized Metropolis*, Basingstoke: Palgrave Macmillan.

Flynn, J. (2016) 'Complete control', *City*, 20(2): 278–86.

Focus E15 (2020) 'Carpenters estate' (https://focuse15.org/category/carpenters-estate/).

Forman, C. (1989) *Spitalfields: A Battle for Land*, London: Hilary Shipman.

Forrest, R. and Murie, A. (1990) 'A dissatisfied state? Consumer preferences and council housing in Britain', *Urban Studies*, 27(5): 617–35.

Forrest R. and Murie, A. (1991) *Selling the Welfare State: The Privatisation of Public Housing*, London: Routledge.

Forrest, R. and Kearns, A. (1999) *Joined-up Places? Social Cohesion and Neighbourhood Regeneration*, York: Joseph Rowntree Foundation.

Foster, J. (1995) 'Informal social control and community crime prevention', *British Journal of Criminology*, 35(4): 563–83.

FPA and GCA (Fletcher Priest Architects and George Cochrane Associates) (2015) *Northumberland Park: Strategic Framework Consultation Report*, London: GCA.

Frediani, A., Butcher, S. and Watt, P. (2013) *Regeneration and Well-being in East London: Stories from Carpenters Estate*, London: UCL.

Fried, M. (1966) 'Grieving for a lost home: psychological costs of relocation', in J.Q. Wilson (ed), *Urban Renewal: The Record and Controversy*, Cambridge, MA: MIT Press, pp 359–79.

Fuller, C. and Geddes, M. (2008) 'Urban governance under neoliberalism: New Labour and the restructuring of state-space', *Antipode*, 40(2): 252–82.

Fullilove, M.T. (2016) *Root Shock*, New York: New Village Press.

Furbey, R. (1999) 'Urban regeneration: reflections on a metaphor', *Critical Social Policy*, 19(4): 419–45.

G15 (2016) *Meeting the Challenge of Urban Renewal: The G15's Contribution to Regenerating London's Estates*, London: G15.

Gans, H.J. (1962) *The Urban Villagers*, New York: Free Press.

Garbin, D. and Millington, G. (2012) 'Territorial stigma and the politics of resistance in a Parisian banlieue: La Courneuve and beyond', *Urban Studies*, 49(10): 2067–83.

Gater, G.H. (1937) *London Housing*, London: LCC.

Gerrard, J. and Farrugia, D. (2015) 'The "lamentable sight" of homelessness and the society of the spectacle', *Urban Studies*, 52(12): 2219–33.

Gest, J. (2016) *The New Minority: White Working-Class Politics in an Age of Immigration and Inequality*, New York: Oxford University Press.

Gidley, B. (2013) 'Landscapes of belonging, portraits of life: researching everyday multiculture in an inner-city estate', *Identities*, 20(4): 361–76.

Gillespie, T., Hardy, K. and Watt, P. (2018) 'Austerity urbanism and Olympic counter-legacies: gendering, defending and expanding the urban commons in East London', *Environment and Planning D: Society and Space*, 36(5): 812–30.

Ginsburg, N. (2005) 'The privatization of council housing', *Critical Social Policy*, 25(1): 115–35.

GLA (Greater London Authority) (2010) *Planning Report 1370c & 1370d/01: Ocean Estate, Stepney*, 2 February, London: GLA.

GLA (2014) *Planning Report D&P/1370g/01: Ocean Estate, Site H*, 29 January, London: GLA.

GLA (2019a) *Housing in London, 2019* (https://data.gov.uk/dataset/ 87c3c78a-e3d6-4a9e-9626-160ea1e4b5c4/housing-in-london-the-evidence-base-for-the-mayor-s-housing-strategy).

GLA (2019b) *Planning Report GLA/2306d/02: Clapham Park Estate*, 15 July, London: GLA.

GLA Intelligence (2013a) *Trends in Housing Tenure*, London: GLA.

GLA Intelligence (2013b) *Housing Tenure by NS-SEC*, London: GLA.

GLA Intelligence (2014) *Trends in Overcrowding*, London: GLA.

GLA Intelligence (2015) *Historical Census Tables* (https://data.london.gov.uk/dataset/historical-census-tables).

Glass, R. (1964) *London: Aspects of Change*, London: Macgibbon & Kee.

Glucksberg, L. (2013) *Wasting the Inner-city: Waste, Value and Anthropology on the Estates*, PhD thesis, Goldsmiths College, University of London.

Glucksberg, L. (2016) 'A view from the top', *City*, 20(2): 238–55.

Glucksberg, L. (2017) ' "The blue bit, that was my bedroom": rubble, displacement and regeneration in inner-city London', in P. Watt and P. Smets (eds), *Social Housing and Urban Renewal: A Cross-national Perspective*, Bingley: Emerald, pp 69–103.

Glynn, S. (2009) *Where the Other Half Lives: Lower Income Housing in a Neoliberal World*, London: Pluto Press.

Glynn, S. (2014) *Class, Ethnicity and Religion in the Bengali East End*, Manchester: Manchester University Press.

GMB (2013) 'Landlords own 40% ex council houses', 5 March (http://archive.gmb.org.uk/newsroom/landlords-own-40-percent-ex-council-houses).

GMB (2015) 'GMB Congress opposes housing estates demolition', 8 June, (http://archive.gmb.org.uk/newsroom/gmb-congress-opposes-housing-estates-demolition).

Goetz, E.G. (2013) 'Too good to be true? The variable and contingent benefits of displacement and relocation among low-income public housing residents', *Housing Studies*, 28(2): 235–52.

Goetz, E.G. (2016) 'Resistance to social housing transformation', *Cities*, 57: 1–5.

Gosling, V.K. (2008) 'Regenerating communities: women's experiences of urban regeneration', *Urban Studies*, 45(3): 607–26.

Gray, N. (2018) *Rent and its Discontents: A Century of Housing Struggle*, London: Rowman & Littlefield.

Green, R. (1997) *Community Action Against Poverty: A Poverty Profile of the Kingsmead Estate in Hackney*, London: The Kingsmead Kabin.

Gunter, A. (2010) *Growing Up Bad? Black Youth, 'Road' Culture and Badness in an East London Neighbourhood*, London: Tufnell Press.

Gunter, A. and Watt, P. (2009) 'Grafting, going to college and working on road: youth transitions and cultures in an east London neighbourhood', *Journal of Youth Studies*, 12: 515–29.

Gustavsson, E. and Elander, I. (2016) 'Sustainability potential of a redevelopment initiative in Swedish public housing: the ambiguous role of residents' participation and place identity', *Progress in Planning*, 103: 1–25.

Hackett, P. (2017) *Delivering the Renaissance in Council-built Homes: The Rise of Housing Companies*, London: The Smith Institute.

Hackney Citizen (2018) 'Success for Northwold Estate residents as Guinness Partnership scraps demolition plans', 13 February (https://www.hackneycitizen.co.uk/2018/02/13/northwold-estate-demolition-plans-scrapped-guinness-partnership/).

Hackney Citizen (2019) 'Handful of leaseholders resist council plans for Woodberry Down redevelopment', 20 August (https://www.hackneycitizen.co.uk/2019/08/20/handful-leaseholders-council-plans-woodberry-down-redevelopment/).

Hackworth, J. and Smith, N. (2001) 'The changing state of gentrification', *Tijdschrift voor Economische en Sociale Geographie*, 92(4): 464–77.

Hamnett, C. (2003) *Unequal City: London in the Global Arena*, London: Routledge.

Hamnett, C. and Butler, T. (2010) 'The changing ethnic structure of housing tenures in London, 1991–2001', *Urban Studies*, 47(1): 55–74.

Hamnett, C. and Randolph, B. (1987) 'The residualisation of council housing in inner London 1971–1981', in D. Clapham and J. English (eds), *Public Housing: Current Trends and Future Developments*, London: Croom Helm, pp 32–50.

Hancock, L. and Mooney, G. (2013) '"Welfare ghettos" and the "broken society": territorial stigmatization in the contemporary UK', *Housing, Theory and Society*, 30(1): 46–64.

Hanna, K. and Bosetti, N. (2015) *Inside Out: The New Geography of Poverty and Wealth in London*, London: Centre for London.

Hanna, K., Oduwaiye, A. and Redman, P. (2016) *Another Storey: The Real Potential for Estate Densification*, London: Centre for London.

Hansard (1981) 'Greater London Council (Housing Transfer)', HC Deb, 31 March, vol 2, cc154-61 (https://api.parliament.uk/historic-hansard/commons/1981/mar/31/greater-london-council-housing-transfer).

Hansard (1983) 'Housing Stock (London Boroughs)', HC Deb, 15 November, vol 48, cc383-7W (https://hansard.parliament.uk/Commons/1983-11-15/debates/cc2fc56d-5515-492a-a7de-fe43e4aeb482/WrittenAnswers).

Hansard (1985) 'GLC Housing Transfer Orders and Nomination Rights', HC Deb 28 March, vol 76, cc728-39 (https://api.parliament.uk/historic-hansard/commons/1985/mar/28/glc-housing-transfer-orders-and).

Haringey Fairness Commission (2020) *Haringey Fairness Commission* (www.haringey.gov.uk/fairness).

Harloe, M. (1995) *The People's Home? Social Rented Housing in Europe and America*, Oxford: Basil Blackwell.

Harris, K. (2006) *Respect in the Neighbourhood*, London: Russell House Publishing.

Harrison, M. and Davis, C. (2001) *Housing, Social Policy and Difference: Disability, Ethnicity, Gender and Housing*, Bristol: Policy Press.

Harrison, P. (1983) *Inside the Inner City*, Harmondsworth: Penguin.

Harvey, D. (1973) *Social Justice and the City*, London: Edward Arnold.

Harvey, D. (1989) 'From managerialism to entrepreneurialism: The transformation in urban governance in late capitalism', *Geografiska Annaler*, 71B(1): 3–17.

Harvey, D. (2003) *The New Imperialism*, Oxford: Oxford University Press.

Harvey, D. (2005) *A Brief History of Neoliberalism*, Oxford: Oxford University Press.

Harvey, D. (2012) *Rebel Cities*, London: Verso.

Harvey, J., Tomkinson, G., Graham, R. and Quayle, Q. (1997) *Mapping Local Authority Estates Using the Index of Local Conditions*, London: DOE.

Hastings, A. (2004) 'Stigma and social housing estates', *Journal of Housing and the Built Environment*, 19(3): 233–54.

HCCHG (House of Commons Council Housing Group) (2005) *Support for the Fourth Option for Council Housing*, London: House of Commons.

Hendon & Finchley Times (2018) 'Jeremy Corbyn and Mayor Sadiq Khan visit West Hendon to announce new estate regeneration guidelines', *Hendon & Finchley Times*, 2 February (www.times-series. co.uk/news/15916343.jeremy-corbyn-and-mayor-sadiq-khan-visit-west-hendon-to-announce-new-estate-regeneration-guidelines/).

Hendry, S. (2019) 'Summer on the farm', *Sunday Times*, 30 June.

Hess, D.B., Tammaru, T. and van Ham, M. (2018) *Housing Estates in Europe*, Cham: Springer.

Heygate Was Home (2014) 'Heygate was home: charting the broken promises of regeneration' [digital archive] (http://heygatewashome. org/index.html).

Hill, Z. (2015) *CPO Report to the Secretary of State for Communities and Local Government: West Hendon Regeneration Area – Compulsory Order No 1*, London: The Planning Inspectorate.

Hirsch, A.R. (1983) *Making the Second Ghetto: Race and Housing in Chicago, 1940–1960*, Cambridge: Cambridge University Press.

Hirschman, A.O. (1970) *Exit, Voice and Loyalty*, Cambridge, MA: Harvard University Press.

Hodkinson, S. (2019) *Safe as Houses: Private Greed, Political Negligence and Housing Policy after Grenfell*, Manchester: Manchester University Press.

Hodkinson, S. and Robbins, G. (2013) 'The return of class war conservatism? Housing under the UK Coalition Government', *Critical Social Policy*, 33(1): 57–77.

Hodkinson, S., Watt, P. and Mooney, G. (2013) 'Neoliberal housing policy – time for a critical re-appraisal', *Critical Social Policy*, 33(3): 3–16.

Holland, M. (1965) *Report of the Committee on Housing in Greater London*, London: HMSO.

Howes, E. and Mullins, D. (1999) *Dwelling on Difference: Housing and Ethnicity in London*, London: London Research Centre.

Hubbard, P. and Lees, L. (2018) 'The right to community?', *City*, 22(1): 8–25.

Hull, A. (2006) 'Facilitating structures for neighbourhood regeneration in the UK: the contribution of Housing Action Trusts', *Housing Studies*, 43(12): 2317–50.

Humphry, D. (2014) *Moving On? Experiences of Social Mobility in a Mixed-class North London Neighbourhood*, PhD thesis, University of Sussex.

Humphry, D. (2020) From residualisation to individualization? Social tenants' experiences in post-Olympics East Village', *Housing, Theory and Society*, 37(4): 458–80.

Huq, E. and Harwood, S. (2019) 'Making homes unhomely: the politics of displacement in a gentrifying neighbourhood in Chicago', *City & Community*, 18(2): 710–31.

Hyra, D.S. (2008) *The New Urban Renewal: The Economic Transformation of Harlem and Bronzeville*, Chicago: University of Chicago Press.

Imrie, R. and Raco, M. (2003) *Urban Renaissance? New Labour, Community and Urban Policy*, Bristol: Policy Press.

Inside Housing (2014) 'Locked out', 2 May (https://www.insidehousing.co.uk/insight/insight/locked-out3-39757).

Inside Housing (2017) 'The battle for Haringey', 23 November (https://www.insidehousing.co.uk/insight/insight/the-battle-for-haringey-53324).

Inside Housing (2019) 'How has Haringey moved on from its development vehicle fight?', 31 May (https://www.insidehousing.co.uk/insight/insight/how-has-haringey-moved-on-from-its-development-vehicle-fight-61622).

Jackson, E. and Benson, M. (2014) 'Neither "deepest, darkest Peckham" nor "run-of-the-mill" East Dulwich: the middle classes and their "others" in an inner-London neighbourhood', *International Journal of Urban and Regional Research*, 38(4): 1197–212.

Jackson, E. and Butler, T. (2015) 'Revisiting "social tectonics": the middle classes and social mix in gentrifying neighbourhoods', *Urban Studies*, 52(13): 2349–65.

Jacobs, K. (1999) *The Dynamics of Local Housing Policy: A Study of Council Housing Renewal in the London Borough of Hackney*, Aldershot: Ashgate.

Jacobs, K. (2019) *Neoliberal Housing Policy: An International Perspective*, New York: Routledge.

Jeffers, S. and Hoggett, P. (1995) 'Like counting deckchairs on the Titanic: a study of institutional racism and housing allocations in Haringey and Lambeth', *Housing Studies*, 10(3): 325–44.

Jeffery, B. (2018) '"I probably would never move, but ideally like I'd love to move this week": class and residential experience, beyond elective belonging', *Sociology*, 52(2): 245–61.

Jephcott, P. (1964) *A Troubled Area: Notes on Notting Hill*, London: Faber & Faber.

John, P. (2015) 'Regenerating Elephant and Castle', in A. Adonis and B. Davies (eds), *City Villages: More Homes, Better Communities*, London: IPPR, pp 85–8.

Johnston, C. and Mooney, G. (2007) '"Problem" people, "problem" spaces? New Labour and council estates', in R. Atkinson and G. Helms (eds), *Securing an Urban Renaissance: Crime, Community and British Urban Policy*, Bristol: Policy Press, pp 125–39.

Jones, A. Pleace, N. and Quilgars, D. (2006) 'Evaluating the Shelter Inclusion Project: A floating support service for households accused of anti-social behaviour', in J. Flint (ed), *Housing, Urban Governance and Anti-social Behaviour*, Bristol: Policy Press, pp 179–97.

Jones, C.A. (2003) *Exploitation of the Right-to-Buy Scheme by Companies*, London: ODPM.

Jones, C.A. and Murie, A. (2006) *The Right to Buy: Analysis and Evaluation of a Housing Policy*, Oxford: Blackwell Publishing.

Jones, H. (1992) *The Conservative Party and the Welfare State, 1942–1955*, PhD thesis, LSE.

Jones, J. (1996) *Community-based Mental Health Care in Britain and Italy: Geographical Perspectives*, PhD thesis, University of Sheffield.

Kallin, H. and Slater, T. (2014) 'Activating territorial stigma: Gentrifying marginality on Edinburgh's periphery', *Environment Planning A*, 46: 1351–68.

Karakusevic, P. and Batchelor, A. (2017) *Social Housing: Definitions and Design Exemplars*, Newcastle upon Tyne: RIBA Publishing.

Karakusevic Carson Architects (2017) 'Bacton estate, UK', in P. Karakusevic and A. Batchelor (eds), *Social Housing: Definitions and Design Exemplars*, Newcastle upon Tyne: RIBA Publishing, pp 133–7.

Karn, J. (2007) *Narratives of Neglect: Community, Regeneration and the Governance of Security*, Cullompton: Willan Publishing.

Kearns, A. and Mason, P. (2013) 'Defining and measuring displacement: is relocation from restructured neighbourhoods always unwelcome and disruptive?', *Housing Studies*, 28(2): 177–204.

Kearns, K.C. (1979) 'Intraurban squatting in London', *Annals of the Association of American Geographers*, 69: 589–98.

Keith, M. and Pile, S. (1993) 'Introduction: the politics of place', in M. Keith and S. Pile (eds), *Place and the Politics of Identity*, London: Routledge, pp 1–21.

Kennelly, J. and Watt, P. (2011) 'Sanitizing public space in Olympic host cities: the spatial experiences of marginalized youth in 2010 Vancouver and 2012 London', *Sociology*, 45(5): 765–81.

Kennelly, J. and Watt, P. (2012) 'Seeing Olympic effects through the eyes of marginally housed youth: changing places and the gentrification of east London', *Visual Studies*, 27(2): 151–60.

Kennelly, J. and Watt, P. (2013) 'Restricting the public in public space: the London 2012 Olympic Games, hyper-securitization and marginalized youth', *Sociological Research Online*, 18(2) (www.socresonline.org.uk/18/2/19.html).

Kilburn, D. (2013) *Together, Apart? Situating Social Relations and Housing Provision in the Everyday Life of New-build Mixed-tenure Housing Developments*, PhD thesis, LSE.

Kintrea, K. (2007) 'Policies and programmes for disadvantaged neighbourhoods: recent English experience', *Housing Studies*, 22(2): 261–82.

Kirkness, P. and Tijé-Dra, A. (2017) *Negative Neighbourhood Reputation and Place Attachment: The Production and Contestation of Territorial Stigma*, London: Routledge.

Kleinhans, R. and Kearns, A. (2013) 'Neighbourhood restructuring and residential relocation: towards a balanced perspective on relocation processes and outcomes', *Housing Studies*, 28(2):163–76.

Koessl, G. and Mayo, M. (2015) *Reversing the Loss of Social Housing via Estate Regeneration in London*, London: UNITE.

Kusenbach, M. (2003) 'Street phenomenology: the go-along as ethnographic research tool', *Ethnography*, 4(3): 455–85.

Kusenbach, M. (2008) 'A hierarchy of urban communities: observations on the nested character of place', *City & Community*, 7(3): 225–49.

Kwest Research (2001) *June 2001 Survey of Canning Town and Custom House Area*, London: Kwest Research.

Labour Party (2019) *Labour Party Manifesto 2019* (https://labour.org.uk/manifesto-2019/).

LAHC (London Assembly Housing Committee) (2015) *Knock It Down or Do It Up? The Challenge of Estate Regeneration*, London: GLA.

Lawless, P. and Beatty, C. (2013) 'Exploring change in local regeneration areas: evidence from the New Deal for Communities Programme in England', *Urban Studies*, 50(5): 942–58.

Lawless, P., Foden, M., Wilson, I. and Beatty, C. (2010) 'Understanding area-based regeneration: the New Deal for Communities Programme in England', *Urban Studies*, 47(2): 257–75.

Lawson, L., Kearns, A., Egan, M. and Conway, E. (2015) '"You can't always get what you want?" Prior attitudes and post-experiences of relocation from restructured neighbourhoods', *Housing Studies*, 30(6): 942–66.

LBB (London Borough of Barnet) (2010) *Housing Strategy 2010–2025*, London: LBB.

LBB (2012) *Delegated Powers Report 1865: West Hendon Regeneration Scheme*, London: LBB.

LBB (2014) *Cabinet Resources Committee: Regeneration Estates Essential Major Works Programme: Discounted Resident Leaseholder Charges*, 2 April, London: LBB.

LBB (2015) *West Hendon Regeneration Area, Compulsory Order No 1, 2014*, London: LBB.

LBB (2016) *Growth and Regeneration Programme: Annual Report, Appendix 1*, London: LBB.

LBB (2017) *West Hendon Fact File, November 2017*, London: LBB.

LBH (London Borough of Hackney) (2002) *Woodberry Down Regeneration Programme – The next steps*, Cabinet, 4 November, London: LBH.

LBH (2014) *Planning Sub-Committee – 05.02.2014*, London: LBH.

LBL (London Borough of Lambeth) (2015a) *Cabinet Report – 27th July 2015, Appendix D – Central Hill*, London: LBL.

LBL (2015b) *Lambeth Council's Estate Regeneration Programme: Development Manager Procurement*, 11 September, London: LBL.

LBN (London Borough of Newham) (2008) *Canning Town and Custom House Supplementary Planning Document*, London: LBN.

LBN (2012) *Greater Carpenters Neighbourhood Redevelopment FAQs*, accessed 23 October (www.newham.gov.uk/Regen/Greater CarpentersNeighbourhoodredevelopmentFAQs.htm).

LBN (2013) *Canning Town and Custom House Regeneration Presentation*, 5 November, London: LBN.

LBN (2015) *Cabinet Report*, 19 November, London: LBN.

LBN (2019a) 'Carpenters Estate: making your views count', Number 1, 1 June, London: LBN.

LBN (2019b) *CDSG Meeting*, 25 July, London: LBN.

LBN (2019c) 'Regeneration progress' (letter), 26 September, London: LBN.

LBN (2019d) *CDSG Meeting*, 9 October, London: LBN.

LBN (2020) 'Regeneration project: Canning Town and Custom House' (www.newham.gov.uk/regeneration-1/regeneration-project-canning-town-custom-house/1).

LBS (London Borough of Southwark) (2005) *East Dulwich Estate – to Present a New Way Forward*, 5 April, London: LBS.

LBTH (London Borough of Tower Hamlets) (2005) *Ocean NDC Regeneration Area: Development Brief*, February, London: LBTH.

LCC (London County Council) (1961) *Housing Londoners: The Part Played by the London County Council, 1945–1960*, London: LCC.

LCC (1965) *London Statistics: Volume VI, 1952–1961*, London: LCC.

Leach, S. (2006) *The Changing Role of Local Politics in Britain*, Bristol: Policy Press.

Lees, L. (2014) 'The urban injustices of New Labour's "New Urban Renewal": the case of the Aylesbury Estate in London', *Antipode*, 46(4): 921–47.

Lees, L. and Ferreri, M. (2016) 'Resisting gentrification on its final frontiers: Learning from the Heygate Estate in London (1974–2013)', *Cities*, 57: 14–24.

Lees, L., Slater, T. and Wyly, E. (2008) *Gentrification*, New York: Routledge.

Lees, L., Shin, H.B. and López-Morales, E. (2016) *Planetary Gentrification*, London: Polity Press.

Lefebvre, H. (1991) *The Production of Space*, Oxford: Blackwell.

Leitner, H., Peck, J. and Sheppard, E. (2007) *Contesting Neoliberalism: Urban Frontiers*, New York: Guilford Press.

Levitas, R. (2005) *The Inclusive Society? Social Exclusion and New Labour* (2nd edn), Basingstoke: Palgrave Macmillan.

Lewicka, M. (2011) 'Place attachment: how far have we come in the last 40 years?', *Journal of Environmental Psychology*, 31: 207–30.

Local Dialogue (2016) *Cressingham Gardens: Consultation on the Future of the Estate*, London: Local Dialogue.

Local Government Association (2020) 'Percent of local authority stock that is non-decent' (https://lginform.local.gov.uk/search?op=Search&s=decent%20homes).

London First (2017) *Estate Regeneration: More and Better Homes for London*, London: London First.

London Geographies (2018) 'Regent's Park Estate', 26 January (https://londongeographies.com/housing/regents-park-estate).

Lowe, S. (1986) *Urban Social Movements*, Basingstoke: Macmillan.

Luba, J. (2012) *Investing in Council Housing: Options for the Future. A Report by the Independent Commission on the Future of Council Housing in Southwark*, London: Southwark Council.

Lupton, R. (2003) *Poverty Street*, Bristol: Policy Press.

Lupton, R. and Fuller, C. (2009) 'Mixed communities: a new approach to spatially concentrated poverty in England', *International Journal of Urban and Regional Research*, 33(4): 1014–28.

Madden, D. and Marcuse, P. (2016) *In Defense of Housing*, London: Verso.

Maeckelbergh, M. (2012) 'Mobilizing to stay put: housing struggles in New York City', *International Journal of Urban and Regional Research*, 36(4): 655–73.

Manley, D., van Ham, M., Bailey, N., Simpson, L. and Maclennan, D. (2013) *Neighbourhood Effects or Neighbourhood Based Problems? A Policy Context*, Dordrecht: Springer.

Manzi, T. and Jacobs, K. (2009) 'From a "society of fear" to a "society of respect": the transformation of Hackney's Holly Street Estate', in R. Imrie, M. Raco and L. Lees (eds), *Regenerating London*, London: Routledge, pp 273–88.

Manzi, T. and Morrison, N. (2018) 'Risk, commercialism and social purpose: Repositioning the English housing association sector', *Urban Studies*, 55(9): 1924–42.

Manzo, L.C. (2014a) 'Exploring the shadow side: place attachment in the context of stigma, displacement, and social housing', in L.C. Manzo and P. Devine-Wright (eds), *Place Attachment*, London: Routledge, pp 178–90.

Manzo, L.C. (2014b) 'On uncertain ground: being at home in the context of public housing redevelopment', *International Journal of Housing Policy*, 14(4): 389–410.

Manzo, L.C. and Devine-Wright, P. (2014) 'Introduction', in L.C. Manzo and P. Devine-Wright (eds), *Place Attachment*, London: Routledge, pp 1–7.

Marcuse, P. (1986) 'Abandonment, gentrification and displacement: the linkages in New York City', in N. Smith and P. Williams (eds), *Gentrification and the City*, London: Unwin Hyman, pp 153–77.

Marriott, J. (1991) *The Culture of Labourism: The East End between the Wars*, Edinburgh: Edinburgh University Press.

Marris, P. (1986) *Loss and Change* (2nd edn), London: Routledge.

Marrs, C. (2017) 'Newham seeks development partner for Carpenters estate regeneration', *Architects' Journal*, 29 August.

Marx, K. and Engels, F. (1968) *Selected Works in One Volume*, London: Lawrence and Wishart.

Matthews, P. (2010) 'Mind the gap? The persistence of pathological discourses in urban regeneration policy', *Housing, Theory and Society*, 27(3): 221–40.

Matthews, P. (2012) 'Problem definition and re-evaluating a policy: the real successes of a regeneration scheme', *Critical Policy Studies*, 6(3): 243–60.

Mayer, M. (2007) 'Contesting the neoliberalization of urban governance', in H. Leitner, J. Peck and E.S. Sheppard (eds), *Contesting Neoliberalism: Urban Frontiers*, New York: Guilford Press, pp 90–115.

Mayo, M. (2017) *Changing Communities*, Bristol: Policy Press.

Mayor of London (2018) *Better Homes for Local People – The Mayor's Good Practice Guide to Estate Regeneration*, London: GLA.

Mayor of London (2019) *Housing in London 2019*, London: GLA.

McKenzie, L. (2012) 'A narrative from the inside, studying St Anns in Nottingham: belonging, continuity and change', *Sociological Review*, 60(3): 457–75.

McKenzie, L. (2015) *Getting By: Estates, Class and Culture in Austerity Britain*, Bristol: Policy Press.

McKenzie, L. (2018) 'Resisting and surviving organised politics: the case of the London housing movement', in A. Fishwick and H. Connolly (eds), *Austerity and Working-class Resistance*, London: Rowman & Littlefield International, pp 17–32.

McKenzie, S. and Hussain, S. (2018) 'We demand fair say in estate's future', *Waltham Forest Echo*, January, 34: 7.

McKibbin, R. (1998) *Classes and Cultures: England 1918–1951*, Oxford: Oxford University Press.

McLaughlin, G. (2015) *Estate Regeneration Sourcebook*, London: Urban Design London.

Merrett, S. (1982) *Owner–Occupation in Britain,* London: Routledge and Kegan Paul.

Merrifield, A. (2014) *The New Urban Question*, London: Pluto Press.

MHCLG (Ministry of Housing, Communities and Local Government) (2015) English Indices of Deprivation 2015 (www.gov.uk/government/statistics/english-indices-of-deprivation-2015).

MHCLG (2019a) Live Tables 100, 253, 670, 684, 685 (www.gov.uk/housing-local-and-community/housing).

MHCLG (2019b) *English Housing Survey: Social Rented Sector, 2017–18*, London: MHCLG.

Miller, D. (1988) 'Appropriating the state on the council estate', *Man: New Series*, 23(2): 353–72.

Millington, G. (2011) *'Race', Culture and the Right to the City*, Basingstoke: Palgrave Macmillan.

Minton, A. (2017) *Big Capital: Who Is London For?*, London: Penguin Books.

Mixed Communities Evaluation Project Team (2010) *Evaluation of the Mixed Communities Initiative Demonstration Projects: Final Report*, London: DCLG.

Moore, R. (1992) 'Labour and housing markets in inner-city regeneration', *New Community*, 18(3): 371–86.

Moore, R. (2016) 'Housing estates: if they aren't broken...', *The Observer*, 31 January (www.theguardian.com/artanddesign/2016/jan/31/council-estates-if-they-arent-broken-lambeth-council-central-hill-estate-social-housing-affordable).

MORI (2003) *Regeneration Developments in Canning Town: Survey of Residents and Businesses*, September, London: MORI.

Morris, A. (2013) 'Public housing in Australia: a case of advanced urban marginality?', *The Economic and Labour Relations Review*, 24(1): 80–96.

Morris, A. (2019) *Gentrification and Displacement: The Forced Relocation of Public Housing Tenants in Inner-Sydney*, Singapore: Springer.

Mortgage Finance Gazette (2019) 'Right-to-Buy Scheme has turned hundreds of ex-council tenants into property millionaires', *Mortgage Finance Gazette*, 15 March (www.mortgagefinancegazette.com/market-news/housing/right-buy-scheme-turned-hundreds-ex-council-tenants-property-millionaires-15-03-2019/).

Mullins, D. and Murie, A. (2006) *Housing Policy in the UK*, Basingstoke: Palgrave Macmillan.

Murie, A. (2016) *The Right to Buy? Selling Off Public and Social Housing*, Bristol: Policy Press.

Musterd, S., Murie, A. and Kesteloot, C. (2006) *Neighbourhoods of Poverty*, Basingstoke: Palgrave Macmillan.

NAO (National Audit Office) (2010) *The Decent Homes Programme*, London: NAO.

National Housing Federation (2017) *How Public Money is Spent on Housing*, September 2017 (www.housing.org.uk/news-and-blogs/news/social-housing-spending-at-record-low/).

Nelson S. and Lewis, J. (2019) 'Resident engagement in the regeneration of social housing: the case of Woodberry Down, London', *International Journal of Housing Policy* (https://doi.org/10.1080/19491247.2019.1683126).

Nevitt, D.A. and Rhodes, G. (1972) 'Housing', in G. Rhodes (ed), *The New Government of London: The First Five Years*, London: Weidenfeld & Nicolson, pp 213–62.

New London Architecture (2019) 'London must engage with communities to win back trust', *New London Architecture*, 15 October (http://newlondonarchitecture.org/news/2019/october-2019/homes-for-londoners).

Newham Recorder (2002) 'Revamp row residents have a say', 3 April.

Newham Recorder (2004) 'Pledges on revamp of housing', 10 March.

Newham Recorder (2017) 'Councillors approve task force to tackle Custom House temporary housing issues', 5 December (https://www.newhamrecorder.co.uk/news/politics/councillors-approve-task-force-to-tackle-custom-house-temporary-housing-issues-1-5309437).

Newham Recorder (2019) 'Have your say on Carpenters Estate proposals', 23 October (https://www.newhamrecorder.co.uk/news/carpenters-estate-redevelopment-meetings-1-6337751).

O'Brien, D. and Matthews, P. (2016) *After Urban Regeneration*, Bristol: Policy Press.

ODPM (Office of the Deputy Prime Minister) (2003) *Factsheet 9: New Deal for Communities*, London: Neighbourhood Renewal Unit.

Olechnowicz, A. (1997) *Working-class Housing in England Between the Wars: The Becontree Estate*, Oxford: Oxford University Press.

Orr, D.J. (2018) *'Only Overcrowded': The Effects of Changes to Social Housing Allocation on Non-emergency Applicants in London*, PhD thesis, King's College, University of London.

Osborne, H. (2014) 'Poor doors: the segregation of London's inner-city flat dwellers', *The Guardian*, 25 July (www.theguardian.com/society/2014/jul/25/poor-doors-segregation-london-flats).

Pahl, R.E. (1984) *Divisions of Labour*, Oxford: Basil Blackwell.

Pain, R. (2019) 'Chronic urban trauma: The slow violence of housing dispossession', *Urban Studies*, 56(2): 385–400.

Panton, M. and Walters, G. (2018) ' "It's just a Trojan horse for gentrification": austerity and stadium-led regeneration', *International Journal of Sport Policy and Politics*, 10(1): 163–83.

Parker, S. (1999) 'From the slums to the suburbs: Labour Party policy, the LCC and the Woodberry Down estate, Stoke Newington', *London Journal*, 24(2): 51–69.

Passmore, M. (2015) *The Responses of Labour-controlled London Local Authorities to Major Changes in Housing Policy, 1971–1983*, PhD thesis, King's College, University of London.

Paton, K. (2014) *Gentrification: A Working-class Perspective*, Farnham: Ashgate.

Pawson, H. and Mullins, D. (2010) *After Council Housing: Britain's New Social Landlords*, Basingstoke: Palgrave Macmillan.

Peck, J. (2012) 'Austerity urbanism', *City*, 16: 626–55.

Peck J. and Tickell A. (2002) 'Neoliberalizing space', *Antipode*, 34(3): 380–404.

Perera, J. (2019) *The London Clearances: Race, Housing and Policing*, London: Institute of Race Relations.

Persak, N. and Di Ronco, A. (2018) 'Urban space and the social control of incivilities: perceptions of space influencing the regulation of anti-social behaviour', *Crime, Law and Social Change*, 69: 329–47.

Porter, L. and Shaw, K. (2009) *Whose Urban Renaissance?*, London: Routledge.

Porter, R. (1994) *London: A Social History*, London: Penguin Books.

Posthumus, H. and Lelevrier, C. (2013) 'How local contexts influence the neighbourhood satisfaction of displaced tenants in the Netherlands and France', *International Journal of Housing Policy*, 13(2): 134–58.

Posthumus, H. and Kleinhans, R. (2014) 'Choice within limits: how the institutional context of forced relocation affects tenants' housing searches and choice strategies', *Journal of Housing and the Built Environment*, 29(1): 105–22.

Powell, R. and Robinson, D. (2019) 'Housing, ethnicity and advanced marginality in England', in J. Flint and R. Powell (eds), *Class, Ethnicity and State in the Polarized Metropolis*, Basingstoke, Palgrave Macmillan, pp 187–212.

Power, A. (1997) *Estates on the Edge: The Social Consequences of Mass Housing in Northern Europe*, Basingstoke: Macmillan.

Power, A. and Tunstall, R. (1995) *Swimming Against the Tide? Polarisation or Progress on 20 Unpopular Council Estates*, York: Joseph Rowntree Foundation.

Power, A. and Tunstall, R. (1997) *Dangerous Disorder: Riots and Violent Disturbances in Thirteen Areas of Britain, 1991–92*, York: Joseph Rowntree Foundation.

Power, R.M. (1982) *Council House Sales in Britain, with Special Reference to London and Incorporating a Case Study of the Borough of Havering*, PhD thesis, LSE.

PPCR Associates (2016) *Northumberland Park Regeneration Survey: What Could the Future Be for Your Neighbourhood?*, London: PPCR Associates.

Provan, B., Belotti, A. and Power, A. (2016) *Moving on Without Moving Out: The Impacts of Regeneration on the Rayners Lane Estate* (CASEreport 100), London: LSE Housing and Communities, LSE.

Pull, E. and Richard, A. (2019) 'Domicide: dis*place*ment and dispossessions in Uppsala, Sweden', *Social & Cultural Geography*, DOI: 10.1080/14649365.2019.1601245

Putnam, R.D. (2000) *Bowling Alone: The Collapse and Revival of American Community*, New York: Simon & Schuster.

Quod (2014) *Living at Woodberry Down*, London: Berkeley.

Qureshi, K., Salway, S., Chowbey, P. and Platt, L. (2014) 'Long-term ill health and the social embeddedness of work: a study in a post-industrial, multi-ethnic locality in the UK', *Sociology of Health & Illness*, 36(7): 955–69.

Rainwater, L. (1970) *Behind Ghetto Walls*, Harmondsworth: Penguin Books.

Ravetz, A. (2001) *Council Housing and Culture*, London: Routledge.

Raynsford, N. (2016) *Substance Not Spin: An Insider's View of Success and Failure in Government*, Bristol: Policy Press.

Relph, E. (1976) *Place and Placelessness*, London: Pion.

Research for Action (2018a) *Debt and Democracy in Newham: A Citizen Audit of LOBO Loans*, London: Research for Action.

Research for Action (2018b) *Cuts and Contempt: Experiences of Austerity and Council Democracy in Newham*, London: Research for Action.

Rex, J. and Moore, R. (1967) *Race, Community and Conflict*, Oxford: Oxford University Press.

Rhodes, G. (1972) *The New Government of London: The First Five Years*, London: Weidenfeld & Nicolson.

Robbins, G. (2017) *There's No Place: The American Housing Crisis and What It Means for the UK*, London: Red Roof.

Roberts, M. (1988) 'Caretaking – who cares?', in N. Teymur, T.A. Markus and T. Woolley (eds), *Rehumanizing Housing*, London: Butterworths, pp 123–31.

Robertson, F. (2016) 'The Estate We're In', BBC, 2 April (www.bbc.co.uk/programmes/b00t0ydd).

Robson, G. (2000) *'No One Likes Us, We Don't Care': The Myth and Reality of Millwall Fandom*, Oxford: Berg.

Romyn, M. (2016) 'Heygate: community life in an inner-city estate, 1974–2011', *History Workshop Journal*, 81(1): 197–230.

Romyn, M. (2019) '"London badlands": the inner city represented, regenerated', *London Journal*, 44(2), 133–50.

Rosbrook-Thompson, J. and Armstrong, G. (2018) *Mixed-Occupancy Housing in London: A Living Tapestry*, London: Palgrave Macmillan.

Rose, D. (1996) 'Economic restructuring and the diversification of gentrification in the 1980s: a view from a marginal metropolis', in J. Caulfield and L. Peake (eds), *City Lives and City Forms*, Toronto: University of Toronto Press, pp 131–72.

Rugg, J. (2016) *Temporary Accommodation in London: Local Authorities under Pressure*, London: London Councils.

Samanani, F. (2017) *Gathering Kilburn: The Everyday Production of Community in a Diverse London Neighbourhood*, PhD thesis, University of Cambridge.

Sassen, S. (2014) *Expulsions: Brutality and Complexity in the Global Economy*, Cambridge, MA: Harvard University Press.

Saunders, C. (2016) *Memory Block* (video) (www.christophersaunders.info/reconstruction3).

Saunders, P. (1990) *A Nation of Home Owners*, London: Unwin Hyman.

Savage, M. (1987) *The Dynamics of Working-class Politics: The Labour Movement in Preston, 1880–1940*, Cambridge: Cambridge University Press.

Savage, M. (2010) 'The politics of elective belonging', *Housing, Theory and Society*, 27(2): 115–35.

Savage, M. (2011) 'The lost urban sociology of Pierre Bourdieu', in G. Bridge and S. Watson (eds), *The New Blackwell Companion to the City*, Malden, MA: Wiley-Blackwell, pp 511–20.

Savage, M. (2015) *Social Class in the 21st Century*, London: Pelican Books.

Savage, M., Watt, P. and Arber, S. (1990) 'The consumption sector debate and housing mobility', *Sociology*, 24(1): 97–117.

Savage, M., Bagnall, G. and Longhurst, B. (2005) *Globalization and Belonging*, London: Sage.

Sborgi, A.V. (2017) 'The day social housing hit mainstream media', *Mediapolis*, 2(3) (www.mediapolisjournal.com/2017/09/the-day-social-housing-hit-mainstream-media/).

Scanlon, K., White, T. and Blanc, F. (2018) *Residents' Experience of High-Density Housing in London: Final Report*, London: LSE.

Sendra, P. and Fitzpatrick, D. (2020) *Community-Led Regeneration: A Toolkit for Residents and Planners*, London: UCL Press.

Sennett, R. and Cobb, J. (1973) *The Hidden Injuries of Class*, New York: Vintage Books.

SEU (Social Exclusion Unit) (1998) *Bringing Britain Together: A National Strategy for Neighbourhood Renewal*, London: The Stationery Office.

Seymour, R. (2017) *Corbyn: The Strange Rebirth of Radical Politics*, London: Verso.

Shamsuddin, S. and Vale, L. (2017) 'Holding on to HOPE: assessing redevelopment of Boston's Orchard Park public housing project', in P. Watt and P. Smets (eds), *Social Housing and Urban Renewal: A Cross-National Perspective*, Bingley: Emerald, pp 37–68.

Shelter (2019) *Building for Our Future: A Vision for Social Housing*, London: Shelter.

Shields, R. (1991) *Places on the Margin: Alternative Geographies of Modernity*, London: Routledge.

Shildrick, T., MacDonald, R., Webster, C. and Garthwaite, K. (2012) *Poverty and Insecurity: Life in Low-Pay, No-Pay Britain*, Bristol: Policy Press.

Sibley, D. (1995) *Geographies of Exclusion*, London: Routledge.

Single Aspect (2014) Cressingham Gardens: housing debate [Blog] (www.singleaspect.org.uk/?p=16735).

Skeggs, B. (1997) *Formations of Class and Gender*, London: Sage.

Skeggs, B. (2011) 'Imagining personhood differently: person value and autonomist working-class value practices', *Sociological Review*, 59(3): 579–94.

Skeggs, B. (2014) 'Values beyond value? Is anything beyond the logic of capital?', *British Journal of Sociology*, 65(1): 1–20.

Skeggs, B. (2015) 'Introduction: stratification or exploitation, domination, dispossession and devaluation?', *Sociological Review*, 63: 205–22.

Slater, T. (2009) 'Missing Marcuse: on gentrification and displacement', *City*, 13(2–3): 293–310.

Slater, T. (2013a) 'Expulsions from public housing: the hidden context of concentrated affluence', *Cities*, 35: 384–90.

Slater, T. (2013b) 'Your life chances affect where you live: a critique of the "cottage industry" of neighbourhood effects research', *International Journal of Urban and Regional Research*, 37(2): 367–87.

Slater, T. (2018) 'The invention of the "sink estate": consequential categorisation and the UK housing crisis', *Sociological Review Monographs*, 66(4): 877–97.

Smith, A.E. (2009) *Ageing in Urban Neighbourhoods: Place Attachment and Social Exclusion*, Bristol: Policy Press.

Smith, D.M. (2005) *On the Margins of Inclusion: Changing Labour Markets and Social Exclusion in London*, Bristol: Policy Press.

Smith, N. (2002) 'New globalism, new urbanism: gentrification as global urban strategy', *Antipode*, 34(3): 427–50.

Smith, T., Noble, M., Noble, S., Wright, G., McLennan, D. and Plunkett, E. (2015) *The English Indices of Deprivation 2015: Research Report*, London: DCLG.

Social Life (2013) *Cressingham Gardens Estate*, London: Social Life.

Social Life (2015) *Understanding Wellbeing on Cressingham Gardens*, London: Social Life.

Social Life (2017) *Living on the Aylesbury Estate*, London: Social Life.

Social Life (2020) *Understanding Woodberry Down*, London: Social Life.

Somerville, P. (1994) 'Homelessness policy in Britain', *Policy and Politics*, 22(3): 163–78.

Somerville, P. (2016) *Understanding Community: Politics, Policy, Practice* (2nd edn), Bristol: Policy Press.

South London Press (2005) 'People power rescues estate flats', 12 April.

Southwark News (1998) 'Tenants plan barricade to beat demolition', 29 October.

Southwark News (2000a) 'Peckham Partnership slammed for estates demolition', 29 June.

Southwark News (2000b) 'I told the council on Friday the lighting's so bad on these estates I wouldn't be surprised if someone was killed. On the Monday, Damilola died', 7 December.

Southwark News (2002) 'Controversial Peckham regen scheme ends', 21 March.

Standing, G. (2011) *The Precariat*, London: Bloomsbury Academic.

Stewart, J. and Rhoden, M. (2003) 'A review of social housing regeneration in the London Borough of Brent', *Journal of the Royal Society for the Promotion of Health*, 123(1): 23–32.

Strauss, P.T. (2007) *Fibre Optics and Community in East London: Political Technologies on a 'Wired-Up' Newham Housing Estate*, PhD thesis, University of Manchester.

Swindon Tenants Campaign Group (2016) *The Case for Cancelling Council Housing 'Debt'*, Swindon: Swindon Tenants Campaign Group.

TCC (The Campaign Company) (2016) *The Future of the Central Hill Estate: Resident Consultation*, Croydon: TCC.

Teernstra, A.B. and Pinkster, F.M. (2015) 'Participation in neighbourhood regeneration: Achievements of residents in a Dutch disadvantaged neighbourhood', *Urban Practice and Research*, 9(1): 1–24.

Telemaque, N. (2015) *South Kilburn's Regeneration: Exploring Young Adults' Experiences of the Regenerating Council Estate*, MSc dissertation, UCL.

The Sun (2018) 'WAR-THAMSTOW: from rampant drug abuse to murder, Vallentin Road in London's Walthamstow has become the UK's most dangerous street', 25 September (https://www.thesun.co.uk/news/7347834/vallentin-road-dangerous-street/).

Tiesdell, S. (2001) 'A forgotten policy? A perspective on the evolution and transformation of Housing Action Trust policy, 1987–99', *European Journal of Housing Policy*, 1: 357–83.

Tinson, A., Ayrton, C., Barker, K., Born, T.B. and Long, O. (2017) *London's Poverty Profile 2017*, London: Trust for London.

Todd, S. (2014) *The People: The Rise and Fall of the Working Class, 1910–2010*, London: John Murray.

Tomlinson, D. (1991) *Utopia, Community Care, and the Retreat from the Asylums*, Milton Keynes: Open University Press.

Torgersen, U. (1987) 'Housing: the wobbly pillar under the welfare state', *Scandinavian Housing and Planning Research*, 4(S1): 116–26.

Totality UK (2015) *Source Magazine*, Spring/Summer, London: Totality UK.

Towers, G. (2000) *Shelter Is Not Enough: Transforming Multi-storey Housing*, Bristol: Policy Press.

Toynbee, P. (2003) *Hard Work: Life in Low-Pay Britain*, London: Bloomsbury.

Toynbee, P. (2008) 'The Labour idealism that saved Clapham Park is dead', *The Guardian*, 12 July.

Transparency International UK (2017) *Faulty Towers: Understanding the Impact of Overseas Corruption on the London Property Market*, London: Transparency International UK.

Travers, T. (2015) *London's Boroughs at 50*, London, Biteback Publishing.

Travers, T., Sims, S. and Bosetti, N. (2016) *Housing and Inequality in London*, London: Centre for London.

Tunstall, R. (2020) *The Fall and Rise of Social Housing: 100 Years on 20 Estates*, Bristol: Policy Press.

Turnbull, P. (2014) 'New Kingshold redevelopment', in GLA (ed), *Written Submissions Received for the London Assembly's Housing Committee Investigation into Social Housing Estate Regeneration: Volume 3*, London: GLA.

Turner, A. (2018) 'A tinted view: negative media portrayals of social housing', *Inside Housing*, 26 April (www.insidehousing.co.uk/insight/insight/a-tinted-view-negative-media-portrayals-of-social-housing-55950).

Tyler, I. (2013) *Revolting Subjects: Social Abjection and Resistance in Neoliberal Britain*, London: Zed Books.

Tyler, I. (2015) 'Classificatory struggles: class, culture and inequality in neoliberal times', *Sociological Review*, 63: 493–511.

Urban, F. (2012) *Tower and Slab: Histories of Global Mass Housing*, New York: Routledge.

URBED (2007) 'Summary of the sixth meeting in the fourth series of TEN, Hackney 18 December 2007', London: URBED.

Vale, L.J. (2013) *Purging the Poorest: Public Housing and the Design Politics of Twice-Cleared Communities*, Chicago: University of Chicago Press.

Vale, L.J. and Freemark, Y. (2012) 'From public housing to public–private housing: 75 years of American social experimentation', *Journal of the American Planning Association*, 78(4): 379–402.

Van Ham, M. and Manley, D. (2010) 'The effect of neighbourhood housing tenure mix on labour market outcomes: a longitudinal investigation of neighbourhood effects', *Journal of Economic Geography*, 10: 257–282.

Viitala, J. (2018) *Participatory Democracy and Transparent City-Planning: Lessons from Haringey, London*, London: Finnish Institute in London.

Wacquant, L. (2008) *Urban Outcasts*, Cambridge: Polity Press.

Wacquant, L. (2019) 'Dispossession and dishonour in the polarized metropolis: reactions and recommendations', in J. Flint and R. Powell (eds), *Class, Ethnicity and State in the Polarized Metropolis*, Basingstoke: Palgrave Macmillan, pp 309–23.

Wainwright, O. (2016) 'A tale of two cities: winners and losers in London's social housing divide', *The Guardian*, 14 March.

Walker, P. (2010) 'South London's Heygate estate mourned by locals – and Hollywood', *The Guardian*, 3 September.

Wallace, Alison (2010) *Public Attitudes to Housing*, York: Joseph Rowntree Foundation.

Wallace, Andrew (2010a) 'New neighbourhoods, new citizens? Challenging "community" as a framework for social and moral regeneration under New Labour in the UK', *International Journal of Urban and Regional Research*, 34(4): 805–19.

Wallace, Andrew (2010b) *Remaking Community? New Labour and the Governance of Poor Neighbourhoods*, Farnham: Ashgate.

Wallace, Andrew (2015) 'Gentrification interrupted in Salford, UK: from new deal to limbo-land in a contemporary urban periphery', *Antipode*, 47(2): 517–38.

Ward, K, Fagan, C., McDowell, L., Perrons, D. and Ray, K. (2007) 'Living and working in urban working-class communities', *Geoforum*, 38: 312–25.

Watson, S. and Austerberry, H. (1986) *Housing and Homelessness: A Feminist Perspective*, London: Routledge and Kegan Paul.

Watt, P. (1996) 'Social stratification and housing mobility', *Sociology*, 30(3): 533–50.

Watt, P. (2001) *The Dynamics of Social Class and Housing: A Study of Local Authority Tenants in the London Borough of Camden*, PhD thesis, King's College, University of London.

Watt, P. (2003) 'Urban marginality and economic restructuring: local authority tenants and employment in an Inner London Borough', *Urban Studies*, 40(9): 1769–89.

Watt, P. (2005) 'Housing histories and fragmented middle-class careers: the case of marginal professionals in London council housing', *Housing Studies*, 20(3): 359–81.

Watt, P. (2006) 'Respectability, roughness and "race": neighbourhood place images and the making of working-class social distinctions in London', *International Journal of Urban and Regional Research*, 30(4): 776–97.

Watt, P. (2007) 'From the dirty city to the spoiled suburb', in B. Campkin and R. Cox (eds), *Dirt: New Geographies of Cleanliness and Contamination*, London: I.B. Tauris, pp 80–91.

Watt, P. (2008) 'Underclass and ordinary people discourses: representing/re-presenting council tenants in a housing campaign', *Critical Discourse Studies*, 5(3): 345–57.

Watt, P. (2009a) 'Housing stock transfers, regeneration and state-led gentrification in London', *Urban Policy and Research*, 27(3): 229–42.

Watt, P. (2009b) 'Living in an oasis socio-spatial segregation and selective belonging in an English suburb', *Environment and Planning A*, 41(12): 2874–92.

Watt, P. (2009c) 'Social housing and regeneration in London', in R. Imrie, L. Lees and M. Raco (eds), *Regenerating London*, London: Routledge, pp 212–33.

Watt, P. (2010) 'Unravelling the narratives and politics of belonging to place', *Housing, Theory and Society*, 27(2): 153–9.

Watt, P. (2013) '"It's not for us": regeneration, the 2012 Olympics and the gentrification of East London', *City*, 17(1): 99–118.

Watt, P. (2016) 'A nomadic war machine in the metropolis: en/countering London's 21st century housing crisis with Focus E15', *City*, 20(2): 297–320.

Watt, P. (2017) 'Social housing and urban renewal: an introduction', in P. Watt and P. Smets (eds), *Social Housing and Urban Renewal: A Cross-national Perspective*, Bingley: Emerald, pp 1–36.

Watt, P. (2018a) '"This pain of moving, moving, moving": evictions, displacement and logics of expulsion in London', *L'Annee sociologique*, 68(1): 67–100.

Watt, P. (2018b) 'Gendering the right to housing in the city: homeless female lone parents in post-Olympics, austerity East London', *Cities*, 76: 43–51.

Watt, P. (2018c) '"Social housing not social cleansing": contemporary housing struggles in London', in N. Gray (ed), *Rent and Its Discontents: A Century of Housing Struggle*, London: Rowman & Littlefield, pp 117–35.

Watt, P. (2020a) 'Class and place', in T. Edensor, A. Kalandides and U. Kothari (eds), *The Routledge Handbook of Place*, London: Routledge, pp 255–64.

Watt, P. (2020b) ' "Press-ganged" Generation Rent: youth homelessness, precarity and poverty in East London', *People, Place and Policy*, 14(2): 128–41.

Watt, P. (2020c) 'Territorial stigmatisation and poor housing at a London "sink estate"', *Social Inclusion*, 8(1): 20–33.

Watt, P. (Forthcoming) 'Home, block and neighbourhood: multi-scalar place attachment among displaced social housing residents in London', *Housing Studies*.

Watt, P. and Jacobs, K. (2000) 'Discourses of social exclusion: an analysis of "Bringing Britain together: a national strategy for neighbourhood renewal"', *Housing, Theory and Society*, 17(1): 14–26.

Watt, P. and Smets, P. (2014) *Mobilities and Neighbourhood Belonging in Cities and Suburbs*, Basingstoke: Palgrave Macmillan.

Watt, P. and Wallace, A. (2014) 'Why can't we have them posh houses? Housing redevelopment and community tensions in London and Salford', in C. Lelévrier and A. Deboulet (eds), *Rénovations Urbaines en Europe*, Rennes: Presses Universitaires de Rennes, pp 215–27.

Watt, P. and Minton, A. (2016) 'London's housing crisis and its activisms', *City*, 20: 204–21.

Watt, P. and Bernstock, P. (2017) 'Legacy for whom? Housing in post-Olympic East London', in P. Cohen and P. Watt (eds), *London 2012 and the Post-Olympics City: A Hollow Legacy?*, Basingstoke: Palgrave Macmillan, pp 91–138.

Watt, P. and Smets, P. (2017) *Social Housing and Urban Renewal: A Cross-national Perspective*, Bingley: Emerald.

Watt, P. and Allen, D. (2018) *Northwold Estate, Hackney: A Report on Residents' Attitudes to the Estate and Its Potential Redevelopment*, London: Birkbeck, University of London.

Watt, P., Millington, G. and Huq, R. (2014) 'East London mobilities: the Cockney Diaspora and the remaking of the Essex ethnoscape', in P. Watt and P. Smets (eds), *Mobilities and Neighbourhood Belonging in Cities and Suburbs*, Basingstoke: Palgrave Macmillan, pp 121–44.

WDCO (2015) *Woodberry Down Community Organisation: Our Key Achievements*, London: WDCO.

WDCO and Eastside Community Heritage (2015) *Woodberry Down: The People's Story*, London: WDCO and Eastside Community Heritage.

Webber, R. and Burrows, R. (2016) 'Life in an Alpha Territory: discontinuity and conflict in an elite London village', *Urban Studies*, 53(15): 3139–54.

Weber, M. (1949) *The Methodology of the Social Sciences*, New York: Free Press.

Weinbren, D. (1998) 'Building communities, constructing identities: the rise of the Labour Party in London', *London Journal*, 23(1): 41–60.

Wessendorf, S. (2014) *Commonplace Diversity: Social Relations in a Super-diverse Context*, Basingstoke: Palgrave Macmillan.

White, J. (2008) *London in the Twentieth Century*, London: Vintage.

Whitley, R. and Prince, M. (2005) 'Are inner-cities bad for your health? Comparisons of residents' and third parties' perceptions of the urban neighbourhood of Gospel Oak, London', *Sociology of Health & Illness*, 27(1): 44–67.

Wilks-Heeg, S. (2009) 'New Labour and the reform of English local government, 1997–2007: privatizing the parts that Conservative governments could not reach', *Planning, Practice and Research*, 24(1): 23–39.

Wills, J., Datta, K., Evans, Y., Herbert, J., May, J. and McIlwaine, C. (2010) *Global Cities at Work*, London: Pluto Press.

Wilson, W. (2009) *The Decent Homes Standard: Update* (SN/SP/3178), 2 September, London: House of Commons Library.

Wilson, W.J. (1987) *The Truly Disadvantaged: The Inner City, the Underclass and Public Policy*, Chicago: University of Chicago Press.

Wohl, A.S. (1977) *The Eternal Slum: Housing and Social Policy in Victorian London*, London: Edward Arnold.

Woodberry Down Memories Group (1989) *Woodberry Down Memories: The History of an LCC Housing Estate*, London: ILEA.

Woodberry Down Regeneration Team (2009) *Woodberry Down Regeneration. A National Mixed Communities Demonstration Project: Framework for Regeneration – 2009*, London: Hackney Council.

Woodward, R. (1991) 'Mobilising opposition: the campaign against Housing Action Trusts in Tower Hamlets', *Housing Studies*, 8(1): 44–56.

Worden, S. (2017) *CPO Report to the Secretaries of State for Communities and Local Government, and for Transport: West Hendon Regeneration Area – Compulsory Order No 2*, London: The Planning Inspectorate.

Young, K. and Garside, P. (1982) *Metropolitan London: Politics and Urban Change 1837–1981*, New York: Holmes & Meier Publishers.

Young, M. and Willmott, P. (1957) *Family and Kinship in East London*, London: Routledge and Kegan Paul.

Young Foundation (2010) *Neighbouring in Contemporary Britain*, London: Young Foundation.

Index

Page numbers in *italic* type refer to figures and photographs; those in **bold** type refer to tables.